Enterprise Digital Transformation

Enterprise Digital Transformation

Technology, Tools, and Use Cases

Edited by
Peter Augustine
Pethuru Raj
and
Sathyan Munirathinam

CRC Press
Taylor & Francis Group
Boca Raton London New York

CRC Press is an imprint of the
Taylor & Francis Group, an **informa** business
AN AUERBACH BOOK

First edition published 2022
by CRC Press
6000 Broken Sound Parkway NW, Suite 300, Boca Raton, FL 33487-2742

and by CRC Press
4 Park Square, Milton Park, Abingdon, Oxon, OX14 4RN

CRC Press is an imprint of Taylor & Francis Group, LLC

© 2022 Taylor & Francis Group, LLC

ISBN: 978-0-367-63589-3 (hbk)
ISBN: 978-1-032-15118-2 (pbk)
ISBN: 978-1-003-11978-4 (ebk)

DOI: 10.1201/9781003119784

Typeset in Garamond
by SPi Technologies India Pvt Ltd (Straive)

Contents

Editors

D. Peter Augustine, PhD, has been working as an associate professor in the Department of Computer Science, CHRIST (Deemed to be University), Bangalore.

He has a PhD in Medical Image Processing in a Cloud Environment, with over 8 years of experience in cloud computing and 5 years in big data analytics. He has authored various research papers published in peer-reviewed journals. He has been involved in a major research project using cloud computing which costs more than 18 lakhs. He has also collaborated with St. John's Medical Research Institute for the research project to diagnose lung diseases using cutting-edge AI and machine learning.

His research interests include artificial intelligence, IoT and big data analysis in the area of healthcare and data mining, and human computer interaction. He has written chapters for the books focusing on some of the emerging technologies such as IoT, data analytics and science, blockchain and digital twin.

Pethuru Raj Chelliah, PhD, has been working as the chief architect in the Site Reliability Engineering (SRE) division of Reliance Jio Infocomm Ltd. (RJIL), Bangalore. He previously worked as a cloud infrastructure architect in the IBM Global Cloud Center of Excellence (CoE), a TOGAF-certified enterprise architecture (EA) consultant in the Wipro Consulting Services (WCS) Division and as a lead architect in the corporate research (CR) division of Robert Bosch. In total, he has gained more than 17 years of IT industry experience and 8 years of research experience.

He finished the CSIR-sponsored PhD degree at Anna University, Chennai, and continued with the UGC-sponsored postdoctoral research in the Department of Computer Science and Automation, Indian Institute of Science, Bangalore. Thereafter, he was granted a couple of international research fellowships (JSPS and JST) to work as a research scientist for 3.5 years in two leading Japanese universities. He has published more than 20 research papers in peer-reviewed journals by publishers such as IEEE, ACM, Springer-Verlag, Inderscience and Elsevier. He also has contributed 35 book chapters thus far for various technology books.

Finally, he has authored and edited 16 books thus far and is focusing on some of the emerging technologies such as IoT, data analytics and science, blockchain, digital twin, containerized clouds, microservices architecture, and fog/edge computing.

Sathyan Munirathinam, PhD, is working as a cloud solution architect manager for ASML Corporation. He is responsible for developing a cloud strategy and roadmap in addressing the dynamic cloud solutions and is working on machine learning/deep learning/IoT delivering innovative and cutting-edge AI and machine learning to the enterprise and developing advancements in AI.

Dr. Munirathinam has a PhD in machine learning, with over 20 years in business intelligence and 15 years in the manufacturing industry. He has authored many papers and is involved in numerous international artificial intelligence and data mining research activities and conferences.

His research interests include artificial intelligence, equipment health monitoring, IoT and big data analysis, statistical machine learning and data mining, ubiquitous computing, and human–computer interaction. He holds a Master of Science from Illinois Institute of Technology, Chicago. He is also a certified business intelligence professional.

Contributors

R. Joshua Arul Kumar
Department of Mechatronics
  Engineering
Rane Polytechnic Technical Campus
Trichy, India

P. L. Chithra
Department of Computer Science
University of Madras
Chennai, India

Savita Choudhary
Statistical Vision Adversarial
  Generation Lab
Department of Computer Science and
  Engineering
Sir M Visvesvaraya Institute of
  Technology
Bengaluru, India

G. Dheepa
Department of Computer Science
University of Madras
Chennai, India

Rathishchandra R. Gatti
Sahyadri College of Engineering &
  Management
Mangalore, India

Vipul Gaurav
Statistical Vision Adversarial
  Generation Lab
Department of Computer Science and
  Engineering
Sir M Visvesvaraya Institute of
  Technology
Bengaluru, India

Nancy Jasmine Goldena
Sarah Tucker College (Autonomous)
Tirunelveli, India

Pradeep Henry
GoodScore Labs
Chennai, India

B. Janet
Department of Computer
  Applications
National Institute of Technology
Trichy, India

Christina Jayakumaran
Department of Computer Science and
  Engineering
Loyola-ICAM College of Engineering
  and Technology
Chennai, India

V. Jayalakshmi
Department of Computer Application
Vels Institute of Science, Technology&
Advanced Studies, (VISTAS)
Chennai, India

Deepa V. Jose
Department of Computer Science
CHRIST University
Bangalore, India

Jinsi Jose
Department of Computer Science
CHRIST University
Bangalore, India

M. Karthigha
Department of Computer Science and
Engineering
Sri Ramakrishna Engineering College
Coimbatore, India

G. Nagarajan
Department of Computer Science and
Engineering
Sathyabama Institute of Science and
Technology
Chennai, India

Ardhendu G. Pathak
Co-founder, Koinvent Business
Solutions (Formerly, Airbus, GE)
Zurich, Switzerland

V. Pavithra
Department of Computer
Application
Vels Institute of Science, Technology &
Advanced Studies, (VISTAS)
Chennai, India

Madhumathi Ramasamy
Department of Computer Science and
Engineering
Sri Ramakrishna Engineering College
Coimbatore, India

A. Mercy Rani
Sri S Ramasamy Naidu Memorial
College
Sattur, India

A. Ranichitra
Sri S Ramasamy Naidu Memorial College
Sattur, India

Ashwath Rao
Sahyadri College of Engineering &
Management
Mangalore, India

Rachel Royan
Loyola-ICAM College of Engineering
and Technology
Chennai, India

K. Sathya
Department of Computer Science
University of Madras
Chennai, India

Shruthi H. Shetty
Sahyadri College of Engineering &
Management
Mangalore, India

Serin V. Simpson
Department of Computer Science and
Engineering
Sathyabama Institute of Science and
Technology
Chennai, India

Thompson Stephan
Department of Computer Science and
    Engineering
Faculty of Engineering and Technology
M. S. Ramaiah University of Applied
    Sciences
Bangalore, India

A. Christoper Tamilmathi
Department of Computer Science
University of Madras
Chennai, India

S. Titus
Department of Electronics and
    Electronics Engineering
K. Ramakrishnan College of
    Engineering
Trichy, India

A. Vijayalakshmi
Department of Computer Science
CHRIST University
Bangalore, India

Chapter 1

Get Technology to Contribute to Business Strategy

Pradeep Henry

GoodScore Labs, Chennai, India

Contents

DOI: 10.1201/9781003119784-1

Transformation Is a Strategic Initiative

Transformation is key to an organization's ability to grow and prosper. The C-suite would consider a transformation initiative to be a success if the initiative eventually generates strategic outcomes. We'll soon describe strategic outcomes, but in the meantime, here's a quick definition: customer value and financial performance that align with an organization's corporate strategy. Given the organization's situation and targeted outcomes, transformation initiatives are strategic initiatives that should contribute – often in direct and measurable ways – to corporate strategy.

A disturbing percentage of transformation initiatives fail to meet the C-suite expectation. Depending on the data source, between 70% and 85% of transformation initiatives fail. Failure could be due to one or multiple reasons. Most reasons covered in the literature are what we might call "soft" reasons such as lack of employee buy-in. However, even if all of the soft issues were addressed, the more fundamental "hard" issues, such as implementing a wrong tech asset, will still fail the initiatives. Before investing in implementation, the organization needs to be sure it is transforming using the right blend of business and tech innovations.

Transformation is not something new. Organizations have always transformed at some point in their existence. Traditionally, transformations were viewed and executed as business process redesign (BPR). Although a process view is obviously required while transforming processes, BPR is not the best approach for transforming an organization, given that today's technologies have the capability to play key roles. On the other extreme end, the power of technology has pushed organizations to think that they can transform by merely using a tech-centric approach and still get strategic business outcomes.

This chapter points out the issues with a tech-centric approach and then provides a process (method) to discover and design the right blend of business and tech assets before organizations invest in implementation.

To Transform an Enterprise, You Need More Than Tech

Transformation initiatives fail for many reasons. Here are three common reasons:

- Implementing an isolated tech asset
- Choosing a tech asset without using a "choosing" process
- Using a tech strategy to drive the initiative

These reasons are common due to a tech-centric approach to transformation. Let's look at how they cause transformations to fail.

Tech-Only Is a Risk

Implementing an isolated tech asset may not transform the organization and generate strategic outcomes. Talking about IT and business change, Joe Peppard [1] explains,

> What also seems to have been forgotten are the lessons from these earlier attempts to leverage IT. Unfortunately, the history of IT investments in most organizations is far from stellar: Research over the years suggests that the overall failure rate of IT projects is around 70%. We know that when IT projects fail, it is usually not because the technology didn't work (although this can sometimes be the case), but because the changes required at an organizational and employee level weren't managed effectively. Quite simply, adding technology does not automatically confer expected benefits; these benefits have to be unlocked and this can only happen through achieving organizational changes.

Technology plays an increasingly bigger role at organizations in many industries. But, even in an organization that wants to create and deliver customer value mostly through technology, a blend of business and tech assets will be required. Almost always, it is a blend that makes a strategic contribution. Unfortunately, what we see more often is organizations executing siloed technology projects.

Tech Chosen without a "Choosing" Process Is a Risk

Take the software development world for example. Collecting requirements is the task that is considered the discovery task. Even a software practice guideline, such as "Develop the right software," suggests getting the right set of requirements. Having the right requirements is of course important, but discovery should be firstly and largely about discovering the right software. Unfortunately, the literature doesn't offer any robust method for discovering the right tech asset. Also, with the large number of shiny new objects in today's digital space, there is an increased probability that we choose the wrong tech assets. Organizations often end up selecting tech assets that can't contribute to corporate goals. With the wrong tech assets, they launch the wrong initiatives.

Tech assets are often suggested by a vendor, consultant, or employee. Suggestions are often triggered by one of the following.

- **The technology is hot**: What's trending need not be the one that the organization needs. The problem with hot technologies is that there could be hype and poor understanding about situations where they really help.
- **The competition has that technology**: Some organizations are competition-obsessed. The problem is: what matters to competition need not matter to the organization's situation at the time. Competition obsession could also stifle purposeful innovation.
- **The technology solves reported problems**: The suggestion for a tech asset may come from employees. This is good. However, the suggestion could be siloed. A suggestion from a business unit may meet the functional goals of that unit, but fail to execute the corporate strategy.
- **The technology solves standard problems**: Often, organizations make a decision to invest in a tech asset based on standard expectations from the functional category to which it belongs or even merely based on standard benefits expected from "automation."
- **The technology is in the portfolio**: The organization might pick a tech asset from a so-called "Strategic IT Portfolio." This approach sounds impressive, but picking from a pre-prepared list may not deliver strategic outcomes.

So, selecting tech assets has been a mere decision-making activity rather than a methodical activity. "Organizations need to ensure that problems and opportunities that have not been properly diagnosed do not become projects – consuming time, money, and other resources – without reasonable confidence that they are valid means of achieving strategic objectives." – Andrew MacLennan [2]. Tech assets should be discovered (or validated if a suggestion exists) using a discovery method that considers factors such as the organization's current corporate strategy.

Tech Strategy Is a Risk

Nigel Fenwick [3] says "The truth is that your company doesn't need a digital strategy." Fenwick goes on to say "You could spend the next five years digitizing your entire business. Many tech vendors will fall over themselves helping you to do just that if you let them. Don't!" Why shouldn't a digital strategy or IT strategy drive your transformation initiative? The reason is that they're potentially siloed and not aligned with the corporate strategy. The tech strategy will likely have the same silo issue that we see in departments within organizations. "I've done some work with a few large corporates in which I compared the corporate strategy with their IT function's strategy – and the match was woeful." – Terry White [4], CXO Advisor. Transformation initiatives that are driven by a "siloed" strategy hurt the organization.

SAS VP Jill Dyché [5]:

> The reality of business siloes means business units have launched their own digital projects. Marketing might be experimenting with real-time product recommendations pushed to customers' smart devices, while manufacturing might be introducing sensors into the supply chain. Each business unit considers its challenges unique. Functional executives pay little heed to the connection, data integration, and analytics technologies that will ultimately be necessary to optimize these efforts.

The organization will therefore have poorly integrated processes and offer poor customer experience. Sure enough, sooner than later, the organization will have to start another project that gets the pieces to work together.

Tech strategy may not be an authentic input for a transformation initiative for the following reasons:

■ **Tech strategy may be outdated**: The Tech strategy may not accurately reflect the organization's current corporate strategy. This is highly likely because many organizations today use a "transient strategy" approach, where strategies are more dynamic (*The End of Competitive Advantage: How to Keep Your Strategy Moving as Fast as Your Business*, Rita McGrath [6]).

■ **Tech strategy cannot suggest the right portfolio**: The so-called strategic IT portfolios are often premature in prescribing a list of tech assets. Such prescribed tech assets are unlikely to be integrated with business.

■ **Tech strategy may not offer directions for business innovation and change**: Forrester Research founder George Colony used the phrase "naked technology" to characterize technology with no business innovation.

■ **Tech strategy may be self-serving**: "Self-serving" need not always be bad; it could deliver tech department level benefits. However, such benefits are more likely functional or standard than strategic.

Transformation requires the most authentic inputs – your organization's corporate strategy.

Operational and Outcome Risks

■ **Poor adoption**: The design of tech assets used to be notoriously poor from a human use perspective, but thankfully human factors are increasingly used in the design. Business factors though are still not systematically used in the design. Where there are poorly designed tech assets, users may find some workarounds or even refuse to use them.

■ **Recurrence**: Recurrence is the situation where one or more old business problems exist even after transformation. Recurrence may be due to a wrong tech asset, that is, the absence of a solution to the problem. Recurrence may be due to simply "automating" a process that already had problems. The accounting process at a restaurant chain remains the same-old after spending money on an accounting software; the existing accounting process is simply embedded in the new software and so if there were problems, those problems remain. A great opportunity to improve the organization was available, but it was squandered.

■ **Degradation**: While deploying new tech assets, changes may be required to one or more connected assets to get everything to work together as one. Such changes are often not foreseen or addressed due to a tech-centric approach that lacks a holistic view. Result: Things such as customer experience may actually get worse instead of better.

Here are a few symptoms of degradation: Different employees give different answers to the same question; different business processes complete the same work, but with different software; decisions by different departments are not coordinated; data are everywhere in the organization, but the information required to make decisions is not easily available.

Implementing and using a silo tech asset or a point solution is often the reason for degradation. Writing about software applications, Ross, Weill, and Robertson [7] describe the silo problem: "Individually, the applications work fine. Together, they hinder companies' efforts to coordinate customer, supplier and employee processes."

■ **Outcome risk**: Poor adoption, recurrence, and degradation deny organizations the business improvements they need to generate strategic outcomes. Also, like oil spills, they will soon require the organization to do difficult, long-drawn-out, and costly "cleanup" work. Cleanup might start with a technology rationalization project to (a) See which tech assets are adding value and which ones are driving costs, and then (b) Make decisions whether to keep or retire them. As a result of this exercise, organizations may have to spend again on one or more cleanup projects such as tech integration, tech re-engineering, and process improvement.

Broken Process

Hoping to mitigate the operational and outcome risks, we improved tech governance and software development practice.

Tech governance improvements: We changed the CIO's reporting and role. We also used strategy frameworks. With the latter, for example, we partly fixed cross-discipline disharmony by getting tech folks to sit closer to business folks in the office, and getting tech folks to talk the language of business folks.

Software development improvements: The software development discipline has been continually improved. We now pay attention to human factors while designing user interfaces (UIs). We use automation in testing to deliver more reliable software.

While both tech governance and software development improvements are necessary, the failure rate of transformation initiatives has not changed. The transformation process itself is broken. Outcomes from transformation are determined at the discovery-and-design stage. We need a corporate-strategy-driven discovery-and-design process that can help a talented team to create a tech-business-blended transformation architecture at the start of a transformation initiative.

Strategy-Driven Discovery-and-Design Process

Every transformation initiative that an organization invests in must show strategic potential right at the start of the initiative. You must know with a fair degree of certainty that your initiative has the potential to generate strategic outcomes. What gives the initiative strategic potential is the architecture. What's in your architecture and what isn't depends on two activities: discovery and design.

Figure 1.1 shows a 3-step discovery-and-design process. Drive every step with corporate strategy. Predict outcomes at the end of every step. At the end of the discovery-and-design process, the major output you have is a tech-business-blended

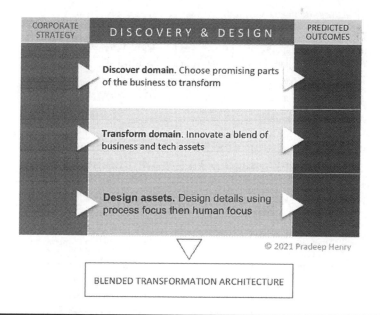

Figure 1.1   Discovery-and-design in transformation.

transformation architecture. Since you use corporate strategy to drive the initiative, you actually translate strategy into architecture. We can therefore call the process "strategy translation."

The tasks, structure, and flow make the discovery-and-design process robust. It's discovery first, design next. Yet, there's flexibility. Move back and forth between the two if needed. For example, while doing Step 2, the team might expand, reduce, or otherwise change the scope of the parts discovered in Step 1. Another example: while designing a specific tech asset in Step 3, the team can make changes to architecture already done in Step 2. In fact, Step 2 might even suggest a better corporate strategy.

Corporate Strategy

Warehouse club Costco's transformation comprised three activities: (1) build a fan base, (2) pioneer a minimum-wage trend, and (3) ditch American Express for Visa. It's easy to imagine that this unified set of activities must have been defined directly from corporate strategy. Also, tech assets must have been discovered as part of the three activities. Result? In just 6 years, Costco's revenue jumped from $76 billion to $114 billion.

A critical and expensive activity like transformation must get its inputs directly from your organization's overall corporate strategy rather than from any other potentially siloed strategy. That's how you can deliver on real organizational needs such as the need to create new revenue streams, the need to sell more customized and personalized offerings, the need for deeper customer interactions, and the need for agile reactions to changes in the environment.

Organizations have goals to achieve while facing a situation that might involve challenges and opportunities. **Corporate goals** are defined broadly in terms of customer value and financial performance. Alternatively, corporate goals are defined in terms of things that will help achieve targeted customer value and financial performance. To achieve corporate goals, organizations devise one or more strategies. A **corporate strategy**, therefore, is an approach or "trick" (in a good sense) that can achieve specific goals.

From the strategy, organizations derive themes, objectives, and outcomes. A **strategic theme** is an important idea that spans multiple processes and gets strategy to work. For example, "Customer delight" could be a strategic theme. You may have one or more themes. **Strategic objectives** are specific and actionable. They're derived from themes or strategies. They're typically defined under 4 categories: Financial performance, customer value, processes, and assets (people, technology, etc.). **Strategic outcomes** define the measure and the target value (Robert Kaplan and David Norton [8]).

How do organizations realize their strategic outcomes? In part, they do it through everyday "business-as-usual" activities. They also do it through new initiatives, which eventually improve business in ways that help realize those outcomes. Can you say what strategic outcomes your initiative is targeting? Eighty three percent of organizations do not know how to use new initiatives to achieve targeted business outcomes. The odds of realizing corporate strategy rise if you start with and keep focus on strategic outcomes.

Customer outcomes: Customer value impacts the organization's ability to acquire and retain customers. Customer value, in turn, determines the financial performance of the organization. Some great examples for customer value come from customers of Uber:

- The car comes to the customer; this eliminates phone calls to potentially disinterested dispatchers.
- Drivers know where to go; no need to try to give them directions.
- Payment is cashless; no need to get stressed about whether nor not you have the right bills and coins.

Financial outcomes: Financial performance in terms of revenues, costs, and profits eventually determines the success or failure of an organization. Cost-related outcomes may be determined by measures such as "reduction in shrinkage" for a retail organization. Revenue-related outcomes may be determined by measures such as "dollars-per-day increase in sales per reservation agent" for a hospitality organization. Profit-related outcomes may be defined considering cost structure and revenue growth.

List targeted strategic outcomes: Listing targeted outcomes is beneficial in the following ways:

- Makes clear what must be pursued in order to improve business and realize the strategy
- Enables business and tech teams to have common objectives and terminology
- Allows discovery and design of the right blend of business and tech assets
- Helps you to focus on things that really matter to the organization
- Confirms the need for business, technical, and project changes
- Demonstrates value from big tech investments.

Targeted strategic outcomes are a key input to strategy translation. Start your initiative by capturing (or helping define) strategic outcomes and stay focused until you know you have an architecture that demonstrates strategic potential.

Step 1: Discover Domain

Choose promising parts of the business to transform. Oil optimists significantly depended on luck when they drilled in our backyards with the hope of striking oil. Nine times out of ten, they ended up drilling a well that was a dry hole. The oil discovery process has advanced since then. They first find an oil reservoir before they invest in further efforts. In business transformation too, we must first find the "reservoir" or domain. The domain comprises "parts" of the business that have the potential to generate strategic outcomes if transformed in certain ways. The parts may be processes, departments, business units, or, in some cases, the entire enterprise.

In a tech-centric approach, the domain would primarily comprise the processes to be encapsulated in one or more tech assets. Allianz [9] instead looked far beyond the boundaries of a tech project. A "simple, engaging customer experience" was a strategic theme at Allianz. So here's what Allianz did. They identified 140 customer journeys, each spanning several touchpoints. From this "lead," they selected about 25 of the most urgent ones. This was their domain. Like an oil reservoir, the domain that Allianz found was promising – it had the potential to realize the theme when it was transformed.

Use a strategic theme or strategic objectives – derived from corporate strategy – to guide you to discover the domain.

The domain is central in any transformation initiative. When **discovered**, the domain shows strategic potential. When **transformed** (Step 2), the significantly or even unrecognizably changed domain has virtually realized the strategic potential. When **operational**, the domain generates strategic outcomes.

Turns out, the domain defines the scope of your transformation initiative.

Step 2: Transform Domain

Innovate a blend of business and tech assets. What business and tech assets should the transformed domain have? How should they be structured and connected? Notice that Step 2 comprises both discovery and design tasks. Make sure to realize the domain's potential identified earlier and the new possibilities from the newly discovered assets and the way they're architected. The resulting output is a tech-business-blended transformation architecture.

Use a strategic theme or strategic objectives – derived from corporate strategy – to guide you to transform the domain.

As regards tech innovations, teams may consider not only cloud, analytics, social, and mobile, but also geolocation-tracking, the Internet of Things, virtual reality, and artificial intelligence. This book guides teams on technologies to consider. Innovation can come not only from the capability of a new technology or tech asset, but also the way it is put to use. If it isn't feasible for an organization to develop a technology or tech asset, it partners with another organization that already has it. Allianz is an insurance and asset management company. So they partnered with Panasonic to launch what might at first appear like an unrelated service: "Panasonic Smart Home and Allianz Assist." This service links Panasonic's monitoring-and-control tech with Allianz's home protection services.

The tech-business-blended transformation architecture is a high-level, business-view diagram, the details of which will be worked out in Step 3. The architecture has far-reaching effects. It is this architecture that will be implemented – and deployed and used. It becomes the business just like civil architecture becomes the building. Once it has been agreed on, it is almost infeasible to fix it. Therefore, the architecture should have in it the right things designed right. Examine the blended architecture to see if it indicates the presence or absence of fit between the initiative and the corporate strategy. Use it while making investment decisions.

Step 3: Design Assets

Design business assets using best practices. Design tech assets at two levels: encapsulated processes first, user interface next. Yet, there's flexibility. Now move back and forth between the two if needed. From the blended transformation architecture, you know the business assets and the tech assets on which you should do further work. Do a high-level design of each identified asset. While doing high-level design, focus on business factors, human factors, and technical factors for technical feasibility. Use a strategic theme or strategic objectives – derived from corporate strategy – to guide you.

> **Business assets**: Business assets may include processes, groups, factories, services, or products. In fact, anything other than a digital/IT asset may be considered a business asset. Clearly, this is such a large range of things we can't even list them. Thankfully, existing best practices are good. There's also a lot of literature to help.
>
> **Tech assets**: All digital/IT assets are considered tech assets. That would include anything that is based on software, hardware, devices, network, or combinations. Tech assets typically have "encapsulated processes" and a user interface. These two need to be purposefully designed.

Design the encapsulated processes: Every tech asset will have one or more processes present in it. Internal assets such as an inventory control system have encapsulated processes. External assets such as a supplier bidding system accessed by bidders have encapsulated processes. Even consumer tech products have encapsulated processes; a typical cab service mobile app, for example, encapsulates at least two processes – Rides and Payments. Most teams are not aware of the tremendous value that could be gained by purposefully designing encapsulated processes. Design these processes with all the rigor that is commonly used in business process design projects.

Design the user interface: The strategic themes or objectives driving Steps 1 and 2 of strategy translation must drive Step 3 as well and right until the end – including the task of designing the UI architecture.

Predicted Outcomes

Predict business outcomes at the end of each of the 3 steps. Although quantitative predictions are often better, qualitative predictions are okay. In fact, at the end of

Step 1, only qualitative predictions will be possible. Remember that we're only in the architecture stage of the transformation initiative. Predicting outcomes at this stage would be a huge advancement and advantage. Along with the corporate strategy and the blended transformation architecture, predicted outcomes help make objective decisions that were not possible before – about what business and tech innovations to invest in.

How to Discover the Right Tech

We just outlined the process for discovery and design. Now we can look at key how-to guidelines. Note however that you discover tech assets in Step 2 while transforming the domain. So, this section is about Step 2. Also, this section covers only the discovery of tech assets.

Discover Tech in the Business Context

Always discover tech assets in Step 2 while creating the tech-business-blended architecture. It's ok to already have a proposed tech idea; in fact, it's highly likely that employees or consultants or vendors would have suggested some ideas. Even in this case, have the proposed tech asset validated by putting it through Steps 1 and 2 of the strategy translation process. By doing so, you make sure that every tech asset you implement will work in synergy with everything else to make a strategic contribution.

Never leap into implementing an asset without first knowing whether or not it has strategic potential. A tech asset implemented and deployed without first validating it in the business context might deliver business benefits that are generic and normally expected from automation or from the functional category to which it belongs, but these benefits may not be the strategic outcomes that the organization needs at the time.

Discover While Exploring Four Things

How did Airbnb generate revenues of $2.8 billion in 2017? "Airbnb has been breathing down hotels' necks for years," says a Digital Trends article. Airbnb started off by providing an alternative to hotel rooms. They let you book someone else's apartment or house for a few days. Then they introduced Airbnb Plus to offer specially curated "beautiful homes" and "exceptional hosts." And then they acquired luxury retreats to introduce Beyond by Airbnb [10]. Most surprisingly, the "don't book hotel rooms" company now lets you book hotel rooms, too.

That's a remarkable amount of serial business innovations. And yet, Airbnb is technology-driven and some even call it a technology company. Airbnb's tech assets, it's fairly clear, were discovered in the business context. It also appears that Airbnb looked at themes, customers, a broad horizon, and new technologies. These are exactly the things to explore in Step 2.

Themes: Derived from corporate strategy, there may be themes that your organization should pursue. Kaplan and Norton list themes such as "just in time" and "relationship management." A theme such as "a delightful customer experience" would involve customer engagements with tech and non-tech assets. A theme could be even bigger and more impactful such as "customer-centricity," which would typically include new customer value delivery through new or better products and services.

Customers: Organizations used to focus on improving internal processes such as accounting. Improvements were often achieved by "automating" the processes. These improvements brought efficiencies and drove down costs. Later, organizations began focusing on customers, but the focus was mostly limited to improving the customer experience. For this, principles were borrowed from human-centric design, which is increasingly informed by technologies involving big data and analytics. Well, good customer experience is extremely important for all organizations; in some cases, it can even turn a company around. However, it's time now to look at the potentially bigger opportunities that could come from innovating products and services themselves.

Broader domain: The simpler an initiative's scope, the higher the chances of completing it successfully – from a project management perspective. However, if you're targeting strategic outcomes, you need to be prepared for something more complex. Multiple businesses and tech assets will likely have to blend to make a strategic contribution. The scope of a transformation initiative should never be defined by the boundaries of a proposed tech asset. A broader scope, if identified using strategic themes or objectives, is likely to present relatively more opportunities.

New technologies: Thankfully, innovation is a constant in the tech space. There's a continual stream of new technologies, some of which may offer opportunities for organizations in certain situations. While some may be used for business-critical purposes, others such as the self-parking TV remote may be used for convenience purposes. All tech assets should be discovered or validated in the corporate strategy context.

How to Design It Right

Designing the wrong thing right squanders time and money. In the discovery-and-design process we described, tech assets are identified in Step 2 and appear in the blended transformation architecture, which is already predicted to have the potential to generate strategic outcomes. This sequentially ensures that organizations don't invest in wrong or non-strategic tech assets. Then you design the chosen tech assets in Step 3. So, this section is about Step 3 and covers only the design of tech assets.

Design Tech in the Business Context

Many teams use what they call a "kindergartener approach" to come up with as many ideas as possible. It is a quick and fun way to experiment. To help with such prototyping, teams use tools ranging from paper napkins and sticky notes to 3D printing and computer simulation. To inspire ideas through prototyping, organizations provide teams with workplaces that range from the merely colorful to the arguably weird.

Prototyping is a useful technique to design almost anything from coffee mugs and everyday products to digital technologies. So, the question is not whether prototyping is required. The question is when. Do not start a transformation initiative by prototyping a proposed tech asset. No amount of prototyping iterations can show whether a proposed tech asset is the right one to implement. Do not design anything before you know it has "strategic potential," that is, a reasonable probability that it is the right thing to work on in the first place. Ignoring this suggestion could be a huge business risk and might turn your project literally into a kindergartener's project. Finish Steps 1 and 2 and you will have one or more tech assets identified in the blended transformation architecture.

In the strategy translation process, prototyping helps you pick the best design for a tech asset. You could use one of three prototyping approaches. (a) Use iterative prototyping to create a prototype (or a design option, if you will), check it for strategic fit as well as for other characteristics that are important, and then improve it. Based on the level of fit, etc., you will then repeat the check-and-improve tasks. (b) Use a parallel prototyping approach to create two or three design options, then check the options for fit, etc., and finally pick the best. (c) Use a combination approach in which you create, say, two options and then "steal" ideas from both to create a third design option.

Design Approach

Keep the right mindset: Products, office interiors, experiments, and pretty much everything is **designed**. Therefore, we have several design approaches. What should be the overall design approach in transformation initiatives? We should approach design with:

- The strategy-focused mindset associated with business model innovation (even if your initiative may not involve designing a business model)
- The disciplined approach associated with process innovation (which is otherwise typically efficiency-focused and does not adequately exploit technology)
- People-sensitivity associated with human-centric design.

Define innovation scope: To define scope, process designers have used categories such as "Radical and Light" and "Simple, Moderate, and Re-imagine." Instead of using categories, consider how an existing design should change to achieve specific customer value and financial performance outcomes.

Design at two levels: The boundaries of a transformation initiative span multiple business and tech assets. And we need to design at two levels: integral and individual. Integral design (Step 2) is the transformation of the domain as a whole. While doing integral design, discover business and tech assets. While doing so, actualize not only the strategic potential earlier identified in the domain, but also a new potential that is possible through innovation and technologies. Individual design (Step 3) is designing individual business and tech assets discovered in Step 2. In this chapter, we talk about the design of tech assets. Every tech asset is designed at two levels. Level 1 is the design of the processes to be encapsulated in the tech asset. Level 2 is the design of the user interface.

Ask questions: Start with the big questions first, which should be derived from the organization's strategic objectives or themes. Skype must have asked, "What if voice calls were free over the internet?" That is a great what-if question because soon, Skype had acquired hundreds of millions of registrations. Ask, What specific changes would help generate strategic outcomes? For this, consider things that matter the most to customers (customer value, for example) and to the organization (customer retention, for example).

Designing the Encapsulated Processes

A company created a new business model that would be primarily driven by technology to provide on-demand cab service. The company became hugely successful due to innovation at the highest level: the business model. However, the company's mobile app had a problem with payments, which is one of the encapsulated processes. Credit card users are forced to pay the fare for the previous trip before booking a new one. Often, the notification came just as the customer was about to book a cab. By the time payment was made, the pricing may have changed or nearby cabs may have been hired by other customers. This not only wastes time but may also create stress or even cause serious problems to the customer depending on the purpose of the customer's ride. It's reasonable to imagine that many customers switched to a competitor.

If "provide superior service" and "retain customers" were among the company's strategic objectives, the company may have failed on both. After innovating at the highest level (business model), the company failed to get an encapsulated process designed right – and failed.

Most software projects merely "automated" a physical or manual process. This is called substitution, where the organization merely uses a tech asset as an alternative or replacement for pretty much the same function they already performed through physical or manual work. Tech substitution is common but it is not the right thing to do. There are a lot of innovation opportunities available in encapsulated processes. We should exploit them.

Process innovation done while designing encapsulated processes is similar to process innovation in conventional process design projects. The team would ask questions such as these: Could we streamline by straightening and shortening the path of flow? Could we do more efficiently what customer or vendor normally does? Could the customer or vendor do some of the work? Could we eliminate some work? Could we eliminate hand-offs, approvals, and anything else that doesn't add value? Importantly, make sure you leverage technology's power.

Designing the User Interface

Once encapsulated processes are designed, you are ready to design the user interface. Although you should start with encapsulated processes, you may go back and improve them while you design the user interface. The two should eventually work together as one.

What is it you should care about while designing the UI? It is a user experience. Definitions for user experience range from a simplistic "user interface design" to a useless "it covers everything." Sure, the term could include many things in which case the line with "customer experience" blurs. So, for the purpose of this chapter, let's focus on the UI. Here's our definition: User experience is the user's perception of a tech asset, where that perception is achieved through the design of the user interface. Easy, quick, and pleasurable are the three most common kinds of experiences that users expect.

Which ones among the three to prioritize depends on the tech asset's purpose and the user's expectations. If the user is playing a video game or even shopping online for some types of products, the top expectation is pleasure. However, when they want to book a cab on your mobile app, they aren't looking for pleasure (they want the ride to be a pleasure, though); instead, they're looking to get the task done as quickly as possible. Speed is also what they want when they're filling out their employer's timesheet application.

To achieve these user experiences through the UI, the following four design disciplines should contribute.

Process design: A study that my team conducted at Cognizant Technology Solutions suggested that about 60% of a large US organization's processes could be executed through user interfaces. Consumer tech products such as online banking and SaaS apps too encapsulate increasing numbers of processes and the process tasks are performed through the UI. If so, it is a powerful idea to view the UI as a process. In fact, many problems thought to be usability problems are actually process problems, which could only be solved through a process view. Consider a bank's loan system that encapsulates origination, processing, underwriting, and closing. If the UI could be designed using a process view, the steps could be completed faster, thus allowing more customers to be served in a shorter time.

So, the process view that you used while designing encapsulated processes should continue into your task of designing the user interface. Using a process view means designing the UI like we would design a process – an approach that determines how work gets done.

Usability design: Human factors experts took over UI design work from programmers, viewed the UI as a medium for human–computer interaction, and cracked the code for usable software. Usability improved and with it, software adoption improved. Usability is the ease of learning, ease of use, and accuracy within the UI realm. Usability is a fundamental quality requirement in every tech asset and for all kinds of user experiences.

Visual design: Good visual design is required for all kinds of experiences. It not only makes UI screens look neat, but it also advances usability by navigating users' eye movements over the screen. It can contribute to pleasure and it can even by itself bring pleasure to users. In some cases, it works better alongside good audio.

Content design: Content is textual information needed by users for the effective use of a tech asset. It comprises labels for UI elements, messages such as error messages, Help text of various kinds including tool tips, and printed manuals.

Getting Your Team to Make a Strategic Contribution
Individual Contribution Is Important

The flow from assets (people, tech, etc.) to processes to customer value to financial performance seems obvious. However, not all of these are measured or understood – in terms of their contribution to a transformation initiative. An organization's financials can be seen in the public domain in the case of public companies. Customer value may be seen in news reports, articles, and in customer complaints and feedback. Process performance may be seen within the organization and in customer complaints and feedback. However, the contribution of assets, particularly human capital, is often not known. People can and should strategic contributions, but the people–financials link is not understood and gets little coverage in the literature. There are at least two reasons:

- **Existence of silos**: Kaplan and Norton introduced a Balanced Scorecard to show the people–task–outcomes link. Unfortunately, the departments or divisions that use balanced scorecards are often themselves siloed and disconnected from corporate strategy.

■ **Focus on team performance**: Collaboration always matters and people must always come together to make strategy work. However, individual performance matters a lot, too. Unfortunately and wrongly, the individual's contribution is being increasingly ignored.

It is important to know individual contributions so you can: (a) Hire the right people and train them appropriately, (b) assign the right people to initiatives, and (c) evaluate and reward them in a fair way.

Potentially Chaotic Team

There's a business analyst/architect group, a process innovation group, a design thinking group, a technology group, and more. Not all of these groups are internal. Some of them are external. Tech vendors try to push new technologies. Management consultants try to push their new or upgraded services. Partner firms want to prove a point. This is complexity. Groups are likely global. Even your own colleagues are located across multiple offices or homes in multiple countries. The group expected to do a particular activity is actually a firm your vendor recently acquired. This firm wouldn't easily work with your vendor's other groups. All this is more complex. Add to it office politics. Each group in this expanding universe believes they are the ones most important to the success of your initiative. Some of them think they can do it all by themselves and that the other groups are unnecessary.

Specialists from multiple disciplines and multiple locations are required in transformation initiatives, but such a team is potentially a big risk. How do you get the team to collaborate?

How to Ensure Collaboration

How do you get a potentially chaotic team to make a strategic contribution to the transformation initiative? Soft skills such as relationship skills are what most pundits recommend. While relationship skills are important, they do not matter if more fundamental "hard" elements are missing. Here are four fundamental elements you should use in order to connect people in a practical way.

Connect them through strategy: Let corporate strategy drive your initiative. The CEO is responsible for corporate strategy, not even the Board [11]. Even where ideas move bottom-up or where strategies need to be different for different markets, the CEO must approve the new or improved strategy.

Connect them through method: To translate strategy into architecture, deploy the strategy-driven discovery-and-design method. Select individuals and groups based on the skillset needed to use the method.

Connect them through roles: Tightly connect roles that are critical to translate strategy into architecture. The link is from team to business leader and/or CIO to CEO. Without this link, the objectives pursued may not be the right ones, to begin with. Since the suggested link connects all the way up to the CEO, there's little chance for conflicts, which may be common otherwise. Even if a conflict arises, say, because a better strategy was just discovered, it will quickly get CEO attention and resolution. The CXOs and business leaders in the link must be employees, while the team and team leader can be external people. Read "Strategy: Who Leads Digital Progress?" [12].

Connect them through portfolio: Give team the ability to see the organization's projects portfolio. Make project deliverables, decisions, and outcomes transparent for more powerful collaboration. Transparency into the organization's portfolio helps in six ways: (1) synergize organizational initiatives, (2) sync initiatives and existing business, (3) generate the right ideas for new initiatives, (4) learn from completed projects, (5) avoid repetition, and (6) retire unnecessary stuff.

Connect them through technology: Software such as the following may help your initiative with transformation or project management tasks.

- **GenSight**: An integrated platform to support strategy and innovation programs; supports the Stage Gate process.
- **GoodScore**: Empowers transformation team to discover and design the right blend of technology and business improvements that can deliver strategic outcomes. GoodScore prompts the team to perform robust discovery-and-design tasks, builds a powerful repository, and provides features to better manage the project.
- **i-nexus**: A single platform for transparency and accountability of strategy which visualizes business-wide progress with clarity of goals, targets, and deliverables. Supports Hoshin Kanri and other methods.
- **Shibumi**: A strategy execution management software that enables business leaders to deliver better business transformation results.
- **Synergy Indicata**: A strategy execution and monitoring and evaluation software.

Product descriptions are reproduced from company websites (Full disclosure: GoodScore is an application from the chapter author's company.)

Managing Transformation Outcomes

An organization runs many initiatives of varying scope and transformation is one of them. A lot of money, time, and effort are invested in these initiatives. The most important question is: what are the business outcomes? Initiatives typically deliver outcomes in the tragic-to-strategic range. Where in this range would you position your organization's different initiatives? Are your transformation initiatives strategic initiatives as they should be? To classify initiatives from an outcome perspective, an outcome quadrants chart is helpful. This tool helps you know where you stand. Over time, it helps you find out what's fundamentally and consistently wrong, so you could then make the needed changes.

To create an outcome quadrants chart, keep corporate strategy and business outcomes handy.

- **Strategy**: Know the corporate goals and know the corporate strategies that were devised to achieve those goals. Consider goals and strategies that were in effect – those that informed the initiative.
- **Outcomes**: Know the outcomes. You need actual or estimated outcomes. Check whether or not an initiative made or will make a strategic contribution.

Create a simple quadrants chart (Figure 1.2). On the chart's X-axis is Strategic Contribution. The range is from None to Strong. On the Y-axis is Outcomes. The range is from None to Strong.

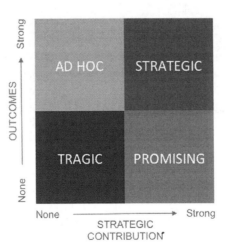

Figure 1.2   Outcome quadrants chart.

The four quadrants represent four broad outcomes.

- **Tragic**: The bottom-left quadrant is the **Tragic** quadrant. Place here those initiatives that generated low levels of business outcomes that were also nonstrategic.
- **Ad hoc**: The top-left quadrant is the **Ad hoc** quadrant. Place here those initiatives that generated significant business outcomes, but those outcomes did not make a strategic contribution. Presence in this quadrant could make organizations think that they're doing fine when in reality, outcomes were not strategic. The presence of too many initiatives in this quadrant probably indicates that the organization lacks strategy translation (corporate-strategy-driven discovery-and-design) capability.
- **Promising**: The bottom-right quadrant is the **Promising** quadrant. Outcomes generated are below target levels, but they made a strategic contribution. A significant number of initiatives in this quadrant indicate that the organization is on the right track and can shoot for greater performance in upcoming projects.
- **Strategic**: The top-right quadrant is the **Strategic** quadrant. This is where you want to see a lot of your initiatives and definitely all of your transformation initiatives.

The outcome quadrants chart is not a maturity model. For transformation initiatives, the target should always be the Strategic quadrant. Position your last several initiatives in the outcome quadrants. What does the classification tell you? What action should you take before you start your next transformation initiative?

References

[1] Joe Peppard, *Strategy Execution*, Routledge, 2010.
[2] Andrew MacLennan, *Strategy Execution*, Routledge, 2010.
[3] Nigel Fenwick, "Digital Myth No. 4 – Your Company Needs A Digital Strategy," *Forrester*, 2018, https://go.forrester.com/blogs/myth-4-your-company-needs-a-digital-strategy/
[4] Terry White, *What Business Really Wants from IT*, Routledge, 2011.
[5] Jill Dyché, *5 Surprises Chief Digital Officers Should Prepare For*, CIO, 2016.
[6] Rita McGrath, *The End of Competitive Advantage*, Harvard Business Review Press, 2013.
[7] Jeanne W. Ross, Peter Weill, David Robertson, *Enterprise Architecture As Strategy*, Harvard Business School Press, 2006.
[8] Robert Kaplan and David Norton, *Strategy Maps*, Harvard Business School Press, 2004.
[9] Allianz, https://media.knowledge-executive.com/human-experience/customer-experience/insurance-cx/allianz-group-biggest-insurer/

[10] Airbnb, *Digital Trends*, https://www.digitaltrends.com/home/airbnb-for-everyone/

[11] Roger L. Martin, *The Board's Role in Strategy*. Harvard Business Review, 2018, https://hbr.org/2018/12/the-boards-role-in-strategy

[12] Gerald C. Kane, Anh Nguyen Phillips, Jonathan Copulsky, and Garth Andrus, "How Digital Leadership Is(n't) Different," *MIT Sloan Management Review*, 2019.

Chapter 2

Introduction to Computer Vision

A. Vijayalakshmi

CHRIST University, Bangalore, India

Contents

DOI: 10.1201/9781003119784-2

23

Introduction

Computer vision is a deep learning technique that has the ability to understand and interpret the images from a given input image or a scene. It generates intelligent information from a visual image or sequence of images or scenes. It is the field of computer science that focuses mainly on replicating the human vision system that helps computers to identify the objects in images and videos in a fashion similar to that of humans. To be specific, they can identify, track, measure, detect and classify objects in images. Machine learning and deep learning techniques can be used to train a model to identify or classify objects in a scene. Computer-vision systems use image processing as a subset to enhance the image for further usage. Image processing is the process of performing a set of operations on an image so that an enhanced image is obtained to extract useful information from it. Some of the applications of computer vision are automatic face recognition, interpretation of facial expression, medical image analysis, its interpretation for diagnosis, etc.

Image Processing

Image processing focuses on processing the images for enhancement. The major goal of image processing is to enhance the quality of the image for it to be suitable for a specific task. Generally, the images captured from the camera are pre-processed to be used for image-processing tasks. The pre-processing of images is carried out to enhance the quality of images. Noise reduction, brightness and contrast enhancements are a few of the examples of pre-processing. The results of image processing will be improved with better pre-processing of images. Image processing helps in object detection, localisation and measurement, identification and verification. The basic steps in image processing are as shown in Figure 2.1.

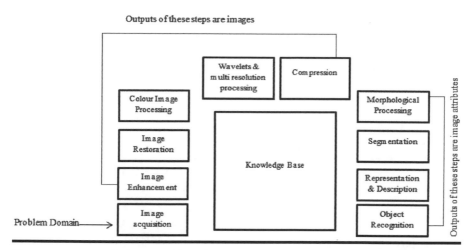

Figure 2.1   Steps in image processing.

Image acquisition is converting the image into its digital form. The binary image is passed through the image-enhancement step to bring out obscured details. Image restoration helps in improving the appearance of an image. Colour image processing includes colour modelling and processing. To reduce the storage to save the image, different techniques are used by compressing the image. Extracting the image components that are useful is called morphological processing. This image is partitioned into different parts in segmentation. Further, the object is recognised. Image segmentation is the most important part of image processing, video processing and computer-vision applications [1, 2] and its purpose is to find meaning from an image.

Image segmentation is the most important step in image analysis. This process is nothing but pre-processing of an image that divides a digital image $f(x, y)$ into continuous non-empty subsets f1, f2, f3,.., fn that helps in extracting features from the image [3]. The basic question in segmentation, while subdividing the image into its constituent parts is the level of segmentation. The level to which subdivision should continue varies with different applications. Having said that, image segmentation is one of the most important and difficult parts of image analysis. The overall analysis of an image greatly depends on the level of image segmentation and it is to be mentioned that if the proper image-segmentation method is applied to an image, the rest of the stages in image analysis becomes easier. Some of the applications of image segmentation are in the field of medical imaging, object detection, video surveillance, etc.

Segmentation

Segmentation is one of the most important problems of computer vision. This marks the transition from low-level image processing to image analysis. The input to segmentation is a pre-processed image. The output will be the region of interest within the given image. In order to represent this region of interest, various techniques are used in the form of boundaries or regions. Once the given image is segmented, the output is used for analysis or classification. The different approaches of image segmentation are discontinuity-based and similarity-based techniques.

Discontinuity-Based Approach

The discontinuity-based approach follows the approach of subdividing the image based on abrupt changes in the level of intensity of the images. The objective of this method is to identify isolated points, lines and edges of an image. In order to identify these features, masks are used.

Operation of Masks

Consider the screen of a window as shown in Figure 2.2, representing x- and y-axes and consider a particular pixel at (x, y).

A 3 × 3 mask can be used to identify points, lines and edges in the image. Figure 2.3 shows the basic representation of a 3 × 3 mask with the weights assigned to the pixel at (x, y) in Figure 2.3 to be $W(0, 0)$ and respective weights to the surrounding pixels.

When this mask is convolved on the image, the R value is computed as given in Equation (2.1).

$$R = \sum_{i=-1}^{1}\sum_{j=-1}^{1} w_{i,j} f\left(x + i, y + j\right) \tag{2.1}$$

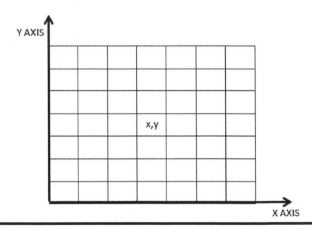

Figure 2.2 Representation of a pixel (x, y).

W(-1,-1)	W(-1,0)	W(-1,1)
W(0, 1)	W(0,0)	W(0,1)
W(1,-1)	W(1,0)	W(1,1)

Figure 2.3 A 3 × 3 mask with weights.

Point Detection

The basic primitive in an image is known as point or pixel which is considered to be the basic type of discontinuity in an image. Convolving on the image with appropriate masks is helpful in identifying the discontinuity. The various masks used for this purpose are shown in Figure 2.4.

The process of applying the mask represented in Figure 2.4 on the original image leading to the convolved image is shown in Figure 2.5.

When the mask is convolved on the image, the response of the image, R, can be calculated using Equation (2.1). If $|R| > T$, where T is the threshold, it indicates that an isolated point is detected at (x,y). Figure 2.6 shows the result of the point detection mask.

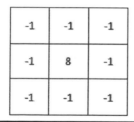

-1	-1	-1
-1	8	-1
-1	-1	-1

Figure 2.4   Mask for convolution.

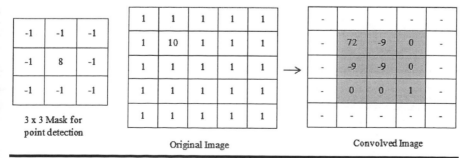

3 x 3 Mask for point detection

Original Image

Convolved Image

Figure 2.5   Applying the mask on an image.

Figure 2.6   Applying point detection mask on an image.

Line-Detection Algorithm

The objects in the visual world are a combination of basic primitive lines. The accurate identification of line segments in an image is one of the most important low-level similarity identification for computer-vision problems like feature matching, vanishing point detection, real-time lane mark detection and construction of 3D images [4, 5].

Include Masks for Line Detection

A line can be represented by the equation of the line using two parameters, (a, b) as

$$y = ax + b \tag{2.2}$$

Equation (2.2) gives the slope-intercept parameterisation form of lines. When the value of x takes 0, i.e., $x = 0$, from Equation (2.2), we get

$$y = b \tag{2.3}$$

Hence, b is the intercept of the given line with the y-axis. a is the slope of the line which can be represented as

$$a = \frac{y2 - y1}{x2 - x1} \tag{2.4}$$

where $(x1, y1)$ and $(x2, y2)$ are the end points of the line.

This form of representation for a line as given in Equation (2.2) cannot represent the vertical line and, therefore, the Hough transform uses the equation given in Equation (2.4) that could be written also as in Equation (2.5) [6].

$$r = x \cos\theta + y \sin\theta \tag{2.5}$$

$$y = -\frac{\cos\theta}{\sin\theta}.x + \frac{r}{\sin\theta} \tag{2.6}$$

The Hough space for lines includes the dimension of r and θ, where $\theta \in [0, 360]$ and $r \geq 0$. A line is represented by a single point and the line-to-point mapping is as represented in Figure 2.7.

One of the major concepts in Hough transform is mapping of the single point to all the lines that pass through that point, leading to a line in the Hough space, as shown in Figure 2.8.

Figure 2.9 shows the algorithm for detecting straight lines [6].

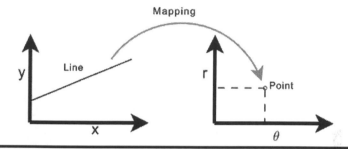

Figure 2.7   Mapping of line to Hough space.

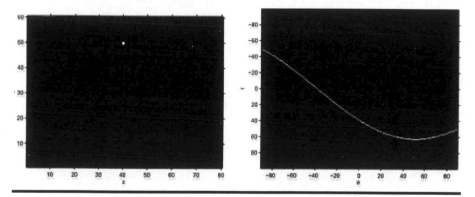

Figure 2.8   (a) point P_0 and (b) all the lines that pass through the point.

Step 1: Detect the edge using canny edge detector.

Step 2: Map the edge point to the Hough space and store in accumulator.

Step 3: Interpret the accumulator to yield lines of infinite length. Interpretation can be done by thresholding.

Step 4:Convert the infinite lines to finite lines

Figure 2.9   Algorithm for detecting straight lines.

Edge-Detection Algorithm

Edge detection is an image-processing technique that plays an important role in segmentation. The edge is a boundary between segments in an image. The objective of edge detection in an image is to reduce the quantity of data during the process. However, the essential information with respect to the shape features of the image is retained which is very much necessary for processing. It helps in identifying meaningful discontinuities in the grey level of an image and helps in image segmentation and data extraction in computer-vision applications. An edge is defined as an abrupt change in the intensity of pixels or the discontinuity in brightness. Edges are a sudden disparity of pixels in an image. Edge-detection algorithms help in extracting the edge line with appropriate orientations. The different types of edges are shown in Figure 2.10.

Spatial masks can be used in detecting the edges in an image. The different edge-detection techniques are explained in this chapter.

Roberts Edge Detection

Roberts edge-detection algorithm for detecting edges in an image was introduced by Lawrence Roberts. This operator finds the edges in an image by approximating the spatial gradient magnitude in an image. The objective of this method is to identify the edges by focusing on the regions with high spatial frequency [7, 8]. For a 2 × 2 window as shown in Figure 2.11, Roberts edge detection consists of horizontal and vertical filters as shown in Figure 2.12. These kernels respond to edges that are at 45° to the pixel grid.

The gradient magnitude can be computed as

$$|G| = \sqrt{G_x^2 + G_y^2} \qquad (2.7)$$

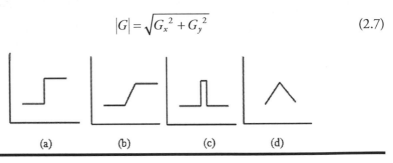

(a)	(b)	(c)	(d)

Figure 2.10   (a) Step edge, (b) Ramp edge, (c) line edge and (d) roof edge.

P1	P2
P3	P4

Figure 2.11   A 2 × 2 window for Roberts edge detection.

+1	0
0	-1

0	+1
-1	0

Figure 2.12   Roberts cross-convolution masks: horizontal (G_x) and vertical (G_y).

In order to make the computation faster, the approximate value is calculated as

$$|G| = |G_x| + |G_y| \tag{2.8}$$

Since the mask is small, the Roberts edge detector is fast but they are subjected to noise. This method cannot detect the edges if they are not sharp.

Sobel Edge Detection

The Sobel method was introduced by Sobel that finds edges by approximating the gradient magnitude of the image. This method uses a horizontal and vertical filter in sequence and sums up the result to detect edges in an image. It finds the high spatial frequency that is directed on the edges by incorporating a 2D spatial gradient on images [8].

The Sobel operator finds the derivative of an image in the x- and y-directions. The 3×3 kernel is used for each of the x- and y-directions. The kernel for the x-direction has negative numbers on the left side and positive numbers on the right. Similarly, the gradient for y-direction has negative numbers at the bottom and positive at the top.

The masks that are represented in Figure 2.13 works on the vertical and horizontal edges. The G_x kernel shown in Figure 2.10 works in the horizontal direction and G_y kernel works in the vertical direction, respectively. The kernel convolved over the image produces separate gradient component measurements in the G_x and G_y orientations.

The gradient magnitude can be computed as

$$|G| = \sqrt{G_x^2 + G_y^2} \tag{2.9}$$

-1	0	+1
-2	0	+2
-1	0	+1

+1	+2	+1
0	0	0
-1	-2	-1

Figure 2.13   A 3 × 3 Sobel mask: horizontal (G_x) and vertical (G_y).

Step1: Accept the sample input image.

Step2: Perform masking on given image.

Step3: Apply algorithm and the gradient.

Step4: On the input image, perform mask manipulation in both the directions.

Step5: Find the absolute magnitude of the gradient.

Figure 2.14   Pseudocode for Sobel edge detection.

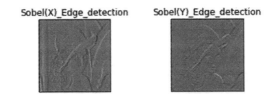

Figure 2.15   Output of Sobel mask on Lena image.

In order to make the computation faster, the approximate value is calculated as

$$|G| = |G_x| + |G_y| \tag{2.10}$$

The angle of orientation is given as

$$\theta = arc\tan\left(\frac{G_x}{G_y}\right) \tag{2.11}$$

This process can be represented in a pseudocode as given in Figure 2.14.

The Sobel operator can be used in segmenting the image as it is very quick to execute. The output of the Sobel operator on the famous Lena image is given in Figure 2.15.

Prewitt Edge Detection

The Prewitt edge-detection algorithm uses a discrete differentiation operator computing the gradient intensity function. The output of a Prewitt operator is a gradient vector when the filter is convolved in horizontal and vertical directions. Prewitt is a faster method of edge detection with less computational power. Prewitt algorithm considers the one with maximum gradient intensity function as an edge. In this case, derivative masks with the following properties are considered, as shown in Figure 2.16. For masks with opposite signs, the sum of masks should be equal to zero; it has two masks for horizontal and vertical edges, respectively.

The output of Prewitt masks on the famous Lena image is represented in Figure 2.17.

-1	0	+1
-1	0	+1
-1	0	+1

-1	-1	-1
0	0	0
+1	+1	+1

Figure 2.16   Vertical and horizontal masks.

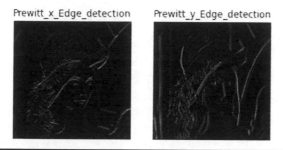

Figure 2.17   Prewitt mask on Lena image.

Kirsch Edge Detection

Kirsch operator, also known as the Kirsch compass mask, is a derivative mask that finds an edge in an image in predetermined eight directions. In this method, a kernel mask is taken and rotated in all the eight compass directions at an increment of 45°. The magnitude of an edge is calculated from the maximum magnitude across all the directions. The compass directions are named as East (E), North East (NE), North (N), North West (NW), West (W), South West (SW), South(S) and South East (SE). These masks are shown in Figure 2.18.

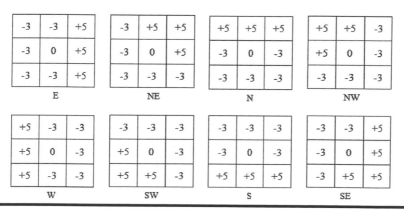

Figure 2.18   Kirsch compass mask.

Robinson Edge Detection

The Robinson edge-detection algorithm is similar to that of Kirsch masks. This is also called a directional mask as one mask is rotated in all the eight compass directions as represented in Figure 2.19. All the eight masks are applied to the pixel neighbourhood and the maximum value is the magnitude of the gradient. The algorithm gives a more accurate magnitude of the gradient but takes more computation power compared to the Roberts algorithm and the Sobel algorithm [9].

Marr Hildreth Edge Detection

In this method, the intensity changes are detected at varied scales that occur in an image. The filter that is used is the second derivative of the Gaussian. The change in intensity at every channel is represented as zero crossings. The image is filtered through two independent channels and the zero crossings are then found from the filtered values [10]. The algorithm for Marr Hildreth edge detection is as shown in Figure 2.20.

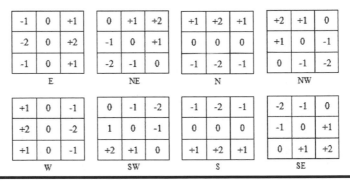

Figure 2.19   Masks in Robinson algorithm.

Step 1: Smooth the image using a Gaussian

Step 2: Apply a two-dimensional Laplacian to the smoothed image.

Step 3: Loop through the result and look for sign changes. If there is a sign change plus the slope across the sign change is greater than some threshold, mark as an edge.

Step 4: To get better results it is possible to run the result of the Laplacian through a hysteresis alike to Canny's edge detection although this is not how the edge detector was firstly implemented.

Figure 2.20   The Marr Hildreth edge-detection algorithm.

LoG Edge Detection

The Laplacian of the Gaussian is one of the most popular edge-detection algorithms. Unlike considering the first derivative in the Sobel algorithm for edge detection, in this case, the second derivative, which is the slope of the first derivative, is considered in identifying an edge from a given image. When the second derivative crosses zero, an edge is said to be occurring [11].

For an image with intensity value I, for any given pixel (x, y), the Laplacian $L(x, y)$ can be mathematically written as Equation (2.12).

$$L(x,y) = \frac{\partial^2 I}{\partial x^2} + \frac{\partial^2 I}{\partial y^2}$$ (2.12)

As the pixels in the image are discrete, the second derivative cannot be calculated directly. Instead, it needs to be approximated using the convolution operator. The two important masks for this are as shown in Figure 2.21.

In order to reduce the noise while computing the second derivative, a Gaussian smoothing filter is convolved with the Laplacian filter. Equation 2.7 shows the combination of both these filters and it is known as the Laplacian of the Gaussian [7].

$$LoG = -\frac{1}{\pi\sigma^4}\left[1 - \frac{x^2 + y^2}{2\sigma^2}\right]e^{-\frac{x^2+y^2}{2\sigma^2}}$$ (2.13)

The output of the Laplacian edge-detection algorithm when applied on the famous Lena image is as shown in Figure 2.22.

0	-1	0
-1	+4	-1
0	-1	0

-1	-1	-1
-1	+8	-1
-1	-1	-1

Figure 2.21   Masks for LoG edge detection.

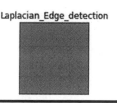

Laplacian_Edge_detection

Figure 2.22   LoG masks on Lena image.

Canny Edge Detection

The Canny edge-detection algorithm, proposed by Canny [12], is known as the optimal edge detector and it is the most appreciated edge-detection algorithm that can detect all those edges in an image with noise suppressed. This algorithm was designed with the following aims:

Detecting the real edge in an image: The main objective was to identify the real edges and marking them as well as decreasing the probability of falsely marking the non-edges as real edges.

Localisation: The method aimed at marking the edges close to the real edges of an image.

Removing multiple responses: This property aims at marking the edge only once. The noise in the image should not create false edges [12, 13].

The Canny edge-detection algorithm works as per the following series of steps:

Step 1: Filter the noise in an image
The first step in this algorithm is to filter out the noise that is present in the original image. In order to remove noise from the image, the Gaussian filter is computed using the simple mask. After computing the mask, the Gaussian smoothing is accomplished through the convolution technique. While convolving, the mask is slid over the image operating on the pixel of the original image. As the size of the Gaussian mask is larger, the detection of noise in the image will be lower.

Step 2: Find the strength of the edge
The strength of the edge is found by taking the gradient of the image. The Sobel operator is used in calculating the spatial gradient measurement on an image. At every point, the strength and gradient magnitude are calculated. For the Sobel operator, a 3 × 3 mask is used for estimating the gradient in x- and y-directions. The edge gradient is computed as per Equation (2.14).

$$Edge_{gradient}(G) = \sqrt{G_x^2 + G_y^2} \qquad (2.14)$$

which can be approximately represented as Equation 2.15.

$$|G| = |G_x| + |G_y| \qquad (2.15)$$

Step 3: Find the direction of the edge
It is very important to find the direction of the edge after computing the gradient in the x- and y-directions. When the gradient in the x-direction tends

to zero, the direction of the edge is 90° or 0° based on the gradient value in the y-direction. If the gradient value in the y-direction is zero, the edge direction will be 0°; else, the edge direction will be 90°. Equation (2.16) represents finding the value of edge direction.

$$\theta = inv \tan\left(\frac{G_x}{G_y}\right) \quad (2.16)$$

Step 4: Relate the edge direction

The edge direction that is computed in step 4 is related to a direction that can be traced in an image. Consider Figure 2.23 where 5 × 5 image pixels are represented.

From Figure 2.23, it can be seen that for the pixel, 'A' the possible directions based on the surrounding pixels are at 0°, 45°, 90° and 135°. The edge orientation will be aligned to one of these directions based on its close proximity to the same. To elaborate on this, consider Figure 2.24. Any edge falling in the R1 region is set to 0°, any edge whose direction is in the region R2 is set to 45°, all those edges falling in the region R3 is set to 90° and all the edges in the region R4 are set to 135°.

Step 5: Non-maximum suppression

Non-maximum suppression is used to suppress all those pixel values that are not considered as an edge. This is carried out by tracing along the direction of the edge which is identified in step 4. The output of this step will be a thin line.

X	X	X	X	X
X	X	X	X	X
X	X	A	X	X
X	X	X	X	X
X	X	X	X	X

Figure 2.23   5 × 5 image pixel.

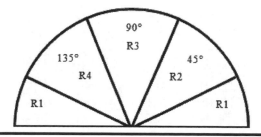

Figure 2.24   Orientation of edges.

Step 6: Hysteresis thresholding

In this step, the hysteresis is used in eliminating streaking. Breaking up of an edge contour above and below the threshold is called streaking. To decide which edges are real edges, two thresholds min and max are used. All the edges with intensity gradients more than max are real edges and those edges below min are non-edges. All the edges that lie between the thresholds are classified as real edges or non-edges based on the connectivity. If these edges are connected to real edges, then they are considered as part of real edges; else, they are ignored.

Figure 2.25 shows three edges A, B and C. the edge A is above the threshold max and hence it is considered to be a real edge. Edge B is below the threshold max, but is connected to the real edge A and hence, B is considered to be a valid edge. Edge C is above min but it is not connected to any of the real edges and hence it is discarded. Figure 2.26 shows the output of Canny edge detection on the famous Lena image.

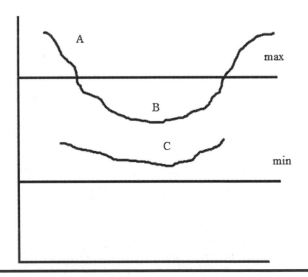

Figure 2.25   Edges with two levels of the threshold.

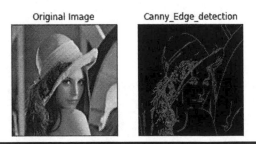

Figure 2.26   Edge detection using the Canny algorithm.

Similarity-Based Approach

In this approach, given an image, segmentation is performed based on the similarity of pixels [1, 3, 14, 15]. The various techniques that follow this approach are thresholding, region growing and region splitting.

Thresholding

Thresholding is a very simple segmentation technique. A threshold value is chosen and all those pixels having values greater than the threshold are assigned to one region and all those pixels with values less than the threshold are assigned to the second region, as shown in Figure 2.27.

Region Growing

Region growing is a method of segmentation wherein the pixels are grouped depending on their similarity based on some predefined similarity criteria to segment images into various regions. The growing region is controlled by these similarity criteria. Apart from the predefined similarity criteria, adjacency spatial relationship among the pixels is also taken into consideration. In this approach, we start from a random pixel and grow the region by appending pixels in the neighbourhood if the neighbouring pixels satisfy the similarity criteria with respect to their intensity, colour and other related properties. Some of the similarity criteria that are considered in this method are listed as follows:

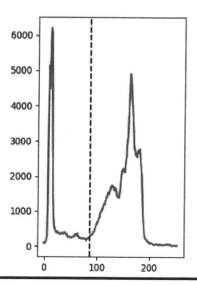

Figure 2.27   Segmentation using thresholding.

Let p(x,y) be the original image that is to be segmented

Let s(x,y) be the binary image where the seeds are located

Let 'T' be any predicate which is to be tested for each (x,y) location

Step 1: All the connected component of 's' are eroded

Step 2: Compute a binary image, P_T where $P_T(x,y)=1$, if $T(x,y)$ is True

Step 3: Compute a binary image 'q', where $q(x, y) = 1$, if $P_T(x, y) = 1$ and (x, y) is 8-connected to seed in 's'

The connected components in 'q' are segmented regions.

Figure 2.28   Algorithm for region growing.

1. The difference in intensity values of the candidate pixel and the neighbouring pixel should be within a specified range.
2. The difference in intensity values between a candidate pixel and the running average intensity of the growing region should be within a specific range.

The basic algorithm for region growing is shown in Figure 2.28.

Region Splitting and Merging

This method uses splitting and merging for segmenting an image. The iterative division of an image into various regions with similar characteristics is called splitting. Combining the adjacent similar regions is known as merging. Figure 2.29 depicts the division of a quadtree.

Figure 2.30 shows the steps followed for region splitting.

Segmentation Based on Clustering

K Means Clustering

K means clustering algorithm is used in segmenting the area of interest from the background of an image. This algorithm works on the basis of centroids. It partitions

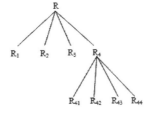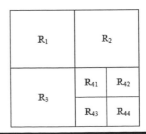

Figure 2.29   Division based on quadtree.

Consider 'p' as the original image and let 'T' be the predicate.

Step 1: Initially R1 is equal to p.

Step 2: Divide each region into quadrants and T(Ri) = FALSE

Step 3: If for every region, T (Rj) = True, then merge adjacent regions Ri and Rj such that T (Ri U Rj) = True.

Repeat Step 3 until merging is impossible.

Figure 2.30   Steps in region splitting.

Table 2.1 K Means Clustering Algorithm

Step 1: Decide the value of the clusters K
Step 2: Choose the centroids at random K points
Step 3: Allocate each point to their appropriate closest centroid to form K clusters
Step 4: Calculate the value of the new centroid and place it for each cluster
Step 5: Assign the data points to the new calculated centroid that is closest to the data points if any

the data into K different clusters based on K centroids. The K means algorithm works with unsupervised data and the goal of the algorithm is to classify data with similarity into a specific number of groups, K. The value of K cannot be obtained from the knowledge on the dataset and this value must be chosen randomly. However, the optimal choice of the value for K will have a great impact on the overall process of clustering. The K means algorithm is given in Table 2.1.

Deep Learning

Deep learning is a subdivision of machine learning that includes multiple processing layers with multiple levels. This representation imitates the function of a human brain in how it understands information underlying a large input data. Deep learning has a variety of models encompassing neural networks, hierarchical probabilistic models and a variety of unsupervised and supervised feature learning algorithms. These algorithms outperform the previous state-of-the-art techniques in several tasks. The development of the neural network is based on the functionality of the human brain, when McCulloch and Pitts (MCP) [16] carried a study to recognise how the human brain produced complex patterns with the use of neurons. They developed a model, known as the MCP model, which has made a significant impact on the growth of artificial neural networks (ANNs). ANNs are designed to solve various problems in pattern recognition, prediction, optimisation, etc.

Neural Networks

The neural network was developed on the working of the biological neural network, where the dendrites receive information from neurons that are connected to it and the information is further processed inside the cell body. The processed information is sent to other neurons through axons. ANN can be represented as a weighted directed graph where the neurons are the nodes and directed edges are the interconnection between the input neurons and output neurons [17]. These directed edges have their own weights. For artificial neurons, MCP suggested binary threshold as the computational model as seen in Figure 2.31. The input signals x_j, where $j = 1$ ... n are the inputs to the neuron where the weighted sum of these input signals are computed and the output is generated. The output will be 1 if the sum is above the threshold; otherwise, it is 0.

MCP neuron has been presented in different ways and one among it is where activation functions are used other than the threshold function. Examples of activation functions include piecewise linear, sigmoid and Gaussian functions. The most frequently used activation function in ANN is the sigmoid function, which is defined as

$$g(x) = \frac{1}{\left(1 + \exp\{-\beta x\}\right)} \tag{2.17}$$

where β is the slope parameter.

Like the biological neural network, the input layer of the ANN receives input data as depicted in Figure 2.32. The lines that are connected to the hidden layers are known as weights and these weights add up to the hidden layers. The processing takes place in the hidden layer and it passes the output to the next hidden layer and finally to the output layer.

Deep Learning Algorithms

Deep learning algorithms have self-learning representations and they depend on the neural networks similar to the human brain computing the information. Training of the samples is done to extract features and group the objects so that the model is able to identify data patterns. This section discusses various deep learning algorithms.

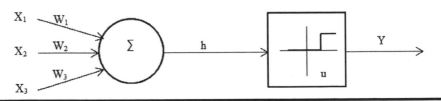

Figure 2.31 Weighted directed graph.

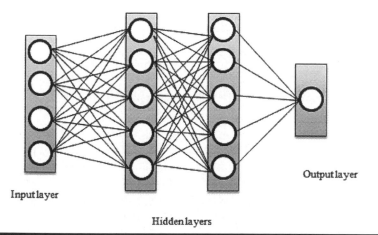

Input layer

Output layer

Hidden layers

Figure 2.32   Artificial neural network.

Convolutional Neural Networks

A convolutional neural network, which is also known as ConvNet or CNN, is a deep learning algorithm which consists of neurons that are self-optimised through learning as seen in Figure 2.33. Each neuron takes the input and performs operations through hidden layers of the neural network [18]. CNN is used in the field of pattern recognition of images.

Convolutional Neural Networks consist of the following layers:

Convolutional layer: This is the first layer in CNN and it extracts features from the input image. A filter of size m × m is slid over the image to get the feature map as the output. The filter in this case is nothing but the weights. The array of the input image is multiplied with the two-dimensional array of weight, also known as filter. When the filter is slid over the input image, the dot product is calculated between the filter and the image. The dot product is calculated between the filter and the filter-sized part of the input image and summed up to a single value. The output of this dot product is the feature map which provides details about the

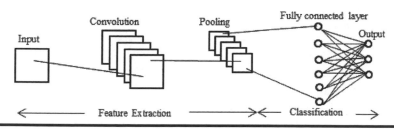

Figure 2.33   Convolutional neural network.

corners and edges of the input image. This feature map is fed as the input to other layers to learn on further features of the image.

ReLU layer: After the feature map is extracted from the image, it is passed to the ReLU layer (Rectified Linear Unit). The function of the ReLU is to perform an element-wise operation to set the entire negative pixel to 0.

Pooling layer: The feature map which is the output of the convolutional layer is converted into a lower resolution which will still be containing the important structural elements. The fine details of the image are eliminated by down-sampling as this will not be useful. In this case, the down sampling is achieved using the pooling layer. It operates on the feature map to generate pooled feature maps. Average pooling and Max pooling are the two functions used in the pooling operation. In the case of average pooling, the average value is calculated for each patch on the feature map. For the Max pooling, the maximum value for each patch in the feature map is considered.

Fully connected layer: Input of this layer is the output from the pooling layer after flattening. The flattened vector is connected to fully connected layers. These fully connected layers are the same as ANNs. Every neuron in one layer will be connected to each neuron in the next layer. The flattened feature map is passed through the fully connected layer to classify the images.

Recurrent Neural Network

Recurrent neural networks (RNNs) are one of the robust neural network algorithms and this is the only algorithm with internal memory. These are algorithms for sequential data as it remembers the input [19] because of its internal memory. This property makes the algorithm suited for machine learning problems which have sequential data like time series data, audio data, video data, sales forecasting, stock forecasting, speech, text, weather, etc. RNNs have internal memory and they can remember the input and predict what is next. RNNs are proved to be forming a deep understanding of a sequence when compared to other state-of-the-art algorithms and hence RNNs are heavily used for retaining sequence information of input data.

In the RNN algorithm, the information in the network cycles through a loop. In order to make a decision, the RNN takes into consideration the current input as well as what the network has learned from the previous input it has received, as shown in Figure 2.34. The RNN uses short-term memory and when the RNN is combined with LSTM, it has a long-term memory. RNN assigns a weight matrix to the current input and previous input to produce output.

Like ANN, in the forward propagation, the weight matrix is assigned to the input to produce output. They map the input to one output whereas the RNN maps one to many, many to many and many to one, as shown in Figure 2.35.

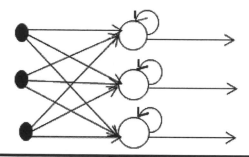

Figure 2.34   Recurring neural network.

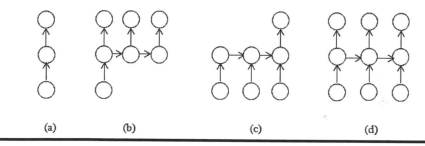

| (a) | (b) | (c) | (d) |

Figure 2.35   (a) One to one, (b) one to many, (c) many to one and (d) many to many.

During the back propagation, the partial derivative of the error with respect to the weights is calculated. This helps in subtracting the value from the weights. This makes it clear that RNN is a sequential neural network that trains neurons with back propagation to retain the sequence of input.

Long Short-Term Memory Network

The long short-term memory network (LSTM) is a type of an RNN which can learn long-term dependency. This method stores the information over a long time interval through recurrent back propagation [20]. LSTM stores information in memory, like the memory of a computer, and can read, write and delete information from its memory. The LSTM is used for time series prediction as they have the capability of remembering previous inputs. Speech recognition is one of the applications of LSTM.

Deep Belief Networks

Deep Belief Networks (DBNs) were invented as a solution for the problems encountered when using traditional neural networks training in deep-layered networks, such as slow learning, becoming stuck in local minima due to poor parameter selection and requiring a lot of training datasets. DBNs are represented graphically and are generative in nature which produces all the possible values. DBN contains multiple layers where there is a relationship between them. This algorithm is a solution to traditional neural network problems like slow learning, problem in local minima due to poor parameter selection, etc. This algorithm is used in generating images, recognising images and also in motion and video sequences [21].

Restricted Boltzmann Machines

Restricted Boltzmann machines (RBMs) are probabilistic graphical models and are inferred as stochastic neural networks. Their computational power and ability to learn faster have helped in applying them to various machine learning algorithms. The RBM is a very useful algorithm for applications like dimensionality reduction, classification, regression, collaborative filtering, feature learning and topic modelling. RBMs are two-layer neural networks which are the building blocks of deep-belief networks. An RBM has two layers: the input layer and the hidden layer. The nodes in an RBM are the places where the calculations take place. Each of the nodes is connected to each other across the layers but there is no intra-layer communication. This is the restriction in the connection of neurons in an RBM. It can be used in comparing the probabilities of observations [22].

Conclusion

For computer vision to analyse the hidden facts of an image or a scene, one of the fundamental steps is to extract data from the image using image segmentation. It is affected by various factors like similarity of images, image continuity, etc. This chapter discusses various methods of segmentation in images. This study gives an overview of computer vision and various segmentation techniques for image processing.

References

[1] D. Kaur, and Y. Kaur, "Various image segmentation techniques: A review," *International Journal of Computer Science and Mobile Computing*, vol. 3, no. 5, pp. 809–814, 2014.
[2] H. Zhang, J. E. Fritts, and S. A. Goldman, "Image segmentation evaluation: A survey of unsupervised methods," *Computer Vision and Image Understanding*, vol. 110, no. 2, pp. 260–280, 2008.
[3] W. X. Kang, Q. Q. Yang, and R. P. Liang, "The comparative research on image segmentation algorithms," *Proceedings of First International Workshop on Education Technology and Computer Science*, vol. 2, pp. 703–707, 2009.
[4] F. Nielsen, *Detecting lines in images: The Hough transform*, 2011. doi:10.13140/RG.2.2.17096.78080

[5] E. J. Almaz, R. Tal, and J. H. Elder, "*MCMLSD: A Dynamic Programming Approach to Line Segment Detection,*" In *Proceedings of the IEEE Conference on Computer Vision and Pattern Recognition*, pp. 2031–2039, 2017.

[6] Duda, R. O., and P. E. Hart, "Use of the Hough transformation to detect lines and curves in pictures", *Communications of the ACM*, vol. 15, no. 1, pp. 11–15, 1972.

[7] Maini, R., and H. Aggarwal, "Study and comparison of various image edge detection techniques," *International Journal of Image Processing*, vol. 3, no. 1, pp. 1–11, 2009.

[8] Easton, Roger L. *Fundamentals of digital image processing*, pp. 1–4, 2010.

[9] J. Burnham, J. Hardy, K. Meadors, and J. Picone, "*A comparison of the Roberts, Sobel, Robinson, Canny, and Hough image detection algorithms,*" In *Image Processing Group: Comparison of Edge Detection Algorithms MS State DSP Conference*, pp. 1–18, 1997.

[10] D. Marr, and E. Hildreth, "Theory of edge detection," *Proceedings of the Royal Society of London. Series B. Biological Sciences*, vol. 207, no. 1167, pp. 187–217, 1980.

[11] S. Savant, "A review on edge detection techniques for image segmentation," *International Journal of Computer Science and Information Technologies*, vol. 5, no. 4, pp. 5898–5900, 2014.

[12] J. Canny, "A computational approach to edge detection," *IEEE Transactions on Pattern Analysis and Machine Intelligence*, vol. 6, pp. 679–698, 1986.

[13] D. Ray, *Edge Detection in Digital Image Processing*, University of Washington, Department of Mathematics, 2013.

[14] F. Y. Shih, and S. Cheng, "Automatic seeded region growing for color image segmentation," *Image and Vision Computing*, vol. 23, no. 10, pp. 877–886, 2005.

[15] L. Grady, "Random Walks for Image Segmentation," *IEEE Transactions on Pattern Analysis and Machine Intelligence*, vol. 28, no. 11, pp. 1768–1783, 2006.

[16] W. S. McCulloch, and W. Pitts, "A logical calculus of the ideas immanent in nervous activity," *Bulletin of Mathematical Biology*, vol. 5, no. 4, pp. 115–133, 1943.

[17] Jain, Anil K., Jianchang Mao, and K. Moidin Mohiuddin. "Artificial neural networks: A tutorial," *Computer*, vol. 29, no. 3, pp. 31–44, 1996.

[18] O'Shea, Keiron, and Ryan Nash. "An introduction to convolutional neural networks." arXiv preprint arXiv:1511.08458, 2015.

[19] Zaremba, Wojciech, Ilya Sutskever, and Oriol Vinyals. "Recurrent neural network regularization." arXiv preprint arXiv:1409.2329, 2014.

[20] Hochreiter, Sepp, and Jürgen Schmidhuber. "Long short-term memory," *Neural Computation*, vol. 9, no. 8, pp. 1735–1780, 1997.

[21] Hinton, Geoffrey E. "Deep belief networks," *Scholarpedia*, vol. 4, no. 5, pp. 5947, 2019.

[22] Fischer, Asja, and Christian Igel. "*An introduction to restricted Boltzmann machines,*" In *Iberoamerican Congress on Pattern Recognition*. Springer, Berlin, Heidelberg, 2012.

Chapter 3

Essentials of the Internet of Things (IoT)

Nancy Jasmine Goldena

Sarah Tucker College (Autonomous), Tirunelveli, India

Contents

DOI: 10.1201/9781003119784-3

Introduction

Instant and endless access to mass information and entertainment is provided through the Internet. It also enables people from around the world to work online and to communicate and work effectively to improve customer service. While people use the Internet with little time, attention and precision, almost 2.5 quintillion bytes of data are generated every single day; the quality of data gathered about real-world things is extremely unfortunate. As the wealth of information matures, this valuable information needs to be used to enhance customer experience by tracking and measuring all data in order to reduce waste, loss and cost.

The Internet of Things (IoT) is an emerging digital age with unconfined new dimensions of technological, communal and economic opportunities. The ways we work, live and play are transformed by existing data analysis capabilities, the Internet connectivity with the combination of connected devices, smart sensors and intelligent operations. It includes all objects in our everyday lives when we say interconnected devices. It will indeed be a worldwide network with computer and computing devices. In order to provide the society with advanced standards of service, all that can be connected to the Internet should be connected to the embedded systems, the integrated electronics and the information technology.

For decades, there has been the concept of the combination of computers, sensors and networks for monitoring and controlling devices, but the IoT is gaining momentum while researchers turn to connected devices to perform their daily tasks. Industries also reinvest in the IoT to achieve optimised performance. Several authentic IoT devices have been created and the market has become open to different professionals, such as IoT product engineers, developers of IoT applications, cloud architects, designers, etc.

The progress of technology development constitutes convenient and faster communication. The IoT-enabled devices relay data to each other. Earlier, this information exchange between devices was often called machine-to-machine (M2M) technology. M2M sim cards enable the sending and receiving of data by devices. This information is then stored on a data-sorting-and-interpreting platform.

As innovative firms build new business models that take advantage of this wealth of data to achieve high operating excellence and ultimately deliver a competitive advantage, the rapid growth of the IoT disrupts virtually every industry. The IoT is the result of further progress in the underlying hardware and software technologies.

The factors driving the rapid adoption of IoT expansion are:

- Technology advances in network connectivity
- Affordable cloud infrastructure
- Low-cost sensors
- High penetration of smartphones and tablets
- Advances in data processing and analytics

Technology advances in network connectivity: Enormous wireless technologies that allow communication between devices are available on the market. Cellular networks provide reliable communication across broadband and support various voice calls and video streaming applications. Some of the most widely used networking technologies include wireless Internet access to Bluetooth, ZigBee, Z-Wave, DECT and Thread. Moreover, peer-to-peer communication technologies such as AllSeen, DLNA and UPnP allow direct device connectivity without the need for an access point.

Affordable cloud infrastructure: The vast advance in cloud capabilities have made IoT more accessible and widespread. Cloud offers quick access to affordable computer resources for information storage and processing over a public network. Cloud infrastructure also allows seamless storage and computing tasks to be offloaded from IoT devices on cloud servers. This makes the IoT one of the driving forces behind innovative and pioneering industries. The IoT has a complementary connexion with the cloud to enhance our daily tasks and are also implemented to simplify complex business issues and optimise industry applications. The IoT generates huge amounts of data and needs the cloud to provide geographic coverage as well as central management and monitoring for the sharing of resources.

Low-cost sensors: During the past few years, the computing expenses, the memory and the cost of wireless connectivity have all been more affordable due to the immense technical advances. The steady decrease in the costs of connected devices and the availability of low-cost sensors has made the IoT a viable technique for businesses. The low-cost portable, mobile and device-sensing systems make the IoT system more intelligent. They provide better data analysis, improve workflow, streamline supply chains, identify problems faster and also increase the production process.

High penetration of smartphones and tablets: The smart phones are also equipped with built-in accelerometers, barometers, thermometers and photometers which measures pressure, humidity, ambient temperature and illumination levels. These small and light-weight portable devices are equipped with wireless, solar power and long-lasting batteries. Smartphones also have an implied store of game play, browsing, image editing, email sending, location-tracking apps that make the user act smarter and play an important role in IoT.

Advances in data processing and analytics: The IoT attracts consumers by presenting information significantly from many devices that interact and exchange large volumes of data in different formats. The data collected can be structured or unstructured, locational or time-based; however, Big-Data-based analytical tools make it possible to convert the data into decision-making statements. Spatial analytics, time series analysis and streaming analysis are some of the techniques used to analyse information in different formats and structures. Progress in data analysis has opened up new opportunities for business optimisation.

Origin and Influences of IoT

The origin of the IoT can be traced back to several decades ago. Machines transmitting information to and from a central network might sound like a device for science fiction, particularly during the pre-Internet era, when things like that didn't exist at all. However, since the beginning of the 1800s, there were visions of machines communicating. Since the telegraph (the first landline) was developed in the 1830s and 1840s, machines have provided direct communication.

The idea of machines that communicate with each other first floated at the beginning of the 1800s and, technically, came to light first in the 1830s with the creation of the telegraph phone that was able to communicate over large distances via electric systems and equipment. The first radio voice transmission, described as "wireless telegraphy," took effect on 3 June 1900, which provided another component necessary for the advancement of the IoT.

In the 1950s, computer development started. M2M technology is an integral part of our workplace and our personal lives, starting with telemetry solutions, and has taken a big step into today's IoT solutions. In 1968, the father of M2M, Theodore Paraskevakos, invented and patented "a device for use in a telephone system," responsible for the "automatic transfer of information from a calling telephone to a called telephone."

John Romkey connected a toaster to the Internet for the first time, in 1990. One year later, a group of students at Cambridge University used a web camera to report on coffee. They came up with the idea of using the first web camera prototype to monitor how much coffee in their computer lab was available in the coffeepot. They programmed the web camera to take pictures of the coffeepot three times a minute. Then the photos were sent to local computers to see if coffee was available.

At the beginning of 2000, in MIT's AutoID laboratory, Briton Kevin Ashton laid the foundations for the IoT. As Proctor & Gamble was searching for ways to enhance their operations by linking RFID information to the Internet, Ashton was one of the pioneers behind the new IoT concept. It was a concept that was simple but very powerful.

He realised that optimisation depends directly on how quickly data are transmitted and handled. The use of Radio Frequency Identification (RFID) has accelerated the process of transferring data directly between devices. He had an idea of things to collect, process and transmit data without human involvement. He decided to refer to it as "the Internet of Things." All objects can communicate and be managed through computers with identifiers and wireless connectivity. An article in the *RFID Journal* was written by Ashton in 1999:

> If we had computers that knew everything there was to know about things—using data they gathered without any help from us we would be able to track and count everything, and greatly reduce waste, loss and cost. We would know when things needed replacing, repairing or recalling, and whether they were fresh or past their best. We need to empower computers with their own means of gathering information, so they can see, hear and smell the world for themselves, in all its random glory. RFID and sensor technology enable computers to observe. Identify and understand the world—without the limitations of human-entered data.

The IoT has become a leading edge in the development of information technologies together with artificial intelligence (AI). The IPSO Alliance has thus created an alliance of companies in 2008 that are promoting the development of technology for the IoT. This was a big step forward for the IoT in real production planning for large-scale enterprises.

As the Internet became more connected with every indication (such as the software) worldwide, a variety of other concepts, including machine-to-machine, RFID, context-aware computing, wearables, ubiquity computing and the web of things, have emerged in accordance with the idea and practice of connecting everything to everything. In Figure 3.1, there are a few milestones in the progress of physical mashing with the digital.

The Internet takes almost every aspect of our lives under its control. We enter a world in which the Internet works constantly and silently for us. They perform all the requisite daily tasks behind the scenes, from home insurance renegotiation, booking holidays, making smarter financial choices, collecting waste and supplying our smart refrigerator with fresh milk.

In the so-called IoT world of interconnected devices from 2020 to 2030, Cisco predicts that 50 billion machines will rise. These connected devices are not as connected devices today, which need the normal human interface.

These devices take almost all form in every corner of our lives. We could have online 3D printers and facilities on plant floors that could react with a virtual assistant built into a personal computer to e-commerce orders from a half-world distance. A motor vehicle could communicate along the road with other connected vehicles that could pick you up from the office and take you to the front door, which your smartwatch would unlock. With welcoming lamplight and warm water for a bath, smart light bulbs and smart metres could also announce your arrival.

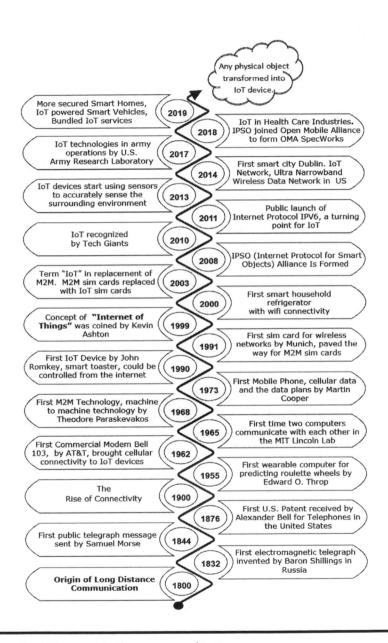

Figure 3.1   Milestones in the progress of IoT.

The IoT has an important positive effect on people, companies and governments, ranging from reducing the cost of healthcare and improving quality of life, reducing carbon footprints, enhancing access to education in remote, unserviced communities and improved safety in traffic.

IoT is also a keyword for a wide range of technologies and services. It relies on use-cases that are part of a broader ecosystem of technology and integrate similar technologies such as Big Data analytics, various communication and connectivity technology, cloud computing technology, artificial intelligence, cybersecurity, blockchain, digital twin simulation, augmented and virtual reality and more.

Basics and Terminology

The IoT's best definition would be "a network of intelligently designed objects that is open and extensive with the ability to organise themselves in the context of situations and environmental changes, share information, data and resources, react and work." Nearly all areas, devices, sensors, software, etc., are interconnected. The ability to access these devices using a smartphone or computer is known as the IoT, and these devices are accessed remotely.

The IoT aims to provide "a connectivity for anything, anywhere, and not just anyone, by giving each and every object its unique identity."

The sensors are linked to physical objects in the IoT networks and are used to keep track of the data, to enable their Internet-tracking. Data are sent by devices, such as sensors. This information is then processed and used for device control or other devices by people or machines. For example, a temperature sensor transfers temperature information to a process that determines that the room temperature is too warm and thus sends a signal for the air conditioning to be activated.

Electronic devices such as TV, washing machine, smartphone, smartwatch, which aid in interacting with the IoT platform, initiate the entire IoT process. Here are four basic IoT system components that will tell us how the IoT works (Figure 3.2).

■ **Sensors/devices:** First, the sensors or IoT devices capture the data every minute from the environment continuously to make smarter decisions. The data collected from the surrounding environment will have different degrees of complexity ranging from a simple sensor to a complex video feed. Integrated with technology, these devices can connect and interact online. Also, they can be remotely monitored and controlled.

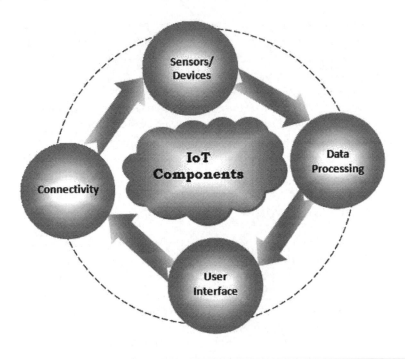

Figure 3.2 Basic IoT system components.

The IoT devices will mainly have/be:
– Low usage and computational power.
– Low cost
– Wireless

Examples include temperature sensors used for calculating the amount of heat energy, hydrostatic pressure sensor used to measure the level of liquid filling, etc. (Figure 3.3).

To transform an everyday object like a house or a car into a smart house or smart car, the object is required to have:
– A unique address – IPv6 address
– A way to connect to a network

In a device, there can be several sensors that can combine, besides sensing, to do something. For example, our phone is a device with a variety of sensors, including GPS, accelerometer and camera. It is extremely vital to have wired or wireless connectivity between devices and processors and often through the Internet.

Because the amount of data collected by IoT devices is very high, storage space, as well as the computing power needed to use this information, is also very high. The benefit of cloud storage and processing solutions is that they are scalable, affordable, have fast response times and are easy to market.

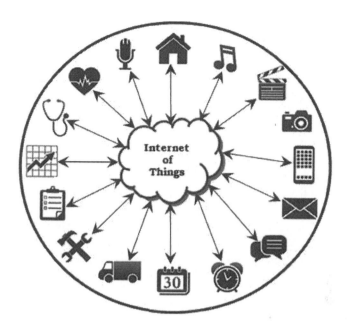

Figure 3.3   Internet of Things.

- **Connectivity:** Subsequently, to be transferred to the cloud infrastructure, the data collected require a means of transport.

    Various communication media, such as satellite networks, mobile networks, Bluetooth, Wi-Fi, Low-Power Wide Area Networks (LPWANs), Wide Area Networks (WAN), etc., can be used to link sensors to cloud infrastructure. Every option we choose contains certain requirements and compensations between electricity consumption, bandwidth and range. Therefore, it is important to select the best IoT connectivity option.
- **Data processing:** The data collected and sent to the cloud are processed by a software. It might be very obvious task such as checking that the temperature reading is acceptable on devices like AC or heaters. Also, sometimes, it may be very complex, for example, using a computer video vision to identify items (e.g., intruders of your house).

    The data collected by the sensors can be processed by the cloud service in various ways. For example, data processing can be done before it is sent to the cloud, which is enabled by edge computing. Edge computing allows the processing of data near its origin (devices with sensors). The data are transmitted from sensor units to a local edge-computing system that then processes and stores the data and then sends it to the cloud.

■ **User interface:** The information is then directed in some way to the end user. This can be done by activating alarms on their phones or by sending information via text messages or emails.

It is also possible for a user to actively check their IoT system via their interface. A user with a camera in his house, for instance, may want to check the video recordings and all the web server feeds.

On the other hand, it's not always that simple and one-sided. The user can also perform a function that can backfire and affect the system in accordance with the IoT application and complexity of the system. For example, the user can remotely adjust the temperature via the phone, if he identifies some changes in the refrigerator.

Some cases also involve the automatic conduct of certain actions. The IoT system can automatically fine-tune settings by creating and implementing certain predefined rules and no person is physically present. If an intruder is sensed, the IoT system will smartly generate a warning not just to the house owner but also to the authorities concerned.

Characteristics of IoT

The fundamental characteristics of an IoT are shown in Figure 3.4:

■ **Hardware:** IoT devices shall be embedded and designed for the outstanding features of design goals intended. The features are the type of sensors to be used, environmental conditions, the volume of data to be aggregated, range and speed required by the device design, the power, their total cost of ownership and the unit cost of the devices.

IoT systems incorporate both physical and digital elements that capture physical device data and opt for delivering actionable and operational insights. IoT devices can be prototyped with custom printed circuit boards (PCBs) using platforms such as Arduino or single-board computers such as the Raspberry Pi.

Prototyping these platforms involves the know-how to create circuits, as well as the programming of microcontrollers and the ability to comprehend protocols for hardware communication such as I2C, serial and SPI, which are also used to create communication with actuators and connected sensors. In general, embedded programmes are built using C++ or C, but for IoT devices, JavaScript and Python are incredibly popular.

■ **Interconnectivity and networking:** When it comes to the IoT, the global framework for information and communication infrastructures will all be interconnected. Connectivity enables compatibility and accessibility of networks. Accessibility can be achieved over a network, while compatibility offers the universal capacity to consume and generate data.

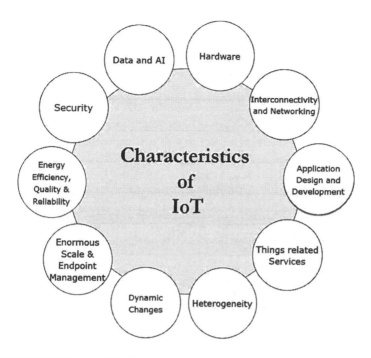

Figure 3.4 Fundamental characteristics of the IoT.

Network design and management within the IoT is a core competency. This is largely due to the size of connected devices and the effect of decisions on network architecture that are potentially large-scale.

In addition to designing the network, developers should be familiar with network standards, specifications and strategies. These include wireless Internet, Zigbee, Low Energy Bluetooth, consumer RFID technology, cellular and LPWAN technology. LPWAN technologies include low-power, long-range wireless communication from LoRa, SigFox and NB-IoT (IoT Narrowband), which is best suited to large-scale and industrial IoT applications.

■ **Application design and development:** The user interfaces (UIs) provided by web and mobile apps enable IoT device interaction and data consumption. However, IoT devices can also have interface designs of their own. Interfaces based on voice and gestures are gaining popularity within the IoT. Augmented reality interfaces provide an exciting opportunity, particularly when it comes to home automation, to cover IoT data in the physical world. Consequently, UI and User Experience (UX) design skills are currently some of the hottest IoT skills.

- **Things-related services:** With constraints, such as privacy and semantic continuity between physical and virtual things, the IoT can provide things-related services. Both technology in the natural world and the world of information will evolve in order to provide services relevant to objects within the constants of things.
- **Heterogeneity:** IoT devices based on different hardware and network platforms are heterogeneous. They are able to communicate with other devices or service platforms via various networks.
- **Dynamic changes:** Device statuses such as connected or disconnected, active or inactive and device context such as location and speed, changes dynamically.
- **Enormous scale and end-point management:** The overall number of devices to be managed and communicated will be at least an order of magnitude greater than those connected to the current Internet. The management and interpretation of the data generated for application purposes will be even more critical. This concerns data semantics and efficient data management as well.

  It is essential to take over the end-point management of the entire IoT system, otherwise, the entire IoT system will fail. For example, the failing IoT system is caused by the ordering of the coffee beans by a coffee machine itself, but by the purchase of the beans from a retailer and we are not attending home for a couple of days. Thus, end-point management is necessary.
- **Energy efficiency, quality and reliability:** IoT equipment may operate in severe weather, relentless surroundings and places that are difficult to reach such as devices in outside spaces or in deep mines. Since equipment can operate in such environments, the high quality, reliability and energy efficiency are important so that batteries do not have to be charged or changed on an ongoing basis.
- **Security:** IoT devices are very vulnerable to the compromise of security. Many companies reported that they were attacked. Many of them, on the other hand, may well have been attacked without knowing it.

  IoT installations and their networks are at significant security risk, which is tackled in the IT department through traditional cybersecurity initiatives. That may not be enough. Organisations which use IoT should use separate operational technology policies that are different from other networks in the company. This should include unique ransomware attack strategies, drills, emergency recovery plans and incident-management policies.

  Security should be inbuilt, not added as an afterthought, at each step of the system design. Data ethics, data privacy and liability are critical issues closely related to security.
- **Data and AI:** In the IoT, AI plays a very important role and has become an essential part of IoT networks. This is due to data explosion, increased storage and power of devices and the adoption of better, customised algorithms.

Intelligent Big Data analytics involves the application of cognitive computing techniques derived from artificial intelligence, machine learning, modelling, statistics and data mining. These techniques can be used in real-time for predictive analytics or for decision-making in reaction to incoming data and also for historical data in order to identify patterns or data anomalies.

IoT Deployment Levels

Level 1: The Level-1 IoT framework has a single device that senses, but can also act, store, analyse and host the application. Level-1 IoT frameworks are appropriate for low-cost and low-complexity solutions, where there is no enormous data and the analytical requirements are not computationally intensive, for example, Home Automation System.

Level 2: The Level-2 IoT framework has a single device that perform local analysis, but can also sense. Usually, the application is cloud-based and the data are stored in the cloud. Level-2 IoT frameworks are appropriate for solutions where data are large, but the key requirement for analysis is not computer-intensive and can be carried out locally, for example, Smart Irrigation.

Level 3: The Level-3 IoT framework has a single device. Usually, the application is cloud-based and the data are stored and analysed in the cloud Level-3IoT frameworks are appropriate for solutions with large data and intensive analytical requirements, for example, Tracking Package Handling.

Sensors such as accelerometers and gyroscopes are used to sense movement or vibrations and to give orientation information respectively. The Websocket service is used because it is possible to send sensor data in real-time.

Level 4: The Level-4 IoT framework has multiple devices that perform local analysis. Usually, the application is cloud-based and the data are stored in the cloud. It includes local and cloud-based observer nodes that can subscribe to and receive data from cloud-based IoT devices. Level-4 IoT frameworks are appropriate for applications with multiple devices, large data and computer-intensive analytical requirements, for example, Noise Monitoring.

Level 5: The Level-5 IoT framework can be used to provide solutions based on Wireless Sensor Networks (WSNs) with large data and computer-intensive analytical requirements. The Level-5 IoT framework is equipped with multiple devices at the end with one coordinating unit. Along with actuation, the end devices perform sensing. Data collected from end devices are transmitted to the cloud by the coordinating unit. The application is cloud-based, the data are analysed and stored in the cloud, for example, Forest Fire Detection.

Detects early forest fires to take action when the fire can still be controlled. The sensors measure the speed of fire spread, wind speed, weather, temperature, smoke, the slope of the earth and flame length.

Level 6: The Level-6 IoT framework is equipped with several independent sensing, but also acting end devices that transmits data to the cloud. Usually, the application is cloud-based and the data are stored in the cloud. The analytical component analyses the data and stores the cloud database results. With the cloud-based application, the results are visualised. The centralised controller identifies the state of all devices in the terminal and sends commands to the end devices Weather Monitoring System.

Sensors are used for measuring the temperature (air, water, soil), wind speed and direction, relative humidity, soil moisture, solar radiation, precipitation, snow depth and barometric pressure.

IoT Terminology

IoT Term	Description
509 digital certificates	A digital certificate using X.509 Protocol for public key infrastructure (PKI) to verify that a public key belongs to the identity of the user, device or service included in the certificate.
6LoWPAN	A communication protocol for sensor or edge devices.
Actuator	A system that translates electrical signals such as motion or pressure into various forms of energy.
AFH	(Adaptive Frequency Hopping) To avoid interference, a mechanism used by Bluetooth devices to provide frequency agility
Address of Device	Used for locating and accessing a device
AllSeen	A non-profit organisation committed to making it easy for the IoT to connect computers, appliances and apps
API	(Application Programming Interface) It is a way for an application to present itself to another
Arduino	An open-source prototyping platform, used to create electronic projects, serves as the system's brain and processes sensor data

(*Continued*)

IoT Term	Description
Big Data	Provides information regarding the ever-growing volumes of data, as well as the concerns that come with the processing of this huge information
Bluetooth	Wireless technology that allows wavelength-based data exchange between devices
BTLE	(Bluetooth Low Energy) A low-power wireless communication technology version of Bluetooth
Cellular Network	A radio network spread over land areas called cells, each served by at least one transceiver at a fixed location, referred to as a base station or a cell site.
C-level	An independent security services firm focused on offering the best security solutions for the non-biased industry
Cloud	That's the Internet. On the Internet, all things are accessed remotely. Information is stored on Internet servers instead of on the hard drive of the local computers
CSA	(Cloud Security Alliance's) A not-for-profit organisation with a mission to "promote the use of best practices for providing security assurance within Cloud Computing and to provide education on the uses of Cloud Computing to help secure all other forms of computing."
Credential	A record that contains the authentication information (credentials) needed to connect to a resource. (e.g., user name and password)
cybersecurity	Responsible for IT infrastructure, edge devices, networks and information security
Data Centre	A place where most of the computer systems are integrated with the computing resources of corporations, or other large organisations
DECT	(Digital Enhanced Cordless Telecommunications) A wireless digital telephony technology that is used both for home and business use

(Continued)

IoT Term	*Description*
DLNA	(Digital Living Network Alliance) It helps you to send content from devices such as laptops, tablets and smartphones to a compatible TV wirelessly, taking the hassle out of sharing home media
Domain	A relevant field of interest
DoS	(Denial of Service) An attack meant that a computer or network would shut down, rendering it unavailable to its intended users
Ecosystem (IoT)	A combination of various IoT layers beginning from the user layer to the connectivity layer
Edge Computing	It enables filtering and analysis of the data before it is sent to the cloud
Embedded Computing Systems	They are made up of both hardware and software and are designed to perform one particular task
EMC	(Electromagnetic Compatibility) A test to observe the interaction between all electrical and electronic devices operating in the same environment
Fog Computing	An extended cloud computing edition that extends some of its services to the end-user level
Gateway	A network device or software running on a network machine that can connect with other networks
GPS	(Global Positioning System) A satellite-based navigation system for evaluating an object's ground location.
GSM	(Global System for Mobile Communications) A standard developed by the European Telecommunications
GSMA	(GSM Association) A business association that serves the interests of worldwide operators of mobile networks
Hosts	Computers that provide (host) some services or resources within a network that can then be accessed and used by other network participants
I2C	A two-wire interface serial protocol to connect low-speed devices

(Continued)

IoT Term	Description
RFID	(Radio Frequency Identification) Electromagnetic fields are used to automatically classify tags attached to objects and track them
IioT	(Industrial IoT) Use of intelligent sensors and actuators to increase production and industrial processes
IoNT	(Internet of Nano-Things) An interrelated system of very tiny devices for data transmission over a network
IoT Service	Enables companies by providing creative IoT strategies to transform business needs into strategic differentiators
IP	(Internet Protocol) The most basic protocol used on the Internet for data communication
IPv6	(Internet Protocol Version 6) A communication protocol that provides an identification and location system for computers on networks and routes traffic across the Internet
LBT	(Listen Before Talk) A collision prevention technique
LoRaWAN	(LoRa Protocol) A wireless technology that provides M2M and IoT applications with low-power, long-range and safe data transmission.
LPWAN	(Low Power Wide Area Network) A wide-area wireless telecommunication network designed to allow long-range communication between connected objects, such as sensors, at a low bit rate
LTE	(Long-Term Evolution) A wireless data transfer protocol that allows you to download your favourite songs, websites and videos very easily
LTE-A	(Long-Term Evolution-Advanced) Built-in security and robust and scalable traffic management services are provided
M2M	(Machine to Machine) A network of closed devices where they can communicate with each other and/or with other systems of control located on the same network

(Continued)

IoT Term	Description
MAC address	(Media Access Control) A unique identifier assigned to a network interface controller (NIC) that can be used in communications within a network segment as a network address
NIST	(National Institute of Standards and Technology's) Promotis U.S. innovation and industrial competitiveness through the advancement of measurement science, standards and technology in ways that boost economic security
NB-IoT	(Narrowband IoT) A low-power wide area (LPWA) standard-based technology designed to support a wide range of new IoT devices and services
NFC	NFC (near field communication) is a collection of wireless technologies that allow data to be shared easily and without contact at a very close distance
Object	Household appliances, wearable technology, surveillance systems or other linked devices may be an "object" in the IoT
OWASP	(Open Web Application Security Project) A non-profit foundation that aims to enhance cybersecurity
OTA	(Over-The-Air) A test to assess the reliability, efficiency and safety of wireless devices
PCBs	(Printed Circuit Board) A thin sheet of fibreglass, epoxy composite or other laminate material. Best candidates to achieve high durability in the production of IoT devices
Peer-to-Peer	A network of personal computers, each of which serves both as a client and as a server, so that files and emails can be shared directly with each other on the network
Pervasive Computing	(Also called Ubiquitous Computing) Incorporating microprocessors into everyday objects to exchange data
PKI	(Public Key Infrastructure) It provides the IoT's requisite authentication and encryption components for data protection, making it an established solution and market-ready platform

(Continued)

IoT Term	*Description*
Radio Frequency	A method for electromagnetic detection of objects (including humans)
Raspberry Pi	A low-cost, credit-card-sized device that uses a regular keyboard and mouse to plug into a computer monitor or TV
RSSI	(Received Signal Strength Indicator) A measurement of the power present in a radio signal received
SAR	(Specific Absorption Rate) A test to measure RF exposure on human dummies to ensure that mobile devices don't cause damage
Sensor	A device which measures and converts physical input from its surroundings into data that can be interpreted either by a human or a computer.
SigFox	World-leading IoT service provider
Spatial Analytics	A form of geographical analysis that seeks to understand human activity patterns and their spatial expression
SPI	A specification for the synchronous serial communication interface used for short-distance communication, mainly in embedded systems
Streaming Analysis	Through the use of continuous queries, analysis of huge pools of current and in-motion data
Tag	A label or other object for the recognition of the physical entity to which it is connected
Thread	Using IP data transfer, a wireless networking protocol
Time Series Analysis	A statistical approach that deals with data from time series or trend analysis and is useful to see how over time a given asset, security, or economic variable changes
UIDs	A globally unique sequence of characters or numbers that is assigned to a single object

(*Continued*)

IoT Term	Description
UpnP	(Universal Plug and Play) A collection of networking protocols that allows networked devices to discover the presence of each other on the network seamlessly and to create sharing, communication and entertainment
WSN	(Wireless Sensor Network) A set of spatially distributed and dedicated sensors to track and document the physical conditions of the environment and to coordinate the data collected at a central location
ZigBee	A low-power radio protocol, based on the IEEE 802.15.4 standard for small amounts of data
Z-Wave	Protocol for wireless communications used mainly for home automation

Goals and Benefits

The IoT's goal is to promote real-time communication with anyone, anything. In order to increase performance and get significant information to the surface more efficiently than a human intervention-based method, the IoT preferably uses every route or network to report in real-time.

The IoT's main objective is to bring everything together in the world, including things, people, places and processes within a common infrastructure to inform and control the state of the objects around us (Figure 3.5).

The IoT is indeed the world of interconnectivity around us and is defined by the technological convergence. The IoT allows an organisation to do more than it has done previously. Efficiency and effectiveness are the hallmarks of the IoT, and it touches all aspects of digital products and services, from regulation to service delivery, components to networks, hardware to software and markets and general public to businesses.

The motives for developing the IoT include creating intelligent environments and self-conscious things for food, energy, climate, digital society, mobility and health applications. Users can rely on analytics to make better decisions as the Internet, data storage, sensors and technology become cheaper, faster, better and more integrated. IoT devices would have a substantial impact in many aspects of our lives, including the way we do things, travel and grow animals and crops.

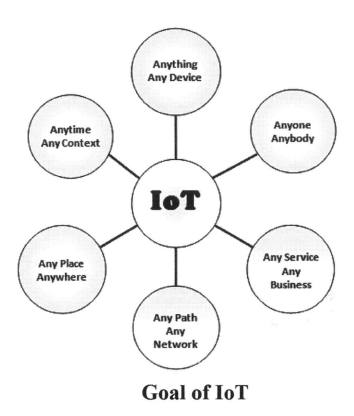

Goal of IoT

Figure 3.5　Goals of the IoT.

The IoT is a major technology that can be greatly improved over time. There are many advantages of connecting things. Here are some of the advantages:

1. **More information means better decision-making:** These devices can collect a large amount of data in many different areas using additional sensors. For example, this updated household item will be able to give you additional information on energy consumption, temperature, average open time and much more, as well as practical elements for knowing which foods are out of date in your smart refrigerator.

   A larger information flow means that a device company can analyse large data trends to improve device features. Many enterprises recognise the potential of this technology and the market is booming greatly.

2. **Capability to monitor and track things:** It also benefits the user significantly as well as the tracking of data for a company. These devices could keep an eye on the current quality of products at home. The state of your items will enable

a homeowner to know when an item needs to be replaced without constantly checking the quality.

3. **Reduce automation workload:** If you have a device that works most for you, you can save time and money. A refrigerator can order a new carton of milk to be supplied when it reaches a certain expiry level. It also leads to devices that need little or no human intervention to operate entirely independently.

4. **Increase efficiency while saving money and resources:** In addition to saving the device owner time, cost savings can also be achieved. You can, for example, save money on electricity bills if lights automatically turn off when you leave the room. Connected devices can provide many useful implementations. The IoT system promotes M2M communication that leads to increased long-term effectiveness for both the business and the user.

5. **Better quality of life:** All the benefits ultimately lead to a better quality of life. Since your equipment tracks and orders things for you, it could turn off light switches and help you manage important tasks you certainly won't have the time to do.

   There is no question of people becoming more occupied over the years. It is difficult to keep track of everything with so many devices being created and new technologies being implemented. It is great that you can do the things you like and take care of the worldly things which you know must be done by a computer.

   In the future, the IoT would also involve improving your lifestyle, healthcare and wellbeing. Those who exercise regularly can, for example, use wearable technology to monitor their heart rate, temperature of the body, hydration and health.

There are several advantages the IoT can bring to your business.

■ **Low-cost access to valuable information:** IoT platforms are designed to collect and process large volumes of data without affecting the performance of the system. In addition to data collection, the IoT is able to perform data analysis and provide it to the right teams readily. This eliminates the need for costly consultants or market research companies to be recruited.

■ **Big Data analysis:** The IoT is a major driver of Big Data analytics projects since it creates and analyses large volumes of data. It can provide massive volumes of data in real-time, in particular. This provides businesses with a complete overview of the real world performance of their products and services, enabling them to improve quickly.

■ **Understand customer behaviour:** IoT platforms provide valuable information which enables businesses to easily evaluate customer demand and the overall buying behaviour. Regardless of the field, businesses can use IoT devices to efficiently adapt their products to meet consumer interests, offer improved customer support and increase the value of the organisation.

■ **Minimise the cost of operation:** The IoT significantly reduces the costs of running an office. Various products are available through IoT that control energy utilisation automatically and interact with other devices in order to reduce overall costs.

■ **Introduce options for remote work:** With the IoT, information can be easily shared and efficiently collaborated with other team members, regardless of where they are. Data can, with a touch of a button, be collected, updated and shared in real-time with all team members. The performance of all employees can be monitored and operations improve via different IoT devices.

IoT solutions are widely used across all industries. The following are some of the most common IoT applications:

Application Type	Description
Wearables	Devices that are designed to be worn all day long, for example, fitness bands, virtual glasses, GPS-tracking belts.
Traffic Monitoring	When mobile phones are used as sensors, they collect and share data via applications like Wazen or Google Maps, and they are used to display the different route conditions and to feed and improve information on various routes to the same location, distance and estimated arrival time.
Fleet Management	The aim is to increase productivity, optimise performance and improve safety for organisation's vehicles and drivers. Sensors are installed in fleet vehicles to ensure an efficient interconnection between the vehicles and their owner and also between the vehicles and their driver. All kinds of vehicle condition data can be understood by both the owner and driver by simply accessing software for data collection, processing and organisation.
Agriculture	It gives farmers the option of accessing detailed knowledge of their soil condition and valuable information. Information such as soil moisture, acidity, presence of nutrients, temperature and many other chemical characteristics help farmers monitor irrigation, increase water quality, determine the best seed times for plants and detect diseases as well.

(Continued)

Application Type	Description
Poultry and Farming	Ranchers, who have early knowledge of the sick animal, are able to collect information on the health and well-being of animals by using IoT applications and help prevent large numbers of sick animals. Ranchers can increase their production of poultry using the data collected.
Hospitality	Various interactions in the hotel industry can be automated by implementing the electronic key that is sent directly to each guest's mobile device. Activities that can be easily handled are the location of guests, submitting details on interest activities, placing orders in the room, automated in-room billing charges and requests for personal hygiene.
Connected Cars	A vehicle equipped with Internet connectivity allows the vehicle to access data, send data, update software and patches, interact with other IoT devices and provide on-board passengers with Wi-Fi. This helps to automatically manage billing, parking, insurance and other similar aspects.
Activity Trackers	A device that detects the body's movements continuously on a three-axis accelerometer. Used for calculating fitness-related measures such as walking or running time, intake of calories and heartbeat.
Parking Sensors	Helps users to detect parking spaces on their phones in real-time.
Connect Health	Enables monitoring of patient health and care in real-time. It contributes to improved medical decisions based on patient information.
Water Supply	Helps to understand consumers' behaviours, detect supply service failures, report results and provide action paths to the service provider company. In a household or industry, an IoT smart water metre monitors the pressure, quality and volume of water consumed. To monitor the flow of water through the entire plant and across the distribution channels, an IoT smart water sensor can be used that also helps to find leaks to minimise water wastage.
Industrial Internet	IIoT has great quality control and sustainability potential. Tracking applications, exchange of stock data from suppliers and dealers in real-time and automated delivery will enhance the efficiency of the supply chain.

(Continued)

Application Type	Description
Tracking and Monitoring	In order to track assets, many companies employ IoT technologies. The GPS or radio frequency (RF) uses IoT-asset-tracking systems. Assets can be identified and verified over long distances.
Internet of Nano-Things	The IoNT consists of very small devices for transmitting data via current telecommunications and network systems.
Smart Thermostats	Thermostats used for home automation are in charge of controlling the heating, ventilation and air conditioning of a home. They allow users to use other Internet-connected devices, such as a laptop or smartphone, to change the heating settings.
Smart Outlets	A device used to turn on or off any appliance remotely. It also allows us to track the energy level of a device and receive personalised reports on our smartphones directly.
Smart City	A city that uses technology to provide services and solve urban challenges is considered as smart city. A smart city enhances mobility and transportation, increases social services and facilitates sustainability.
Smart Home	A smart home encapsulates a home's connectivity. It contains fume sensors, home equipment, light bulbs, windows, door locks, etc.
Smart Grid	It enables better electrical network monitoring and control. Information can be obtained, such as fault detection, decisions taken and repair thereof. It also provides valuable information for consumers on their consumption patterns and how best their energy spending can be reduced or adjusted.
Smart Retail	Offers retailers the opportunity to connect with their customers to enhance their experience in and out of the store. They may also monitor the path of consumers in a store and improve the shop layout and place premium products in high traffic areas.
Smart Supply Chain	Helps to track goods on the road in real-time, or allows suppliers to exchange information about stocks.

(Continued)

These are only some examples of how towns, farmers and healthcare providers improve the world's life with the IoT. This new technology empowers users to make more informed, data-driven decisions about our shared resources. The IoT may link them to an even better future, whether those people live in a crowded city or on a remote farm.

The future of IoT is more fascinating than where thousands of things talk to one another with less human intervention. In the way we live and work, the IoT will bring macro changes.

Risks in IoT

The IoT enables sensors to collect, communicate, analyse and act on information, and provides a new way of creating value for technology, the media and telecommunications companies that also create new opportunities to compromise this information. Not only do more data are shared by the IoT, but more sensitive information is shared among many more participants which leads to exponentially greater risks.

Everything with a connection to the Internet is susceptible to threats. As the saying goes, "There are two kinds of parties, one hacked, and the other not aware of being hacked." While the IoT is increasingly offering organisations new benefits, it is also creating major cybersecurity risks. However, many organisations fail to understand the level of risk they are exposed to while using connected devices and are left behind in managing such threats.

Many threats, whether in the IoT industry or on a website, are endorsed and generated by human beings. The intruder's intent may differ depending on the target:

- Depending on human use and handling of IoT devices, a hacker may need gain the unwanted human access.
- The intruder may want to gain confidential information by tapping the wireless IoT devices.
- Low power and less computer capacity are used for IoT devices. This makes it impossible for them to afford complex security protocols. Thus for intruders, it becomes an easy target.

The simplest and easiest threat that can be detected in IoT devices is its vulnerability which can be of two types: hardware and software. Hardware vulnerability is often difficult to detect or penetrate. However, repair or revision of the damage is even more difficult. A vulnerability of software points to a poorly written algorithm or a backdoor line of code. This backdoor can easily access intruders at such times.

IoT systems are not resilient to third-party disclosure in most situations and are either accessible or open to everyone. This means that an attacker may either simply steal the device, attach the device to another harmful-data-containing device or attempt to extract cryptographic secrets. The intruder may also change programming or even replace malicious devices that are completely controlled by the intruder.

Another type of risk is the human threat or a natural threat. Any natural threat, like seizures, hurricanes, floods or fires, could seriously damage IoT equipment. In these cases, we often take backups to protect the data or create contingency plans. However, no physical damage to the devices can be restored.

Human attacks against IoT devices can be identified as follows:

Cyber reconnaissance: Where a targeted user is spied on by an intruder using the cracking methods and malicious software to gain or sabotage secret information on existing systems.

Brute force attacks on passwords: Intruders try to devise the user's passwords by means of automated software that attempts countless times until the correct password provides access.

Stalking or tracking: The user can be tracked or traced by the UID of the IoT at every movement. Tracking a user gives their exact location when the user wants to be anonymous.

Controlled attacks: Some examples of controlled attacks are Denial of Service (DoS), Trojans, or viruses. In these cases, the intruders develop a certain virus which is programmed to work to kill the host device. Programmers and developers need to be careful as they work on current IoT solutions because hackers are strongly proficient today to launch cyberattacks worldwide.

Some threats to the IoT security in organisations are as follows:

Botnets: Cyber criminals can use botnets to attack IoT-connected devices such as smartphones, laptops and desktops.

Denial of service: Service denial may be used to slow down or hinder a service that damages the organisation's credibility.

Man-in-the-middle: Attackers can block multiple IoT device communication, leading to critical device defects.

Identity and data theft: Hackers can target IoT devices for sensitive information on multiple users and groups, such as smart metres, smartwatches and smart home appliances.

Social engineering: An attacker may illegally access personally identifiable information to obtain confidential information, including bank details, purchasing history and address for social engineering attacks.

Advanced persistent threats: Cyber criminals can target IoT devices for gaining access to personal or business networks.

Ransomware: Hackers can block and deny access to users from using their IoT-enabled devices until they get a ransom.

Remote recording: Attackers can secrete audio and video recording using zero-day exploits in IoT devices.

The fundamental reasons why the current IoT environment creates security risks are as follows:

1. No privacy and security programme
2. Complete absence of ownership and governance to promote privacy and security
3. Failure to integrate security into product design and environmental systems
4. Insufficient knowledge of safety and practice for engineers and architects
5. Lack of product privacy and security for IoT/IIoT resources
6. Inadequate system and network control for security incidents
7. Failure to manage post-market security and privacy risk
8. Absence of visibility or complete inventory of the product
9. Risk identification and treatment of existing and field products
10. Inexperienced or immature response to incidents

The factors for businesses looking to incorporate Security by Design in IoT products are as follows;

- **Understanding product safety and establishing a cyber strategy:** Whether to design connected products or acquire these products in-house, evaluate how products and their production data are safe and establish a cyber strategy to improve the quality of products.
- **Development of safety measures by design:** Incorporate safety into product design or ecosystem architecture design using requirements, risk and safety assessments and modelling.
- **Set "tone-at-the-top":** Make sure that the exact people have ownership of the process – from leaders to the relevant product managers, safety experts to product teams.
- **Having a committed team and ensuring enough support for them:** It is unfair to require company security teams to cover tasks without fresh resources being added. To increase knowledge, as necessary, develop a dedicated team with product-based experience and training.

■ **Use customary resources in the industry:** Instead of developing and distributing your device vendors with unique questionnaires, utilise publicly available industry resources.

In order for the IoT to be secure and productive in relation to risk, safety and performance, the technology industry, the government and the consumers should always work on the same page.

The following measures can be taken to improve the IoT environment:

■ It is important that organisations bridge the gap between understanding and practice.
■ Individuals across the IoT ecosystem need to understand technology threats better and organisations need to ensure that IoT security is taken seriously by the management at all levels.
■ A full-fledged framework for IoT risk management is essential to ensure that the IoT security complies with defined risk tolerances.
■ Organisations need a more effective and reliable but validated IoT control verification model.

Challenges in IoT

Organisations can face the challenges of implementing an IoT solution when designing the IoT, managing IoT data and related security issues (Figure 3.6).

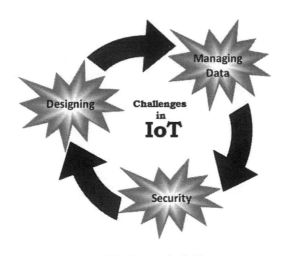

Challenges in IoT

Figure 3.6   Challenges in the IoT.

Challenges in Designing IoT

Connectivity, continuity, compliance, coexistence and cybersecurity are the challenges in designing IoT.

- **Connectivity:** Highly complex wireless network is a major IoT challenge to enable efficient data flow to and from a device, manage dense data, infrastructure, cloud and applications. However, even in the toughest environments, mission-critical IoT devices should function reliably without fail. Rapidly evolving wireless standards make it difficult for engineers to keep up with the latest technology while ensuring that devices can run smoothly across an entire ecosystem.
- **Continuity:** Battery life is one of the most important aspects of IoT devices. In consumer IoT devices, long battery life provides a great competitive advantage. A five or ten year battery life is the common expectation for industrial IoT devices. Device life can mean the difference between life and death in medical devices, such as pacemakers. And battery failure is certainly not an option.
- **Compliance:** IoT devices must comply with global regulatory requirements and radio standards. Tests of conformity include radio standards, carrier acceptance tests and regulatory tests of conformance such as RF, EMC and SAR tests. Design engineers frequently struggle to meet tighter timelines of product introductions and ensure that global market entry is smooth and updated according to the latest regulations.
- **Coexistence:** The congestion in the radio station is a problem that only gets worse with billions of devices. Standard bodies have developed test methods to assess device operations in the presence of other signals for the management of wireless congestion. The adaptive frequency hopping (AFH) system allows a Bluetooth device to drop channels with high data collisions in Bluetooth, for example. Additional collision prevention techniques (listen before talk [LBT]) and co-operative collision prevention (CAC) also improve the efficiency of transmission. But in a mixed-signal environment, the efficiency is unknown and collisions and data losses occur if the radio format does not detect each other.
- **Cybersecurity:** Network and cloud are the main focus of traditional cybersecurity protection tools. Vulnerabilities at the endpoint and over-the-air (OTA) are often ignored. Although mature technologies such as Bluetooth and WLAN are used in many applications, little action has been taken to deal with OTA vulnerabilities. The complexity of these Wireless Protocols means that device radio implementations may have potential unknown pitfalls which could enable hackers to access or control a device.

Challenges in Managing Data

A wealth of valuable information is gathered by the IoT which is transmitted as data. Increased data transmission and shared information presupposes many challenges, whether it involves smart home appliances, smart business technology or the Industrial IoT (IIoT). Some of the issues that IoT data are facing are as follows:

- **Security:** Security or, in fact, cybersecurity in terms of information technology is the most important and probably immiscible challenge. Not only is the collected data vulnerable, but all connections to the actual hardware are vulnerable.
- **Privacy:** Many firms actively decide not to use encryption (the data are locked behind software keys and without appropriate authorisation, cannot be decrypted or translated). It's particularly bad to store sensitive digital content in a plain text file, such as user accounts, passwords and personal information.
- **Reliability:** When the power falls out or the local Internet provider fails, all systems go offline. Emergencies or natural disasters may also affect data centres and most IoT solutions need to operate appropriately.
- **Resource consumption:** The use of electronics requires energy and IoT equipment is no exception. Worse still, they need to actively communicate data 24/7 and also support other technologies, including network adapters, gateways and much more.

  Data require physical storage in addition to electricity. There is still a remote server connected to the network that supports digital content, even with cloud and edge solutions. Excessive energy is required by the servers, like data centres that require large-scale cooling systems for heavy loading.
- **Fragmentation:** The IoT world comprises thousands of devices from every single brand and developer. Each is designed with separate mobile apps, tools and gateways to support the proprietary ecosystem. The fragmentation is unbelievable and it can truly hold the industrial world back. In some industries, such as the medical industry, it could be disastrous where clear and highly reliable solutions must be in place.

Challenges in Security

The IoT has great potential, but it can facilitate cyberattacks without adequate security. The following are some of the challenges concerning IoT security:

- **Security:** IoT devices significantly expand the "attack surface" or the potential area to penetrate a secure network for cybercriminals.

- **Regulation:** The lack of strong IoT regulations makes the IoT a serious security risk and is likely to worsen, as the attack surface potentially expands to include increasingly crucial devices.
- **Compatibility:** Continued IoT device compatibility also requires users to update and patch their devices.
- **Bandwidth:** Connectivity is a major IoT issue. As the IoT market is growing in size, certain experts worry that bandwidth-intensive IoT applications such as video-streaming will soon be battling for space on the current IoT server–client model.
- **Customer expectations:** Many IoT companies have learnt this the hard way, with IoTstartups often failing and confused customers. If the customer expectations and product reality fail, system failures, orphaned systems and loss of productivity can be the result.

Smart objects are associated with the IoT to allow various intelligent services. The implementation of IoT meets several challenges, such as IoT applications and network monitoring and management, programing existing IoT systems, complexity, long-term service provisioning, under-used resources, isolation and scalability. The lack of flexibility and intelligence also need to be addressed by current IoT networks.

Fundamental Concept and Methodology

The IoT is a framework of interconnected computers, mechanical and digital devices, objects, animals or persons with unique identification (UIDs) that transmits data without human-to-human or human-to-computer interactions over a network.

An object or a thing on the Internet can be a cardiovascular implant, a farm animal with a biochip transponder, an automobile with built-in driver-warning sensors when the pneumatic pressure is low or another natural or man-made object, which is assigned an IP address and which can transmit data via a network.

Sensor-connected IoT, IoT gateway, IoT cloud and IoT analytics are the four layers of the IoT technology ecosystem (Figure 3.7).

Layer 1 – IoT devices: IoT devices include transducers such as actuators, wireless sensors and myriad objects that are often referred as "smart" or "intelligent." These are the tiny, memory-restricted electronic devices, mostly battery-operated electronic devices. These can either function as standalone sensing devices or are integrated into a larger sensing and control machine. A sensor is a system that tracks, detects or indicates a particular physical quantity, such as moisture, heat, vibration, light, movement, electrical pulses or related entities. Sensors sense and send data, while acting and activating actuators. The actuator receives a signal and starts to activate what is needed to be done on/within an environment. Actuators use data acquisition to trigger "something" in the physical world. These devices are linked

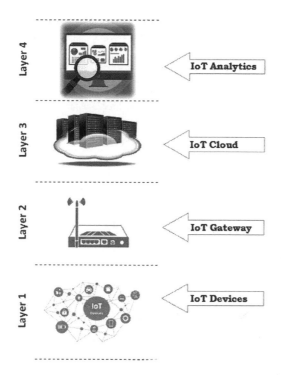

Figure 3.7 Layers of IoT technology ecosystem.

over the Internet and enable them to continuously communicate data online between them. Analysis and decision-making based on those data are automatic and real-time.

The typical features of the IoT device are:

■ detects and records data
■ performs light calculations
■ connects to a network and communicate the data
■ is secure and reliable

These devices are composed of energy, sensing, power management and RF modules. RF modules manage communication via Bluetooth, Wi-Fi, radio transceiver, ZigBee, duplexer and BAW. Sensing modules use different active and passive measuring devices for sensing.

Proximity sensors, light sensors, image sensors, acoustic sensors, pressure sensors, humidity sensors, temperature sensors, RFID gas and microflow sensors, accelerometers, gyroscopes and magnetometers are some of the measurement devices used in IoT.

Layer 2 – IoT gateway devices: Various Layer-1IoT devices are connected to the Internet through a networking device called the IoT gateway. Similar to a Wi-Fi router, the IoT gateway can therefore aggregate information from various sensing devices into the cloud, helping us connect many phones, tablets and laptops to the Internet.

An IoT gateway is a key element of the IoT ecosystem and acts as a link between various communication technologies. IoT gateways usually have several communication capabilities (such as Bluetooth, Zigbee, LoRa WAN, Sub GHz proprietary protocol) for talking to IoT devices on one end and an Internet connection on the other (over Wi-Fi, Ethernet or Cell Link).

An IoT gateway can be either hardware, software or a combination of both. IoT gateways are responsible for data pre-processing, aggregation, encryption and decryption. They also perform other crucial functions, such as the analysis of the different protocols that exist in the overall panorama of the IoT era, IoT edge computing, IoT system management and onboarding, remote control and management.

Layer 3 – IoT Cloud: On servers hosted within the cloud, all sensor data transmitted through IoT gateways is stored. For analysis and decision-making purposes, these servers capture, store and process information, which also allows decision-makers to screen and make strategic decisions based entirely on data to create live dashboards. Nowadays, for IoT solutions, almost all cloud infrastructure companies have custom built carrier offerings.

Layer 4– IoT Analytics: The raw data collected is then turned into actionable enterprise knowledge that could help enhance business operations and productivity or even predict future events such as machine disasters. Different data science and analytical techniques are used in this layer, along with machine learning algorithms, to identify statistics and enable corrective action.

IoT Design Methodology

The computing idea behind the IoT is that the normal physical gadgets are linked to the Internet and are recognised with other devices. It is a complex system of automation and analytics that combines sensing, networking, Big Data and artificial intelligence technology which provides complete system for a product or service. These systems allow any organisation or system to have more accountability, control and overall performance when implemented.

The process of developing an IoT system that integrates hardware devices with high-level software services needs an additional level of planning and Figure 3.8 provides ten steps for IoT designing and planning:

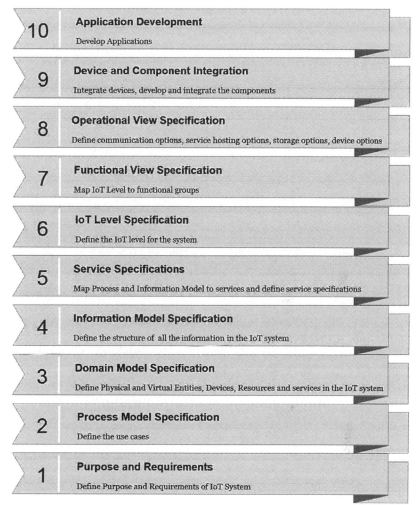

Figure 3.8   IoT design methodology.

Step 1: Purpose and requirement specification
The purpose of designing the system, its actions and the system's specifications are captured during this phase. The requirements such as data collection, data analysis, system management, user interface, data privacy and security are collected.

Step 2: Process model specification
During this phase, the process specifications are specified. IoT use-cases are theoretically dependent on and derived from the purpose specifications and requirements.

Step 3: Domain model specification

In this phase, the key concepts, entities and objects to be built in the IoT framework domain, independent of any particular technology or platform are specified. The domain model specifies object attributes and relationships between objects. The designers of the IoT framework will understand the IoT domain for which the system should be designed.

Step 4: Information model specification

This phase describes the structure of all information, such as attributes of virtual entities and relationships, in the IoT framework. The information model does not define the details of the representation or storage of information. First, virtual entities specified in the domain model are described in the information model definition. The information model provides virtual entities with more data by describing their characteristics and relationships.

Step 5: Service specification

Service requirements are specified in this phase. Service requirements describe the IoT device facilities, service types, service inputs/outputs, service prerequisites, service effects, service endpoints and service schedules.

Step 6: IoT level specification

The level of IoT deployment of the system is decided during this phase.

Step 7: Functional view specification

This phase describes the functions of the IoT systems grouped into various Functional Groups (FGs). Each Functional Category either provides functionality for interacting with instances of concepts specified in the Domain Model or provides information related to these principles.

Step 8: Operational view specification

Different options related to the deployment and operation of the IoT system are specified at this phase, such as application hosting options, service hosting options, device options, storage options, etc.

Step 9: Device and component integration

This phase integrates the devices and components.

Step 10: Develop applications

IoT application development is carried out at this phase.

IoT Technology and Communication Protocols

In the IoT, various protocols and communication technologies are used. Some of them areWi-Fi, Wi-Fi-Direct, Bluetooth, Radio protocols and LTE-A. These IoT communication protocols fulfil the basic functional specifications of an IoT device and comply with them.

- **Bluetooth:** Bluetooth is a major short-range IoT communications protocol/ technology that has become very relevant in computing and in many consumer goods. In many cases, Bluetooth is expected to be essential for wearable devices, particularly those connecting to the IoT probably through a smartphone. A significant protocol is now branded as the latest Bluetooth Low-Energy (BLE) or Bluetooth Smart for IoT applications. Importantly, It was designed to provide significantly low power consumption while offering a range comparable to Bluetooth.
- **ZigBee:** Like Bluetooth, ZigBee is used extensively in industrial environments. It has some important advantages in complex systems that provide high security, high functionality, low power and robustness. It is well suited to take advantage of wireless control and sensor networks in IoT applications.
- **Z-Wave:** Z-Wave is a wireless protocol that uses low-energy radio waves to help intelligent devices or appliances communicate with each other effectively. Z-Wave is specifically designed for home automation devices, such as lamp controllers and sensors. A simpler protocol is used by Z-Wave, which can allow faster and simpler development. Sigma Designs is the only chip manufacturer compared to various outlets for other wireless technologies, such as ZigBee and others.
- **Wi-Fi:** One of the most common protocols for IoT communication is Wi-Fi connectivity. For many developers, it is often a simple choice, especially given the accessibility of Wi-Fi within LANs within the domestic setting. In addition to providing rapid data processing and the ability to handle high data volumes, there is a wide-ranging infrastructure. 802.11n is in fact the most common Wi-Fi standard used in homes and many businesses, covering a range of hundreds of megabits per second, which is ideal for file transfers, but for many IoT applications it might be too power-consuming.
- **Cellular:** Any IoT device requiring service over longer distances will take advantage of the capabilities of GSM/3G/4G cellular connectivity. Although the cellular network is obviously able to transmit massive amounts of data, especially 4G, for many applications, the cost and power consumption would be too high. But it may be sufficient for sensor-based, low-bandwidth data projects that transmit very small amounts of data over the Internet.
- **NFC:** NFC is an IoT technology that allows electronic devices and smartphones to communicate easily and securely, allowing clients to perform transactions in which they do not have to be physically present. It allows users to communicate and access digital content on mobile devices. It increases the ability of contactless card technology and allows devices to exchange data at a distance of less than 4 cm.

■ **RFID:** RFID provides simple, energy-efficient and adaptable options for identifying and accessing tokens, connection bootstrapping and payments. To recognise and monitor tags associated with objects, RFID technology uses 2-way radio transmitter-receivers.

■ **LoRaWAN:** One of the common IoT technologies targeting WAN applications is LoRaWAN. To support low-cost mobile secure communication, the LoRaWAN architecture is designed to provide low-power WANs with features specifically required for the IoT, smart city and industrial applications. In particular, LoRaWAN meets low power consumption requirements and supports large networks of millions of users, with data rates from 0.3 to 50 kbps.

Characteristics and Architecture

The main task of IoT systems is to collect data from environments and to make the data available and functional when appropriate. The IoT differentiates itself in the following ways relative to conventional Internet services (Figure 3.9):

■ **Large amounts of devices and data:** The huge amount of information produced by the large number of IoT devices must be handled efficiently by the network. Data must be continually uploaded to a central cloud or processed

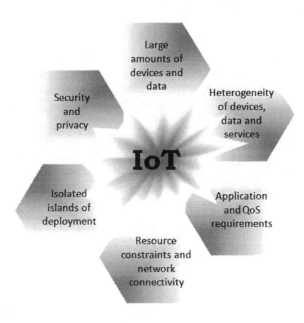

Figure 3.9   Characteristics of the IoT compared to Internet services.

locally. Continuously uploading data to a central cloud will cause heavy traffic and some local computing resources and distributed algorithms are needed to process the data locally.

■ **Heterogeneity of devices, data and services:** Networks and connected devices are heterogeneous with regard to capabilities, power and the amount and type of data produced. Individual nodes are capable of producing large quantities of data without having great computational capabilities. Only small triggered updates are generated by other nodes. Similarly, application requirements also state that services require high energy consumption, low computational complexity, low latency or elevated cloud bandwidth.

■ **Application and QoS requirements:** Internet applications, including high-quality audio, video and variable data speeds, have a limited set of specifications. An application-dependent set of specifications is introduced by the IoT. For example, it needs high bandwidth and low latency for remote e-health service, but remote water metering requires low bandwidth and can withstand high latency.

■ **Resource constraints and network connectivity:** In terms of resources, many IoT devices and networks are more constrained than traditional Internet services. Cheap and energy-efficient devices, low-power and low-bandwidth communication networks, often allow large and long-term installations to function independently without a continuous power supply. The IoT devices may also be isolated from the entire network, on an irregular basis due to changing network conditions or power-saving device duties.

■ **Isolated islands of deployment:** In an isolated domain, many IoT implementations are closed local systems where most communication occurs. Reliance on proprietary device-to-device communication solutions, a lack of open IP-based networking, or a willingness to shield the system from external access may be the reasons for this. At the same time, communication with other parts of the network might be needed by certain stakeholders for accessing more data, for remote controlling or for providing data selected for an open ecosystem.

■ **Security and privacy:** IoT devices often gather sensitive data. Since personal information can be disclosed about the user or people nearby, IoT services can also allow certain physical equipment to be monitored. Protecting access to IoT data and resources is therefore essential. Restricted devices may not have the computing capacity to perform the required cryptographic operations. Furthermore, uncoordinated deployments and network interruptions make it difficult to maintain contact with the network security, which prevents key setup and identity formation by IoT devices.

The above IoT characteristics present challenges in constructing a speedy, reliable and efficient infrastructure for networks.

IoT Architecture

■ **Conventional architecture:** One of the simplest IoT reference architecture is the conventional IoT architecture/three-layer IoT architecture model. As shown in Figure 3.10, perception layer, network layer and application layer are the three layers.

The **perception layer** is the physical layer, which has actuators, sensors and smart devices to detect and capture environmental information. It detects certain physical parameters in the environment or identifies other smart objects. Using conventional network technologies and regional RF networks, communication from this layer to the outside world is cloud-driven and controlled.

The **network layer** connects devices, other smart things and servers to the network. In this layer, sensor data processing and transmission are performed. Their function is to detect and move smart devices in the perception layer into the network and allow them to interact with the applications.

The **application layer** is a part of the cloud and servers and is responsible for supplying the client with application-specific services. This layer describes the various applications such as smart health, smart cars and smart cities, in which the IoT can be implemented.

A prerequisite called the support layer was later added for more efficient and transparent communication between the application layer and the networking layer.

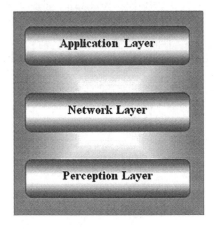
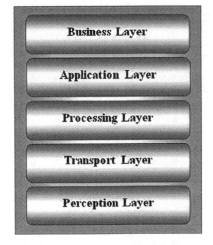

Figure 3.10   (a) Conventional IoT architecture and (b) five-layer IoT architecture.

■ **Five-layer IoT architecture:** Five-layer IoT architecture model is an extension of the three-layer approach. The two additional levels added are the business layer and the processing layer.

Networks like wireless, 3G, Bluetooth, RFID, LAN and NFC are used by the **transport layer** to transfer sensor data from the perception layer to the processing layer and vice versa.

The **processing layer**, also known as the middleware layer, collects, stores, analyses and handles large volumes of transport layer data. The lower layers can be managed and a diverse range of services can be offered. It utilises many technologies, such as databases, cloud computing and the study of Big Data. The **business layer** governs the entire IoT system, including software, business and benefit models and the privacy of users.

■ **Seven-layer IoT architecture:** The IoT architecture with seven layers is the most widely used by users when seeking to describe the appearance and layout of the IoT ecosystem (Figure 3.11).

Layer 1 – The things: The IoT ecosystem requires a number of devices, sensors and controllers to enable their interconnection. In addition to standard sensors, actuators include microcontrollers, laptops, smartphones, etc. This implies that the end point of an IoT system would include connected systems.

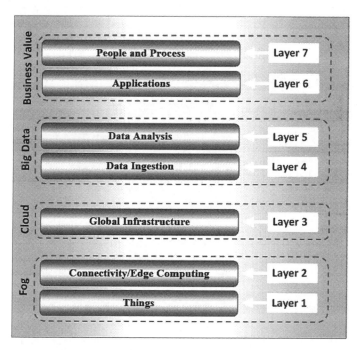

Figure 3.11   Seven-layer IoT architecture.

Layer 2 – Connectivity/edge computing: portrays the environment and the location where all links within the IoT ecosystem are made before data are shared. It specifies all protocols for communication and creates an edge-computing network. This indicates a distributed architecture and that data processing is located close to the network edge.

Layer 3 – Global infrastructure: It is a platform for developing software applications that focuses on cloud technology. This is because most IoT systems depend on the integration of cloud services. This is an inescapable approach from a business perspective of recent times, as the cloud offers a complete upgrade from the customer's point of view.

Layer 4 – Data ingestion: It is the layer of data entry that is inevitably termed Big Data, as well as data cleaning and storage. Also, as a building block of data ingestion, data streaming procedures are present in this layer.

Layer 5 – Data analysis: It is obviously related to systematic process of collecting and organising information in order to draw meaningful conclusions from it.

Layer 6 – Application layer: Applications are based on the user's intentions and needs. Different context elements are often thing-specific, so a certain application layer is needed, otherwise within the IoT ecosystem they cannot be standardised. At this level, the convergence of users and objects take place on the lowest design level. In some IoT architecture studies, this layer is often referred as the application integration layer, where the UI being implemented at the top, the same layer can be viewed as a service layer.

Layer 7 – People and processes involve all corporate organisations as a consortium of IoT ecosystems. At the same time, stakeholders engage in data-based decision-making.

■ **Cloud- and fog-based IoT architecture:** As there is an increasing need for data analysis in real systems, such as smart grid environments, as well as monitoring and pre-processing in local IoT environments, a new layer has been introduced between the physical layer and the transport layer.

The **cloud-based architecture** shown in Figure 3.12 is becoming common in the IoT and centralised data control is achieved using cloud services in most IoT architectures. The IoT framework has a cloud-centred architecture, which allows the cloud between the applications and network of things. Since cloud computing offers great versatility and scalability, it is given primacy. It offers the core, storage infrastructure, software and platform. Developers through the cloud can provide their tools for data mining, storage, software, visualisation and cloud-based learning.

As shown in Figure 3.12, the **fog architecture** presents a layered approach which inserts security, storage, pre-processing and monitoring layers between the physical and transport layers. Monitoring layer is responsible

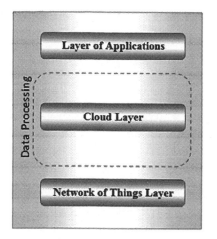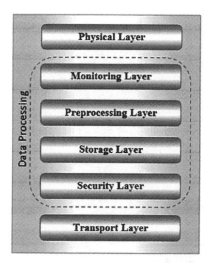

Figure 3.12 (a) Cloud-based IoT architecture and (b) fog-based IoT architecture.

to monitor resources, power, responses and services. Sensor data filtering, processing and analytics are performed by the pre-processing layer. The temporary storage layer performs storage functions such as data replication and distribution. Finally, encryption/decryption is carried out by the security layer and guarantees data integrity and privacy. At the network edge, monitoring and pre-processing is done before data are sent to the cloud.

Services and Security Mechanisms

IoT services include application management, data analytics, strategic consulting and development, to make it easier for enterprises to solve their business problems and use IoT technology to tap into new revenue streams.

The IoT is an arrangement of Internet-connected devices for transmitting and sensing data without much human interference; since the IoT is meant to make the user intelligent, this technology is used by different industries and realms to get various services.

This technology allows remote contact with the device. The main point is that it will contribute to the creation of a centralised structure from which all devices can be regulated. It is possible to enjoy the IoT technology either by being on the same network or the public network. It takes the input from the other device accordingly, depending on the type of device, and gives the required output. It takes the input from the other device accordingly, depending on the type of device, and gives the required output.

By improving their efficiency, the IoT is designed to make devices smart. Diverse sectors and fields have leveraged this technology to accelerate the challenge. Some of the useful services provided by the IoT are shown in Figure 3.13.

1. **Medical treatment:** There are IoT-developed instruments that assist the patient during treatment. On the one hand, it is much too costly to stay in hospital to get the care completely and on the other hand, having such IoT-enabled systems makes it affordable for patients to continue treatment at low costs. The most common device is used to fight diabetes in this field.
2. **Remote control:** The IoT lets us control distant geographically located equipment. The function of IoT-connected devices is that they can accept data from other Internet-connected devices. Cell phones are widely used to transmit commands to a computer remotely. In such situations, the Internet is typically favoured, while computers will communicate using Wi-Fi if they are connected to the same network.
3. **Enhancing lightning experience:** To make the experience and interaction with light-emitting devices possible, the IoT can be used to add many functionalities. We may imagine making the lights shine in such a way that it just lights up while someone is walking, which might lead to power usage saving loads. By making the lighting systems smart enough to recognise when to shine and follow a pattern, this can be done.
4. **Detecting machine failure:** The devices used these days are too difficult to understand and a device that can predict the malfunction of the devices can be

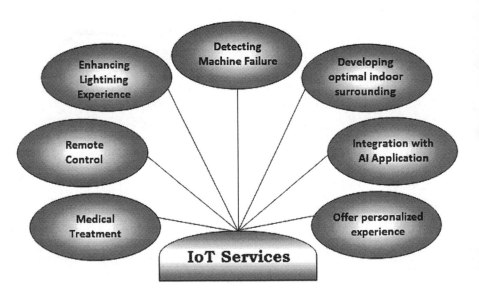

Figure 3.13 IoT services.

established by making use of the IoT. These machines are used to alert the customer to the unsafe operation of some aspect of the system that would be useful to maintain the product's consistency. It may also be used to avoid a fatal accident occurring to machine users.

5. **Developing an optimal indoor surrounding:** The environment could be made very smart and optimal by using IoT-enabled devices. Smart equipment reduces power consumption and increases performance. This will lead to a safer working environment as it is the place that needs to be well planned with fewer resources being used and it can be seen that the IoT is the best alternative to help such environments.

6. **Integration with AI application:** The next major thing is any smart device uses artificial intelligence to increase performance. In order to render things much simpler and to improve processing capacity, IoT principles and functionality should be combined with AI-based applications. Effective devices which leverage both AI and the IoT are already in the market.

7. **To offer a personalised experience:** Millions of clients on online websites are reliant to purchase the items that they need. The e-commerce sites often recognise the value of providing their consumers with personalised services so that their website can make their customers feel secure, and that the IoT can be used for this reason. This makes it conveniently easier for consumers to use the online portal to concentrate on what they need to purchase.

IoT Security

IoT security is the technological field for the security of devices and networks connected to the Internet.

The IoT has been an inevitable concept that identifies ten billion devices that can be detected or controlled by the Internet. The IoT contains everything from wearable fitness bands, sophisticated home appliances to plant monitoring systems, diagnostic instruments and even automobiles. Until now, the security of such instruments has not been a high priority. Some of the most intimidating vulnerabilities on IoT devices have further reinforced IoT security in a pile of problems.

Every IoT solution or framework must tackle the following challenges with regard to privacy:

■ **Profiling and tracking:** Association with an identification with one person is a threat, and this may lead to surveillance and follow-up. One of the key problems, however, is to disallow certain IoT behaviours and take certain preventive steps.

■ **Localisation and tracking:** As systems seek to evaluate and document the position of individuals through time and space, localisation is another threat. One of the IoT's major security solutions challenges is developing protocols for IoT interactions which prevent such behaviour. It is very common in e-commerce applications to profile information belonging to a certain person to infer preferences through similarity with other profiles and data. The huge problem lies in matching the needs of corporations with the privacy criteria of consumers for identification and data collection.

■ **Secure data transmission:** Another precaution is for data to be safely transferred to anyone in the public media without concealing information and thereby avoiding unauthorised information gathering on things and individuals.

Common steps to be taken for IoT security are:

■ **Integrate security at the design level:** At the beginning of any industrial product design and development, IoT developers should provide security. It is necessary to enable security by design, in addition to providing the most current operating systems with reliable hardware.

■ **PKI and digital certificates:** Public key infrastructure (PKI) and 509 digital certificates have crucial roles in designing protected IoT devices to have the trust and control required for the dissemination and authentication of shared encryption keys, secure transmission of data across networks and identity verification.

■ **API security:** Security of the Application Performance Indicator (API) is necessary to maintain data transfer privacy from the IoT to back-end systems and to ensure that only authorised devices, developers and applications are linked to APIs.

■ **Identity management:** It is essential to ensure that each device has its own unique identity, to take into account the details of the device, its functions, the other devices with which it communicates and the required security measures to be taken.

■ **Hardware security:** End-point-hardening requires making products that are tamper-proof or tamper-evident. This is especially important when an equipment is used or is not physically monitored in tough environments. Good encryption is essential for safe communication between devices. Data should be encrypted during rest and transit using cryptographic algorithms and it can be carried out by key lifecycle management.

■ **Network security:** Securing an IoT network involves keeping ports safe, avoiding port forwarding and port opening when not using antimalware, firewall and intrusion detection/intrusion prevention technology. Also, blocking unwanted IP addresses and ensuring up-to-date patching of systems.

■ **Network access control:** Network access control (NAC) can help to classify IoT devices linked to a network and to inventory them. This will provide a basis for tracking and monitoring of devices.

- **Security gateways:** The security gateway serves as an interface between the IoT devices and the network, which has more processing capacity, memory and functionality than IoT devices and includes features such as firewalls to ensure that hackers do not access the IoT devices they are linked to.
- **Patch management/continuous software updates:** Providing means of updating devices and applications through either network connections or automation is important. It is also important for the upgrading of software as quickly as possible to provide a structured disclosure of vulnerabilities. End-of-life strategies are also important to consider. Security staff need to be up-to-date with current or unfamiliar technology, understand emerging architectures and programming languages and also need to be prepared for new security threats, as the IoT and operating system security are crucial. C-level and cybersecurity teams should undergo consistent training in order to keep up with modern threats and compliance initiatives.
- **Integrating teams:** In addition to training, it may be helpful to combine disparate and silo-free teams. In the production process, for instance, an application developer working with security professionals would help to ensure careful inspection of devices.
- **Consumer education:** Consumers need to be educated about the dangers of IoT systems and steps to keep them safe, for example, by using security patches and upgrading default credentials. Consumers can demand that device manufacturers produce reliable products and refuse to use products that do not meet stringent safety requirements.

For the IoT, various organisations have developed security guidelines. These include:

- The IoT Security Foundation's "Best Practice Guidelines"
- The Open Web Application Security Project's (OWASP) "Security Guidance"
- Groupe Spéciale Mobile Association's (GSMA) "GSMA IoT Security Guidelines & Assessment"
- The U.S. Department of Commerce National Institute of Standards and Technology's (NIST) Special Publication 800-160 (the "Guidance") on implementing security in IoT devices
- The Cloud Security Alliance's (CSA) "Future Proofing the Connected World: 13 Step to Developing Secure IoT Products"

Case Study: Using the Meshlium Scanner for Smartphone Detection

The radio interfaces supported by the Linux router, Meshlium, are ZigBee, Bluetooth, 3G/GPRS, Wi-Fi 2.4 GHz and Wi-Fi 5 GHz. A GPS module for mobile and automotive applications can also be incorporated into the Meshlium and powered by solar and battery power. Together with an IP67 aluminium enclosure, these features allow Meshlium to be mounted anywhere outdoors. Meshlium comes with the Manager System, a web application that offers quick and easy monitoring of Bluetooth, Wi-Fi, ZigBee and 3G/GPRS settings, as well as storage options for the acquired sensor data. In reality, it is smart enough to recognise all sorts of hands-free devices such as Android and iPhone that broadcast on air.

The fundamental principle of technology is to measure the number of vehicles and people present at a given pointof time, to facilitate the study of the evolution of congestion. For this concept to work, the users don't have to do anything to be identified or visible on a network. As long as the Wi-Fi and Bluetooth radio installed in their mobile device are running, the router can still sense its existence. The Meshlium router detects the user, based on the following:

- wireless interface MAC address that enables it to be uniquely defined;
- signal intensity (Received Signal Strength Indicator [RSSI]) that indicates the average device distance from the scanning point;
- the mobile device vendor (Apple, Nokia, etc.); the user's access point (Wi-Fi); and the Bluetooth-friendly name (users not linked to a access point would be identified as a "free user"); and
- the class of device (CoD) that enables the system to distinguish the device type in the case of Bluetooth and enhances the distinction between vehicles and pedestrians.

In addition, the coverage areas can be changed by altering the power transmission of the radio interfaces, enabling the formation of separate scanning zones from a few metres, enabling the study of a specific point for dozens of metres (studying the entire street or even the whole floor of the shopping centre).

The Meshlium or any other similar scanner can focus on:

1. **Vehicle traffic detection:** In this procedure, it is possible for the system to:
   - monitor the number of vehicles moving to a certain point on roads and highways in real-time.
   - detect average vehicle stance time to prevent traffic congestion
   - observe average vehicle speed on all roads and highways
   - when congestion is observed, provide travel times on alternative routes
   - calculate the average vehicle speed on the road by observing the time at two different points
2. **Shopping and street activities**: Similar to automobile traffic monitoring, an optimal mobility of individuals can be tracked at a shopping centre, airport or stadium to enhance the user experience and create a disparity between a good visit and a bad one.

Case Study: Seedbed Based on IoT

In delivering decision support systems that address many real-world issues, the WSN and the IoT are commonly used. The IoT is the best way to address agricultural problems related to seedbed resource optimisation, which facilitates seed-breeding decision-making and monitoring.

Environmental Factors and Seed Breeding

The processing of seeds relies on the conditions of the environment in which they are produced. There are several factors in the environment, primarily, air temperature, soil temperature, air humidity, soil humidity, ambient temperature and light. In terms of the quality and productivity of seed breeding, these climate variables are independent but are also interrelated and should not be individually considered without regard to the impact on others. A thorough understanding of these variables and their relationships can allow a farmer or any other user of the seedbed being monitored to become more informed of possible problems.

Temperature influences most seed development phases, such as photosynthesis and flowering, and these should be maintained at an optimum level depending on the seed used.

Humidity regulates the loss of humidity from the plants, allowing the water and oxygen to leave them and consume more CO_2. High humidity may cause fungal diseases to spread and thus reduce the transpiration process.

Light is a significant factor in the process of seed breeding, as seeds and plants obtain their energy from sunlight through photosynthesis.

Soil humidity is an important factor in deciding when and in what quantity of water to be supplied. The water loss percentage is measured by the flow of air, the ambient temperature, the relative humidity in the air and the state of the soil. If the soil is over moist, the roots can never expand because they are unable to absorb water and nutrients from the soil.

Monitored Seedbed Construction Automation and Development

The soil humidity sensor monitors the soil humidity (i.e., the water retained in the spaces between soil particles). Contact-based sensors are used to measure soil temperature, air temperature, soil humidity and air humidity. All these measurements are compared with an extra space temperature sensor for accurate measurements.

Automation and measurements are entirely controlled by Arduino UNO which controls the heat from the heat seals.

Forty-nine tomato seeds were used within the monitored seedbed and 49 tomato seeds were used in an indoor environment to compare the breeding process. Tomato seeds need between 24°C and 27°C air temperature and between 60% and 70% air humidity. The breeding of tomato seeds in indoor seedbed conditions was seven days slower than the breeding of tomato seeds in the monitored seedbed.

And the plants in the monitored seedbed were also ready for transplantation after the ninth day. On the other hand, in comparison to those raised in the monitored seedbed with regulated soil humidity, temperature and air humidity, it was noted that most of the tomato seeds left in an indoor seedbed did not grow at all and also the rest were seven days behind in height.

The temperature and humidity stability along with the suitable soil humidity provided by the monitored seedbed for the tomato seeds have evidenced a favourable environment for faster breeding. Compared to monitored seedbed, indoor climate conditions were less desirable for tomato seed growers.

References

[1] Keith, D., D. Foote, "A Brief History of the Internet of Things", [E-book], August 16, 2016, Available: https://www.dataversity.net/brief-history-internet-things/
[2] SIMON IoT, "The Rise of IoT: The History of the Internet of Things", November 20, 2020, [Online]. Available: https://www.simoniot.com/history-of-iot/
[3] Sinh, Shubham, "Introduction to Internet of Things: IoT Tutorial with IoT Application", September 11, 2020, Available: https://www.edureka.co/blog/iot-tutorial/#Birth_of_IoT.
[4] TutorialsPoint, "Internet of Things (IoT) Tutorial", 2021, Available: https://wwwtutorialspoint.com/internet_of_things/index.htm.
[5] Pujar, Shamprasad, K.V. Satyanarayana, "Internet of Things and Libraries", September 2015, 62, 186–190, Available: https://www.researchgate.net/publication/286224381_Internet_of_things_and_libraries
[6] IoTnow, "5 challenges still facing the Internet of Things", 2021, Available: https://www.iot-now.com/2020/06/03/103228-5-challenges-still-facing-the-internet-of-things/
[7] IoTEvolution, "The Top Five Challenges of IoT", June 22–25, 2021, Available: https://www.iotevolutionworld.com/iot/articles/445866-top-five-challenges-iot.htm
[8] Matthews, Kayla, "Five Major Challenges When Managing IoT Data", January 24, 2020, Available: https://theiotmagazine.com/five-major-challenges-when-managing-iot-data-1bb97d890465
[9] Bahga, Arshdeep, Vijay Madisetti, "Internet of Things: A Hands-On Approach", 2014, ISBN:978-0996025515, Available: https://www.slideshare.net/pavanpenugonda1/chapter-5-iot-design-methodologies
[10] WikiBooks, "I Dream of IoT/Chapter 8: IoT and Case Study", Available: https://en.wikibooks.org/wiki/I_Dream_of_IoT/Chapter_8_:_IoT_and_Case_Study

[11] Kalathas, J., D.V. Bandekas, A. Kosmidis, V. Kanakaris, "Seedbed based on IoT: A Case Study", *Journal of Engineering Science and Technology Review*, 9, 1–6, Available: https://www.researchgate.net/publication/305377999_Seedbed_based_on_IoT_A_case_study

[12] Sethi, Pallavi, Smruti R. Sarangi, "Internet of Things: Architectures, Protocols, and Applications", *Journal of Electrical and Computer Engineering*, 2017, Available: https://doi.org/10.1155/2017/9324035.

[13] Patel, Keyur, S. Patel. "Internet of Things-IOT: Definition, Characteristics, Architecture, Enabling Technologies, Application & Future Challenges", *International Journal of Engineering Science and Computing*, 6(5), 2016, Available: http://ijesc.org/DOI10.4010/2016.1482, ISSN 2321 3361

[14] Gupta, Ashish, Jigsaw Academy, "4 Layers of the Internet of Things", 18 October, 2018, Available: https://www.jigsawacademy.com/4-layers-of-the-internet-of-things/

[15] Thales, "Are There Security Guidelines for the IoT?", Available: https://cpl.thalesgroup.com/faq/internet-things-iot/are-there-security-guidelines-for-the-iot

Chapter 4

The Internet of Things Architectures and Use Cases

Jinsi Jose and Deepa V. Jose

CHRIST University, Bangalore, India

Contents

DOI: 10.1201/9781003119784-4

Introduction

The Internet of Things (IoT), the buzz word of the modern world, has significant influence in the day-to-day life of human beings. This technology has made a variety of activities quite easily manageable for us which were considered to be difficult or even impossible. This demonstrates the power of IoT applications. As the name indicates the IoT is a combination of 'Internet' and 'things.' Things can be any physical objects which can sense, communicate, and act accordingly. In the IoT, the interconnected devices can realise the atmosphere of the surrounding deployed area with the help of sensors and perform tasks according to the situational demand [1], as represented in Figure 4.1. Any IoT devices will have sensors, minimal processing, storage capability, and wired or wireless communication mechanisms to connect to each other and the centralised system [2]. Such an interconnected network can provide enormous services and applications in our day-to-day life, in health care and surveillance applications, business and agriculture, engineering and medical fields, and so on. According to the literature, the influence of the IoT has reached to such an extent that it will cross over 20 billion users by 2025 [3].

The rapid progression of information technology and its casual availability prompted us to give more importance to IoT devices in our daily life. Currently, the adoption of IoT devices is very massive, and in the future, it might take the superior ship all over the world, including rural areas. The IoT devices consist of sensors, actuators, communication interfaces, operating systems, system software, embedded

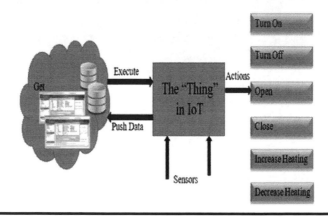

Figure 4.1 An IoT scenario.

Figure 4.2 Perspective of IoT.

applications, and lightweight services. The primary accountability of smart things is to gather information from devices by using sensors and perform actions using actuators. The IoT has emerged from the computer science perspective, with its first and foremost goal to develop a network with interconnected devices capable of making self-decision, which function on top of the current Internet with intelligence. It comprises different hardware, software, standards, communication protocol, and languages, which helps create intelligence in devices [4]. The IoT is aimed to develop an infrastructure for a network with appropriate communication protocols and make the 'Things' smart [5] to enable communication with anybody at any time, as represented in Figure 4.2.

Traditional Network Versus the Internet of Things

Before the inception of the concept of the IoT in 1999 by Kevin Ashton [2], the traditional networks were the only way of communication which was prevalent. Traditional networks are a collection of different network devices such as a router or switches, which can connect through wired or wireless media. Each network device has fixed functions that altogether help the network to operate well, based on predefined commands. In the case of the conventional network, user control is required for monitoring the network continuously. Focusing on the security part of the traditional network, it needs more manual supervision and substantial resources; because the add-on security is reactive [5, 6]. The Internet is not a mandatory part of the traditional network. It does not have any constraints on memory or processing

Table 4.1 IoT Network Vs Traditional Network

IoT Network	Traditional Network
The Internet is the heart and supporting part of the IoT	The Internet is not a mandatory element
Actions are performed by using predefined commands and computational intelligence	Actions are always performed by predefined commands
Machine-to-machine (M2M) communication possible	Manual intervention is always needed
Large technological heterogeneity	Lesser technological heterogeneity
The IoT uses lightweight algorithms for security purposes to adapt to resource constraints	Sophisticated algorithms can be used for security purposes as resource constraints do not matter much

resources, which supports embedding complex security algorithms for ascertaining high-end security.

The IoT network comprises a variety of interlinked devices that can communicate with each other through wireless and wired means. The Internet is a vital part of IoT [7]. The building blocks of the IoT are Wireless Sensor Networks (WSNs) and ad -hoc networks that collect data from the environment via different sensors and actuators [5]. The IoT has significant technological heterogeneity [6]. The decision -making capability is the most key ability that makes the IoT differ from the traditional network. Table 4.1 showcases the major differences between an IoT network and the traditional network.

Challenges in IoT

Even though IoT applications diminish manual efforts and offer ease of life, it is prone to several challenges too, either from the software or hardware side. In practice, the challenges of IoT application varies in different scenarios. The top highlighted ones which apply to all IoT applications are related to security, privacy, and trust issues [2, 8]. The prime cause of these issues is the lack of standardised architecture and policies for IoT devices, which leads different IoT inventors to develop various IoT products without following standards in manufacturing and deployment as well [2, 8, 9]. Tables 4.2 and 4.3 mentions the various challenges in the IoT domain based on security constraints and security requirements, respectively, in various security perspectives.

IoT Challenges Based on Security Constraints

Table 4.2 IoT Challenges Based on Security Constraints

Hardware based: It includes all the constraints related to hardware. ▪ Computational and energy constraint ▪ Memory constraint ▪ Tamper resistant packaging ▪ Lack of common standard
Software based: It includes all the constraints related to software. ▪ Inbuilt software constraint ▪ Lack of active security patch
Network based: It includes all the restriction based on network. ▪ Mobility ▪ Scalability ▪ Hetrogeinity

Hardware-Based Security Constraint

Hardware concern is significant in the case of IoT devices primarily on four elements, such as; computation power and energy, memory, tamper resistance, and reliability. Computational and energy constraints are always an issue to be addressed as it lacks high memory, processing, and power backup facilities due to its inherently small size. The majority of the IoT devices are plug and play, which use low-power CPUs with low clock rates. Hence, lightweight algorithms only can be adopted for device protection instead of sophisticated cryptographic algorithms.

One of the main attractions of IoT devices is the ease of deployment in restricted environments without or with minimal human intervention. It can easily be embedded in any device or environment which is possible because of its tiny size. They can also be deployed in any type of geographical location; hence, appropriate security should be ensured. An intruder can easily tamper the device or alter the contents by device capture and even insert new devices in the network. Besides this, because of environmental factors, also the device can be damaged. To avoid this, IoT devices have to have an inbuilt tamper-resistant package as well as energy-efficient security measures [1, 8–11]. Reliability is another area of concern as it is quite necessary; otherwise, the intent of the entire IoT network deployment may go futile. The lack of universal standards for all devices is risky as it is reasonably challenging to identify whether the devices are lawful or not to connect to the Internet. Drastic usage of IoT devices produces tremendous amounts of data. All these data have to be preserved against data theft and other security breaches, which is always a tremendous concern as the majority of these applications gather personal and private data [2].

Software-Based Security Constraints

The main security constraints related to software are inbuilt software constraints and lack of active security patches, because of the lack of standardizsed rules, policies, and also dropping out of IoT vendors from the market. IoT devices have software embedded security constraints that use the real-time operating system with minimal network protocols, which leads to the drip of security modules. Even though security patches are available, dynamic updations are difficult. Remote reprogramming is not possible all the time due to the unreliability and low bandwidth [1, 9]. Besides all, the most threatening factor is the lack of IoT literacy among the majority of the users.

Network-Based Security Constraints

The network-based security constraints are mobility, scalability, and heterogeneity. Mobility is one of the features of IoT devices. The devices should adapt to an existing network without any other configuration, which is difficult in real-time. Furthermore, the number of IoT devices is increasing exponentially, which upturns issues in the secure connectivity of mass IoT devices. Here, scalability is a significant concern. The devices getting connected to the IoT network are heterogeneous, in their functions, communication medium, protocols used, and even the network topology. All these add on to the network-related security issues [1, 9].

IoT Challenges Based on Security Requirements

Three factors have to be considered while inspecting the challenges based on security requirements: the information level, access level, and the functional level, as summarised in Table 4.3. Information-level security requirements include all the factors considered for ensuring data security and privacy, maintaining integrity, and preventing unauthorised access from the third party and providing data confidentiality and non-repudiation [1, 3].

Access-Level Security Requirements

This level of security requirements includes all the constraints which are related to accessing the data. An authentication procedure guarantees that the valid user receives data from the correct source and vice versa. Authentication is crucial in the case of accessing data. Authorisation makes sure that those that receive the network services and resources are authorised devices and users. Access control relates to controlling the data accessing by ensuring all the authorised IoT devices access only the authorised data [1].

Table 4.3 IoT Challenges based on Security Requirements

Information level: Security of data. ■ Integrity ■ Security and privacy ■ Data confidentiality ■ Non-repudiation
Access level: Accessing the data. ■ Authentication ■ Authorization ■ Access control
Functional level: Functions of data. ■ Availability ■ Resiliency ■ Self organization

Functional-Level Security Requirements

All the constraints which are related to the functions of data belong to this level. They are availability, resiliency, and self-organisation. Availability guarantees that all the services by IoT devices to authorised users are in a proper way even though distractions occur. It indicates the competency of devices to provide minimum-level services in case of a power loss or any failure. Resiliency is the readiness to provide security schemes to protect against various kinds of attacks. Through self-organisation, even though one of the IoT devices may fail, the other device will be equipped to recognise and maintain the level of connectivity in a secure manner [1].

IoT Features and Issues

The various characteristics of the IoT give it a unique identity. These specific characteristics differentiate the IoT device from traditional devices, networks, and services. Nonetheless, there are some issues also related to this explicit nature, which are briefed in the subsequent sections.

■ **Heterogeneity** – The IoT includes a variety of software, hardware, operating systems, protocols, platforms, policies, etc. The main issue with heterogeneity is the lack of universal security service. There is no standard architecture to follow the development of IoT devices currently. It results in various security issues, mainly insecure protocols, IoT botnet, and malware propagation. The challenge is to defend the fragment of security, cross-domain identification, and trust. To overcome this, we can use dynamic configuration and intrusion detection systems to a certain extent [12, 13].

- **Interdependence** – The number of IoT devices is increasing, and communication between the devices becomes complex and needs to reduce human intervention. Usually, there is no direct communication amongst the IoT devices; most of the time, clouds are subtly controlled by other devices or environments. This type of dependence between the IoT devices is known as the interdependence of IoT features. The main issues are access control and privilege management [13].
- **Resource Constraint** – Resources are constrained in the IoT. Hence, they face problems with computational requirements, storage capabilities, as well as energy requirements. Specific lightweight algorithms have to be designed to optimise the available memory and battery capacity [12]. These limited resources pave the way for many security attacks that have to deal consciously. Remote attestation and trusted lightweight execution mechanisms serve the purpose of a certain outspread [13].
- **Dynamic Environment** – The IoT environment is dynamic because of mobility and connectivity concerns. For addressing the enormous application's requests, flexibility and scalability is required for IoT communication protocols. According to the Cisco report, the usage of IoT devices will increase by up to 50 billion [14] by 2021. Subsequently, flexibility and scalability ensuring security will be the primary requirement of any IoT network. The main issues to be addressed are insecure configuration and privacy leak, which can resist by using homomorphic encryption and anonymous protocols [13].
- **Intelligence** – Intelligence is a pivotal and critical feature of the IoT. IoT devices are special-purpose devices. Computational intelligence will improve the function of devices. Many of the IoT devices need significant computational intelligence and speed. Intelligence helps to achieve smart analytics based on the huge data generated within a shorter duration.

Components of IoT

To understand and evaluate the functionalities of the IoT, it is necessary to identify and examine the nature of IoT components, their network infrastructure, and interoperability. The IoT environment has five major components: IoT devices, coordinator, sensor bridge, IoT services, and controller [1].

IoT devices are hardware components that help the entity to be a part of the digital world. It consists of various sensors, communication interfaces and software, and lightweight services. An IoT device can communicate with other IoT devices like Information and Communication Technology (ICT) systems. The main objective of smart things is to collect the contextual information with the help of sensors and to do specific actions through actuators [1, 15]. For example, a smart pump set perceives the level of water in well as well as in the water tank, and pumps water accordingly.

A coordinator should act as the main controller of the entire system. It is a device that acts as a device manager and coordinates one or more smart things under a single coordinator. The primary aim of a coordinator is to examine the performance and activities of smart things and report the same to the service provider. Considering the previous example of a smart pump set, the smart pump set has to pump the water to the paddy field, based on the moisture level and probabilities of rainfalls. Here, moisture-level sensors, two water-level sensors, and weather forecasting sensors are operated by the same coordinator. First, the action of water pumping to the field should get triggered when the water level of the tank becomes empty. The water-level sensor sends information with appropriate commands to the coordinator for pumping the water to the tank after which the coordinator forwards the command to the pump set. At last, the coordinator generates a report which includes all the information about the events and sends it to the IoT service provider.

The sensor bridge is also known as the IoT gateway or multi-protocol device. It pretends as a hub between the local IoT network and IoT cloud service [16]. It also behaves like a connector between asymmetric local IoT networks. For example, the sensor bridge device enables ZigBee IoT devices to talk with Z-wave IoT devices.

Typically, the cloud is the storage area of IoT services so that users can access the services from anywhere at any time. The primary responsibilities are device management, IoT process automation, and decision-making. All IoT devices are controlled by using various kinds of controllers; it may be a remote, a smartphone or a tablet, or any other remote control device. For instance, a user can use his smartwatch to issue commands to smart home appliances even remotely [15].

IoT Architecture and Protocol Stack

The rapid growth of technology and mass usage of IoT conveyed considerable changes in the end user's daily lives. The IoT can work together with WSNs, Radio Frequency Identification (RFID) objects, and any network anywhere at any time. The security and privacy of the IoT is a critical problem. With the help of RFID sensors or actuators, intelligent devices can make the self-decision and pass the information to the user safely [17]. According to various studies by Gartner, IBM, and Cisco, the physical world will be fully oriented with connected devices, which are able to make predictions, take appropriate solutions, improve the processes, and reduce the human efforts remarkably [18].

Even though there exists no standardised format for IoT architecture, the most existing architecture models follow the layered approach. Several stakeholders and research groups recommend layered architectures. The models are not from an entirely technical point of view, but mixed with business and processes together. Table 4.4 shows a summary of the different layered architectures of the IoT based on altered perspectives available in the literature. From this, it can be summarised that

Table 4.4 Summary of the Different Layered Architectures of the IoT

Number of Layers	Major Technologies	Article
Three Layers	Wireless Sensor Network (WSN), Cloud Servers, Application.	[10]
	Perception, Network, Application.	[7, 19]
	Sensing, Transport, Application.	[20]
Four Layers	Sensing, Networking, Middleware, Application	[17, 21]
	Local environment, Transportation, Storage and Data Mining, Availability.	[18]
	Physical, Network, Perception, Application.	[3]
	Sensors and Actuators, Networking, Data Processing, Application.	[22]
Five Layers	Physical, Data Link, Network, Transport, Application	[16]
	Edge Nodes, Object Abstraction, Service Management, Service Composition, Applications.	[10]
Seven Layers	Edge Nodes, Communication, Edge Computing, Data Accumulation, Data Abstraction, Applications, Users, and Centres.	[6, 10, 23]

there are four types of layered architectures, mainly: three-layered, four-layered, five-layered, and seven-layered. Even though in each category of a layered architecture, different authors give different names for each underlying layer, the functionalities remain the same. The following sections give a detailed briefing about the various layered architectures in the IoT.

Three-Layered Architecture

Three-layered architecture is the most commonly used architecture of the IoT [7, 10, 19, 20]. Three layers are Perception, Network, and Application – each layer dedicated to performing specific tasks and functions. Figure 4.3 gives a symbolic depiction of the three-layered architecture.

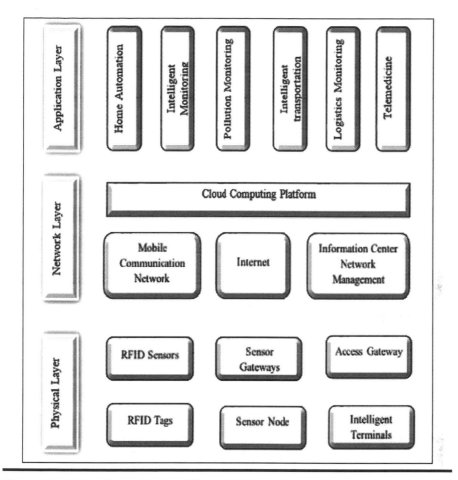

Figure 4.3 Three-layered IoT architecture.

The first layer, the perception layer, is also known as the physical layer or sensor layer or the WSN layer. The crucial function of this layer is to sense the events using sensors to collect information from the environment. For the additional processing, it transmits data to the network layer and also handles node collaboration in the IoT in a local and short-range network. The perception layer includes various types of sensors, RFID, Barcodes, etc.

The second layer is the network layer, which is also called the transport layer or the cloud server layer. It acts as the main component in the entire network. The network layer sends the data collected from the sensing layer to appropriate layers ensuring data security. Mainly, this layer focuses on data routing. The network layer also focuses on network security, which includes core network security, local network security, as well as different technologies, 3G/4G access network security, ad-hoc network security, and Wi-Fi security.

The next preceding layer is the application layer, which can provide various services to the users. The main focus of the application layer is to develop a smart environment like the structural health of buildings, waste management, air quality, noise monitoring, traffic congestion, city energy consumption, smart lighting, etc. The application layer provides security to the IoT applications. The application layer focuses on data integrity, data confidentiality, and data authenticity. The application layer protocols define the application interface with the lower layer protocols to transfer the data over the network.

Four-Layered Architecture

The four-layered architecture [3, 17, 18, 21, 22] is similar to the three-layered architecture mentioned above, with an added extra layer known as the middleware layer. The functionalities of each layer in this architecture are described as follows:

- **Sensor Layer:** It is also known as the physical layer, mainly focused on sensors and actuators to collect the data from the external world and perform an action based on sensed data. The different types of sensors are ultrasonic sensors, camera sensors, smoke-detection sensors, temperature, and humidity sensors.
- **Networking Layer:** The primary purpose of the networking layer is data routing and transmission to different IoT hubs and devices over the Internet as well as mobile networks. For this, it uses cloud computing platforms, Internet gateways, and switching and routing devices used by some recent information technologies such as Wi-Fi, LTE, Bluetooth, 3G/4G/5G, Zigbee, etc. The network gateways act as the negotiator between different IoT nodes by aggregating, filtering, and from different sensors.
- **Middleware Layer:** The main principle of this layer is based on Service-Oriented Architecture (SOA). It is a software layer between the network and application layer. Mainly, this layer will be focusing on the authenticity, integrity, and confidentiality of the exchanged data which need to be operated and managed. In the IoT architecture, the intelligent part of the layer will overcome all ubiquitous sensor networks and create a dynamic mechanism for the physical world in the digital/virtual world. This layer provides the Application Program Interfaces to fulfil the demands of the application layer. The middleware layer also includes brokers, persistent data stores, queuing systems, machine learning, etc.
- **Application Layer:** This layer provides services to the end users. The application layer provides all functionalities to the users with the help of standardised protocol and service technologies. Providing data protection, security, and privacy is the primary concern of this layer (Figure 4.4).

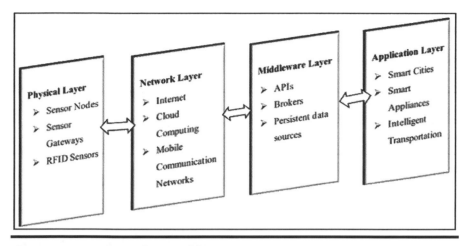

Figure 4.4   Four-layered IoT architecture.

Five-Layered Architecture

According to the five-layered architecture of the IoT [10, 16], the layers are named Physical, Data Link, Network, Transport, and Application layers.

The five-level model contains edge nodes, object abstraction, service management, service compositions, and application layers. It is a substitute model that enables the communication between different sections of applications through decompositions of complex systems into simpler forms [10]. Figure 4.5 gives a pictorial representation of a five-layered IoT architecture.

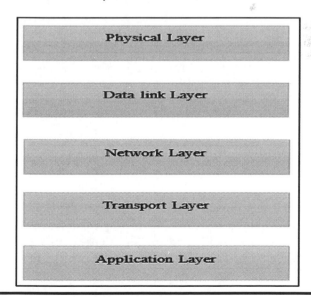

Figure 4.5   Five-layered architecture.

Seven-Layered Architecture

The seven-layered architecture is an extension of the previous three- and five-layer models. CISCO proposed a seven-layer model in 2014 where data flow is considered to be bidirectional. The layers and their main components are as follows:

- Layer 1: Computing nodes, smart controllers, and various sensors are the major components in this layer. Data confidentiality and integrity are the foremost concerns of this layer.
- Layer 2: All the components required for transmitting commands and information is involved in this layer. Communication between the different layers is the functionality of this layer.
- Layer 3: Here, the main focus is on data processing using signal processing and algorithms to reduce the computation load and provide fast responses.
- Layer 4: Data gathering for further analysis and converting the data into appropriate formats for higher-level processing is the functionality of this layer.
- Layer 5: Data abstraction being the main focus, collective operations of are normalisation, denormalisation, indexing, and appropriate data storage are performed
- Layer 6: This layer, often called the application layer level, emphasises on data interpretation.
- Layer 7: The layer consists of users and centres [6, 10, 23].

As we are taking a tour of this IoT architecture, which is mentioned above, we can understand that three layers are common for all categories. The layers are the Physical/Perception layer, Network/Communication layer, and Application layer. So, we would like to hold on to this three-layered architecture for all further study.

Protocol Stack

IoT protocols help each layer to communicate with each other. For this purpose, three main requirements have to be satisfied, namely, a low-power communication stack, a highly reliable communication stack, and an Internet-enabled communication stack [24]. When we consider the three-layered architecture, each layer has its protocols and is described further.

- **Perception Layer** – It is also known as the physical layer. This layer includes a variety of sensors and actuators for data-sensing and collection [25]. It is for frequency selection, modulation, and demodulation. In this layer for communication, use different hardware and software. For the identification and addressing, it uses EPC (Engineering, Procurement, and Construction), uCode, and RFID tags. Hardware such as smart things, sensors, Arduino, and Raspberry, and software operating systems such as Contiki, tinyOS, Android, LiteOS, etc. [26].

■ **Network Layer** – The main objective of this layer is to acquire data from different devices and to forward it to the application layer. This layer is responsible for connecting smart devices, network devices, and servers [25, 26]. There are different protocols used in the layer for better communication, like 6LoWPAN, Routing Protocol (RPL), IPv4/IPv6, IEEE 802.15.4, etc. [21].

  – IPv6 over Low power Wireless Personal Area Network (6LoWPAN) is a popular standard for wireless communication. It is encapsulated with an IPv6 long header and IEEE 802.15.4 small packets [27]. 6LoWPAN devices can communicate to all IP-based devices on the Internet [28].

  – Routing Protocol for Low power and Lossy network (RPL) is another protocol used in this layer. The main aim of the RPL is to provide different levels of security. Data authenticity, semantic security, protection against replay attacks, and confidentiality are provided by the RPL. RPL attacks include selective Forwarding, Sinkhole, Sybil, Hello Flooding, Wormhole, Black hole, and Denial of Service [27]. Internet Protocol Version4/Version6 is useful for communication in the IoT domain. Compared to other IPv6 is the best protocol for IoT domain communication due to its scalability and stability [25].

  – IEEE 802.15.4, which is the most generally used IoT standard for MAC, gives an idea about frame format, headers with source and destination address, and how to communicate each node with others. This frame format is not suitable for low power in multihop networking in IoT. To upkeep low power communication, IEEE 802.15.4e, an extended version of IEEE 802.15.4 [27, 29], is used.

■ **Application Layer** – This layer provides application-based services to users. The main objective of this layer is object tracking, raw data processing, and decision-making [26]. The application layer uses different protocols, depending on the requirement of the application. The most commonly used application protocols are Message Queue Telemetry Transport Protocol (MQTT), Advanced Message Queuing Protocol (AMQP), Constrained Application Protocol (CoAP), Extensible Messaging and Presence Protocol (XMPP), Data Distribution Service (DDS) [21], etc.

  – MQTT is a lightweight protocol based on the publish/subscribe model that runs on TCP. It includes three main components: publishers, subscribers, and brokers. The clients are publishers/subscribers, and the server acts as a broker to which clients connect through TCP.

  – AMQP is the open standard application layer that follows publisher/subscriber and point-to-point models. It is dedicated to the middleware messaging protocol. The main features are message orientation, queuing, switching, reliability, and security.

  – CoAP follows the request-response model for web transfer protocol. It is dedicated to the constrained environment with constrained resources and networks and was designed by IETF Constrained RESTful Environment (Core) working group to cooperate and work with HTTP.

– Extensible Messaging and Presence Protocol are especially for chatting and messaging applications. XMPP can handle real-time communication and streaming for XML data between network entities. It supports both the publisher/subscriber and request/response model. The main applications of this protocol are messaging, syndication, gaming, multi-play chatting, and voice/video calling.

– The Data Distribution Service follows the publisher/subscriber model. Object Management Group designs it. The DDS is a data-centric protocol for the machine-to-machine (M2M) communication, and it gives configurable reliability and quality of service [19, 25, 27].

Applications and Use Cases

Nowadays, every object can be connected to the Internet and hence every device can interconnect to other devices with the help of IoT technology. There are many applications in IoT, which are capable of making self-decision based on the needs of the users and stakeholders. The stakeholders in the IoT perspective can be a person, group of persons, or a company that is directly or indirectly involved in any application process. Stakeholders based on the roles can be segregated into four categories, such as manufacturer, developer, consumer, and provider [23], as mentioned in Figure 4.6.

The manufacturer is the person who is making IoT hardware and IoT products. A developer is the one who is implementing the IoT solutions for the consumer who is using IoT objects in different areas in daily lives. The persons or companies who provide IoT services to the consumer belong to the IoT provider category.

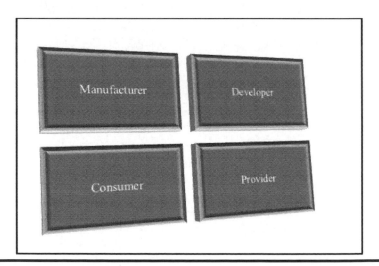

Figure 4.6 IoT stakeholders.

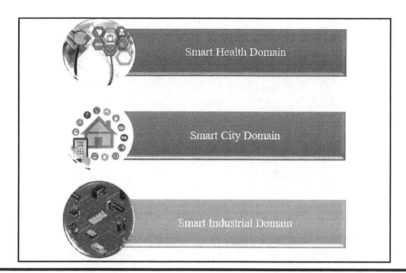

Figure 4.7   IoT applications.

There are many applications available in different domains such as smart cities, smart appliances, smart homes, smart cars, smart agriculture, animal farming, smart retail, smart aviation, industrial systems, critical infrastructure, and the E-healthcare system. These domains can we broadly categorise into three such as a health domain, smart city domain, and industrial domain, as shown in Figure 4.7.

■ **Smart Health Domain** – This domain includes any kind of health monitoring such as endorsement, automatic data collection, and sensing [16] using IoT applications. It can be achieved by using IoT healthcare devices installed either in hospitals or at home or as wearable devices. Smart health domain provides an additional facility for remote surgery, remote patient monitoring, and remote diagnostics [30]. The main focuses of IoT in healthcare are patient monitoring, personal health monitoring, and remote patient monitoring by using less cost and increasing the quality of life [9]. To obtain this goal, smart devices are used in the hospitals [31] and also in the form of Personal Medical Devices (PMDs), which can monitor the patients. PMDs are small devices implanted in the patient's body, either internally or externally [2]. These devices are wireless, which are capable of communicating with the base station and read the device status, medical reports, control the parameters of a device, or update the states on the devices. Security and privacy are the main issues in wireless devices. It will affect the patient's safety and privacy. There are different types of attacks on medical devices such as DoS, eavesdropping, routing diversion, and botnet attacks [2, 9, 16], which has to be taken care of. Figure 4.8 shows different levels of smart health domain applications.

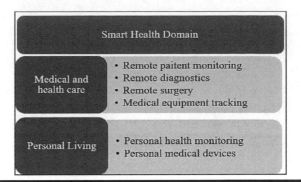

Figure 4.8 Category of smart health.

The main categories of the smart health domain are medical and healthcare and personal living. Nowadays, most of the people focusing on different IoT devices in the area of healthcare, especially during this pandemic period, IoT devices place a vital role in both medical and healthcare and personal living. Table 4.5 shows some of the IoT devices/proposed systems available for the smart health domain.

■ **Smart City Domain** – Smart cities help proper usage of computation and communication resources which helps human lives be much better. It included various IoT applications such as home automation, environmental monitoring, security and emergencies, transportation, and critical infrastructure. Figure 4.9 depicts the classification of the smart city domain.

  – **Home Automation:** Smart homes can monitor an authorised person by using different IoT devices either in the home or outside. While implementing this, one should be aware of how different devices can communicate with each other by using IP (Internet Protocol) addresses. Service platforms, smart devices, home gateways, and home networks are the main parts of the smart home [2]. It has many features like home security: temperature monitoring, smoke detector, surveillances, etc. [9], smart appliances, smart gardening [30]. When using IoT devices in smart homes, the primary issue is Zombie ransomware. 'Zombie' devices are devices that have no update and support from the company because of invisibility from the market as the problem is that they went off from the business or altogether discontinued the support of the devices. These devices remain without future support for security and control in-home networks [31], which is a security loophole to be dealt with severely.

  – **Environmental Monitoring:** Smart things are using environmental monitoring by using various kinds of embedded sensors. These are very capable of giving fast responses to perform a specific action based on information received from the situation [10]. Environmental monitoring IoT devices are fire detection in forests, early prediction of earthquakes, and detection

Table 4.5 Examples of Proposed IoT Devices in the Smart Health Domain

Sl. No	Proposed Device	Description
1	A Distributed Key Authentication and OKM-ANFIS-Centred BC Prediction System [32].	The proposed system predicts breast cancer based on a distributed key authentication and OKM-ANFIS. The proposed method had five steps. 1) Mobile authentication: performed by patients through registration, login, and verification. 2) Data retrieval: by using a bra which includes seven sensors. 3) Secure data transfer: by using the DK-AES algorithm. 4) Hospital cloud server: store the data securely in the hospital public cloud server.5) Hospital monitoring and management system: performs pre-processing and breast cancer prediction and send the notifications to the registered mobile number.
2	A Fuzzy Ontology-Based Diabetes-Monitoring System [33].	The authors proposed a system for constant nursing of diabetic patients by using a fuzzy-ontology-based system. The proposed method developed and maintained a fuzzy ontology with the help of the Protege tool: it is able to be cognitive by various plugins. They used fuzzy owls for adding fuzzy sets to fuzzy variables and SWRL to manage fuzzy rules. For computing results and answers, they used DL and SPARQL queries. This fuzzy ontology-based system is espoused to conclude the health condition and diet status of patients based on the results and give accurate recommendations.
3	A Review on IoT-Based Healthcare-Monitoring System [34].	The proposed system is a Linux-based Raspberry Pi working framework, which converted into an android app. By using different sensors such as temperature sensors, accelerometer, gyroscope, and heart rate, the sensors continuously monitoring the patient's well-being condition. These data are transferred to the server with the Raspberry pi interface. The server frequently sends the data to the site. Using the patient's IP address, anyone can check the health condition of the patient. If the system goes off state, it will automatically send reminders to patient's specialists and relatives. The android application gives alert about daily routine and remedies.

(Continued)

Table 4.5 (Continued) Examples of Proposed IoT Devices in the Smart Health Domain

Sl. No	Proposed Device	Description
4	An IoT-Guided Healthcare-Monitoring System for Managing Real-Time Notifications by Fog Computing Services [35].	This proposed system, mainly focusing on real-time IoT, has driven the health care system using fog computing. Mainly, they have discussed wearable devices, smart clothing, and smart goggles on how to help the patients to get details about his/her health without consulting with anybody. Fog computing facilities are used to identify certain complex diseases. In these techniques, data are collected from the integrated framework as metadata cubes for an understanding of the patient's diseases and suggesting the nutriment.
5	Designing ECG Monitoring Healthcare System Based on Internet of Things Blynk Application [35].	The proposed work is an IoT Blynk application, which uses the AD8382 ECG sensor for collecting patients' data. It also consists of Arduino Uno, ESP8266 Wi-Fi module. Using this application, the doctor can remotely access the patient's ECG rate by using the Blynk application installed on his smartphone. In the cloud database, store the details of the patient and health history. The doctor can analyse the current ECG and send consultative reports to the patient.

Figure 4.9 **Classification of smart city domain.**

of the landslide in the particular geographical area, monitoring the level of snow falling in the altitude area, and pollution monitoring. These are the disasters that directly affect human life also in animals. So, the security in IoT devices is more important [21]. Nowadays, the government sectors are very conscious of using smart things for a better life.

– **Critical Infrastructure:** Critical infrastructure includes smart grid, telecommunication grid, independent refineries, and autonomous water or power distribution [30]. These are very important in critical infrastructure because the above mentioned are their issues that will affect critically in a specific region or nation. Security is essential and vital in critical infrastructure.

- **Security and Emergency:** Security and emergency is the most basic needed facility in IoT applications. Security is the method to prevent unauthorised access to anybody from the restricted area. Security applications can deploy to identify susceptible goods and data. Surveillance monitoring, in any property, the detection of leakage of hazardous gas in industrial and chemical factories and the detection of radiation level in nuclear power reactors or cellular base stations [21], etc., are a few to mention.
- **Smart Metering and Smart Grids:** The applications associated with various measurements, monitoring, and management in smart metering and smart grids are typical nowadays. Monitoring electricity consumption by using smart metering in a very professional way helps to be aware of the energy use and optimise it at both domestic and commercial levels. Smart metering also used to measure the performance of solar energy, monitoring of water, oil, and gas levels in storage tanks, etc. [21].
- **Transportation:** For making a city smart, a smart transportation is unavoidable as it is very much required to make life more comfortable. Smart transportation can be implemented in airlines, marine shipping, rail, and road means. For example, in airlines, it is elementary to handle the luggage and store the passenger's information [16] using this technology. The various levels in transportation are smart vehicles, traffic control, luggage tracking, tracking of real-time engine performance, real autonomy and crewless ships, smart navigation, and cargo management [30].
■ **Smart Industrial Domain** – IoT devices provide a wide range of chances to make industrial systems and applications to be smart. An intelligent IoT system can perform many actions fast in industry and reduce manual work. The IoT provides the ability to connect, track, and monitor the system by using meaningful information through collecting the data. There are various applications in the industrial domain, such as industrial automation, predictive maintenance, and asset tracking [30] in the field like smart agriculture and animal farming, construction management, smart retail, and food supply chain, as mentioned in Figure 4.10.
  - **Agriculture and Animal Farming:** Smart agriculture and animal farming is an IoT application which helps to make more productivity. It includes monitoring soil moisture, micro-climate control, controlling humidity, and temperature [21], and animal tracking [9]. IoT applications will help in improving quality in both agriculture and animal farming. It can make more profit, high yield, easier agriculture land monitoring, and effective utilisation of water compared to traditional farming [9]. Animal tracking is also essential to monitor the activities and health and security of animals by using different sensors.
  - **Construction Management:** The main aim of the IoT in construction management is the monitoring of modern infrastructure. It will help to make all kinds of construction in a smart way like railway tracks, bridges,

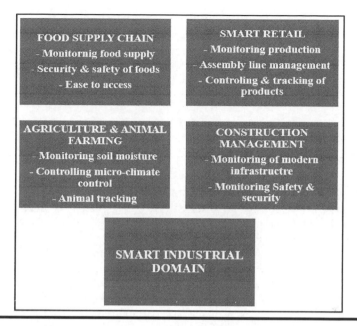

Figure 4.10   Different areas of the smart industrial domain.

buildings, and toll centres. The IoT will provide monitoring safety and security in construction [10].

- **Smart Retail:** In this are monitoring of production, assembly line management, and controlling and tracking of products. IoT applications are used in the retail sector for monitoring the storage conditions of goods and the supply chain of products. Different smart applications provide recommendations to customers based on their habits, preferences [10, 21].
- **Food Supply Chain:** The food supply chain is helping to measure the safety and security of foods and ease of access. It will provide more information to managers of this chain [10]. Currently, the food supply chain has become smarter than the ancient time. They can track food, customers, and employees. The food supply chain is a very booming and attractive application of IoT.

Conclusion

The IoT and its applications will grow further in the future as the technology is evergrowing. It provides immense comfort in all walks of our life, including healthcare, agriculture, business, surveillance and monitoring, scientific and engineering areas, and so on. While embracing the good side of this technology, we also have to be vigilant of the pitfalls, which can lead to many disasters if not wisely used. This chapter provides an overall understanding of the IoT technology, the components of it, the main architectures adopted, and the various applications highlighting the different relevant security concerns which can be further addressed by the researchers.

References

[1] M. M. Hossain, M. Fotouhi, and R. Hasan, "*Towards an analysis of security issues, challenges, and open problems in the Internet of Things,*" *Proc. – 2015 IEEE World Congr. Serv. Serv. 2015*, pp. 21–28, 2015.

[2] M. Abdur, S. Habib, M. Ali, and S. Ullah, "Security issues in the Internet of Things (IoT): A comprehensive study," *Int. J. Adv. Comput. Sci. Appl.*, vol. 8, no. 6, 2017.

[3] S. A. Kumar, T. Vealey, and H. Srivastava, "Security in Internet of Things: Challenges, solutions and future directions," *Proc. Annu. Hawaii Int. Conf. Syst. Sci.*, vol. 2016, pp. 5772–5781, 2016.

[4] D. S. Sousa Nunes, P. Zhang, and J. Sa Silva, "A survey on human-in-The-loop applications towards an internet of all," *IEEE Commun. Surv. Tutorials*, vol. 17, no. 2, pp. 944–965, 2015.

[5] F. A. Fadele Ayotunde Alaba, Mazliza Othman, Ibrahim Abaker Targio Hashema, "Internet of things Security: A Survey Fadele Ayotunde Alaba," *J. Netw. Comput. Appl.*, vol. 88, pp. 1–35, 2017.

[6] M. C. B, *Advances in Security in Computing and Communications*. Springer Singapore, 2017.

[7] J. Deogirikar and A. Vidhate, "*Security attacks in IoT: A survey,*" *Proc. Int. Conf. IoT Soc. Mobile, Anal. Cloud, I-SMAC, 2017*, pp. 32–37, 2017.

[8] S. Tweneboah-Koduah, K. E. Skouby, and R. Tadayoni, "Cyber security threats to IoT applications and service domains," *Wirel. Pers. Commun.*, vol. 95, no. 1, pp. 169–185, 2017.

[9] Z. Mohammad, T. A. Qattam, and K. Saleh, "*Security weaknesses and attacks on the internet of things applications,*" *2019 IEEE Jordan Int. Jt. Conf. Electr. Eng. Inf. Technol. JEEIT 2019 – Proc.*, pp. 431–436, 2019.

[10] A. Mosenia and N. K. Jha, "A comprehensive study of security of internet-of-things," *IEEE Trans. Emerg. Top. Comput.*, vol. 5, no. 4, pp. 586–602, 2017.

[11] I. Yaqoob, I. A. T. Hashem, A. Ahmed, S. M. A. Kazmi, and C. S. Hong, "Internet of things forensics: Recent advances, taxonomy, requirements, and open challenges," *Futur. Gener. Comput. Syst.*, vol. 92, no. May, pp. 265–275, 2019.

[12] S. R. Oh and Y. G. Kim, "*Security requirements analysis for the IoT,*" *2017 Int. Conf. Platf. Technol. Serv. PlatCon 2017 – Proc.*, 2017.

[13] Y. Zhang, A. Peng, Y. Jia, P. Liu, and W. Zhou, "The effect of IoT new features on security and privacy: New threats, existing solutions, and challenges yet to be solved," *IEEE Internet Things J.*, pp. 1–1, 2018.

[14] D. Evans, "IoT by Cisco 2011.pdf," *Cisco Internet Bus. Solut. Gr.*, no. April, pp. 1–11, 2011.

[15] M. Abomhara and G. M. Koien, "Cyber security and the Internet of Things: Vulnerabilities, threats, intruders and attacks," *J. Cyber Secur. Mobil.*, vol. 4, no. 1, pp. 65–88, 2015.

[16] M. Nawir, A. Amir, N. Yaakob, and O. B. Lynn, "*Internet of Things (IoT): Taxonomy of security attacks,*" *2016 3rd Int. Conf. Electron. Des. ICED 2016*, pp. 321–326, 2017.

[17] Y. Lu and L. Da Xu, "Internet of things (IoT) cybersecurity research: A review of current research topics," *IEEE Internet Things J.*, vol. 6, no. 2, pp. 2103–2115, 2019.

[18] B. Dorsemaine, J. P. Gaulier, J. P. Wary, N. Kheir, and P. Urien, "*A new approach to investigate IoT threats based on a four-layer model*," *13th Int. Conf. New Technol. Distrib. Syst. NOTERE 2016 – Proc.*, no. Notere, 2016.

[19] S. N. Swamy, D. Jadhav, and N. Kulkarni, "*Security threats in the application layer in IoT applications*," *Proc. Int. Conf. IoT Soc. Mobile, Anal. Cloud, I-SMAC, 2017*, pp. 477–480, 2017.

[20] A. Oracevic, S. Dilek, and S. Ozdemir, "*Security in Internet of Things: A survey*," *2017 Int. Symp. Networks, Comput. Commun. ISNCC, 2017*, no. i, 2017.

[21] V. Hassija, V. Chamola, V. Saxena, and D. Jain, "A survey on IoT security: Application areas, security threats, and solution architectures," *IEEE Access*, vol. 7, pp. 82721–82743, 2019.

[22] P. Varga, S. Plosz, G. Soos, and C. Hegedus, "*Security threats and issues in automation IoT*," *IEEE Int. Work. Fact. Commun. Syst. – Proceedings, WFCS*, 2017.

[23] H. A. Abdul-Ghani and D. Konstantas, "A comprehensive study of security and privacy guidelines, threats, and countermeasures: An IoT perspective," *J. Sens. Actuator Networks*, vol. 8, no. 2, p. 22, 2019.

[24] M. R. Palattella et al., "Standardized protocol stack for the internet of (important) things," *IEEE Commun. Surv. Tutorials*, vol. 15, no. 3, pp. 1389–1406, 2013.

[25] P. Sethi and S. R. Sarangi, "Internet of Things: Architectures, Protocols, and Applications," vol. 2017, 2017.

[26] I. Makhdoom, S. Member, M. Abolhasan, and S. Member, "Anatomy of threats to the Internet of Things," *IEEE Commun. Surv. Tutorials*, vol. 21, no. 2, pp. 1636–1675, 2019.

[27] T. Salman and R. Jain, "Networking protocols and standards for internet of things," *Internet Things Data Anal. Handb.*, pp. 215–238, 2017.

[28] S. Deshmukh and S. S. Sonavane, "*Security protocols for Internet of Things: A survey*," *2017 Int. Conf. Nextgen Electron. Technol. Silicon to Software, ICNETS2 2017*, pp. 71–74, 2017.

[29] M. R. Palattella et al., "Standardized protocol stack for the internet of (Important) Things," vol. 15, no. 3, pp. 1389–1406, 2013.

[30] E. P. For, I. Of, and T. Security, "Internet of Things security foundation," vol. 7, pp. 21–42, 2019.

[31] K. Fu et al., "Safety, security, and privacy threats posed by accelerating trends in the Internet of Things," *CRA Rep.*, pp. 1–9, 2017.

[32] V. Savitha, N. Karthikeyan, S. Karthik, and R. Sabitha, "A distributed key authentication and OKM-ANFIS scheme based breast cancer prediction system in the IoT environment," *J. Ambient Intell. Humaniz. Comput.*, no. 0123456789, 2020.

[33] F. Yahmed and M. Abid, "*The impact of digital technologies on public health in developed and developing countries*," *ICOST 2020 Impact Digit. Technol. Public Heal. Dev. Dev. Ctries.*, vol. 12157, pp. 277–286, 2020.

[34] P. Kshirsagar, A. Pote, K. K. Paliwal, V. Hendre, P. Chippalkatti, and N. Dhabekar, "A review on IOT based health care monitoring system," *Lect. Notes Electr. Eng.*, vol. 570, pp. 95–100, 2020.

[35] N. Mani, A. Singh, and S. L. Nimmagadda, "An IoT guided healthcare monitoring system for managing real-time notifications by fog computing services," *Procedia Comput. Sci.*, vol. 167, no. 2019, pp. 850–859, 2020.

Chapter 5

Challenges of Introducing Artificial Intelligence (AI) in Industrial Settings

Ardhendu G. Pathak

Co-Founder, Koinvent Business Solutions, Zurich, Switzerland

Contents

DOI: 10.1201/9781003119784-5

> Amara's Law:
>
> We tend to overestimate the effect of a technology in the short run and underestimate the effect in the long run [1]

Introduction

Andrew Ng, a Computer Science professor at Stanford and one of the leading lights in the field of Artificial Intelligence (AI), has been quoted as saying, 'Artificial Intelligence is the new electricity' [2]. The implication is that this technology will leave almost no industry unchanged and the transformative effects of AI could be felt for decades to come.

The introduction of electricity on the industrial scale by Edison and Tesla was certainly a transformative technology with far-reaching effects. We are still experiencing the changes brought about by electricity, more than a century after Edison built power stations at Pearl Street in Manhattan, USA, and Holborn, London, in 1881.

At that time, though the potential for electricity appeared clear, it did not lead to an immediate change from a steam-based economy. More than two decades later, less than 5% of drive power in America was coming from electric motors. Those who did adopt early were often disappointed [3].

One principal reason why this happened was that electric drives and electrical energy were not simply drop-in replacements for the way steam energy and engines worked. Electricity was fundamentally different and could do more. For example, various machines in a factory did not have to run off a central shaft nor there had to be one big steam engine supplying power to the entire plant. The electrical energy could be easily distributed, and smaller electrical machines were also efficient, unlike small size steam engines. This meant that the factory layout could be dictated by the production flow rather than the position of the driveshaft. It was also easy to switch off and on electrical machines, leading to fundamental ways in which workers were expected to work. Added to this was confusion regarding the specific technology to use. Edison insisted that A/C – alternating current technology, as opposed to D/C – direct current technology he supported as dangerous and predicted that rival Westinghouse's alternating current technology will kill customers 'just as certain as death' [4].

To realize the potential of the electricity, everything from factory layout to production lines, labor training, and work shifts had to be changed. It took almost four decades for the productivity changes to show up in statistics for American factories due to the changes brought about by electricity.

The challenges related to AI will be no different. It is also a transformative technology in the sense that it is not merely a drop-in replacement for the existing way of doing work. The only change perhaps from the electricity example above is the pace at which the transformation is taking place.

The specific challenges related to AI can be categorized into the following broad, but overlapping, categories:

1. Strategy and Organization: when and how to implement the changes across the organization, how to organize the enterprise to leverage the changes,
2. Technology: specific risks associated with the technology, and finally,
3. People and Process: type of skills and knowledge required to fully benefit from the new technology wave, what kind of organizational processes and decision-making processes are needed to take advantage of the transformation.

We will go through each of the above facets in detail in the following sections. We will then end the chapter with some advice for the companies which are just starting their journey or are in the early stages of their digital transformation journey.

Strategy and Organization

A decision to explore digital transformation in general, and applications of AI in particular, usually starts with some excitement and curiosity in C-suite. Due to incessant buzz about AI in the business and financial media, there is a desire not to miss the AI bus. The decision may also be linked to the need to justify earlier investments, for example, in product- or customer-connectivity solutions (e.g., products with internet connectivity or customer-facing apps). These solutions may be generating a huge amount of data that may be lying unused or underutilized. The desire for AI-based solutions may also be driven by sporadic requirements from manufacturing to improve throughput, reduce defects, etc.

However, very few companies have relevant expertise in the senior management team to decide on the path to implementation. Executives are afraid of new jargon and no one wants to be seen as ignorant. This results in a situation of either a very slow uptake ('this is a fad', 'we are different') or in working toward unreasonable goals that are not within the reach of the current state-of-the-art.

This may be one reason why the data shows that although many organizations have begun to adopt AI, the pace and extent of adoption have been uneven. Almost half of the respondents in a 2018 McKinsey survey on AI adoption say their companies have enabled their business processes with AI; the proportion of large companies who have adopted AI across enterprise workflows is just 3% [5].

Strategy

An Executive Briefing Note by McKinsey Global Institute points out that executives cite: (1) development an AI strategy with clearly defined benefits and (2) lack of leadership ownership, and commitment to AI on the part of leaders as barriers to adoption of AI, in companies across various sectors [6].

As noted above, often the top management setup has no expertise in the new technologies. This typically results in hiring an external Digital Tzar (Chief Digital Officer or equivalent) or hiring a management consultant to prepare a roadmap for digital transformation. The company may end up burning a lot of cash upfront with cloud platforms and generic analytics tools that may or may not help to solve the business problems. There is also confusion between routine IT investments and AI solutions hosted in a cloud. This issue is further compounded by disparate and legacy IT systems within different functions. Since no one wants to lose the existing investment, generally it is the IT head who gets approached first for implementing AI solutions. In most companies, the IT infrastructure function may not be well placed to identify and implement the change management process associated with AI implementation needed to solve business-critical problems.

A decision to implement AI-driven solutions in a company must start with the business strategy being articulated about the larger digital transformation of the company. AI implementation requires a strategic approach, senior management backing and involvement, clear identification of business objectives, a plan with periodic review and adjustments mechanism, stakeholder management, etc.

Organization

For large companies with multiple business units or a vertically aligned functional structure, the challenge is fitting the new AI initiatives within the existing structure. It appears the structures that are adopted range between two extremes: on one side is a structure akin to the Greek City States – every division has its own data boss to ensure ownership and to find value propositions. On the other extreme is the 'Roman Empire model' with control of everything from strategy to execution resting with the corporate headquarter.

In the case of central control of everything, the end user has no skin in the game. Vendors don't know whom to listen to: the end user or the central funding group. Also, the middle management ends up focusing too much on bid management and distribution of pilot projects to multiple vendors, rather than on value generation. On the other hand, in the case of a distributed model, there's potential for duplication, wastage, and lost opportunities for scaling up.

What appears to be working well is a sort of middle ground, where the corporate office sets the governance structure, security, and absorbs set-up costs that allow time to understand RoI, while uses-cases/value generation is the responsibility of the business units.

Technology

There are several steps involved in the design, testing, and implementation of AI-based solutions. AI tends to give superior results when the complexity and 'dimensions' of the problem are large, but training such models for a complex problem also requires large amounts of data that is properly curated. Once the models are ready, modification of the existing processes, even for testing, can also be expensive and time-consuming due to regulatory, safety, or operational requirements. Finally, the way the AI models are developed and implemented does not make them a natural fit in the existing workflow process of the company. Packaging the AI models in such a way as to fit seamlessly into the existing workflow can sometimes take more time and effort than the development of AI solutions.

In the following sections, we will consider specific aspects related to input data, model testing and validation, and data-related risks.

Data

The current state of the art in AI/ML is such that to create solutions, a lot of data is needed that is accurate, annotated, and accessible. Data collection, labeling, and validation take time and effort (someone has said 'data scientists spend 80% of their time in pre-processing the data, and the rest 20% complaining about it'!). While companies do tend to have a lot of data, they are either incomplete, are not labeled properly, or are locked up in organizational siloes.

But, more often, business-critical problems span across the functions. But with data collection happening in silos across functions or business units leads to data being stored in different formats, in different databases, and with varying access rights. For example, data related to employees may be scattered across HR and Finance databases or product-related data may be stored in different ways in Engineering, Production, and Supply Chain databases.

The data annotation requirements for AI model development can take several forms ranging from, say, sensor calibration information and units for engineering-oriented data to, say, notes and annotations of a radiologist for medical images. AI models can give inaccurate or misleading predictions if the data does not have the required markers (or features).

Another frequent problem with data quality is missing or incomplete data. The data may be missing due to several reasons. It may be due to a faulty data collection plan, i.e., some relevant data is simply not recorded. Or it may be due to factors such as sensors going on a blink or failure of communication network, etc. While statistically rigorous methods to deal with missing data have been in use, nothing can be done if a particularly important parameter is not recorded at all.

Data ownership and open access within an enterprise can be another challenge. Such issues may arise due to several reasons. This may happen due to security and regulatory constraints. For example, EU GDPR regulations (and similar national requirements elsewhere) might restrict the access. Another reason is the sensitivity of the data, for example, personal data or financial records. Privacy requirements are a key issue while dealing with employee data, healthcare data, or financial data. If the data belong to customers, then regulatory and legal hurdles may prevent wider access within the organization to the data for building AI models.

In almost all cases, what is needed is a single source of truth with all the relevant features recorded in one place. Often reaching this stage itself is the first step for the implementation of AI initiatives. This requires making sure that a modern and efficient IT infrastructure consisting of microservices, APIs, and containerization is implemented across the enterprise. Also, it helps to put in place a data strategy (collection plan, data lake, quality checks, storage, access policy, etc.) for the types of problems sought to be solved. One may also have to install additional sensors or even build special gadgets to collect the data. A newly built AI group at a major aviation company found that they needed high-quality boroscopic images used in the inspection of the equipment. Since such data was not readily available in the required form, the group ended up developing a special attachment to collect the videos from a boroscope and then processed the videos to get the required images.

Testing and Validation

Integrating AI into your existing systems is more complicated than adding an app to your phone or installing a package on the computer. It is not unusual for the new versions of a software to be deployed frequently, sometimes even on an hourly basis. Large companies are continuously doing A/B testing to check consumer preferences for everything from checking a specific shade of blue on the website to the place-ment of icons, etc. [7]. The software industry has developed tools and processes to deal with such continuous deployment. As a result, the incremental cost of such deployments is close to zero. Moreover, even if problems show up in the field, the situation can be reversed quickly.

However, the situation is not the same for hardware-related changes. Implementing AI solutions may need modification of the hardware (in the form of, say, IoT solutions) to collect the data. Hardware-related modifications or replace-ments may also be needed to deploy the solutions. This immediately leads to several challenges. First, the hardware changes tend to have significant marginal costs. A visit to any well-established manufacturing plant will reveal old process equipment, machine tools, and computers operating on outdated operating systems, etc. For example, only recently did Indian Railways announce that they are all set to over-haul its almost-century-old safety system based on Red–Green signaling. Capital costs and a comfort level with the way things have always been done keeps hardware around for much longer, thus hindering the efficient generation of data and deploy-ment of AI-driven models. Next, it is not enough that a new hardware is installed, and new models are developed. The implementation is not a one-shot process, and somebody is needed to 'turn the knobs' to fine-tune and improve the models. All these need to be accomplished without hindering the ongoing operations. In an industrial setting, this is akin to changing tires while the car is being driven. Also, as the McKinsey report points out, one of the significant issues that are not easy to tackle is integrating the AI-generated insights into the operating processes and the mindset of the people [4].

The solution calls for a well-thought-out change management program, with wider participation in the implementation process and feedback mechanism from the value chain.

Technology Risks

One of the challenges of AI technology, as it exists today, is that the extrapolation from the current status to the generalization can be incorrect and sometimes dangerous. An AI program that identifies people's faces with accuracy better than humans has no idea what a face is, what it means to be human, or the cost of incorrect identification. The programs are only as good as the programmers who wrote them and the data on which the models were trained. Amazon reportedly had to scrap its AI-backed recruiting tool since it turned out that the decisions were inherently biased against women due to the training set used [8]. A chatbot developed by Microsoft quickly started spewing racist abuses based on the conversations it had with internet users in less than 24 hours and was shut down [9].

The AI models tend to be much higher dimensional in nature, trained on very large data sets. Hence, statistically, it is quite possible to find almost perfect correlations between some parameters and the output. But correlation does not imply causation. For example, a radiology image analysis program was found to be using the presence or absence of a ruler in the image as a classification parameter, a kind of error a well-trained radiologist will never do.

Errors like the above can have profoundly grave consequences. First, lawsuits involving losses due to AI-driven automated investment are now in courts [10]. Legal liability of the damages if an AI system causes damage or injury is yet to be determined. Therefore, regulatory authorities in the field such as aviation and healthcare are being very careful about ceding the final say to algorithms. Such caution is also required when dealing with new AI implementations involving plant automation, customer data, or product safety.

The chart in Figure 5.1 shows the perceived risks by executives across different enterprises in AI adoption [11].

The two top risks cited by 'mature practitioners' were 'Unexpected outcomes/ predictions' and the 'need to control for the interpretability and transparency of ML models'. This group was also more likely to implement model quality checks.

Unfortunately, while legitimate uses may have several obstacles, it is being put to use by actors with criminal intent. In the social and political sphere, 'deep-fakes' are creating confusion and havoc. Cyberattacks are getting more powerful because of AI. Cyber defense systems are also evolving to match these challenges with even

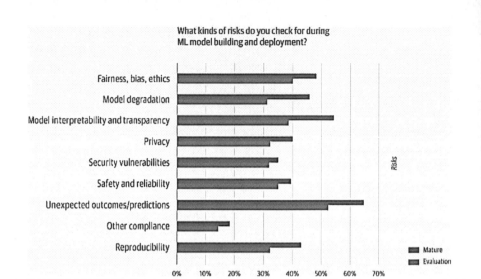

Figure 5.1   Risks checked for during ML model building and deployment (with AI adoption maturity level).

more powerful AI systems. 'Learning' malware and ransomware that learns as it spreads, globally coordinated cyberattacks mediated by ML, use of analytics to customize attacks are all real possibilities or are already a reality. Cybersecurity may be many enterprises' first foray with AI.

People and Process

Here, we will consider a few aspects of the process of AI implementation within an organization. We will briefly consider challenges related to skilled resources required to develop AI solutions, typical decision-making process, identification of the type of problems to be solved first, and whether to develop the solutions in-house or outsource them to specialized firms.

People

For companies that are not 'digital natives', there is often a lack of internal, trained resources to work on AI solutions. When resources are hired from outside, generally young graduates who have acquired proficiency in AI/ML and related areas, they lack the domain knowledge of the industry. Not surprisingly, the existing workforce and the new group tend to view each other with a bit of suspicion and sometimes hostility. This can lead to missed opportunities and delays, not to mention heartburn.

Several companies have found a work around this challenge. Some, like a well-known industrial conglomerate, have adopted a strategy based on a problem-solving approach. This consists of a two-pronged initiative. The first part consists of testing the externally available resource pool and calibrate talent (such as from IITs, Indian Statistical Institute, etc.) to gauge what can be potentially done. The second part is about systematically training interested internal resources (who already possess the domain knowledge) to identify and solve business-critical problems. With such kind of approach in place, it is also easy to isolate and outsource work packages to partners that may be labor-intensive (such as data cleaning and labeling) or work that calls for specialized expertise (infrastructure management, front end/back-end developments, etc.) that may not be core to the enterprise.

Process

In this section, we will consider a few aspects of the process of implementing the AI solutions within an enterprise. First, we will consider the decision-making itself, followed by the types of problems to attack first, followed by a decision to decide the balance between in-house development vs outsourcing.

Decision-Making

A PwC Digital IQ report points out that 'about two thirds of an enterprise's technology expenditure is outside the CTO's budget' [12]. Also, other key leaders who handle technology aspects, such as the Chief Digital Officer or Head of Data and Analytics may also have a say in the AI/ML introduction and adoption within the company.

This can result in business stakeholders across various functions independently investing in technology solutions, some of which can be (or should be) AI/ML-based. It creates pockets within the company where AI solutions are adopted without the knowledge of other stakeholders. This can result in the creation of a patchwork of solutions, with the sum of the parts being less than the whole.

This leads to a situation where there is no single leader or organization that is responsible and accountable for AI/ML implementation within the company. This is linked to the organizational structure issue discussed before. As mentioned earlier, it is important to create a balance between centralized governance and autonomy to achieve the business goals.

Type of Problem

AI/ML investments can be a significant shift for most companies, and naturally, the desire to see the retunes of investments relatively quickly is high. Therefore, the selection of the right business use-cases to solve with AI/ML is very important.

Identifying the 'right problem' to solve takes time, effort, and buy-in from the people deep within the organization. Asking external consultants to prepare road-maps in a vacuum without a clear understanding of the business can result in disappointment and wasted resources. It is easy to pick a problem that is straightforward, where clean data is available, and the contours of the solution can be guessed by the experts to 'test AI'. On the other extreme, there is a tendency to pick a problem for which there is hardly any consistent data, and a solution, even if found, makes no difference to the business since an efficient workaround already exists. An example of this is about trying to predict boiler tube failures. The physics is highly complex, and sufficient data may not exist to train the models. A simple work-around, already in use, is to keep a spares stock ready and simply replace it whenever there is a failure. Arjun Bhattacharyya, VP and GM at SymphonyAI, a B2B AI solutions company based in Bangalore, calls these types of mistakes 'going micro or going mega'.

An ideal problem is the one that, if solved, has immediate tangible business benefits, and is high dimensional enough for which other tools do not exist or are too expensive. This includes complex problems that can potentially replace human judgment based on sight, sound, or speech, and/or can be implemented in real-time. Otherwise, it becomes difficult to assess the results produced by AI and compare them with the success measures of the investment.

Make/Buy

Once a decision is made to at least explore applications of AI in the company, the immediate challenge is to decide how one is going to execute in terms of resourcing it. One way is to commit your own resources and set up a group or a dedicated division. The second option is to treat this as a non-core aspect of the business, at least to begin with, and outsource everything. In between these two extremes, there is a spectrum of choices in terms of what is called a make-vs-buy decision in supply chain jargon.

Just as in the case of hiring specialized resources, AI for business is an emerging field. The big tech companies and consulting giants are talking with the CEOs directly to offer tools, technologies, and tales of triumph in often unrelated fields. Jargon-filled marketing pitches and the reluctance of the senior managers to ask simple questions at the cost of appearing ignorant makes the decision-making even more difficult.

Different companies have chosen different paths in this regard, with varying success. GE Healthcare (GEHC), a leading global medical technology and life sciences company, is using open innovation to develop innovative solutions backed by AI. They are developing an open platform called Edison-X where anyone can introduce their solutions via APIs and microservices. This allows GEHC to tap external creativity, agility, and specialized expertise while retaining control over the key features such as safety, security, compliance, and integration with the hardware. A few other companies have successfully tapped into the thriving start-up ecosystem in IITs and elsewhere to start their journey into AI applications.

To summarize, the make/buy decision and the challenge of evaluating a vendor/ partner is a non-trivial one and needs to be kept in mind while drawing up the plans to explore or implement AI-backed solutions. In certain areas, the AI solutions are well established and may only require minor customization to suit the business needs. These include applications such as supply chain analytics or HR analytics. In such cases reinventing the wheel for your specific needs may be an overkill and, in all likelihood, result in a suboptimal solution. On the other hand, in areas that require deep institutional knowledge, it may be a better idea to co-develop the solutions along with an external partner.

Advice for Implementation

In this chapter, we have outlined several challenges of introducing AI into an industrial setting. We will now conclude this chapter by giving a few pointers for those who are in the early stages of introducing AI into their business or those who are still undecided.

First, this wave of change led by AI and other digital technologies is unstoppable. At some point, your customers and their customers are going to demand this. If you are a part of the global supply chain, the demand for change will reach you sooner or later. It is not a question of if but when. Those who do it faster will gain an advantage in the marketplace. With powerful open-source frameworks, almost free educational material in the form of MOOCs, and the easy availability of the latest servers in the cloud, the entry barriers are low.

Second, sponsorship of the top management in the initial period till success can be demonstrated is absolutely needed to make a lasting impact. It is important to keep in mind that the success is not guaranteed by technology alone. Start with the customer in mind and with a focus on business benefits, both short-term and long-term.

Third, think big but act small. Define end points and build incrementally, with rapid turnaround of projects. Use an agile framework to build the momentum and drive the progress. At least in the early stages, ensure creating plug-and-play solutions, without expecting the mainstream businesses to change the standard operating procedures (SOPs) overnight to accommodate the new solutions. In other words, if your solution is to gain acceptance, then don't create additional work for the 'shop'.

Fourth, remember that digital is another toolkit in your kitty. As with every other investment decision, don't get taken in by the jargon or shiny new tools. A proper, upfront homework is required. Clearly articulate the value proposition and the roadmap to achieve it. 'Don't jump into ocean first and then try to figure out how to swim' as Dr. Ravi Malladi of McKinsey puts it.

Fifth, the availability of the right kind of data is critically important. Ensure you know what data you have, and what you can potentially generate. Build quality-data-generation opportunities in your operations, develop quality metrics, and ensure you have an enterprise-wide data strategy in place. AI developments closely mirror the dominant trends in software architecture. Therefore, your IT operations will also need to be modernized. AI teams will need to recognize that the legacy data will never be 'clean' and hence they will need to develop models that detect and correct anomalies in the input data. Data governance is a key aspect and should not be ignored. Depending on the industry you work in, regulatory, legal, and ethical considerations related to data quality and security can have serious repercussions.

And last, ensure that AI teams, whether internal or those of partners, work closely with the people who have the knowledge of the business context, own the data, and are looking to have some specific problem solved. It is a mistake to look at this as a simple replacement of technology. Instead, serious AI implementation requires a change management program. Get a buy-in from the stakeholders, especially the end users. General awareness and training of the workforce should be part of your overall plan. Institutional support remains the biggest barrier to AI adoption. If Ai is a priority for you, then you should be prepared to spend time to articulate and communicate the expectations to all stakeholders within the enterprise.

Summary

In this chapter, we have reviewed some of the challenges of implanting AI in an industrial setting, specifically for traditional companies whose core business is not really about anything viewed as 'digital'. We have seen challenges ranging from strategy and organization design to the aspects that are rooted in the very nature of the AI technology. Each aspect has also been illustrated with examples of how different companies are dealing with it. Finally, we close with a few pieces of advice to those who are thinking of diving into digital transformation in general, and implementing AI solutions in particular.

Acknowledgments

The author wishes to acknowledge many helpful discussions and comments on the draft by Nitin Joglekar, Arjun Bhattacharyya, Ravi Malladi, Alok Nanda, Sanjay Anikhindi, and Dileep Mangsuli, among others.

Abbreviations

AI	Artificial Intelligence
RoI	Return on Investments
ML	Machine Learning
EU	European Union
GDPR	General Data Protection Regulation

References

[1] Wikipedia Contributors, "Roy Amara," Wikipedia, The Free Encyclopedia, 7 December 2020. [Online]. Available: https://en.wikipedia.org/wiki/Roy_Amara. [Accessed January 26 2021].

[2] *WSJ D.Live Asia conference.* [Interview]. [Accessed June 9 2017]

[3] T. Harford, "Why didn't electricity immediately change manufacturing?," 21 August 2017. [Online]. Available: https://www.bbc.com/news/business-40673694. [Accessed September 7 2020]

[4] Wikipedia Contributors, "War of the currents," 23 August 2020. [Online]. Available: https://en.wikipedia.org/w/index.php?title=War_of_the_currents&oldid=974608739. [Accessed September 7 2020]

[5] J. M. A. J. Bughin, "The promise and challenge of the age of artificial intelligence," 15 October 2018. [Online]. Available: https://www.mckinsey.com/featured-insights/artificial-intelligence/the-promise-and-challenge-of-the-age-of-artificial-intelligence#. [Accessed September 7 2020]

[6] N. v. Z. Jacques Bughin, "Artificial intelligence: Why a digital base is critical," 26 July 2018. [Online]. Available: https://www.mckinsey.com/business-functions/mckinsey-analytics/our-insights/artificial-intelligence-why-a-digital-base-is-critical. [Accessed September 7 2020].

[7] "Why Google has 200m reasons to put engineers over designers," *The Guardian*, 5 February 2014. [Online]. Available: https://www.theguardian.com/technology/2014/feb/05/why-google-engineers-designers

[8] J. D. 8. M. READ, "Amazon scraps secret AI recruiting tool that showed bias against women," *Reuters Technology News*, 10 October 2018. [Online]. Available: https://www.reuters.com/article/us-amazon-com-jobs-automation-insight-idUSKCN1MK08G.

[9] A. Kraft, "Microsoft shuts down AI chatbot after it turned into a Nazi," *CBS News*, 25 March 2016. [Online]. Available: https://www.cbsnews.com/news/microsoft-shuts-down-ai-chatbot-after-it-turned-into-racist-nazi/.

[10] N. K. Thomas Beardsworth, "Who to sue when a robot loses your fortune," *Boomberg*, 6 May 2019. [Online]. Available: https://www.bloomberg.com/news/articles/2019-05-06/who-to-sue-when-a-robot-loses-your-fortune.

[11] S. S. Roger Magoulas, *AI Adoption in the Enterprise 2020*, O'Reilly, 2020.

[12] PWC 2015 Global Digital IQ® Survey, "Lessons from digital leaders 10 attributes driving stronger performance," September 2015. [Online]. Available: https://www.pwc.dk/da/presse/2016/digital-iq-survey.pdf.

Chapter 6

Blockchain-based Circular-Secure Encryption

K. Sathya and P. L. Chithra

Department of Computer Science, University of Madras, India

Contents

Introduction

Passwords provide the primary line of defence against unauthorized access to a computer and private information. Creating strong passwords for all of your accounts

DOI: 10.1201/9781003119784-6

will make them more secure against hackers and malicious software. Robust authentications furnish vital defence from financial swindling. Simple and widely used authentications permit intruders to merely obtain access and influence a computer. A password is a phrase, word, or collection of characters used to identify a legitimate user or method (for the purpose of granting access) from a fraudulent user, or, to put it another way, a secret key is used to demonstrate one's character or authorise access to an asset. Stronger, diversified passwords make security breaches harder. The more different the passwords, the harder it'll be to hack all or any of the accounts.

We can add another layer of assurance by guaranteeing that each secret phrase is strong. We'd prefer to choose a secret phrase that's lengthy enough, at least 16 characters, and includes numbers, photos, capital letters, and lower-case letters, as well as a variety of characters, no ties to your own data, and no word reference to make the secret phrase more difficult to crack. Samples of weak passwords include qwert12345, Gbt3fC79ZmMEFUFJ, 1234567890, 987654321, Norton password, PASSWORD.

One of the easiest ways for a hacker to ask for your own data is by taking your login certifications through a digital assault. The Better Business Bureau (BBB) and most experts suggest continuous secret phrase changes. The suggested recurrence can go from each 30, 60, to 90 days. An example of a robust password is "Maroon-Doggy-30-Drinks-Shops". It is long, contains all four character types, and is straightforward to recollect. There are 4 uppercase letters, 18 lowercase letters, 2 numbers, and 4 symbols, totalling 28 characters. John the Ripper ("JtR") is one of those indispensable tools. It's a quick password cracker that identifies users' weak passwords on a server that supports Windows and a variety of Linux versions. It's incredibly versatile and may crack pretty much. JtR could be a free password-breaking software method. It can run on 15 specific stages, originally created for the UNIX OS (11 of which are design-explicit adaptations of UNIX, DOS, Win32, BeOS, and OpenVMS).

A rainbow table might be a group of all conceivable plaintext permutations of encoded passwords explicit to a provided hash calculation. Rainbow tables are frequently utilized by password-breaking programming for network security attacks. During a rainbow table creation, an arrangement starts with a discretionary plaintext, hashes it, reduces the hash to an alternate plaintext, and hashes the new plaintext, and so on. Tables are typically used in recuperating a key induction work up to a specific length comprising of a restricted arrangement of characters. Instead of the word "novatashy," the value stored in the rainbow table will be a series of numbers, depending on the hashing method or algorithm employed. A rainbow table is utilized to authenticate clients by looking at the hash estimation of the entered secret phrase against the one stored in the rainbow table. It assumes a basic part of network protection. When hackers line up of a rainbow table, password-breaking becomes tons simpler.

Specialists accept that the preeminent powerful method of fighting rainbow table assaults is password salting. The strategy includes adding "salt" or arbitrary information to encode a password. That way, each hash gets novel for each client. Indeed, even reused passwords are more secure from hacking since each has extra irregular information sprinkled in. In this case, even if a coder figures out how to decode the rainbow table, the hashes will not match. Note, notwithstanding, that there are different rules to ensure the viability of secret word salting. The salt should not be too short in the light of the fact that an attacker with a high-memory disk drive can in any case effectively break it by means of guessing.

Usernames should not be utilized as salt as these are not difficult to accumulate. Never utilize obsolete hashing calculations in rainbow tables since they're currently simple to break. Try not to utilize a firm salt, that is, an identical salt for each hashed secret phrase. That may be exceptionally ineffectual, particularly for reused passwords. In the event that a hacker guesses one, the individual in question additionally opens different records with a comparable secret phrase. Besides encryption, the most straightforward technique to stop rainbow table assaults is by keeping attackers from accessing your secret word data set.

It might be ideal to have a security solution in situ that instantly identifies and impedes compromise attempts. All organizations should use powerful and proactive security solutions which will identify and put an end to unapproved network access. The password-cracking tool for breaches of security mostly uses rainbow tables. All smart systems require password-based verification and stores pieces of information of passwords related to user accounts, typically encoded rather than plaintext as a safety measure. The below figure shows the outline of the client verification measure.

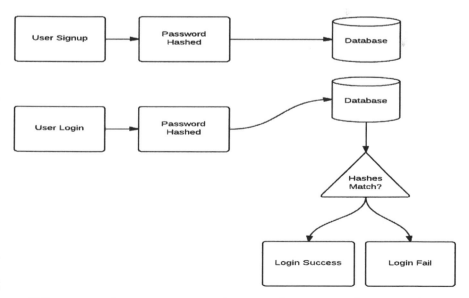

When an attacker accesses a system's password repository, the password hacker compares the rainbow table's precompiled group of potential hashes to hashed password phrases within the repository. The rainbow table associates plaintext possibilities with each of these hashes, which the attacker can then exploit to reach the network as a legitimate user. Rainbow tables make password-breaking much quicker than prior strategies, similar to brute-force and dictionary attacks. Depending on the real software, rainbow tables are often won't break the 14-character alphanumeric secret key in around 160 seconds. However, the methodology uses huge loads of RAM on account of an outsized amount of knowledge in such a table.

Rainbow tables have just become feasible in recent times because the amount of possible RAM in earlier computers was lacking. One rainbow table for a common alphanumeric file is on the brink of 4 gigabytes (GB). Adding new symbols to a combination, as well as each magnification in encryption, increases the amount of memory required. To protect against attacks using rainbow tables, system administrators must add security measures to encoding passwords; similarly, the addition of randomly produced characters (salt) to password hashes eliminates the use of obsolete password-hashing algorithms.

The reason why they are called rainbow tables is that every column applies a special reduction function. Since each reduction feature has a special colour, and at the rock bottom, you have starting plaintexts at the highest and final hashes, and it might seem like a rainbow. The three advantages of a rainbow table over other password attacks are that it is often used repeatedly to attack other passwords, quicker than dictionary attacks and therefore the quantity of memory required on the machine is considerably minimized. Hash tables are built by hashing the entire word with a password dictionary. The password-hash duads are stored when a table, classified by the hash value. To employ a hash table, just have the hash and conduct a binary search in the table to determine the first password, if it's available.

Building a rainbow table requisites two aspects: a reduction and hashing function. The hashing function for a provided set of rainbow tables should be equivalent to the hashed password to get back. The reduction function needs to convert a hash into something workable as a password. A simple reduction function is to Base64 encrypt the hash, and then compress it to a specific number of characters. Rainbow tables are built of "bonds" of a certain length: 100,000 for instance. To make the bond, start with a random seed value, then apply hashing and reduction to the existing seed, as well as its result, then repeat 100,000 times. The seed and the final value alone are stored in the table. Recurrence this approach to produce as many bonds as needed. To retrieve a password through rainbow tables, the password hash experiences the above approach for the same length: in this case, 100,000, but every link in the bond is maintained.

All links in the bond are compared with the ultimate value of every bond. If it is similar, the bonds are repeatedly recreated by holding both the result of every hashing operation and the result of every reduction task. The power of a hash table is that it can quickly retrieve a password, so the person building it can choose what enters into the sort equation here. The defect compared to rainbow tables is that hash tables should save each individual hash-password dyad. The below figure shows an announcement from eBay to change the password due to a cyber-attack.

Rainbow tables have the advantage that the person creating those tables can select what proportion of memory is necessary by choosing the number of links in all bonds. The increased the number of links between the seed and the last value, the more passwords are detected. One problem is that the person who creates the links does not choose the passwords they store; therefore, rainbow tables are useless for common passwords. Furthermore, password retrieval necessitates identifying lengthy hash bonds, making it an upscale operation. The longer the bonds, the more the number of passwords getting caught in them; nevertheless, it takes longer to find a password inside. Hash tables are adequate for ordinary passwords; rainbow tables are acceptable for complicated passwords.

The easiest technique would be to retrieve as many passwords as possible using hash tables and/or traditional breaking with a dictionary of the highest N passwords. Whenever a password is saved on a system, it's generally encoded utilizing a "hash", or a cryptographic alias, making it unfeasible to formulate the first password without the related hash. So as to divert this, spammers maintain and distribute directories that saved passwords and their equivalent hashes, frequently constructed from foregoing hacks, diminishing the time it takes to interrupt a system. The below figure shows the output of the Kali Linux password-cracking tool.

Many calculations are completed prior to the attack being implemented, making the method much quicker. The pitfall for cybercriminals is that the absolute amount of feasible combinations means rainbow tables are often massive, commonly numerous gigabytes in size. Though, rainbow tables are enormous, unmanageable things. They need major computing capacity to run and a table becomes purposeless if the hash it's trying to seek out has been "salted" by the inclusion of arbitrary alphanumeric letters to its password prior to hashing the algorithm. There has been speculation about using salted rainbow tables; however, these would be extremely large and impossible to use in practise. They might probably only work with a predetermined "random character" set and password characters less than 12 alphanumeric letters since the size of the table would be restrictive to even state-level spammer otherwise. However, many servers do not retain the password in any form, including encrypted or with salt. Albeit encrypted and salted, the tables are created with hash and salt for concern passwords. To beat this, we introduced a unique Blockchain-based circular fused encryption and it is explained in detail in the next section.

Password Vulnerability

Modern researchers propose that even programmers don't apply proper hash functions to guard passwords, since they will not have sufficient security knowledge. We can organize password-guessing attacks into three kinds: brute force, rainbow tables, and dictionary. Modern password-guessing tools, like JtR and Hash Cat, allow clients to get several millions of passwords per second against password hashes. These tools may employ password generating rules to extend password dictionaries in addition to basic dictionary assaults, such as word concatenation (e.g., "password123456"), where "password" becomes "p4s5w0rd." While these rules work well in practice, it can be a labour-intensive job that requires advanced skills to develop and extend them to model more passwords.

Authors [1] suggested using the Keccak hashing algorithm with the integrated development environment CUDA for a General Processing Unit (GPU) within the heterogeneous GPU+CPU framework to implement high-speed rainbow table generation. The various precomputed hash chains form a rainbow table. Philippe Oecshlin developed the concept of the rainbow table as a quick sort of time-memory trade-off and is mentioned in his paper "Making a Faster Cryptanalytic Time-Memory Trade-Off" [2], which appeared in 2003 in *Lecture Notes in Computer Science*. The widest method utilized in password-cracking is to fully guess, which incorporates a variety of attacks such as brute-force attacks, dictionary attacks, rainbow attacks, hybrid of dictionary and brute force [3], etc.

Precomputed hash values are used in rainbow table attacks [4]. The time needed to crack is reduced to make it necessary to move through the list. Rainbow table attacks are frequently used, for example, [5, 6] there are many web services that use this form of attack, such as the use of rainbow tables for online MD5 cracking.

They're used to eliminating surplus labour. Online guessing and offline guessing are mostly carried out by password-cracking [7]. The hacker communicates with the scheme with online guessing, while the hacker accesses the password table or file with offline guessing and uses all his tools. One solution that can boost the protection of hashing passwords is the algorithm of circular fused encryption and wedges (CFW). By using sorting and concatenation algorithms, it was developed to secure a hash. The random text is sorted alphabetically by the algorithm on the plain text, while the concatenation algorithm is used to rearrange all private information together. Generally, the randomness of the digest is enhanced when the circular fused encryption technique is applied.

It is kind of difficult to manage the password register. Password-hashing methods are the last line of defence against an offline cracker who has stolen the password digest saved during a password file operation. Attackers may use different kinds of attacks that do not protect password-hashing [8] to get the password hash or digest inside the password file. By comparing the stolen password hashes to an inventory of password-hash value pairs, the hacker is able to crack [9]. A dictionary attack on WordPress was similarly carried out by Kyaw et al. [10] (a Content Management System). They were ready to guess the seven-character password of a WordPress user. Bosnjak et al. [11] were also experimenting with a brute-force dictionary attack on the hashed password. The results show that a coffee to mid-range single (GPU) can crack 95 percent of passwords in 3–5 days. As the hacker gains access to user passwords stored in the databases, business establishments and organizations get compromised [12].

Password-Cracking Attacks

A file containing 90,000 military e-mail usernames and hashed passwords [13] was leaked by hackers. This assault was called Monday's Military Meltdown. In December 2009, when the rock-you.com website was targeted by SQL injection, 32.6 million user passwords were revealed [14]. The leaked password list was released on the Internet and is now being used for dictionary attack tests by researchers and security analysts. Password-cracking attacks, such as Brute-Force attacks, rainbow tables attacks, and Dictionary attacks [14, 15], are also executed using various methods of password-guessing. The hacker attempts to crack the system using password applicants obtained from personal user information or dictionary files in these kinds of attacks. A dictionary assault has been used to perform most real-life hacks. It makes use of a massive dictionary file called the wordlist [16], which may contain passwords or a combination of wordlists.

The time-memory trade-off approach is taken into account in the rainbow table attack [17]. There are two stages in the method: table generation and online attack [18]. With rainbow tables Attack, if the password hashes value exists inside the precomputed lookup table, the cracker checks. The plaintext password is exposed if it is contained inside the table [12]. In order to detect weak UNIX passwords [19], JtR is mainly used. Single-mode (JtR-S), Incremental-mode (JtR-I), Wordlist mode (JtR-W), and Markov-mode (JtR-M) [20] support multiple cracking modes. RainbowCrack (rCrack) is a hash-cracking software programme that uses a large-scale time-memory trade-off technique [21]. It is an application of the technique of Philippe Oechslin that cracks hashes with rainbow tables [22]. It uses encryption technologies such as UNIX crypt (3), Standard DES-based, Big Crypt, Extended DES-based BSDI, MD5-based FreeBSD (Linux and Cisco IOS), Blowfish-based OpenBSD, Kerberos/AFS, LM Windows (DES-based), DES-based trip codes, hashes SHA-crypt (newer versions of Fedora and Ubuntu), hashes SHA-crypt, and SUNMD5 (Solaris) [23].

Authors [24] indicated that the info protection model involves generating OTP for the user authentication method using HMAC (Hash-based message authentication code) and includes comparative MD5 and SHA algorithms for higher-model implementation. The time-memory trade-off attack that Hellman devised in 1980 [25] indicates a response that occurs between two options. The time of precomputation remains on the order of 2^n, but the memory complexity is $2^{2n/3}$ and thus only $2^{2n/3}$ function evaluations are needed for the inversion of one value.

Common Causes of Knowledge Breaches

Credentials that are vulnerable and stolen – Despite recognizing that it is such a bad idea, people want to reuse their passwords. It may result in an out-sized lump of cash for corporations. For additional security, organizations can attempt to inform workers and introduce two-factor authentication. Breaches can begin with the reuse of a password by an employee at work – this happened with Dropbox.

Phishing – The attacker attempts to disguise himself as a legitimate or trust-worthy person during this attack to urge entry to sensitive data, for example, numbers of credit cards, passwords, etc. It could also be widely used, that is, to help execute other attacks, to distribute malware.

Social engineering – This may include tricks to exploit confidential information to urge them. It may be manipulating feelings, giving a reward, etc. It is also solved through appropriate training and education of the employees.

Threats from insiders – This involves persons who have access to confidential data and have malicious, criminal intent. For private benefits, they can use these details. A restaurant server, for instance, copies the MasterCard numbers of clients.

Application vulnerabilities – This is often something that can't be completely eliminated, but just lessened; non-patched or badly designed systems that are not modified often leave organizations with privacy violations and other issues. This can be reduced by promising frequent device updates, and the implementation of testing will also help to minimize the risk.

Ransomware – It's not a substitute technique, but it's becoming more and more successful. During a Ransomware attack, data is frequently compromised, and access is restricted until the deal is completed. Most of these are triggered by unpatched computers and poorly configured systems.

Loss and physical theft – Violations of data are typically owing to digital issues, but material violations cannot be overlooked either; most organizations also lack security measures and fail to understand that far more damage can be done by offenders physically than technologically.

Preventive Steps for Violations of Data

- **Appropriate training** – A worker of an organization has obtained confidential materials of the organization and can create severe hazards. In order for them to know the value of protection, they should be given sufficient safety knowledge and training to be able to identify dangers such as phishing. Policies on protection should be observed and revised regularly. Cyber-security sessions should be conducted in order to educate employees on the methods and strategies which are used by hackers in order to help the employees reduce threats and become safer.
- **Evaluation of vulnerabilities and penetration testing** – Most of the vulnerabilities are triggered in an application or device by the manipulation of technological flaws. The probability of software vulnerabilities can only be reduced and cannot be totally eliminated. The evaluation of vulnerabilities and penetration testing helps detect weaknesses until they are abused by anyone. It also helps to recognize potential situations that may be used by an offender to penetrate into a device.
- **Data breach response strategies** – We can do everything to prevent an infringement, but it is not always possible. The security group should also be established with appropriate duties and obligations for handling the breach. Infringements should be adequately recorded and sufficient protocols should be taken to prevent this from occurring again.

Blockchain Structure

The Blockchain may also be a collection of blocks containing individual data, but in a safe and genuine way that is clustered as peer-to-peer within a network. According to the genesis block, the first block inside the Blockchain is identified. Of all the blocks inside the Blockchain, it is the universal parent. In other phrases, if individuals start at any block and monitor the sequence counter-clockwise, they eventually go to the block of genesis. Each node continually starts with a Blockchain of at least one block since it is not possible to change the genesis block. Each node immediately identifies the hash and specification of the genesis block. It also acknowledges the fixed time when it was produced and also its performance.

Thus, for the Blockchain, each node has a starting line, a stable "root" from which to construct a trusted Blockchain. Blockchain technology may also be a unique innovation that has resulted in the digital world's much-needed defence and security. The Blockchain agreement is defined as a structured back-linked registry of blocks of transactions. It is also stored in a transparent repository or as a directory. Each block is commonly recognized by a hash generated on the header of the block using the SHA256 cryptographic hash algorithm. In the "previous block hash" section, inside the block header, each block mentions a previous block, often known because of the parent block.

The block includes a header that contains metadata, in the midst of a long transaction history that advances its duration. The block header is 80 bytes and could therefore be a minimum of 400 bytes for the typical transaction. Nearly 1900 transactions are included in the general block. With all transactions, a whole block is almost 10,000 times stronger than the header of the block. Typical block metadata includes the version – the version of the block structure, the previous block header hash – the reference to the parent block of this block, Merkle root hash – the cryptographic hash of all the transactions used in this block, time – the time this block was formed, nBits – this complexity used to construct this block, nonce ('number used once') – a random value that can be managed by the maker of a block, but they chose to do so.

Hash Functions in Blockchain

Hash functions transform an arbitrarily large bit of data into a hash output of a fixed length. They're one-to-one: the same hash data will always be given by the same input. They are one-way functions: "work backward" is impossible and the input provided a hash value can be reconstructed. There are also some common hashing systems found here. Bitcoin uses the SHA-256 hashing algorithm for proof of labour for comparison. Due to hashing, even one bit of the block header editing would end during a unique hash. Therefore, to cross-check with these difficulty rules, modifying the nonce would generate a substitute hash value. For each new possible block, this process must be repeated over and over until a valid hash is identified.

Hashing in Password Security

The method is relatively easy; users enter their information on the authentication form of the website. The detail is being sent to the authentication server where all user credentials on file are checked with the information. The system will improve security when a match is identified and make them accessible to their accounts. Use a singular salt for each user account or password and store that salt with the password. An extra layer of system-wide salt that's not stored with the password can also add extra strength if the database is stolen because it isn't stored with the passwords but is known to you.

A hashing process utilizes a plaintext password as an input and converts it into a hash value that requires three elements into account: (i) hashing function; (ii) repetitions; (iii) salt. More precisely, the central parameter of a hashing method is that hash functions such as MD5 are used. The iteration factor is optional and defines the number of consecutive hash function operations used to calculate the hash value. As an explanation, if the MD5 hash function is used by a hashing method and then the number of steps is 100, then the password hash will be computed by 100 consecutive MD5 executions. The number of cycles is generally adjusted such that the hash value calculation takes an undefined quantity of computational cost (also mentioned as key stretching). Iterations are often used to adversely affect password-guessing attacks in this way. The salt is also optional with regard to the last component, and it is a random string that provides the hash code together with the password with the inputs to the hash function. Rainbow tables become ineffectual employing arbitrary salts. That is, an intruder would not realize what the salt value is in advance and will therefore not precomputed a rainbow table.

Every password that the user creates is saved in the server database, along with the corresponding hash. The password database contains the hashed password and the hashed salt. To urge authentication from the server during online transactions, the user should enter a password and a couple of important credentials like the first name, last name, user id, password, etc. Albeit users enter much personal information, a password alone is taken as an important one for access authentication. Most of the server stores the password without using any encryption algorithm within the database. If salt is added to a password, it's difficult to crack the hashed password. Nowadays, rainbow tables are created with salt which helps the hacker to access the password within a few seconds.

Once the hacker has access to the server database, the hacker will be able to use all of the credentials. The below figure shows how the password goes to be hashed, salted, and then stored within the database. The password database was built primarily using a hashing method that hashed a password with salt and raw salt. While logging in, users should submit their passwords together with other personal information. The password is then compared to a database-stored precomputed hashed password with salt or without salt. If the proper user is found, access is granted; otherwise, access is refused. In a similar manner, the hacker searches for the correct password using a rainbow table created with a recomputed hashed password and salt. The below table shows the password database with hashing and salting.

PASSWORD HASHING AND SALTING

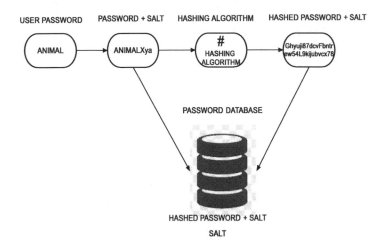

Password	Salt	Hash Function	Database (HexMD5Hash)
passwords	45hj54jikonyew78	Hash = H(password + salt)	u i h j e r w n c i 8 7 5 4 m 93d09w2e4r5y9hjbn
qwerty	rjekwl5o6k7n5m4n	Hash = H(password + salt)	q o 2 k 3 m 4 n 8 b 5 g 4 j 3 h5k6l7i4h3b5n6m7i
12345	3jdk6l8m9k3n5gsj	Hash = H(password + salt)	O 5 j d m n s h r i 3 o 5 j s n a bdvcur85j9s3k85
I love you	endisoalfopkntfsr	Hash = H(password + salt)	J i n f k l w o 0 9 4 3 j k m s 84jdgei4o3ns8emv
P@$$w0rd	Jkryeiwoqp873nfh	Hash = H(password + salt)	J f k d l s o e u i t r n m v c 7h9j3u2o1j4n5b8e

The first password database has the list of all hashed passwords rather the rainbow table is made with a password and their hash. If the hacker gets access to the first password database, then it is easy to seek out the password by comparing the hashed password within the original password database and therefore the precomputed hashed password within the rainbow table.

Blockchain-Based Circular Fused Encryption

In this chapter, the authors introduced a unique method to store the hashed password within the database to secure the knowledge from hackers. All the login details with passwords are hashed, salted, and then stored in Blockchain-based circular form either within the right circular (a right adjacent record) or left circular (a left adjacent record). For instance, five users (user1, user2, user3, user4, and user5) created a login for a specific website. User1's hashed passwords are going to be stored either in user2's place or in usrer5's place. User2's hashed passwords are going to be stored either in user3's place or in usrer1's place then on. The below figure shows the block diagram of circular fused password encryption.

CIRCULAR FUSED PASSWORDS

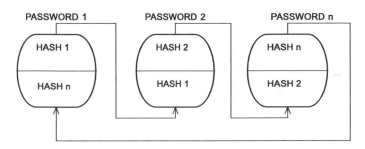

It makes it a little harder for hackers to seek out the precise user id even after they cracked the password successfully with the assistance of a rainbow table. After creating the password, it's salted and reduced to store within the database and here, the authors used random characters for salting. The password is then supplemented with information such as the time it was created, the user's given name, last name, and salt. Further, the reduction process is applied to store it in fixed length. On the other hand, CFW algorithms generate and use a random salt internally during the hash calculation. The below figure shows the snapshot of a password database.

	firstname	lastname	user	passwd	email
60.					
61.					
62.	George	Korfiatis	gkorfiat	gkorfiat	gkorfiat@stevens.edu
63.	Maureen	Weatherall	mweather	mweather	mweather@stevens.edu
64.	Eric	Rosenberg	erosenbe	newpassword	erosenbe@stevens.edu
65.	Ralph	Giffin	rgiffin	rgiffin	rgiffin@stevens.edu
66.	Randy	Greene	rgreene	rgreene	rgreene@stevens.edu
67.	Fred	Regan	fregan	fregan	fregan@stevens.edu
68.	Barbara	DeHaven	bdehaven	bdehaven	bdehaven@stevens.edu
69.	Constantin	Chassapis	cchassap	cchassap	cchassap@stevens.edu
70.	Michael	Bruno	mbruno	mbruno	mbruno@stevens.edu
71.	Lex	McCusker	lmccuske	lmccuske	lmccuske@stevens.edu
72.	Dinesh	Verma	dverma	dverma	dverma@stevens.edu
73.	Anthony	Barrese	abarrese	abarrese	abarrese@stevens.edu
74.	Lisa	Dolling	ldolling	ldolling	ldolling@stevens.edu
75.	Robert	Zotti	rzotti	rzotti	rzotti@stevens.edu
76.	Charles	Suffel	csuffel	csuffel	csuffel@stevens.edu
77.	Laurence	Russ	lruss	lruss	lruss@stevens.edu
78.	Christos	Too long	christod	christod	christod@stevens.edu
79.	Henry	Dobbelaar	hdobbela	hdobbela	hdobbela@stevens.edu
80.	Annette	Feliciano	afelicia	afelicia	afelicia@stevens.edu
81.	Daniel	Gallagher	dgallagh	dgallagh	dgallagh@stevens.edu
82.	Shivam	Raval	sraval	sraval	sraval@stevens.edu
83.	Siva	Thangam	sthangam	00$ITwork	sthangam@stevens.edu
84.	Keith	Sheppard	ksheppar	ksheppar	ksheppar@stevens.edu

Wedges Algorithm for Adding Salt

The salting process is nothing but adding some random or fixed text to reinforce the safety of the password. Conventionally, adding salt is either within the beginning or at the top of the password. But, in this work, the authors insert the random text between the password texts after concatenating all the private information together. The Wedges technique is used to insert random text into concatenated personal information in alphabetical order. Assume we have the H password hash function and the "Pass" numerable password collection. The aim is to precompute an information construction that, provided any output h of the hash code, can either detect a password p in the *Pass* such that H(p) = h, or find out that there's no such p in the *Pass*. On the other hand, preserving the table includes n (H $_{len}$ + p $_{len}$) bits of space, where n is the number of passwords, H $_{len}$ is the length of the output hash value, and p $_{len}$ is the length of p. Hash chains are a means of reducing this requirement for space.

The definition is to describe a reduction function R that maps the hash values back to the Pass values. Chains of alternating passwords and hash code are created by replacing the hash function with the reduction function. The only prerequisite for the reducing feature is that it is ready to return a "password" value for a given size. The reduction function might still be a function that produces the hash code from the corresponding password choice. The reduction function is not one that is evaluated; for each and every rainbow table, it's unique. The reduction function of Rainbow crack, for example, is sometimes described as: "R = H mod N". Here, R is the reduction function, H is the hash value, and N is the total number of options for a password. Under the rainbow table, the reduction function is not too complex a function. An equivalent password candidate is typically created from various hash values termed password candidate collision when using a simple reduction feature.

$$w_{alg1} = concat\left(tm, \ln, fn, uid, pw\right) \tag{6.1}$$

$$w_{alg2} = sort\left(rand_t\right) \tag{6.2}$$

$$w_{alg3} = wedge\, w_{alg2}\left(w_{alg1}\right) \tag{6.3}$$

$$w_{alg4} = reduction\left(w_{alg3}\right) \tag{6.4}$$

Equation 6.1 to 6.4 explains the wedges algorithm: w_{alg1} concatenates all the private information like time of making the password, last name, given name, user identification details, and password; w_{alg2} sorts the random text alphabetically; w_{alg3} wedges the random text into the w_{alg1}; w_{alg4} applies a reduction process on w_{alg3} with 100 iterations.

John the Ripper 1.9.0 and HashCat 5.1.0 are used to execute dictionary attacks. The dictionary file [26] is the Rockyou.txt wordlist, which is combined with Kali Linux and includes 14,341,564 unique passwords. We collected some rainbow tables in freerainbowtables.com to conduct our test successfully. For the plaintext of the hash specified in a paper, rCrack software conducted a lookup on current rainbow tables. Numerous rainbow tables which include only lower alphanumeric with 1–9, lower-alpha with space and 1–9, and mixed alphanumeric with 1–9 are utilized within the experiment. A huge precomputed registry list is used by crackstation. net and hashkiller.co.uk to break the hash value of passwords. The search tables are used to convert the hash of a password into the proper password for that hash. For fast search, indexing is applied within the hash values. The below table depicts the comparison between the exiting hash function and the CFW hash function.

Hash Algorithm	Dictionary Attack	Brute-Force Attack	Rainbow Table Attack	Online Cracking Attack
MD5	Cracked	Cracked	Cracked	Cracked
SHA1	Cracked	Cracked	Cracked	Cracked
CFW (this work)	Non-cracked	Non-cracked	Non-cracked	Non-cracked

If the hash value remains in the online database, the plain text of the password is always exposed in seconds. The password digest created by the CFW approach produced a hash that was undetectable by the standard password-cracking tools using dictionary, brute-force, and rainbow table attacks. An equivalent refers to online cracking attacks carried out. The MD5 algorithm belongs to the hash algorithm group, and the only exception, much like that of SHA, is that SHA executes the message in 80 rounds, while MD5 handles the message in 64 rounds. SHA also provides more security than MD5, but SHA is rather MD5 in execution. But, CFW requires 100 rounds and offers protection in contrast to the current encryption algorithm. The outcome summary of the attacks conducted during the trial is shown in the below table.

Conclusion

There are several hashing techniques in the Blockchain-Based CFW Algorithm system. The method developed a trendy password digest that the prevalent password-cracking techniques do not recognize. This is also verified by the various forms of attacks carried out using the CFW technique. As the digest length created by the method differs from the plaintext of the user's password, it is extremely resource-consuming to execute a brute-force attack. The intruder might assume the hashing feature used by random wedges salt and concatenation system while using the CFW method, which creates the hacking procedure impossible. It is therefore reported that a safe approach for hashing passwords could be the CFW technique.

References

1. Thuong Nguyen Dat, Keisuke Iwai, Takashi Matsubara, and Takakazu Kurokawa, "*Implementation of high speed rainbow table generation using Keccak hashing algorithm on GPU*", *2019 6th NAFOSTED Conference on Information and Computer Science (NICS)*, pp. 166–171.
2. Philippe Oechslin, "*Making a faster cryptanalytic time-memory trade off*", *Advances in Cryptology – CRYPTO 2003, CRYPTO 2003*. Lecture Notes in Computer Science, 2729, pp. 617–630, 2003, https://lasec.epfl.ch/pub/lasec/doc/Oech03.pdf.
3. J. A. Cazier and D. B. Medlin. Password security: An empirical investigation into e-commerce passwords and their crack times. *Information Security Journal: A Global Perspective*, vol. 15, no. 6, pp. 45–55, 2006.
4. K. Theocharoulis, I. Papaefstathiou, and C. Manifavas. "*Implementing rainbow tables in high-end FPGAs for super-fast password cracking*," *International Conference on Field Programmable Logic and Applications*. September 2010. pp. 145–150.
5. Oechslin P. *Making a faster cryptanalytic time-memory trade-off*. In *Proceedings of the CRYPTO'03, volume 2729 of LNCS*, pp. 617–630. Springer, 2003.
6. N. Mentens, L. Batina, B. Preneel, and I. Verbauwhede. "*Time-memory trade-off attack on FPGA platforms: UNIX password cracking*," *Proceedings of the International Workshop on Reconfigurable Computing: Architectures and Applications*. Lecture Notes in Computer Science, vol. 3985, pp. 323–334, Springer, 2006.
7. F. Yu and Y. Huang, "*An overview of study of password cracking*," *Proceedings of the 2015 International Conference on Computer Science and Mechanical Automation (CSMA), 2015*, pp. 25–29, 2016.
8. K. S. M. Moe and T. Win, "*Improved hashing and honey-based stronger password prevention against brute force attack*," *2017 International Symposium of Electronics Smart Devices, ISESD, 2017*, vol. 2018, pp. 1–5, 2018.
9. J. Blocki, B. Harsha, and S. Zhou, "On the economics of offline password cracking," *Proceedings of the IEEE Symposium on Security and Privacy*, vol. 2018, pp. 853–871, 2018.
10. A. K. Kyaw, F. Sioquim, and J. Joseph, "*Dictionary attack on Wordpress: Security and forensic analysis*," *2015 2nd International Conference on Information Security and Cyber Forensics, InfoSec 2015*, pp. 158–164, 2016.
11. L. Bosnjak, J. Sres, and B. Brumen, "*Brute-force and dictionary attack on hashed real-world passwords*," *2018 41st International Convention on Information and Communication Technology, Electronics and Microelectronics, MIPRO 2018 – Proceedings*, pp. 1161–1166, 2018.
12. E. I. Tatli, "Cracking more password hashes with patterns," *IEEE Trans. Inf. Forensics Secur.*, vol. 10, no. 8, pp. 1656–1665, 2015.

13. P. Bright, "'Military Meltdown Monday' – 90K Military USERNAMES, HASHES RELEASED," *Wired Business*, 2011. [Online]. Available: https://www.wired.com/2011/07/booz/.

14. J. Jose, T. T. Tomy, V. Karunakaran, V. Anjali Krishna, A. Varkey, and C. A. Nisha, "*Securing passwords from dictionary attack with character-tree,*" *Proceedings of the 2016 IEEE International Conference on Wireless Communications Signal Processing and Networking, WiSPNET, 2016*, pp. 2301–2307, 2016.

15. A. K. Kyaw, F. Sioquim, and J. Joseph, "*Dictionary attack on Wordpress: Security and forensic analysis,*" *2015 2nd International Conference on Information Security and Cyber Forensics, InfoSec 2015*, pp. 158–164, 2016.

16. J. A. Dev, "*Usage of botnets for high-speed MD5 hash cracking,*" *2013 3rd International Conference on Innovative Computing Technology INTECH, 2013*, pp. 314–320, 2013.

17. M. D. A. Chawdhury and A. H. M. A. Habib, "*Security enhancement of MD5 hashed passwords by using the unused bits of TCP header,*" *Proceedings of the 11th International Conference on Computer and Information Technology ICCIT, 2008*, vol. 5, no. Iccit, pp. 714–717, 2008.

18. L. Zhang, C. Tan, and F. Yu, "An improved rainbow table attack for long passwords," *Procedia Comput. Sci.*, vol. 107, pp. 47–52, 2017.

19. "John the Ripper password cracker," *Openwall*, 2019. [Online]. Available: https://www.openwall.com/john/. [Accessed: July 9 2019].

20. S. Ji, S. Yang, A. Das, X. Hu, and R. Beyah, "Password Correlation : Quantification, Evaluation, and Application," 2017.

21. T. Kakarla, A. Mairaj, and A. Y. Javaid, "A real-world password cracking demonstration using open source tools for instructional use," *IEEE Int. Conf. Electro Inf. Technol.*, vol. 2018, pp. 387–391, 2018.

22. "RainbowCrack," RainbowCrack Project. [Online]. Available: http://project-rainbowcrack.com/index.htm. [Accessed: July 9 2019].

23. https://www.varonis.com/blog/john-the-ripper/ [Accessed: August 29 2020].

24. S. Shanmuga Priya, A. Valarmathi, and D. Yuvaraj. "The personal authentication service and security enhancement for optimal strong password," *Concurrency Computat Pract Exper.*, e5009, 2018. https://doi.org/10.1002/cpe.5009

25. M. Hellman. "A cryptanalytic time-memory trade-off," *IEEE Trans. Inf. Theory*, vol. 26, pp. 401–406, 1980.

26. Mati Aharoni, "Official Kali Linux Documentation," Offensive Security. [Online]. Available: https://www.kali.org/kali-linuxdocumentation/.

Chapter 7

Security Challenges and Attacks in MANET-IoT Systems

Serin V. Simpson and G. Nagarajan

Sathyabama Institute of Science and Technology, Chennai, India

Contents

DOI: 10.1201/9781003119784-7

Introduction

Internet of Things (IoT) is an emerging technology, which aims to interconnect physical objects in our surroundings. The main advantage of having an interconnected network is the ease of access. It reduces the human efforts to maintain and monitor physical objects. The IoT offers robust network management and data sharing among the nodes without the need for human interference. The IoT reduces the scalability and accessibility issues present in the networks. It reduces the scalability issues by implementing a distributed computing approach among the interconnected nodes. The backbone of the IoT is wireless sensor networks (WSN). The IoT uses the routing principles of WSN. The sensor nodes are connected to each other to make the communication among themselves for various needs. The end-sensor will sense the data and send them to the server with the help of neighboring nodes. The IoT network can be connected to cloud servers to reduce the computational overhead of lightweight IoT sensors. The individual components in IoT networks have only limited capabilities in terms of energy, computation capacity, bandwidth and memory. The IoT has a wide range of applications. The IoT can be applied in health care, home automation, farming, traffic management, etc. The IoT networks are mostly affected by Denial of Service (DoS) attacks. Since it has a heterogeneous structure with numerous individual components, the chances of having the DoS attacks are high [1–5].

The mobile ad hoc network (MANET) was introduced to have mobility in communication. The traditional communication technology was not capable of including moving components as their end nodes. The MANET changed the fixed infrastructure environment to an infrastructure-less environment. The MANET is capable of handling the dynamic topology changes happening due to mobility. Routing became a challenging process because of the continuously changing topology. Individual nodes in a MANET have the capacity to act both as a router and a normal node. The lack of fixed infrastructure demands a self-healing ability in a MANET. The link breakage and coverage issues are common in a network due to the mobility. The

MANET was designed to self-configure based on the changing topology and was not developed for a small community. The whole world is using the same technology and is communicating without considering the boundaries. Thus, each protocol and application in a MANET must be capable of addressing scalability issues expected to be present in the long run. The broadcasting and multicasting features in MANETs offer hassle-free communication in the network. The more the capabilities of the network, the more the chances of intruders. The intruders have a wide scope in the pure form of the network. They can get the data, destroy the network, masquerade as other legitimate nodes and even simply disturb the network. The integrity and confidentiality of data need to be assured in every communication. Thus, all the existing protocols in the network required some security-aware enhancements to incorporate additional capabilities. Authentication protocols, encryption schemes, secure routing approaches and malicious node identification have been introduced in the MANET due to the presence of attackers. The initial task of an attacker is to find the vulnerabilities of the network. The attacking pattern always depends on the need of an attacker and the vulnerabilities of the network. Thus, an attack is hard to identify.

The MANET-IoT system was introduced to have mobility in IoTs. The main part of an IoT is a sensor network. It became possible to have mobility in sensor nodes after the introduction of the MANET to IoT-based smart environments. That in turn reduced the deployment cost of additional components required to have mobility in an IoT-based network. The MANET-IoT system gave the ability to sensor nodes to move within the range of the MANET. The combination of the MANET and the IoT has welcomed new challenging issues in the network. The authentication and the things-to-things interaction will be carried out in IoT networks and the communication with the heterogeneous networks will be carried out with the help of traditional ad hoc networks. The IoT is less concerned about the quality of service (QoS) whereas the main focus of a MANET is on QoS. A MANET is less concerned about energy optimizations, whereas IoT networks require continuous restructuring for optimizing the energy-management schemes. Thus, maintaining the equilibrium among those two factors is the most challenging task of MANET-IoT integration. This chapter is mainly focused on the security aspects of MANET-IoT systems. Since the MANET-IoT system uses the existing routing protocols of MANETs, the existing routing issues have to be expected in a MANET-IoT system. This chapter discusses a few of the attacking patterns in all layers of the network and mainly focuses on routing attacks present in MANET-IoT systems [6–20].

Routing is the process of deciding the path to forward the packets toward the destination. Mostly, the destination will be at a long distance that cannot be reached by direct communication. Thus, the incorporation of neighboring nodes is required to deliver the packets to the destination. A good network will have more than one path to the destination. An intermediate node must be capable of identifying the best route to the destination. The network considers different criteria like distance, available bandwidth, delay and the presence of attackers, while deciding a path to the destination. Finally, the best path will be chosen based on these considerations.

Sometimes, the communication demands the shortest path on the basis of distance to the destination. In some cases, the network bandwidth may be considerably low. Thus, the intermediate node needs to find a congestion-free path to the destination. Some networks may be affected by external and internal reasons, which may contribute to delay in communication. In such cases, the nodes need to find the amount of delay expected in each path. The most important consideration is the presence of an attacker in the network. The routing must happen through a malicious free path. An attacker is capable of tampering with the data packets. Identifying such attacks can reduce the risks involved in communication. An intermediate node must be capable of finding a forward path to the destination without having the presence of the attacker [21–25].

The MANET-IoT system needs reassessment in regular intervals due to its dynamic topology. All intermediate nodes must be updated properly to consider the topology changes while choosing the next hop to the destination. It requires enough control packets to gather and distribute the information. The use of control packets increases the overall overhead of the network. Increased overhead may affect the performance of the network tremendously. Thus, proper maintenance is required to keep the network stable and secure. The computation power of all the nodes must be high to compute the best path to the destination. In some protocols, the computation is required in all individual nodes in a path. Due to some reasons, there is a chance to form a loop while routing. An endless loop will drastically affect the network. Thus, the loop formation must be prevented by some mechanisms. Packets in the network are pre-added with a time stamp for eliminating the risk of never-ending loops. The routing process becomes complex due to all these considerations. A protocol designed for the MANET-IoT system must be capable of addressing all the issues present in a network and able to provide a stable and secure communication. This chapter is organized in the following manner: the next section discusses the classification of routing protocols in the MANET-IoT system. The latter sections of this chapter discuss the existing routing approaches, classification of attacks in a MANET-IoT system, existing routing attacks, available defense mechanisms in the network, the security issues present in the MANET-IoT system, open-research challenges in routing attack defense mechanisms, and the scope of future works in MANETs.

Classification of Routing Protocols in MANET-IoT Systems

The MANET is always exposed to dynamic changes due to link breakage, node failure and mobility. All these dynamic changes come to the network without any notification. Thus, the network must be capable of adapting to the sudden changes. The routing protocols can be classified into static and dynamic. The static approach can also be called a proactive or table-driven approach. The routing process in the proactive approach happens based on the saved data. Sudden network changes cannot be considered in static routing. Thus, the routing decisions will be the same for good and worst network conditions. The dynamic approach can also be called a reactive or on-demand approach. As the name suggests, it could react to sudden changes in the network. Dynamic decision-making is possible in reactive routing with respect to network changes. Also, it doesn't need to strictly follow the initial decision. The dynamic decision changes will happen with respect to sudden network changes.

Table-Driven Approach

In a table-driven approach, all the routing data will be kept in a table. Each node has a table of data about its neighbors. The routing decision will be taken purely based on the table. The table has to be updated in regular intervals. It is useful in small networks. It can provide comparatively high security than all other approaches. This approach is necessary when a source needs to provide the path to the destination along with the packets. The route can be computed based on the available table data. Since it depends only on the table data, it does not require complex routing algorithms. It will not respond to sudden failures of network or network entities. Thus, it does not require additional resource support for maintaining the ongoing transmission. In the case of failure, the transmission will be interrupted and the routing process will re-initiate from the beginning [26–30].

On-Demand Approach

The on-demand approach was introduced to make routing more efficient in large networks. The table-based approach is not adaptable to a large network. It requires a dynamic approach to handle the dynamic changes in the network. In the table-driven approach, the role of the routing protocol lies mainly in the source node. Since each node is supposed to play the role of a router, the routing protocol has to be configured at each node in the case of dynamic routing. It considers all the dynamic changes of the network while routing the packets. Thus, it requires complex routing algorithms to compute the best path. Each node automatically calculates the next best hop based on the present constraints of the network. In order to assess the present network conditions, the routing approach requires additional resources. A non-demand routing approach can assure only less security due to its operational constraints. In an on-demand approach, a link breakage during an ongoing transmission will not affect the overall transmission. The route will be recomputed from the immediate previous node of the affected node and the packets will be forwarded toward the destination through the next available path [31–35].

Existing Routing Approaches in MANET-IoT Systems

The previous section elaborated a general classification of MANET protocols based on dynamic and static routing. This section discusses a classification of the routing approach based on the network coordination process. The network can be controlled by both centralized and distributed coordination. In the centralized approach, the routing process will be completely controlled by a centralized authority. In the case of the distributed approach, all nodes in the network will join together to control the routing process. Each node in the network will do its own part and leave the rest to other responsible nodes. Some additional algorithms are required to coordinate the activities of individual nodes in the distributed environment.

Centralized Routing

The centralized authority has complete control over the network. The centralized authority will monitor and control the routing process. The individual nodes will send all the state information to the central node and the central node distributes the state information if required. All routes in the network will be decided by the centralized authority. Thus, the network can produce consistent results. Also, it is easy to maintain the same time at every node due to the presence of a global clock at the server node. Thus, synchronization is an easy process in centralized routing. But, it has several limitations. The centralized authority could itself be a single-point failure of the network. All data will be lost if the system fails without proper backup. This vulnerability has become the easiest entry point for the attacker. Attackers are able to get all the data from a single point and they can even destroy the system permanently. The server maintenance is difficult due to the large data residing at the server. The increase in the number of network entities will increase the burden of the server. Thus, a centralized system cannot scale well. It is cost-efficient only for small systems with limited requirements. It is not possible to handle a large network by a centralized routing approach even if we increase the software and hardware capabilities of the server node. A bottleneck effect will be experienced when the applications require large-scale server support within a limited time [36, 37].

Distributed Routing

The main advantage of centralized routing is the capacity of the centralized authority to monitor all the individual components in the network. But, it is not possible for a centralized system to handle the increased number of nodes. The distributed routing approach can handle any number of systems because the individual nodes in the network coordinate together to accomplish the network needs. It uses a message-exchange mechanism and performs individual computations required to coordinate the overall network. The system is capable of adapting to topological changes.

All state information will be exchanged with neighboring nodes. That plays an essential role while finalizing the path for routing the packets. There is no chance for a single-point failure in a distributed system. The failure of an individual node can be resolved by rerouting the path through the neighboring nodes. The distributed environment may encounter issues related to loop formation. Such vulnerabilities may produce inconsistent results in the network. Also, the lack of a global clock is a major drawback of the distributed system. Each node in the distributed environment keeps individual clocks. Thus, some special algorithms are required to synchronize the communication without any error. One major limitation of distributed routing is the absence of a superior node. Thus, it is hard to handle a big task, which needs to be accomplished with the help of several individual nodes. Even though the node failure and link breakage can be handled effectively, it is hard to get the details of the failed node. Also, it is difficult to identify the responded node for a route request. But the routing can be done without any error using the available information [38–40].

Classification of Attacks in MANET-IoT Systems

The routing process is always complex due to the increased number of nodes and dynamic changes. But, the heavy workload at the server is not actually because of routing. It is due to the presence of malicious attacks. An attacker tries to intrude on the network to fulfill the needs by using the vulnerabilities present in the network. Though the attacks cannot be classified specifically, they can be classified based on the attacking pattern and the layers of the network affected by the attack. The same kind of attacking pattern can be executed in different layers. The aim and effect of the attack will vary in different layers. This section gives an overview of the attacks present in the MANET-IoT system.

Basic Classification

The attacks can be classified into active attacks and passive attacks, based on the attacking pattern. The passive attacks will not affect the communication. During passive attacks, the communication will happen normally without knowing the presence of an attacker. The attacker tries to get the data and tries to make use of it. The attacker will not alter the data or any other network resources. The active attacks are harmful to the network. It will affect either the communication or the network resources. The attacker may alter the data and try to make use of it. Also, the attacks may affect the routing process drastically. A routing protocol must be capable of identifying and eliminating this kind of attack. The basic classification of security attacks is shown in Figure 7.1.

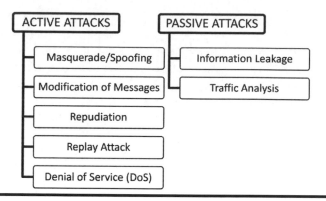

Figure 7.1 Basic classification of security attacks in MANET-IoT systems.

Active Attacks

Active attacks can be further divided into five categories, based on the effect of the attack. They are masquerade/spoofing attack, modification attack, repudiation attack, replay attack and DoS attack.

- **Masquerade/Spoofing attack:** It is an attacking strategy where the attacker uses the identity of a legitimate node. Thus, a request from the attacker will be counted as an authorized request and the receiver node will serve the malicious node unknowingly. The attacker uses the IP address of a legitimate node for getting network access. After getting the access, the attacker can get the data, study the network activities and even destroy the network by using any other type of attack [41].
- **Modification attack:** It is the process of modifying the data packets for confusing the receiver about unauthorized access. This kind of attack can contribute delay to the network. It can be done either by simply delaying the message or by altering some of the data packets. This can also be done by reordering the packets that are expected to receive in the correct order [42].
- **Repudiation attack:** The repudiation attack is an internal attack. Both the source node and the receiver node can execute the repudiation attack by simply denying a packet. The repudiation attack reduces the reputation of both source and receiver nodes if the network fails to identify the source of the attack [43].
- **Replay attack:** Initially, the attacker will try to eavesdrop on the data transmitting through a network. After getting some information or packets, the attacker will do some kind of malpractice with the data for misdirecting the receiver. The malpractice includes delaying and resending the packets. The attacker needs to get access to the receiver node where the attacker wishes to intrude [44].
- **DoS attack:** It is the widely used attacking strategy of malicious nodes. The main aim of the attacker is to make the resource unavailable. Most of the routing attacks come under DoS attacks. The DoS attack may disturb the

communication temporarily or permanently. The attacker may not get any data from the DoS attack, but it can interrupt the communication and find the advantage by interrupting the network [45].

Passive Attacks

Passive attacks can be further divided into information leakage attacks and traffic analysis attacks.

- **Information leakage:** These kinds of attacks never disturb the communication. It will not make any damage to the network resources. The attacker will simply monitor the data transmission and try to get the information. The attacker will neither alter the message nor affect the routing process [46].
- **Traffic analysis:** This attack can be done by an external attacker by simply monitoring the packet transmission. The attacker does not aim to access the data. By this attack, the attacker can understand the type of data and the type of communication. It is easy to distinguish the type of communications such as email, chat or webpage requests by analyzing the traffic. This kind of attack is also not contributing any damage to the network resources [47].

Layer-Based Classification

The attacks can be classified based on the layers of a network where the attacker tries to deploy the attack. The Open Systems Interconnection (OSI) model presents a seven-layer classification of networks. Among those layers, we are considering five basic layers for the layer-based classification of attacks. Based on the functionalities of each layer, the attacker introduces different attacks to each layer. The layer-based classification is illustrated in Figure 7.2.

Application Layer

This layer is responsible for handling user interactions. In this layer, the data are represented in a user-friendly manner. The data will be visible to the applications in this layer without encryptions. But only the intended users will have access to the data. Repudiation attacks and data-corruption attacks are the most commonly seen attacks in this layer.

- **Repudiation:** The source node or the receiver node can deny that they have already shared a message. This attack comes under active attacks. This attack can badly affect the communication. X. Lv et al. [48] proposed a secure group communication to defend against repudiation attacks. Here, the repudiation attack is prevented by using public–private key encryption technique. The proposed method ensures the confidentiality of data by the same techniques.

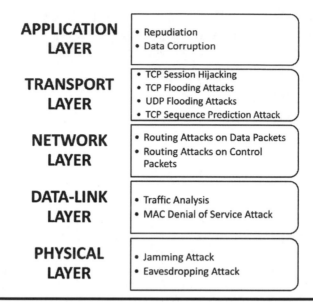

Figure 7.2   Layer-based classification of security attacks in MANET-IoT system.

The public keys are publicly known to all nodes. If a node wishes to transmit a message, then the node has to make a request to get the public key of the destination. The message will be encrypted by the received public key. The encrypted message can be decrypted only by the destination. The public key request followed by an encrypted data exchange ensures a non-repudiation environment. The encryption technique is the right solution to achieve non-repudiation. Additionally, the proposed system offers a reduced cipher text size than other existing systems. The proposed encryption method offers reduced rounds, fewer message requirements and high security.

■ **Data corruption:** This attack involves modification of messages by an external attacker. The attacker can make use of viruses or worms for executing the attack. Both are malicious codes that can be programmed with respect to the need. L. Han et al. [49] introduced a method to detect malicious codes. The malicious codes are identified by behavior study. The malicious codes may be self-regenerative or never-ending loops. Such codes behave differently than the usual program codes. That can be identified by closely assessing the codes before execution. The malicious behavior of the code can be reading file behavior, ending file behavior or cumulative execution behavior. The detection scheme must be capable of identifying all of the above. The proposed method outperforms the existing detection schemes. The comparative study is performed by introducing the known set of malicious codes to the newly developed system and also to other existing systems. The proposed system is able to identify 80% of test cases. But the existing systems fail in many cases.

Transport Layer

The transport layer is responsible for flow control and error control. It uses transport-layer protocols for flow control. The attacks in this layer are mainly on the transport-layer protocols. The most common transport-layer protocols are Transmission Control Protocol (TCP) and User Datagram Protocol (UDP). The TCP needs an end-to-end route setup before the transmission and the UDP does not bother about the route setup phase.

- **TCP session hijacking:** The attacker initially uses a spoofing attack to get access to an ongoing communication. Then, the attacker node captures all the communications that have happened so far. After that, the attacker node will resume the communication with the destination node. In other words, the attacker node hijacks an ongoing communication using a spoofing attack. Minghan Chen et al. [50] combined existing methods to produce an integrated security strategy. The TCP session hijacking is possible only when there is a chance to do a spoofing attack. An efficient encryption algorithm can prevent a spoofing attack. Rather than identifying a spoofing attack, the encryption scheme avoids the chances of performing the spoofing attack. The proposed integrated approach joins the functionalities of existing cryptographic and key exchange algorithms. It uses the Rivest–Shamir–Adleman (RSA) approach for both key generation and signature generation. It uses a Diffie–Hellman (DH) key exchange algorithm and SHA1 for verification purposes. This method is not an exact solution for TCP session hijacking, but it can successfully eliminate the identity attack. The TCP session hijacking attack cannot be initiated without a spoofed ID of a legitimate node.
- **TCP flooding attacks:** In a TCP flooding attack, the attacker node continuously sends ping messages to the targeted node. The targeted node will start responding to the ping messages. The victim node will stop working when it receives a large number of packets that are unable to handle. Rana Deepak et al. [51] made a study about the causes of having TCP flooding attacks in the network. Based on the observations, the TCP flooding attack has been introduced to the network for the behavior study. A C language code is used to flood the server with packets. The C code spoofs the identity of a legitimate node to make a communication with the server. A random IP generation function is incorporated with the code to regularly change the address of the attacker. C script then sends a large number of packets to the server. It is possible due to the vulnerabilities present in the TCP handshaking procedure. The reply argument packets are used to mitigate the flooding attack. One other defense method is used to accommodate the flooded packets at the server. It is achieved by maximizing the backlog queue of the server node.
- **UDP flooding attacks:** The UDP flooding attack is a combination of a spoofing and a flooding attack. The attacker node uses the identity of one

legitimate node and floods UDP packets to the targeted port of the victim node. Singh Aarti et al. [52] designed a software-agent-based approach to defend against UDP flooding attacks in a distributed environment. The flooding attack can cause drastic damage in the network due to the connectionless routing behavior of the UDP protocol. Rather than establishing an end-to-end connection between the source and the destination node, the UDP protocol broadcasts all the packets to the network. Thus, a flooding attack is hard to identify in the UDP protocol-based system. A flooding attack may be counted as normal network congestion due to legitimate communication packets. As a solution to this problem, a software agent is deployed in every node to observe the immediate neighboring nodes. The software agent will identify the flooding attack and will do the necessary to eliminate the malicious node from the network.

■ **TCP sequence prediction attack:** The TCP sequence prediction attack uses a combination of flooding and spoofing. Here, the attacker will select an ongoing communication and targets the end node of the communication. Then, the attacker floods packets to other nodes till that node becomes unable to participate in the communication. After that, the attacker resumes the communication with the help of spoofed ID of blocked node and correct sequence number. F. Zeng et al. [53] implemented a system to eliminate the TCP sequence prediction attack. It is an example of an active replay attack. The attacker aims to predict the initial sequence number of a packet. The sequence number indicates the freshness of a packet. All nodes in the network will verify the sequence number of the received packet. If the sequence number of the packet is less than the expected value, then the packet will be discarded. That packet might be an older version or a packet from an attacker. An intruder can participate in the communications of TCP-based systems, only if the attacker has enough knowledge about the present sequence number. For getting the sequence number, the attacker will join an ongoing communication by using a spoofed ID. After that, the attacker will be able to inject malicious packets into the network with an incremented sequence number. The proposed system uses 'chaotic adding-weight dynamic local predict model' to defend against both TCP sequence prediction and TCP reset attack.

Network Layer (Routing Attacks)

The path determination and actual routing process happen in a network layer. Thus, the attacks present in this layer can also be called routing attacks. The network has two types of packets. One is actual data packets and the other is control packets. The attacks in this layer can be classified based on the attacks on data packets and control packets. The detailed classification is discussed in the next section of this chapter.

- **Routing attacks on data packets:** Some of the routing attacks target directly at the data packets. Such attacks reduce the integrity of data delivery. The common attacks on data packets are packet-drop and delay attacks. Both attacks come under DoS attacks [54].
- **Routing attacks on control packets:** Control packets help the network for adapting to new conditions, based on new protocols. As the constraints increase, the overhead will also increase. Thus, the control packets have a major role in the routing process. Most of the routing attacks are targeting the control packets [55]. The most common routing attacks on control packets are rushing attacks, Sybil attacks, worm-hole attacks and flooding attacks. All these attacks are detailed in an upcoming section of the chapter.

Data Link Layer

The data link layer handles transmission by using a physical address. Thus, the attacker can perform a traffic-analyzing attack in this layer. The active DoS attacks are also performed in the data link layer.

- **Traffic analysis:** Attackers aren't able to get the data through this attack. The data might be encrypted or in a scrambled form. Even if the attacker can get some information regarding the type of data, it is easy to identify a mail communication or web page request by analyzing the network traffic. F. Kausar et al. [56] developed an attacking model to infer the data by analyzing the traffic. The authors explain timing attack as an example of the traffic analysis attack. The first step of a traffic analysis attack is creating a web page crawler. The crawler can perform the analysis automatically like a bot. After the successful creation of a crawler, the attacker can sniff the network to get the traffic flow. The sniffing process is implemented to execute the timing attack. After getting the traffic flow, the packets will be parsed to extract the features. Based on the extracted features, the attacker can classify the user activities into known categories like web page requests, e-mail communication, etc. The classification can be done using the k-nearest neighboring algorithm. The performance of the attack model is evaluated based on true positive and accuracy levels.
- **Medium Access Control (MAC) DoS attacks:** This attack can be performed on a single connected node. The attacker will make the link busy for a long time. Thus, the node does not have access to the network. It is a kind of DoS attack. V. Gupta et al. [57] introduced a mechanism to detect and eliminate MAC DoS attacks in the network. The MAC protocol can be tampered with by malicious nodes. Thus, the MAC protocol must be strong enough to withstand the attacks. The authors suggest some solutions, based on the following experimental observations. The role of neighboring nodes in eliminating a malicious node is really high. A malicious node is not that much capable of

doing a DoS attack on a node which is far away from the attacker node. The end-to-end authentication scheme fails when two nodes are agreed to cooperate for performing an attack. The main aim of a DoS attack on a MAC layer is to make the resource unavailable for a while. The authors suggest that a new system needs to be designed based on the above observations.

Physical Layer

The actual data transmission happens in this layer. The digital data will be converted to electronic signals in this layer. Thus, the attackers mainly focus on the vulnerabilities of transmitted signals and transmission technologies.

- **Jamming attacks:** An attacker with a powerful transmitter can overwhelm the communication signals in the network. A jamming attack can disturb the network tremendously. Pulse and random noise are commonly used signals for jamming attacks. Kanika Grover et al. [58] collected and analyzed the details of existing jamming and anti-jamming techniques. The authors added a complete overview of jamming attacks. The jamming attacks can be classified into elementary and advanced levels. The elementary level can be further divided into proactive and reactive. Similarly, the advanced-level jamming attacks can be divided into function-specific and smart-hybrid approaches. The strength of a jamming attack depends on the placement of jammers. The exact placement of jammers based on the attacking strategy causes more damage than a random deployment. The anti-jamming approach does not need high-power equipment. The detailed study about the placement of jammers gives an optimal solution to this problem. Anti-jamming can be done effectively by using knowledge about jammer placement.
- **Eavesdrop attack:** Attackers using eavesdrop attacks in the physical layer focuses on the transmitted signals. They will try to fetch the data from the signals. This attack will not alter the signals or data (passive attack). Tiep M. Hoang et al. [59] introduced a method to defend against eavesdrop attacks occurring at the physical layer by using a support vector machine (SVM) classifier. The method is experimented with in an environment where one access point and one eavesdropper are present. The initial step for defending the eavesdropper is the creation of a dataset based on some features. The dataset will be given as an input to the SVM classifier. The feature extraction happens at different levels. The first observation is at the access point. The received signal at the access point will be evaluated. Based on the evaluation, three different features, MEAN, SUM and RATIO will be defined. During the communication, artificial training data will be generated. Based on the extracted features and the created artificial training data, the SVM classifier could identify the eavesdropper. The system produces a 90% accuracy level.

Routing Attacks and Existing Defense Mechanisms

This chapter mainly focuses on routing attacks present in the network layer. Such attacks can be classified into two: routing attacks on data packets and routing attacks on control packets. Rather than getting information from the communication, the attacker tries to destroy the network by routing attacks. All routing attacks come under the DoS attack category. External attackers always aim at the control packets rather than the data packets. The data in a network must be in an encrypted format. It is hard to make use of data flowing through the network. That is the reason why the attacks on control packets became popular among the routing attacks. The attacker can make at least a delay in the network by altering/discarding the control packets. Attackers can make such delays fruitful for their needs. The classification of routing attacks is shown in Figure 7.3.

Routing Attacks on Data Packets

The routing attacks on data packets can be further divided into packet-drop attacks and delay attacks. The packet-drop attack is the simplest attack that a node can perform without any background knowledge. A delay attack can be implemented either by reordering the packets or by holding a packet for a while.

■ **Black-hole attack:** Black-hole attack is the basic form of packet-drop attack. All packets coming to an attacker node will be discarded. A node will try all the possible ways to be a part of all nearby communications. Aly M. El-Semary et al. [60] proposed a mechanism to prevent black-hole attacks based on a chaotic map. The proposed work is an enhancement of the Secure Ad-hoc

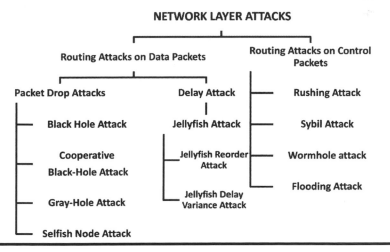

Figure 7.3   Classification of routing attacks.

On-demand Distance Vector (SAODV) protocol [61]. Black-hole-protected ad hoc on-demand distance vector routing (BPAODV) addresses the issues of SAODV while identifying black-hole nodes in the network. Also, BPAODV is capable of resisting cooperative black-hole attacks by the chaotic map. BPAODV considers the best three paths for routing the packets and finds the best among the three by using the features of the chaotic map. In addition to normal control packets used for the route setup phase, BPAODV adds one more packet called CONFIRM to inform the destination node about the selected path. By using this approach, BPAODV can also find the attackers those who appear normally during normal conditions and drop packets during communication. Divya Sai et al. [62] introduced a technique for black-hole attack conformation, by using honeypot. The authors mainly contribute toward the detection of false black-hole identification. The legitimate nodes will be removed due to false detection. The proposed method removes the drawbacks of the existing systems by eliminating the risk of false detection. The method maintains an attack history table to generate observations about the detected node. The final decision will be based on the observations by using the honeypot method. It uses a black-hole attack tree for analyzing all the possible ways of black-hole attack in the network. Such an observation will compare with the attack history of a detected node. By honeypot analysis, it is possible to distinguish the legitimate and false detection of a black-hole attack. Manoranjini et al. [63] designed a trust detection algorithm to improve the QoS and avoid the black-hole attacks in MANET. The algorithm computes the trust value based on the communications and the mobility of the nodes. The algorithm uses direct trust, indirect trust and mutual trust for computing the final trust value. Direct trust can be obtained from individual nodes. The indirect trust is an assessment value obtained from the neighbors of the node. The neighboring nodes will consider the forwarded packet count and the drop count to compute the indirect trust. Mutual trust is obtained by considering the overall performance of the node during the communication. Threshold-based trust value assessment reduces the risk of having black-hole nodes and increases the privacy of the network.

■ **Cooperative black-hole attack:** It is a collective packet-drop attack where more than one node participate together to disrupt the network. All packets will be dropped in this attack. The collective effort is mainly used for being a part of legitimate communication. Nai-Wei Lo et al. [64] implemented a security-aware routing protocol (CBDAODV) to defend against a cooperative black-hole attack in a MANET. The proposed method prevents the cooperative black-hole attack by making changes in the traditional route-discovery process. The proposed protocol is added as a modification to the existing AODV protocol. The route setup phase of AODV considers only one path to the destination. The destination node will respond only to the first-received Route Request (RREQ) packet. Here in CBDAODV, the source node will select two paths to the destination. The paths will be checked for confirming the absence of cooperative nodes. Here, the cooperative nodes are identified by the nature of packet drop. No nodes among the attackers will forward a blacklist about one of the attackers. By analyzing this behavior, the network can identify the presence of a cooperative attack. Dorri, A. [65], used an Extended Data Routing Information (EDRI) approach for identifying and eliminating the cooperative black-hole nodes in a MANET. It proposes an EDRI table for the successful detection of cooperative nodes in a selected path. Each node in the network has to maintain the EDRI table and record the details of incoming and forwarding packets. The EDRI table has a column to add the detected black-hole attacker nodes. Such nodes will be excluded from further communications. The presence of a black-hole node is identified by circulating a data-control packet. The data-control packet contains the node's ID, the next hop details and a random number. The routing process has three phases, route finalization, verification of path and malicious node identification. The proposed technique uses only data-control packets for identifying the cooperative black-hole node. Thus, the proposed work has less overhead than the existing methods. J Chang et al. [66] found out that a Cooperative Bait Detection Approach (CBDA can reduce the cooperative attacks in MANET. The proposed system uses a reverse-tracing technique to find out the source of packet drop. The packet drop in a path reduces the packet delivery ratio at the destination node. The drastic reduction in the delivery ratio will be notified to the network controller. The method also uses the advantages of the table-driven approach for computing the route during the reverse-tracing phase. At first, the destination node computes the address of each node in the path. It is possible to detect the attacker by verifying each node in the route. The cooperative attack can be executed only among one-hop neighbors. Thus, the neighbors of the detected node will also be verified for eliminating the risk of having cooperative attacker nodes in the network.

- **Gray-hole attack:** It is a variant of a black-hole attack. In this attack, the packet will be dropped selectively. Not all packets will be dropped during this attack. Thus, it is hard to distinguish it from a normal network packet drop due to resource constraints. Gurung, S. et al. [67] achieved performance improvement in MANETs by introducing Mitigating Gray-Hole Attack Mechanism (MGAM) for handling gray-hole attacks. The gray-hole detection is done by installing a new set of nodes called gray-hole intrusion detection system nodes to the network. The system deploys enough number of nodes to the network. Those nodes have the capability to identify and measure the number of packet drop. The detection system follows a threshold-based identification process. If the neighbor of a gray-hole intrusion detection system node drops packets more than a threshold value, then the node will be eliminated from the communication. The gray-hole is hard to detect due to the normal behavior of the node during most of the communication. Thus, this kind of special node has to be deployed in the network for the successful detection of gray-hole nodes. N. Schweitzer et al. [68] proposed Denial Contradictions with Fictitious Node Mechanism (DCFM) for minimizing the gray-hole attack in ad hoc networks. It is a contradiction-based approach. The centralized authority verifies the messages received about a node based on the topological information. If any contradiction occurs between the compared data, then the node will be checked for finding the presence of malicious nature. It is identified based on the dropped packets and the offered packets. In a gray-hole attack, the attacker node drops the packets randomly. Thus, a normal mechanism is not able to distinguish the presence of a gray-hole. The proposed contradictory-based approach could eliminate the gray-hole, better than the existing approaches. The packet-drop count is evaluated during simulations by introducing different attackers to the network. The packet-drop count is less while comparing with the normal detection algorithms. P. Rani et al. [69] combined the concepts of artificial neural network (ANN) and the swarm-based Artificial Bee Colony (ABC) optimization technique for identifying gray-hole and black-hole attacks. The basic concept of this work is to find the best nodes for routing. Since the proposed method eliminates both black-hole and gray-hole attacks, it can be considered as a dual attack elimination approach. It uses swarm-based ABC for optimization. Using this optimization approach, the nodes are categorized into several sections. During this categorization process, the gray-hole and the black-hole nodes will come into the same category. Based on the ANN concepts and packet-drop count, the gray-holes and black-holes can be differentiated. As per the simulation, it is clear that the mechanism increases the throughput and delivery ratio by successfully eliminating the attacker nodes from the network.

■ **Selfish node attack:** Selfish node attack is an internal attack. The attacker node tries to save its own resources for the attacker's personal use. All nodes in the network face this constraint. Whenever a node wishes to transmit the packets, the node may fail to use its own recourses due to the already-committed transmissions of other nodes. A selfish node commits all the requests but drops packets depending on personal needs. Guaya-Delgado et al. [70] utilized the node's reputation value to identify the selfish nodes. The selfish behavior of a node is examined based on the reputation value. All nodes in the network will compute the reputation value of every other node in the network using proposed equations. The individual reputation value is used to compute the reputation of a path. The reputation of a path will be calculated before finalizing a path to send the data. If a path includes a node with a lower reputation, then that route will be excluded. Every node in the network will perform better to achieve a good reputation among the neighboring nodes. The nodes with lower reputation value cannot be a part of any communication. This approach will not eliminate the selfish node from the network. But the selfish node will forcefully reduce its selfish behavior to become a part of network communications. Annadurai, P. et al. [71] also applied a Highly Reputed Authenticated Routing mechanism for mobile Ad-hoc Networks (HRARAN) to find the selfish nodes. The proposed work helps to detect the selfish nodes in authenticated routing. It also proposes the method to find the reputation of individual nodes and paths. It computes the individual reputations based on the difference between received and forwarded packets. The ratio gives an average count of packet drop in the network. The reputation of the path is determined by using the individual reputation values and the distance from the source to each intermediate node. The proposed work has been implemented as an extension to the existing SAODV [61] protocol. It uses the same routing principles of traditional AODV with the added extensions. The concept of eliminating the selfish node is the same as the previously mentioned work, but the reputation calculation function is different. Josh Kumar et al. [72] introduced a Token-Based Umpiring Technique (TBUT) to eliminate the selfish node from the network. Each node in the network will be issued a token by the centralized authority. The token will have a node ID and an initial reputation value. The reputation value of the node will be updated further, based on the shares from the neighboring nodes. The path determination process also uses the same token to get the reputation value. A reputation-based categorization is also proposed in this work. Based on the reputation value, the nodes are classified into green and red zones. A node with a green flag is allowed to participate in the communication. But the node with a red flag will be excluded. This mechanism is also based on reputation value. Thus, we can conclude that the existing prevention mechanisms for the selfish node attacks are all based on reputation values.

■ **Jellyfish attack:** Rather than dropping the packets, in a jellyfish attack, the attacker node delays the packets using different methods. It has two variants: the jellyfish reorder attack and the jellyfish delay variance attack. In the reorder attack, the packets will be reordered and the receiver fails to rebuild them in the initial order. In a delay variance attack, a random delay will be added to the packets going through the attacker node. It is hard to identify the jellyfish attack since the attacker node obeys all the rules present in the network. For example, S. Doss et al. [73] point out that normal routing attack detection schemes cannot identify the jellyfish attack. They have proposed Accurate Prevention and Detection of Jelly Fish Attack Detection (APD-JFAD) mechanism for the accurate prediction of jellyfish attacks. The proposed work applies SVM concepts to an authenticated routing framework. The packet forwarding is observed and analyzed by the SVM classifier. The proposed method only allows the legitimate nodes to participate in the communication. The nodes are classified by the hierarchical trust evaluation method. The trust value is computed based on forwarded packets, ping messages, residual energy, and the overall delay. As per the simulation results, the throughput and the delivery ratio of the newly proposed algorithm are larger than the existing algorithms. Due to the successful elimination of jellyfish attackers, the over-all delay has decreased. Satheeshkumar, S. et al. [74] developed an enhanced version (ACO-CBRP) of the CBDS [66] for defending against jellyfish attacks. The older version of this work addresses only the black-hole and cooperative black-hole attacks in a MANET. Even though the jellyfish attack comes under the attacks on data packets, it is different from others. All other data-related attacks are performing packet-drop attacks, whereas the jellyfish attack is con-tributing delay to the network. The jellyfish attacker behaves like a normal node in the network. Thus, the attack is hard to identify. The proposed work uses a cluster-based approach to defend against jellyfish attacks. In the pro-posed method, the cluster head monitors the activities of the cluster members. It also monitors additional delays happening at a particular node at a ran-dom time. Based on the observed data, the CH node can identify the jellyfish attack. Samad F. et al. [75] proposed Jellyfish Attacks Mitigator (JAM) for the successful identification and the elimination of jellyfish attacks. It mainly addresses the jellyfish attack present along with the TCP protocol. The ulti-mate aim of an attacker is to contribute delay to the network. Normally, the jellyfish attack achieves the goal by reordering the packets. But in TCP-based systems, it is easy to delay by strictly obeying the protocol rules. A packet drop in such a network will initiate the slow start mechanism in transmission. The attacker needs to do only a legitimate packet drop. It can be done by claim-ing a resource constraint while dropping the packet. The attacker can mislead the network and can initiate a slow start approach. This will add delay and considerable performance degradation to the network. The proposed method focuses on identifying the packet drop from a maliciously compromised node.

Routing Attacks on Control Packets

The routing attacks on control packets can be implemented in several ways. Some of the common attacks are rushing attacks, attacks on the voting-based system, worm-hole attacks and flooding attacks. The voting/accusation-based system can be attacked either by a cooperative blackmailing attack or by a Sybil attack. In the cooperative blackmailing attack, the malicious nodes will collectively accuse a legiti-mate node to keep it away from the network. The Sybil attack is a variant of the cooperative blackmailing attack.

■ **Rushing attack:** The ultimate goal of routing is finding the best path to the destination. That will be chosen based on the first arriving route request. The initially received route request will be replied and all other redundant requests will be discarded. Here, the attacker node aims to deliver the route request packets to the destination node quickly, even if the shortest path does not exist between the attacker and the destination. This kind of attack is known as a rushing attack. If the node wins to do the same, then all the remaining communications will go through the attacker node. Yi Ping et al. [76] designed a flooding attack prevention (FAP) technique to prevent both rushing and flooding attacks. The attack is identified by analyzing the packet receive rate. A centralized authority will monitor all the network transmissions. The sudden increase in network communication will be observed by calculating the receive rate of each node. If the receive rate is higher than the threshold value, then the attacker node will be closely monitored for a small period to confirm the malicious behavior. The rushing attack can only be done along with any other DoS attacks like flooding attacks. The successful identification and the elimination of flooding attacks, in turn, reduce the chances of having a rushing attack in the network. A rushing attack is more harmful than a flooding attack because the attacker is able to get the benefits of the rushing attack for a long time. S. Ghoreishi et al. [77] introduced an integrated secure routing protocol for defending against rushing attacks. In proactive routing, the effect of rushing attacks will remain in the network for a long time. The proposed method combines the legitimate neighbor detection and trusted route formation for the successful elimination of rushing attacks. The authors classify the rushing attack based on the position where it appears. During the simulations, the proposed work is analyzed by deploying the attacker in all possible positions. That includes, near the source node, near the destination node and anywhere in the network. The proposed works have performance variations with respect to the position of the attacker. The attacker node near the source is easy to identify. The attacker node placed at the random space is taking more time for detection. Yih-Chun Hu et al. [78] implemented Rushing Attack Prevention (RAP) mechanism for the successful avoidance of rushing attacks. Nodes in a network will fail to find paths beyond their two-hop neighbors if the rushing attack is present in the network. Even a comparatively weaker node is also capable of performing a rushing attack effectively, making it more challenging. The authors discuss the reasons for the failure of existing security mechanisms toward rushing attacks and propose a new prevention mechanism for the MANET. The main advantage of the proposed work is no-cost routing. The proposed mechanism contributes no additional cost to the network till the source fails to discover a new route when the network finds the presence of a rushing attack. The proposed method is mainly designed for reactive routing protocols. Thus, it works well with AODV and SAODV.

■ **Sybil attack:** It comes under the attacks performed on voting-based systems. A malicious node can contribute falsified data to the voting system. Such types of attacks are known as cooperative blackmailing attacks. The Sybil attack is different in execution. A node tries to claim the identities of more than one node. A combination of Sybil and a cooperative black mailing attack can destroy a voting-based system. L. Xiao et al. [79] found out that the Sybil attack can easily be prevented in a physical layer. They have proposed a Sybil attack prevention mechanism that works well in the physical layer by analyzing the signals. The first step of the proposed scheme is identifying Sybil and legal nodes in the network. This method can be integrated with any other existing attack solutions. Generally, this scheme can be used along with any of the spoofing detection schemes. The proposed work compares the nodes in the network and claimed identities. If the signal rate from the claimed identity and the actual node differs, it can be considered as a Sybil attack. The successful prevention of Sybil attack increases the stability of the network. They have done simulations and also an experimental verification of the proposed work. The method performs well in small-scale and large-scale networks. Faisal, M et al. [80] also applied the detection mechanism for Sybil attack on a physical layer. A signal-based analysis is the best way to identify the Sybil attack. The main reason for the Sybil attack is the lack of centralized authority. It is difficult to detect an identity-based attack in a distributed environment. The Sybil attack is prevented by doing a signal-level assessment of the attacker node. The network knows the physical location of each node and the distance between each node. Thus, the expected signal strength can be calculated based on the physical distance. The signal strength of the received signal will also be calculated. A slight variation between the expected and actual signal strength can be neglected. But the large-scale variation between those two data indicates the presence of Sybil attack. This method outperforms the existing methods as per the simulation results. S. Abbas et al. [81] used the same physical-layer-based mechanisms proposed in the previous works. It uses special hardware for distance calculation and also for signal strength assessment. The proposed work gives a solution to two types of Sybil attacks. If the attacker node discards the previous identity when it creates new, then the attacker holds only one ID at a time. In this case, the attacker seems normal and is difficult to identify. On the other hand, the attacker can keep more than one ID and do concurrent attacks. The previous methods address the second type of attack. But the proposed scheme is capable of detecting both attacks. That in turn increases the network throughput and packet delivery ratio. The proposed work has been experimentally evaluated under various conditions. The movement of a node and the varying distance are the primary considerations for the simulation.

■ **Worm-hole attack:** It is a combination of tunneling and replay attacks. Two malicious nodes agreed to play tunneling attack can replay the packets to the network at the other end. This type of attack is known as a worm-hole attack. Jamali S. et al. [82] combined artificial immune systems and fuzzy logic to defend against worm-hole attacks. It uses fuzzy logic to find the high-performance route. It categorizes the routes into different levels. Based on the categorization, the method finds the best path by using the inference engine. The worm-hole attack is detected and prevented by using an artificial immune system. The proposed method, Defending Against Worm-hole Attack in MANET (DAWA) is implemented on top of the AODV protocol. In the AODV protocol, the path selection is based on the first-received Route Reply

(RREP) packet. The proposed work collects all the RREP packets received for a single request. Then, the routes will be analyzed by the artificial immune system based on the best path knowledge obtained using the inference engine. This analysis will end up with the detection of a worm-hole attacker present in the network. Shahram Jamali et al. [83] also used the artificial immune system to detect worm-hole attacks. This work proposes a method to bypass the worm-hole attacker nodes. Since the worm-hole attack uses the tunneling approach, two nodes from the system have to be detected and eliminated. It also has the same routing modifications as the previous method. The system considers all the received RREP packets and finds the best-performing path using the artificial immune system. This work uses a path evaluation mechanism by sending test packets. After this phase, the system will check the efficiency and the security of obtained paths by the artificial immune system. The proposed work was implemented by changing the routing concepts on SAODV [61] protocol. As per the simulation results, the technique outperforms the existing methods. Sharma D. et al. [84] proposed a signature-based mechanism to prevent and eliminate worm-hole attacks. The proposed work uses a clustered architecture and an identity-based signature generation to cope with worm-hole attacks. The initial phase of the work explains the key generation process. The public/private key generation process is assigned to cluster heads. The generated keys are used in every communication for encryption and identity verification. The algorithm is capable of detecting the worm-hole nodes during the route setup phase itself. It identifies the presence of worm-hole by analyzing the route reply packets and the nodes present in the obtained route. As per the simulation results, it is clear that the artificial immune system-based analysis is more reliable than this signature-based method. The signature-based method can provide only a surface-level protection from worm-hole attacks.

■ **Flooding attack:** It is the normal flooding attack by using the route request packets. The targeted node cannot participate in any other communications due to the queued malicious route requests. Gurung, S et al. [85] proposed a method to detect the selective route request flooding attack. The attacker can implement the flooding attack in two ways. Either the attacker can flood the packet all over the network or the attacker can do the same selectively to targeted nodes. All the existing systems are focusing only on basic flooding attacks. Thus, those systems fail to identify the selective flooding attack. The proposed system introduces a specialized node called the flooding attack detection node. Such nodes will be deployed in the network. Those nodes will monitor the packet flow and report the unusual data flow to the coordinator. The selective flooding attack can only be identified by this type of close monitoring. It can also detect normal flooding attacks because the flooding attack detection nodes can identify all the abnormal data flow happening through the network. Mohammadi, P et al. [86] contributed statistical-analysis-based flooding attack detection to dynamic source routing. The dynamic source routing is a reactive routing approach where the routes will be computed only when it is required. It follows a source-routing mechanism. The system initially checks the status of all nodes in the network. During the same time, the source node collects the misbehavior information about the nodes in the path. The flooding attack detection is based on the average packet transmission of RREQ packets. Route request packets are the primary choice of an attacker to perform the flooding attack. Thus, a statistical study on the average packet transmission will make the system efficient to identify the flooding attack. The same method can be applied along with all other reactive routing protocols which follow source routing. Nithya B. et al [87] introduced a Fuzzy-based Flooding Attack Detection System (FFADS) to identify the RREQ flooding attack in the network layer. The proposed system applies fuzzy logic to identify the flooding attack. Most of the defending mechanisms use node-specific parameters to detect the flooding attack. In this work, the network-specific parameters are mostly used. Overhead, throughput and packet-drop measures of the network are fed to the fuzzy inference system. Based on the fuzzy inference rules, the output will be generated. The proposed system can find the flooding attacks through these computations. But the system fails to identify the source of the flooding attack from the inferred data. The proposed method is intended to detect and overcome the impacts of flooding attacks. Based on this assessment, no legitimate nodes will be falsely added to the black list.

Classification of Existing Defense Mechanisms

The existing defense mechanisms are classified based on their contributions to make the MANET-IoT system more secure. The layer-based classifications and attack-based basic classifications of defense mechanisms are given in Table 7.1.

Discussion

This section mainly focuses on the existing research challenges in the area of routing attack defense mechanisms. The potential issues present in the existing systems are also analyzed under this section.

Analysis of Existing Defense Mechanisms

There are many defense mechanisms available to identify and prevent the security attacks present in a MANET-IoT system. The routing attacks can be classified based on the affected layers of the MANET-IoT system. Attacks on each layer require different kinds of defense mechanisms. The application layer attacks can be prevented by encryption mechanisms. Also, a type of software attack is present in the application layer. Such attacks can be prevented only by detecting such codes. The transport layer is responsible for the end-to-end packet delivery. The attacks on the transport layer mainly aim to utilize the vulnerabilities present in the transport-layer protocols. The attacks in this layer can easily be eliminated by adding countermeasures to the existing transport layer protocols. The data link layer maintains the traffic flow in the network. The attacks in this layer are not able to alter the data. Thus, the attackers try to derive the metadata from the available information. Attackers can perform only DoS-and-analyses attacks in this layer. The physical layer is responsible for signal transmission. The attackers in this layer perform attacks on the transmitted signals. Jamming attacks and eavesdrop attacks are possible in this layer.

The network layer is prone to several types of DoS attacks. Since the data packets are in encrypted form, the attackers can gain the benefit only through DoS attacks. The main drawback associated with the existing defense mechanism is the inability to defend the attacks other than the ones for which the mechanism was developed. Next, the defense mechanisms have limitations due to the strategically varying attack patterns. If we consider the packet-drop attack, the normal packet-drop attack is easy to identify. But the attacker may behave differently during some periods. At that time, the packet drop will be less in count. The defense mechanism may consider such attacks as a normal packet drop due to resource constraints. Thus, a defense mechanism becomes inefficient due to these varying attack patterns. Also, we couldn't find an effective mechanism to isolate the selfish node in the network. The existing mechanism is capable of preventing the selfish nodes by reputation mechanism. But that cannot be considered as an effective isolation scheme. The false accusation in a voting-based scheme is also an area effectively untouched by existing defense mechanisms.

Open-Research Challenges

Based on the above observations, we can say that the existing defense mechanism still has limitations. Some of the challenging areas of the defense mechanisms are as follows.

Identification of Strategically Different Packet-Drop Attacks

A few varieties of packet-drop attacks are discussed in this chapter. The dropping of a packet happens differently for different attacks. Some attacks drop the packets completely. Some drop only 50% of the received packets. Some behave normally most of the time. The attacking pattern is always different. The existing mechanisms may be efficient to identify one particular attack, but it fails to defend the different versions of packet-drop attacks. The packet-drop attack is a big concern for the network. A single packet loss may affect the communication badly. The network engineers are trying to increase the reliability of the network by increasing the efficiency of resources. But the packet drop by an attack reduces the reliability of the network tremendously. Thus, a system needs to be developed that can identify and distinguish all kinds of packet-drop attacks.

Cooperative Node Attacks

A majority of the defense mechanisms are developed to address single node attacks. But the same attack can be done by the cooperation of more than one node. Thus, all nodes need not behave like an attacker every time. The existing defense mechanisms work based on a cumulative calculation of the node's behavior. Thus, the nodes performing a cooperative attack are able to maintain a value lower than the threshold. Due to this reason, the existing mechanisms cannot perform well to identify the attacker nodes. A system must be capable of identifying both single and cooperative attacks present in the network. There are effective defense mechanisms for cooperative black-hole attacks. But the same cooperation can be expected in all other routing attacks. Still, we do not have a complete system to identify both single and cooperative routing attacks simultaneously.

Identity-Based Attacks

The attacker plays a spoofing attack to get legitimate access to the network. The spoofing attack can be applied in all layers of the network. As per the defense mechanism, the malicious node will be isolated. A Malicious activity performed by a spoofed node will be added to a legitimate node's account. Whenever the malicious activity increases, the accused legitimate node will be eliminated. If the same process repeats, the normal node ratio will decrease. A combination of spoofing and any other attack can degrade the network performance at a large scale. The network is capable of identifying the attacks by the existing defense mechanisms but it fails to identify the spoofing attack altogether. Thus, the normal nodes will be excluded from the communication. This is a major threat to all existing defense mechanisms.

Conclusion and Future Works

This chapter discusses the security attacks and the existing defense mechanisms present in MANET-IoT systems. An attacker could try to destroy the stability of a network by using any methods like packet drop, delay, flooding, jamming, etc. The most common category of attack is the DoS attack. An attacker can perform the DoS attack in almost all layers of the network. The attacking strategy of an attacker is unpredictable. It is not possible to defend against all kinds of attacks by using a single method. But it is possible to include the necessary modifications to existing

Table 7.1 Classification on Defense Mechanism

Sl. No.	Proposed Approach	Citation	Attack Classification		Contributions	Performance Metrics
			Layer	Attack Type		
1	Secure group communication	[48]	Application Layer	Repudiation Attack (Active – Repudiation)	• Public/private key exchange mechanism • Reduction in cipher text size	• No. of rounds • Broadcast message size • Unicast message size
2	Malicious code detection model	[49]	Application Layer	Data-Corruption Attack (Active – Modification of Message)	• Malicious code detection method based on behavior association • Improved detection	• Performance analysis based on known malicious codes like Key. Trojan.a, Vidio. Trojan.win, etc.
3	Encryption algorithm for TCP session hijacking	[50]	Transport Layer	TCP Session Hijacking (Active – Masquerade/ Spoofing)	• Defense mechanism for TCP session hijacking • Integrated security strategy using existing schemes	• Time complexity

(Continued)

Table 7.1 (Continued) Classification on Defense Mechanism

Sl. No.	Proposed Approach	Citation	Attack Classification		Contributions	Performance Metrics
			Layer	Attack Type		
4	Detection of TCP flooding attack	[51]	Transport Layer	TCP Flooding Attacks (Active – DoS)	• Prevention by utilizing reply argument packets • Maximizing the Backlog queue of the server node	• Packet rate on a victim server per second
5	Agent-based prevention mechanism	[52]	Transport Layer	UDP Flooding Attacks (Active – DoS)	• Software agent-based solution • Flooding attack prevention in a distributed environment	• Theoretical study
6	Chaotic adding-weight dynamic local predict model	[53]	Transport Layer	TCP Sequence Prediction Attack (Active – Replay Attack)	• Prevention system for TCP sequence prediction attack • Successful elimination of TCP reset attack	• TCP Initial sequence number prediction count • Slipping window characteristics

7	Methods to infer data through traffic analysis	[56]	Data-Link Layer	Traffic Analysis (Passive – Traffic Analysis)	• A timing attack model • Methods to sniff the traffic	• True positive • Achieved accuracy
8	MAC DoS detection scheme	[57]	Data-Link Layer	MAC DoS Attack (Active – DoS)	• Introduced the concept of giving extra capabilities to nodes. • A robust MAC protocol	• Throughput • Traffic pattern
9	A survey on Jamming and anti-jamming techniques	[58]	Physical Layer	Jamming Attack (Active – DoS)	• Detailed study of jamming attack • Classification of jammers	• Theoretical study
10	Eavesdrop-Attack detection based on SVM	[59]	Physical Layer	Eavesdrop Attack (Passive – Information Leakage)	• Creation of structured dataset • 90% accuracy	• True positive • False positive
11	BP-AODV (based on the chaotic map)	[60]	Network Layer	Black-Hole Attack (Active – DoS)	• Enhanced detection of Black-hole attack • Detection of cooperative black-hole attack	• Avg. throughput•Avg. end-to-end delay • Avg. packet delivery ratio (PDR)

(Continued)

Table 7.1 (Continued) Classification on Defense Mechanism

Sl. No.	Proposed Approach	Citation	Attack Classification		Contributions	Performance Metrics
			Layer	Attack Type		
12	Honeypot-based black-hole attack confirmation technique	[62]	Network Layer	Black-Hole Attack (Active – DoS)	• Eliminating the false detection of attacks • Mechanism to confirm the black-hole	• Avg. detection rate of symptoms • Symptom strength • Attack history • No. of observations
13	Improved trust detection algorithm	[63]	Network Layer	Black-Hole Attack (Active – DoS)	• Trust calculation method • Enhanced data privacy	• Packet loss • Consumption of energy • Overall throughput • Trust level
14	CBDAODV	[64]	Network Layer	Cooperative Black-Hole Attack (Active – DoS)	• Detection of cooperative nodes • Increased packet delivery ratio	• Avg. end-to-end delay

15	EDRI-based approach	[65]	Network Layer	Cooperative Black-Hole Attack (Active – DoS)	• Extended data routing information table-based cooperative node detection • Decreased packet overhead	• Delay • Number of RREQ packets • False detection • Network throughput
16	CBDS	[66]	Network Layer	Cooperative Black-Hole Attack (Active – DoS)	• A cooperative bait detection approach • Efficient system for eliminating cooperative black-hole nodes	• Packet delivery ratio • Routing overhead • End-to-end delay • Throughput
17	MGAM	[67]	Network Layer	Gray-Hole Attack (Active – DoS)	• Mitigating gray-hole attack mechanism • Gray-hole-intrusion detection system	• Packet loss rate • PDR • Average throughput • Routing overhead

(Continued)

Table 7.1 (Continued)   Classification on Defense Mechanism

Sl. No.	Proposed Approach	Citation	Attack Classification		Contributions	Performance Metrics
			Layer	Attack Type		
18	Improved DCFM	[68]	Network Layer	Gray-Hole Attack (Active – DoS)	• Improved denial Contradictions with fictitious node mechanism • Enhanced gray-hole detection	• Packet drop
19	Swarm-inspired algorithm	[69]	Network Layer	Gray-Hole Attack (Active – DoS)	• ANN-based gray-hole detection • Best node identification technique	• Delay • Throughput • PDR
20	Reputation-based source-routing protocol	[70]	Network Layer	Selfish Node Attack (Active – DoS)	• Reputation-based routing protocol • Method to compute the reputation of nodes and path	• Average reputation

21	HRARAN	[71]	Network Layer	Selfish Node Attack (Active – DoS)	• Mechanism to detect selfish node in authenticated routing • Method to compute the reputation of nodes and path	• Packet loss rate • Average path length • Average route latency • Packet delivery ratio • Throughput
22	TBUT	[72]	Network Layer	Selfish Node Attack (Active – DoS)	• Token-based umpiring technique • Lower overhead	• Packet delivery ratio • False negative • False positive • Overhead
23	APD-JFAD	[73]	Network Layer	Jellyfish Attach (Active – DoS)	• SVM-based attack classifier • Hierarchical trust evaluation	• Throughput • Dropped packet ratio • End-to-end delay • PDR
24	ACO-CBRP	[74]	Network Layer	Jellyfish Attach (Active – DoS)	• Enhance version of CBDS [66] • Trust calculation	• Packet delivery ratio • Lifetime • Overhead

(Continued)

Table 7.1 (Continued) Classification on Defense Mechanism

Sl. No.	Proposed Approach	Citation	Attack Classification		Contributions	Performance Metrics
			Layer	Attack Type		
25	JAM	[75]	Network Layer	Jellyfish Attack (Active – DoS)	• Security scheme for identifying a jellyfish attack • Decreased delay	• Packet drop • Delay
26	FAP	[76]	Network Layer	Rushing Attack (Active – DoS)	• Flooding attack prevention technique to defend both rushing and flooding attack • Better prevention during a flooding attack	• Receive rate
27	An integrated protocol	[77]	Network Layer	Rushing Attack (Active – DoS)	• Legitimate neighbor detection • Trusted route formation	• Packet drop • Delay

28	RAP	[78]	Network Layer	Rushing Attack (Active – DoS)	• Rushing attack prevention • No cost mechanism	• Packet delivery ratio • Median latency • Packet overhead • Byte overhead
29	Enhanced authentication method	[79]	Network Layer	Sybil Attack (Active – DoS)	• Physical layer Authentication • Signal comparison method	• Avg. false alarm rate • System bandwidth
30	Sybil attack detection method	[80]	Network Layer	Sybil Attack (Active – DoS)	• A physical layer solution • Signal-analysis-based Sybil attack detection	• False positive • True positive
31	Detection approach in the physical layer	[81]	Network Layer	Sybil Attack (Active – DoS)	• Hardware-based Sybil attack detector • Physical layer detection	• Node movement • Distance • Throughput • PDR
32	DAWA	[82]	Network Layer	Worm-Hole Attack (Active – DoS)	• Best path identification • Worm-hole detection	• Detection rate • Packet delivery Rate • False positive rate • Packet loss

(Continued)

Table 7.1 (Continued) Classification on Defense Mechanism

Sl. No.	Proposed Approach	Citation	Attack Classification		Contributions	Performance Metrics
			Layer	Attack Type		
33	Worm-hole detection based on the artificial immune system	[83]	Network Layer	Worm-Hole Attack (Active – DoS)	• Bypass mechanism • Worm-hole detection	• PDR • End-to-end delay • Packet drop
34	Signature scheme	[84]	Network Layer	Worm-Hole Attack (Active – DoS)	• Identity-based signature mechanism • Prevention of worm-hole attack	• PDR • End-to-end delay • Throughput
35	Mitigating floodingattack mechanism	[85]	Network Layer	Flooding Attack (Active – DoS)	• Mechanism for selective flooding attack detection • Improved normal flooding attack detection	• PDR • PLR (packet loss rate) • Average throughput • Average overhead • Normalized routing load

| 36 | Statistical analysis-based flooding attack detection | [86] | Network Layer | Flooding Attack (Active – DoS) | • Flooding attack prevention in dynamic source routing
• Statistical analysis method | • Avg. packet loss rate
• Avg. PDR
• Avg. end-to-end delay
• Avg. throughput |
| 37 | FFADS | [87] | Network Layer | Flooding Attack (Active – DoS) | • Fuzzy-based RREQ packet flooding mechanism
• Network-specific parameter-based detection | • Flooding level
• Throughput
• Packet loss ratio
• Routing overhead |

protocols for defending the expected attacks in a network. The aim of an attacker is always the same but the methods he/she chooses for the attack will be different with respect to the system setup. All attacks behave differently with different systems. Thus, a system-specific defense mechanism is required to prevent security breaches in the network. The heart of network communication is the routing process. A small disturbance in the routing can badly affect the communication. Thus, the attackers always prefer to choose the network layer to intrude on the network. Routing attacks have to be identified and eliminated from the network at the earliest. Thus, the recent research is concentrated on routing attacks. The routing process can happen in many ways as the protocol suggests. The attackers can have a wide range of attacking strategies in a network layer due to the proposal of various routing protocols. All newly proposed protocols are able to eliminate the attacks which are intended to be eliminated by the proposal. But, sometimes those protocols fail to identify other types of attacks. Thus, a robust system needs to be developed to cope with the varying strategies of the attackers.

References

[1] H.A. Abdul-Ghani and D. Konstantas, A Comprehensive Study of Security and Privacy Guidelines, Threats, and Countermeasures: An IoT Perspective, *Journal of Sensor and Actuator Networks*, Vol. 8, No. 22, pp. 1–38, 2019.

[2] F.S. Dantas Silva, E. Silva, E.P. Neto, M. Lemos, A.J. VenancioNeto, and F. Esposito, A Taxonomy of DDoS Attack Mitigation Approaches Featured by SDN Technologies in IoT Scenarios, *Sensors*, Vol. 20, No. 3078, pp. 1–28, 2020.

[3] H.-C. Lin, P. Wang, and W.-H. Lin, Implementation of a PSO-Based Security Defense Mechanism for Tracing the Sources of DDoS Attacks, *Computers*, Vol. 8, No. 88, pp. 1–16, 2019.

[4] A. Mathur, T. Newe and M. Rao, Defence against Black Hole and Selective Forwarding Attacks for Medical WSNs in the IoT, *Sensors*, Vol. 16, No. 118, pp. 1–25, 2016.

[5] J. Galeano-Brajones, J. Carmona-Murillo, J.F. Valenzuela-Valdés and F. Luna-Valero, Detection and Mitigation of DoS and DDoS Attacks in IoT-Based Stateful SDN: An Experimental Approach, *Sensors*, Vol. 20, No. 816, pp. 1–18, 2020.

[6] Alnumay Waleed, Ghosh Uttam and Chatterjee Pushpita, A Trust-Based Predictive Model for Mobile Ad Hoc Network in Internet of Things, *Sensors*, Vol. 19, No. 6, pp. 1–14, 2019.

[7] P. Bellavista, G. Cardone, A. Corradi and L. Foschini, Convergence of MANET and WSN in IoT Urban Scenarios, *IEEE Sensors Journal*, Vol. 13, No. 10, pp. 3558–3567, 2013.

[8] Sankar Mukherjee and G.P. Biswas, Networking for IoT and Applications Using Existing Communication Technology, *Egyptian Informatics Journal*, Vol. 19, No.2, pp. 107–127, 2018.

[9] Rasa Bruzgiene, LinaNarbutaite and Tomas Adomkus, MANET Network in Internet of Things System, Ad Hoc Networks (Book Chapter), 2017.

[10] Alam Tanweer and Benaida Mohamed, The Role of Cloud-MANET Framework in the Internet of Things (IoT), *International Journal of Online Engineering (iJOE)*, Vol. 14, pp. 97–111, 2018.

[11] D.G. Reina, S.L. Toral, F. Barrero, N. Bessis and E. Asimakopoulou, *The Role of Ad Hoc Networks in the Internet of Things: A Case Scenario for Smart Environments, Internet of Things and Inter-cooperative Computational Technologies for Collective Intelligence, Studies in Computational Intelligence*, Springer, Vol.460, 2013.

[12] I. A. Alameri, MANETS and Internet of Things: The Development of a Data Routing Algorithm, *Engineering, Technology & Applied Science Research*, Vol. 8, No. 1, pp. 2604–2608, 2018.

[13] J. Gowrishankar, P. Senthil Kumar, T. Narmadha and N. Yuvaraj, A Trust Based Protocol ForManets In Iot Environment, *International Journal of Advanced Science and Technology*, Vol. 29, No. 7, pp. 2770–2775, 2020.

[14] Munisha Devi and Nasib Singh Gill, Mobile Ad Hoc Networks and Routing Protocols in IoT Enabled Smart Environment: A review, *Journal of Engineering and Applied Sciences*, Vol. 14, No.3, pp. 802–811, 2019.

[15] Munisha Devi and Nasib Singh Gill, Novel Algorithm for Enhancing MANET Protocol in Smart Environment, *International Journal of Innovative Technology and Exploring Engineering*, Vol. 8, No. 10, pp. 2278–3075, 2019.

[16] Tanweer Alama and Baha Rababahb, Convergence of MANET in Communication among Smart Devices in IoT, *International Journal of Wireless and Microwave Technologies*, Vol. 2, pp. 1–10, 2019.

[17] Mahmood Ibrahim Alsaydia, Analysing MANET Ability to Work with WSN in IoT Environment using IPv6, *International Journal of Innovative Research in Computer and Communication Engineering*, Vol. 5, No. 8, pp. 1–12, 2017.

[18] Mamata Rath and Chhabi Rani Panigrahi, Prioritization of Security Measures at the Junction of MANET and IoT, *ACM*, No. 127, pp. 1–7, 2016.

[19] Alsumayt Albandari, Haggerty John and Lotfi Ahmad, Using Trust to Detect Denial of Service Attacks in the Internet of Things Over MANETs, *International Journal of Space-Based and Situated Computing*, Vol. 7, No. 43, pp. 1–22, 2017.

[20] Sana Zeba and Md Hussain Ahmad, Survey on Attacks in MANET Based Internet of Things System, *IJSRD –International Journal for Scientific Research & Development*, Vol. 7, No. 6, pp. 1–7, 2019.

[21] S. Vadhana Kumari and B. Paramasivan, Defense Against Sybil Attacks and Authentication for Anonymous Location-based Routing in MANET, *Wireless Network*, Vol. 23, pp. 715–726, 2017.

[22] K. Cumanan et al., Physical Layer Security Jamming: Theoretical Limits and Practical Designs in Wireless Networks, *IEEE Access*, Vol. 5, pp. 3603–3611, 2017.

[23] X. Wei, Analysis and Protection of SYN Flood Attack, Advances in Computer Science, Intelligent System and Environment, *Advances in Intelligent and Soft Computing*, Springer, Vol. 106, pp. 183–187,2011.

[24] D.B. Roy and R. Chaki, *Detection of Denial of Service Attack Due to Selfish Node in MANET by Mobile Agent, Recent Trends in Wireless and Mobile Networks, Communications in Computer and Information Science*, Springer, Vol. 162, pp. 14–23, 2011.

[25] Z. Shi, R. Sun, R. Lu, J. Qiao, J. Chen and X. Shen, A Worm-hole Attack Resistant Neighbor Discovery Scheme With RDMA Protocol for 60 GHz Directional Network, *IEEE Transactions on Emerging Topics in Computing*, Vol. 1, No. 2, pp. 341–352, 2013.

[26] M. Marimuthu and I. Krishnamurthi, Enhanced OLSR for Defense Against DOS Attack in Ad Hoc Networks, *Journal of Communications and Networks*, Vol. 15, No. 1, pp. 31–37, 2013.

[27] Z. Wang, Y. Chen and C. Li, PSR: A Lightweight Proactive Source Routing Protocol For Mobile Ad Hoc Networks, *IEEE Transactions on Vehicular Technology*, Vol. 63, No. 2, pp. 859–868, 2014.

[28] Hicham Amraoui, Ahmed Habbani, AbdelmajidHajami and EssaidBila, *Security-Based Mechanism for Proactive Routing Schema Using Game Theory Model*, Vol. 2016, pp. 1–18, 2016.

[29] Y. Ye, S. Feng, M. Liu, et al, A Safe Proactive Routing Protocol SDSDV for Ad Hoc Network, *International Journal of Wireless Information Networks*, Vol. 25, pp. 348–357, 2018.

[30] H. Kanagasundaram and A. Kathirvel, EIMO-ESOLSR: Energy Efficient and Security-based Model for OLSR Routing Protocol in Mobile Ad-Hoc Network, *IET Communications*, Vol. 13, No. 5, pp. 553–559, 2019.

[31] S. Krco and M. Dupcinov, Improved Neighbor Detection Algorithm for AODV Routing Protocol, *IEEE Communications Letters*, Vol. 7, No. 12, pp. 584–586, 2003.

[32] N. Meghanathan, A Location Prediction-Based Reactive Routing Protocol to Minimize the Number of Route Discoveries and Hop Count per Path in Mobile Ad Hoc Networks, *The Computer Journal*, Vol. 52, No. 4, pp. 461–482, 2009.

[33] H. Nakayama, S. Kurosawa, A. Jamalipour, Y. Nemoto and N. Kato, A Dynamic Anomaly Detection Scheme for AODV-Based Mobile Ad Hoc Networks, *IEEE Transactions on Vehicular Technology*, Vol. 58, No. 5, pp. 2471–2481, 2009.

[34] M. Rao and N. Singh, *An Improved Routing Protocol (AODV nthBR) for Efficient Routing in MANETs*, Advanced Computing, Networking and Informatics, Vol. 2, Smart Innovation, Systems and Technologies, Springer, Vol. 28, 2014.

[35] S.R. Malwe, N. Taneja and G.P. Biswas, Enhancement of DSR and AODV Protocols Using Link Availability Prediction, *Wireless Personal Communications*, Vol. 97, pp. 4451–4466, 2017.

[36] Zhan Jing, *Centralized Routing and Distributed Routing Protocol for Dynamic Routing*, World Automation Congress 2012, Puerto Vallarta, Mexico, pp. 1–4, 2012.

[37] S. Vassilaras, D. Vogiatzis and G. S. Yovanof, Security and Cooperation in Clustered Mobile Ad Hoc Networks with Centralized Supervision, *IEEE Journal on Selected Areas in Communications*, Vol. 24, No. 2, pp. 329–342, 2006.

[38] A. Anand, H. Aggarwal and R. Rani, Partially Distributed Dynamic Model for Secure and Reliable Routing in Mobile Ad Hoc Networks, *Journal of Communications and Networks*, Vol. 18, No. 6, pp. 938–947, 2016.

[39] N. Chauhan, L.K. Awasthi, N. Chand and A. Chugh, *A Distributed Weighted Cluster Based Routing Protocol for MANETs*, Computer Networks and Information Technologies, CNC 2011, Communications in Computer and Information Science, Springer, Vol. 142, pp. 147–152, 2011.

[40] L. Li and R. Liu, Securing Cluster-Based Ad Hoc Networks with Distributed Authorities, *IEEE Transactions on Wireless Communications*, Vol. 9, No. 10, pp. 3072–3081, 2010.

[41] G. Liu, H. Dong, Z. Yan, X. Zhou and S. Shimizu, B4SDC: A Blockchain System for Security Data Collection in MANETs, *IEEE Transactions on Big Data*, Vol. 14, No. 8, 2015.

[42] T. Tsuda, Y. Komai, T. Hara and S. Nishio, Top-k Query Processing and Malicious Node Identification Based on Node Grouping in MANETs, *IEEE Access*, Vol. 4, pp. 993–1007, 2016.

[43] Yi-Chi Lin, and Jill Slay, Non-Repudiation in Pure Mobile Ad Hoc Network, School of Computer and Information Science (SCIS) & Edith Cowan University, pp. 59–66, 2005.

[44] Z. Feng, J. Ning, I. Broustis, K. Pelechrinis, S. V. Krishnamurthy and M. Faloutsos, *Coping with Packet Replay Attacks in Wireless Networks, 8th Annual IEEE Communications Society Conference on Sensor, Mesh and Ad Hoc Communications and Networks*, Salt Lake City, UT, 2011.

[45] G. Vaseer, G. Ghai and D. Ghai, Novel Intrusion Detection and Prevention for Mobile Ad Hoc Networks: A Single- and Multiattack Case Study, *IEEE Consumer Electronics Magazine*, Vol. 8, No.3, pp. 35–39, 2019.

[46] J. Sigholm and M. Raciti, *Best-Effort Data Leakage Prevention in Inter-organizational Tactical MANETs*, MILCOM 2012–2012 IEEE Military Communications Conference, Orlando, FL, pp.1–7, 2012.

[47] A.G.S. Trujillo, A.L.S. Orozco, L.J.G. Villalba, et al., A Traffic Analysis Attack to Compute Social Network Measures, *Multimedia Tools and Applications*, Vol. 78, pp. 29731–29745. 2019.

[48] X. Lv and H. Li, Secure Group Communication with Both Confidentiality and Non-repudiation for Mobile Ad-Hoc Networks, *IET Information Security*, Vol. 7, No. 2, pp. 61–66, 2013.

[49] L. Han, M. Qian, X. Xu, C. Fu and H. Kwisaba, Malicious Code Detection Model Based on Behavior Association, *Tsinghua Science and Technology*, Vol. 19, No. 5, pp. 508–515, 2014.

[50] Minghan Chen, Fangyan Dai, Bingjie Yan, Jieren Cheng and Longjuan Wang, Encryption Algorithm for TCP Session Hijacking, Cryptography and Security (cs. CR), arXiv:2002.01391v1 [cs.CR], pp. 1–12, 2020.

[51] Rana Deepak, Garg Naveen and Chamoli, A Study and Detection of TCP SYN Flood Attacks with IP spoofing and its Mitigations, *International Journal of Computer Technology and Applications*, Vol. 3, pp. 1–5, 2012.

[52] Singh Aarti, AARTI and Juneja Dimple, Agent Based Preventive Measure for UDP Flood Attack in DDoS Attacks, *International Journal of Engineering Science and Technology*, Vol. 2, No. 8, pp. 3405–3411, 2010.

[53] F. Zeng, K. Yin and M. Chen, *Research on TCP Initial Sequence Number Prediction Method Based on Adding-weight Chaotic Time Series*, IEEE – The 9th International Conference for Young Computer Scientists, Hunan, pp. 1511–1515, 2008.

[54] Bhattacharyya Aniruddha, Banerjee Arnab, Bose Dipayan, Saha Himadri and Bhattacharyya Debika, Different types of attacks in Mobile ADHOC Network, arXiv2011.

[55] M. S. Khan, D. Midi, M. I. Khan and E. Bertino, Fine-Grained Analysis of Packet Loss in MANETs, *IEEE Access*, Vol. 5, pp. 7798–7807, 2017.

[56] F. Kausar, S. Aljumah, S. Alzaydi and R. Alroba, Traffic Analysis Attack for Identifying Users' Online Activities, *IT Professional*, Vol. 21, No. 2, pp. 50–57, 2019.

[57] V. Gupta, S. Krishnamurthy and M. Faloutsos, *Denial of Service Attacks at the MAC Layer in Wireless Ad Hoc Networks*, MILCOM 2002, Proceedings, Anaheim, CA, Vol. 2, pp. 1118–1123, 2002.

[58] Kanika Grover, Alvin Lim, and Qing Yang, Jamming and Anti-jamming Techniques in Wireless Networks: A Survey, *International Journal of Ad Hoc Ubiquitous Computing*, Vol. 17, pp. 197–215, 2014.

[59] Tiep M. Hoang, Trung Q. Duong, Hoang Duong Tuan, Sangarapillai Lambotharan, Emi Garcia-Palacios and Long D. Nguyen, Physical Layer Security: Detection of Active Eavesdropping Attacks by Support Vector Machines, Signal Processing (eess. SP), arXiv:2003.01048v1 [eess.SP], 2020.

[60] Aly M. El-Semary and Hossam Diab, BP-AODV: Blackhole Protected AODV Routing Protocol for MANETs Based on Chaotic Map, *IEEE Access*, Vol. 7, pp. 95197–95211, 2019.

[61] S. Lu, L. Li, K.-Y. Lam, and L. Jia, "*SAODV: A MANET Routing Protocol That Can Withstand Black-hole Attack*," in *Proceedings of the International Conference on Computational Intelligence and Security*, Beijing, China, 2009, pp. 421–425.

[62] Divya Sai Keerthi Tiruvakadu and Venkataram Pallapa, Honeypot Based Black-Hole Attack Confirmation in a MANET, *International Journal of Wireless Information Networks*, Vol. 25, pp. 434–448, 2018.

[63] J. Manoranjini, A. Chandrasekar and S. Jothi, Improved QoS and Avoidance of Black-Hole Attacks in MANET Using Trust Detection Framework, *Journal for Control, Measurement, Electronics, Computing and Communications*, Vol. 60, pp. 274–284, 2019.

[64] Nai-Wei Lo and Fang-Ling Liu, *A Secure Routing Protocol to Prevent Cooperative Black-hole Attack in MANET*, *Intelligent Technologies and Engineering Systems*, Lecture Notes in Electrical Engineering, Vol. 234, pp. 59–65, 2013.

[65] A. Dorri, An EDRI-based Approach for Detecting and Eliminating Cooperative Black-Hole Nodes in MANET, *Wireless Network*, Vol. 23, pp. 1767–1778, 2017.

[66] J. Chang, P. Tsou, I. Woungang, H. Chao and C. Lai, Defending Against Collaborative Attacks by Malicious Nodes in MANETs: A Cooperative Bait Detection Approach, *IEEE Systems Journal*, Vol. 9, No. 1, pp. 65–75, 2015.

[67] S. Gurung and S. Chauhan, A Novel Approach for Mitigating Gray-Hole Attack in MANET, *Wireless Network*, Vol. 24, pp. 565–579, 2018.

[68] N. Schweitzer, A. Stulman, R. D. Margalit and A. Shabtai, Contradiction Based Gray-Hole Attack Minimization for Ad-Hoc Networks, *IEEE Transactions on Mobile Computing*, Vol. 16, No. 8, pp. 2174–2183, 2017.

[69] P. Rani, Kavita, S. Verma and G. N. Nguyen, Mitigation of Black-hole and Gray-hole Attack Using Swarm Inspired Algorithm With Artificial Neural Network, *IEEE Access*, Vol. 8, pp. 121755–121764, 2020.

[70] L. Guaya-Delgado, E. Pallarès-Segarra and A.M. Mezher, A Novel Dynamic Reputation-based Source Routing Protocol for Mobile Ad Hoc Networks, *Journal of Wireless Communications and Network*, Vol. 77, pp. 1–16, 2019.

[71] P. Annadurai and S. Vijayalakshmi, Highly Reputed Authenticated Routing in MANET (HRARAN), *Wireless Personal Communications*, Vol. 83, pp. 455–472, 2015.

[72] J.M.S.P. Josh Kumar, A. Kathirvel and N. Kirubakaran, A Unified Approach for Detecting and Eliminating Selfish Nodes in MANETs Using TBUT, *Journal of Wireless Communications and Network*, Vol. 143, pp. 1–11, 2015.

[73] S. Doss, Anand Nayyar, G. Suseendran, Sudeep Tanwar, Ashish Khanna, Le Hoang Son and Pham Huy Thong, APD-JFAD: Accurate Prevention and Detection of Jelly Fish Attack in MANET, *IEEE Access*, Vol. 6, pp. 56954–56965, 2018.

[74] S. Satheeshkumar and N. Sengottaiyan, Defending against Jellyfish Attacks Using Cluster Based Routing Protocol for Secured Data Transmission in MANET, *Cluster Computing*, Vol. 22, pp. 10849–10860, 2019.

[75] F. Samad, Q. Abu Ahmed, A. Shaikh and A. Aziz, *JAM: Mitigating Jellyfish Attacks in Wireless Ad Hoc Networks, Emerging Trends and Applications in Information Communication Technologies, Communications in Computer and Information Science*, Springer, Vol. 281, pp. 432–444, 2012.

[76] Yi Ping, Z. Dai, S. Zhang and Y. Zhong, A New Routing Attack in Mobile Ad Hoc Networks, *International Journal of Information Technology*, Vol. 11, pp. 83–94, 2005.

[77] S. Ghoreishi, S. AbdRazak, I. F. Isnin and H. Chizari, *Rushing Attack against Routing Protocols in Mobile Ad-Hoc Networks, International Symposium on Biometrics and Security Technologies (ISBAST)*, Kuala Lumpur, pp. 220–224, 2014.

[78] Yih-Chun Hu, Adrian Perrig and David B. Johnson, *Rushing Attacks and Defense in Wireless Ad Hoc Network Routing Protocols, WiSe '03: Proceedings of the 2nd ACM Workshop on Wireless Security*, pp. 30–40, 2003.

[79] L. Xiao, L. J. Greenstein, N. B. Mandayam and W. Trappe, Channel-Based Detection of Sybil Attacks in Wireless Networks, *IEEE Transactions on Information Forensics and Security*, Vol. 4, No. 3, pp. 492–503, 2009.

[80] M. Faisal, S. Abbas, and H. Ur Rahman, Identity Attack Detection System for 802.11-based Ad Hoc Networks, *Journal of Wireless Communications and Network*, Vol. 128, pp. 1–16, 2018.

[81] S. Abbas, M. Merabti, D. Llewellyn-Jones and K. Kifayat, Lightweight Sybil Attack Detection in MANETs, *IEEE Systems Journal*, Vol. 7, No.2, pp. 236–248, 2013.

[82] S. Jamali and R. Fotohi, DAWA: Defending against Worm-holeAttack in MANETs by Using Fuzzy Logic and Artificial Immune System, *The Journal of Supercomputing*, Vol. 73, pp. 5173–5196, 2017.

[83] Shahram Jamali and Reza Fotohi, Defending against Worm-hole Attack in MANET Using an Artificial Immune System, *New Review of Information Networking*, Vol. 21, No. 2, pp. 79–100, 2016.

[84] D. Sharma, V. Kumar and R. Kumar, *Prevention of Worm-hole Attack Using Identity Based Signature Scheme in MANET, Computational Intelligence in Data Mining*, Springer, Vol. 2, pp. 475–485, 2016.

[85] S. Gurung, and S. Chauhan, A Novel Approach for Mitigating Route Request Flooding Attack in MANET, *Wireless Network*, Vol. 24, pp2899–2914, 2018.

[86] P. Mohammadi and A. Ghaffari, Defending Against Flooding Attacks in Mobile Ad-Hoc Networks Based on Statistical Analysis, *Wireless Personal Communications*, Vol. 106, pp. 365–376, 2019.

[87] M. Faisal, S. Abbas, and H. Ur Rahman, Identity Attack Detection System for 802.11-based Ad Hoc Networks, *Journal of Wireless Communications and Network*, Vol. 128, pp. 1–16, 2018.

Chapter 8

Machine and Deep Learning (ML/DL) Algorithms for Next-Generation Healthcare Applications

V. Pavithra and V. Jayalakshmi

VELS University, Chennai, India

Contents

DOI: 10.1201/9781003119784-8

Introduction

The healthcare division is completely distinctive from other industries. It is a basic human demand, and each individual expects the highest quality of care and administration. It did not accomplish the social desire, although it devours a colossal rate of the budget [1]. Generally, the translations of restorative information are being done by the restorative master. In terms of picture elucidation by the human master, it is very restricted due to its subjectivity and complexity of the picture; broad varieties exist over diverse translators and weariness. After the victory of deep learning (DL) in other real-world applications, it has additionally given energizing arrangements with great precision of therapeutic imaging and is seen as a key strategy for future applications in the well-being sector. Gone are the days when healthcare information was microscopic. Due to the colossal headway in picture-securing gadgets, the information is very expansive (moving to huge information), which creates it challenging and curious for picture examination. This quick development in therapeutic pictures and modalities requires broad and tedious efforts by the therapeutic master that's subjective, inclined to human blunder, and may have expansive varieties over the diverse master. The elective arrangement is utilizing machine learning (ML) procedures to computerize the determination handle in any case; conventional machine learning strategies are not adequate to bargain with a complex issue. High-performance computing with machine learning guarantees the capacity to bargain huge therapeutic picture information for exact and proficient determination.

Deep learning will aid in the selection and showcasing of important qualities for recent models that evaluate data and provide relevant prediction models to help doctors more effectively. ML and Artificial Intelligence (AI) have advanced quickly in later a long time. Procedures of ML and AI have played a vital part in the restorative field like therapeutic picture handling, computer-aided conclusion, picture elucidation, picture combination, picture enlistment, picture division,' image-guided treatment, picture recovery, and investigation. Methods of ML extricate data from the pictures and speak to data successfully and proficiently [2].

Experts can use machine learning and artificial intelligence to study and predict disease risks more precisely and quickly, allowing them to avoid the risks sooner. These procedures improve the capacities of specialists and analysts to understand that how to analyze the bland varieties which will main to illness. Deep learning-based computations appeared to be promising in terms of execution and speed in a variety of disciplines, including discourse recognition, content recognition, lip reading, computer-aided conclusion, face recognition, and sedate-finding. The aim of this section is to provide a full overview of deep learning-based computations in corrective image investigation issues, both in terms of present research and future directions. This chapter provides basic facts and outline the level of craftsmanship in the field of regenerative picture handling and analysis approaches of deep learning. Deep learning algorithms incrementally learn from elevated highlights. Machine learning calculations are reasonable for issues with the direct tall sum of information. It takes up to a few hours to prepare the calculation. Deep Learning calculations are more reasonable for issues with gigantic sums of information that it takes much longer to prepare the calculation. But during the test time, deep learning calculations take less time to work. These machine learning computations are divided into two groups: supervised and unsupervised. Supervised learning is when learning work and preparing a calculation that maps an input to a yield based on case input–output sets. Unsupervised learning could be (self-organized) learning that finds already unfamiliar designs in data set without names. Advanced Deep Learning could be a segment of machine learning as given in Figure 8.1. Deep learning is propelled by the structure and capacity of a human neuron called the Artificial Neural Network (ANN) [3]. ANN has predominance over most other ML calculations due to its capacity to utilize directed, semi-administered, and unsupervised learning on assorted sorts of information.

Significant learning applies significant neural frameworks with various layers and fundamentally a bigger number of data than standard ML estimations and from this time onward, it needs more prominent models and more figuring. It's also useful because the performance of typical AI computations can't be enhanced if the proportion of data is increased after a certain point, and the display of significant learning figures is related to the entirety and arrangement of data. Counterfeit Neural Networks are systems that understand how to perform exercises that are subject to models but do not have a clearly stated program. ANN configuration is

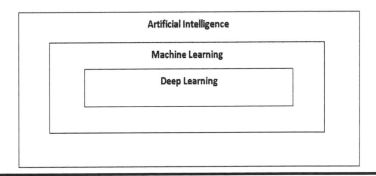

Figure 8.1 Deep learning structure.

made of three layers: data layer, yield layer, and one covered layer. Significant neural frameworks are ANNs with various layers among information and yield layers, for instance, different disguised layers. Deep Neural Network, Deep Convict Network, Recurrent Neural Network, and Convolution Neural Network are important deep learning computations. Massive Neural Networks are a powerful tool for learning. Andrew Ng, a Coursera instructor who is also the Chief Scientist at Baidu Science and the founder of Google Brain, has had great success in the field of education through a variety of Google businesses. He spoke and discussed a lot about vital appreciation, which is a great place to start. During his early visits to large learning, Andrew described in-depth learning about conventional phone neural frameworks.

The Significance of Deep Learning Using Natural Language

The assurance of deep learning in the field of normal dialect preparation is the increased production of models that would need more data but less etymological mastery in preparation and work [4]. There's a lot of build-ups and expansive statements around deep learning techniques, but beyond the build-up, deep learning strategies are producing state-of-the-art outcomes on difficult topics. Strikingly planning for modern dialect. In this chapter, you will find assurances that deep learning techniques are in place to resolve the issues of characteristic dialect training.

The Promise of Deep Learning

1. Deep learning becoming more acquainted with strategies is well known, specifically because they are giving over on their guarantee. That is not to say that there is no publicity surrounding the innovation, but rather that the promotion is primarily based on real results that have been approved over a system of rigorously testing produced insight concerns from PC innovative and poor eyesight, as well as typical language preparation. Regular language handling, especially discourse acknowledgment, has shown some of the first significant demonstrations of the intensity of deep information gathering. Recently, there has been an increase in PC interpretation. Five deep learning ways to monitoring home-grown language management are assured in this segment. Promises made feasible by scientists and field experts late, citizens who may be more significant than the simple guarantees that are suggested, may also be more notable. They are as follows:

2. **The promise of drop-in replacement styles.** That is, the current home-grown language systems may be implemented as replacement templates, which can increase comparably or more effectively.

3. **Fresh NLP models' pledge.** In other terms, a deep selection of systems knowledge offers the ability to evaluate new display techniques for home-ground language challenges, such as succession arrangements.

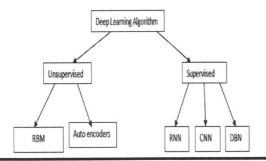

Figure 8.2   Deep learning algorithms.

4. **Function learning pledge.** This ensures that comprehensive information on approaches will look at the focuses in the handmade language required by the model process, rather than the need to concentrate on and exclude the highlights from a specialist's guide.
5. **The pledge to change continually.** This ensures that the general implementation of the emphasis on natural language preparation is focused largely on genuine effects and that the changes prove to persist and can be conceived.
6. **End-to-end models pledge.** It would be that a monstrous beginning to deeply collect model knowledge will organize characteristic language issues and give a step-by–step, more ordinary, and successful approach.

Deep Learning Algorithms

Deep neural systems are not simple to prepare with back proliferation due to the issue of vanishing angle which impacts the time taken for preparing and decreases exactness. Fake Neural Systems decide to choose a fair work based on the net contrast between the Neural Network's expected yield and the genuine yield within the preparation information. Figure 8.2 implies that, depending on the fetched, the weights and predispositions are changed after each preparation, until the death toll is as low as it possibly can be. The rate at which a number of casualties is taken changes depending on weights and predispositions [5].

Restricted Boltzmann Machine (RBM)

The Restricted Boltzmann Machine may (RBM) be a shallow 2-layer Neural Arrange with each neuron in one gather associated to each neuron within the other bunch without having any associations inside a gather. In Figure 8.3, the two bunches are obvious (input) and covered-up layers of neural organization. RBMs are prepared to recreate the input information. The preparing strategy of RBM is forward-passed; in the reverse pass, compare the result to input. In the forward pass, each input is

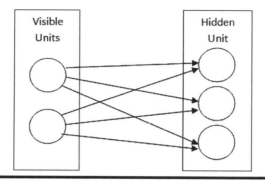

Figure 8.3   Deep layers.

combined with its weight and a single inclination. Within the reverse pass, each neuron is combined with a weight and a by-and-large predisposition and the result is passed to an unmistakable layer for remaking. The show in an unmistakable layer is compared with the initial input. This handle is rehashed with different weights and inclinations till the input and reproduction are exceptionally comparative [6].

Autoencoders

Autoencoder may be a specialized Counterfeit Neural Arrange which learns a representation (encoding) for a set of information, by preparing the arrange to disregard flag clamor. It also tries to retrieve the initial input from the deteriorated encoding a representation [7] in Figure 8.4. As the framework learns to ignore noise, the way of re-erasing the input makes a difference in dimensionality reduction. An autoencoder may have any number of covered-up layers. Both RBMs and autoencoders support unsupervised learning and are utilized in generative models since both methods endeavor to reproduce the input.

Deep Belief Networks (DBNs)

Deep Belief Networks (DBNs) may be characterized as a straightforward combination of unsupervised learning calculations suck as RBMs and autoencoders. In Figure 8.5, the structure of a DBN might seem indistinguishable from an MLP but the preparation is like that of a stack of RBMs which is valuable in diminishing the vanishing slope issue. Straightforward structures of autoencoders or RBMs are consecutively put for illustration; the covered-up layer for the primary RBM gets to

Figure 8.4   Autoencoders.

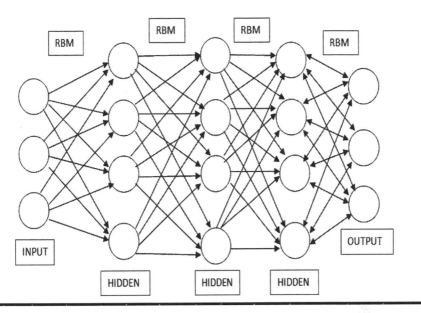

Figure 8.5   Deep neural networks.

be the Unmistakable layer for another RBM. Common applications of DBNs are in Image/Video/Confront acknowledgment.

NN is utilized when the yield must be successive like in picture-captioning and dialect interpretation, as shown in Figure 8.6. In a standard MLP, each layer has its claim weights and inclinations and consequently cannot be combined. To combine these layers, utilization of the same weights and predispositions is made (repetitive layer). This guarantees that the neuron recollects the existing state and based on this state, another yield is produced.

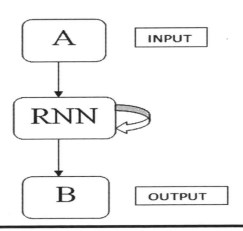

Figure 8.6   Recurrent neural network.

Convolutional Neural Network (CNN)

Convolutional neural networks (CNNs) is a deep learning algorithm which contain layers like Input layer, kernel, Pooling, and Fully Connected Layers [8]. The input layer takes image as the input and filters only an important portion of the images to the next layer; to distinguish the features, it employs an array known as the Filter or Feature Extractor. In the convolution Layer, an established function is applied, which assists in receiving non-linearity and getting productivity based on the input. The triggering applications are ReLU, Sigmoid, and so on. The frequently used CNN is ReLU.

The pooling layer is the next and it assists in shrinking the parameters, because the pictures may be large. There are numerous pooling methods based on constraints, but the most commonly used one is Max Pooling, which is defined as the most concentrated area of the resulting record. A 1-dimensional array will be injected into the entirely related network after the derived feature record is destroyed. This network serves the same goal as other neural networks, and after some backpropagation, the most appropriate categorization is displayed. Other than image investigation, the CNN is also used in Optical Character Recognition to transfer the handwritten document into a digital document, which is an element of Natural Language Processing.

Natural Language Processing

The regular handling of natural language such as speech and text through software is usually specified. Natural linguistic analysis has been learned for over 5 decades and has grown with the development of machines beyond the realm of concepts. Human language relates to how humans talk to each other – chat and text usually– and they are found in the document. Imagine how many texts each day you notice: signs, menus, letters, instant messages, websites, etc. There's no limit to the list. Imagine chatting now. It will communicate with someone more than it will compose as a group. It is much easier to speak than it is to write. The way you connect with someone is through speech and email. Given the importance of this evidence, strategies for understanding and rationalizing natural language should be accessible.

Challenges of Natural Language

It is not clear how to work with natural language info. It's been studied and tested over the previous 50 years. It's tough from the viewpoint of the infant who has gained a language after many years. It is tough for adult language beginners, rough for the physicist who wants to model the subsequent phenomenon, complicated for the architect who attempts to construct systems dealing with the feedback or efficiency of natural languages. These tasks are so overwhelming that natural language will make them easier to address.

English is primarily rough when it's confusing. Few laws remain. So most of the time, it can be accurately known. The vocabularies of people are quite complicated. It tends to evolve and grow. Persons are excellent at language growth and language acceptance and can communicate, perceive, and understand rather specific concepts. Individuals, therefore, are excellent vocabulary consumers and very bad at embracing and explaining language-ruling policies accurately.

From Linguistics to Natural Language Processing

- **Linguistics** – Linguistics, along with its syntax, emancipation, and phonetics, is technical language learning. Standard linguistics is concerned with language preparation and evaluation. The official syntax and semantic methods were developed tremendously, but clean mathematical formalization resists the thrilling problems of natural language interpretation. In general, a linguist is a language student, though more colloquially. An autonomous linguist can take care that he/she is out on the field. The tool of research is mathematics. Real language mathematicians may use their research as mathematical linguistics, focusing solely on the use of discrete mathematical formalisms and natural language premises.
- **Computational linguistics** – Computational Linguistics is a new branch of linguistics research that employs computer science approaches. Because the use of computer software and concepts has surpassed most areas of research, a computer linguist of today would have been a computer linguist of yesterday. The learning of a machine structure to accept and generate natural language is computer linguistics. The typical role of machine linguistics is to evaluate theoretical linguists' grammars.

Medical Imaging Analytics and Diagnostics

PC visualization is how computers know how to see and recognize from pictures and videos. PC visualization is an effort to duplicate the individual imaginary structure to analyze and recognize picture facts to formulate a decision. The intellectual organization can make decisions that are constructed with special deep knowledgeable methods like DBN and CNNs [9]. This segment can talk about the application of CNN in PC visualization, i.e., picture-captioning, medical image analysis, and robots' direction-finding. This function of CNN knows how to be used for a lot of dissimilar necessities like do research and identification of diseases. Here, there are numerous types of medical images that are used, like X-rays, MRIs, and ultrasounds. The X-rays create a 2-dimensional reflection at the same time the MRI creates a 3-dimensional image of the unit and the ultrasound is a live capturing of conditions like pneumonia, TB, and cardiomegaly utilizing X-rays. X-rays diagnosis of pneumonia and tuberculosis can be identified using the CNN's simple categorizing method. The analysis of TB with upper body X-rays will be considered in two dissimilar ways. The initial step is feature extraction by local and global filters or feature descriptors.

The next approach is where the feature extraction is completed with pre-trained CNN networks. In all of the above methods, the categorization of the features is completed with SVM algorithms. To use the pre-trained statistics several times, the current data must be downsampled. In this method, information may be missed out and that's why the first way proposes the use of local and global filters. The pre-trained networks are tested for accuracy using the Image Net dataset in the following proposal. The best way to detect tuberculosis from an upper-body X-ray is to perform a comparison or transaction between these methods. Separation of images is the technique of partitioning it for enhanced study or simplifying the figure in a PC visualization.

Semantic segmentation is when all pixels of the picture are classified. In semantic segmentation, a complicated system comparable to a regular CNN is used; except that, the fully linked layers that are generally generated toward the system's conclusion are lacking. In this MRI image of the brain, FCN is used to segment lesions. FCNs are quick to divide and robust in learning the form of the object from the 3-dimensional representation. Yet, it has two main disadvantages. First, the FCN fails to spot the borders of the injury. To solve this problem, segmentation is completed through an area-wise sample so that the forecast is dependent on the local samples. However, an FCN is likely to misclassify items that are of excessive sizes; therefore, the next difficulty is that FCN is not aware of organizing information with uneven class ratios. As a result, the approaches for solving both problems are as follows: first, a sample of the original photographs is finished in 3-dimensional patches, and the patches are guided such that the class ratio is not extreme. The identification of further diseases such as prostate cancer is achievable through CNNs.

Define a CAD

The CAD is to identify Prostate cancer. Initially, images are gathered from a DWI volume that is an MRI result image dataset [10]. Then, the next step is prostate segmentation or description. This segmentation procedure depends on three major ways. They are appearance, prior shape, and spatial relationship, which gives more efficiency. The third step is feature extraction; different features are recognized from the images to differentiate them into malignant or benign.

Machine Learning

ML provides strategies for solving analytic and statistical disorders in several diagnostic disciplines, approaches, and instruments. The definitions of medical parameters and their diagnostic variations are used for researching ML. Also, ML is used to evaluate the data, such as the discovery of regularities in the data through treating insufficient data, the realization of constant data in an Intensive Care Unit, as well as intellectual alert resulting in reliable and accurate control. It is claimed that the effective introduction of the ML application scan allows computerized healthcare programmers to support and strengthen the efforts of medical experts and ultimately develop the quality and excellence of medical care. Some of the essential medical ML uses are as follows [11].

A very important aspect of an intellectual method is the medical diagnostic study. This framework provides frameworks for inventing theories from medical reports for expert structures and model-related schemes. Unfortunately, specialists cannot classify, in different situations, which evidence they use to solve their problems. The integration of information management and learning skills to specialist programs is achieved utilizing symbolic learning approaches that offer an example for a sequence of scientific cases. Methods of ML that can give systematic clarification to certain science features that only differentiate scientific conditions enable learning of intellectual structures to be accomplished. Facts should also be represented clearly as a strategy or as a decision-making tree. KARDIO, which was designed to explain ECGs, is a common example of this sort of method. This method will be broad in situations where the study and interpretation of medical evidence were not previously practiced. Moreover, these models may be presented in an investigation scenario as an early hypothesis that can be worked out in advance.

Patient statistics find it challenging to learn because databases are marked by incompleteness, error, sparsity, and inaccuracy. ML creates methods to manage the singularity of medical datasets [12]. Sub-symbolic learning technology, in particular, the neural networks, can accommodate these datasets and is used to align samples and to allow medical decision-making progress. Biomedical signal processing is another region of application. Although our knowledge of the biological system is not total, the physiological signals do not explicitly indicate essential elements and details. Furthermore, there is no consistent impact on the various subsystems. Important incoherence, either by impulsive internal processes or external stimulation, characterizes biological signals. Relationships between the multiple criteria can be too complex for the conservative proposals to overcome. ML models use these data sets and can be more conveniently formed to display the nonlinear interactions between these data as well as to eliminate parameters and functionality that can enhance the medical problem. The computerized study of patient representation is one of the most significant fields in which medical analysis is assisted. The extension of these structures is often calculated to mimic the physician's capacity to distinguish malignant regions in imagery behavior. The goal is to enhance the capacity of the specialist to recognize malignant regions by reducing their involvement requirements and preserving their analytical precision.

Furthermore, a wider field, examining live tissue in vivo, perhaps remotely, may be examined, and therefore poor biopsies may be minimized, for example, patient pain, diagnostic holdup, and insufficient tissue samples. Early detection approaches need to be more successful, such as those provided by computer-assisted medical diagnostic systems. ML is considerably high in the field because it helps us to collect, modify, and update data in intelligent medical image analysis systems using computational methods and learning mechanisms that enable us to induce examples or statistics. ML techniques can be helpful, particularly in simple persistent imagery events involving new values of imagery. Due to a lack of prior understanding and/or medical knowledge in the healthcare system, where algorithmic solutions are not available, known model flaws are present, or the evidence concerning the field of application is poorly established, such as fluorescence imaging and laser scanning, where algorithmic solutions are not available, known model flaws are present, or the evidence concerning the field of application is poorly established; the healthcare system is highly reliant on computer technologies. The usage of ML methods may provide realistic support to help surgeons in many situations, remove human wear and tiredness concerns, easily detect abnormalities, and promote real-time detection.

Applications of ML in Treatment

- **Image interpretation** – As described above, medical photographs are usually used in laboratory practice and professional physicians and radiologists examine and evaluate these images. They offer textual radiology detail for each portion of the body that was inspected in the studies to explain the effects of the photographs being analyzed. However, in many situations, it is quite difficult to compose certain material. For a specialist radiologist, a tough and time-consuming approach for generating high-quality records may be annoying for those patients who come every day. Therefore, the complexity in the NLP and ML approaches was sought by many researchers. For medical radiology studies, a treatment-based approach is usually recommended. For routine labeling and monitoring of medical photographs, a multi-task ML-based system is designed. Architecture with the combination of CNN and RNN has grown in a related analysis. For the automated production of data in an initial multi-model using a CNN and LSTM network.
- **ML in real-time health-monitoring** – Timely follow-up is important and is a central element in the healing practice. Constant tracking of health using wearable gadgets, IoT sensors, and smartphones is growing people's knowledge. Health information is gathered periodically via the wearable tracker and the mobile and then sent for review via ML/DL system to the cloud for continuous health-monitoring. The findings are then returned to the system for necessary intervention. The structure is built using PPG signals to integrate the smartphone and cloud heart rate tracking. A study of the multiple methods of ML for the detection of human action for remote control of wearable patients is also conducted. The dissemination of cloud fitness data for potential research poses many threats to privacy and protection.

Applications of ML in Medical Workflows

- **Disease prediction and diagnosis** – One of the interesting uses of ML approaches is in the timely prediction and identification of diseases from medical history. There will be an analysis of various ML methods to classify rare diseases. There is a key justification to use ML-based cancer detection and prediction techniques.

- **ML in computer-aided detection or diagnosis** – The CADe or CADx programs are typically configured to auto-analyze medical photos to help the medical practitioner. The framework is focused on diversified functions such as ML/DL, traditional device monitors, and image processing methods. However, any role in the medical picture or signal test computerized by the ML/DL feature models can be considered as CADe or CADx systems.

- **Medical reinforcement learning** – The key objective of enhancement learning is to examine a policy challenge for making specific decisions to use cumulative returns in a dubious setting. RL methods for effective analysis and recovery of individuals with diverse features are used in clinical medicine. The evaluation of the efficiency of numerous RL techniques for a septic cure in ICU with real-world health data is achievable. Sepsis is a serious organ failure that is a leading cause of death owing to exclusive and suboptimal care. The data collection comprises of the behavioral well-being trajectory of a patient which delivers life or death care at all stages by a counselor. The research shows that easy and tabular learning will review useful sepsis-care policies and their analysis is as strong as the nuanced method of continuing state-space therapy.

- **ML for medical time-series data** – The creation of medical time series data is the primary duty of medical workflows. Health time series concept features include the forecasting of medical procedures in CNN and LSTM intensive care units. In a recent report, treatment models for ICU prediction control were used by combining multi-variate and sequence calculation data into medical data. The challenge of unintended breathing decomposition using ML techniques is explored in a simultaneous analysis.

- **Medical natural language processing** – Medical evidence is a widely employed method for communicating the status of patients. The usage of medical records is important since it provides vital information repeatedly. To achieve improved medical efficiency and analysis, the implementation of the Medical NLP method would be incorporated into the next medical program for gathering associated data from unstructured medical notes. For example, the usage of acronyms, language gaps, inadequate layout, uncertainty on efficiency, Medical NLP indicate exclusive difficulties. A study of the medical NLP approaches would also provide criteria and possibilities for contact other than English. A method is known as CLAMP, which includes NLP strategies for medical data processing of different statuses.

- **Medical speech and audio processing** – Doctors would prepare several patient data, approval summaries, and radiology in their medical setting. Dr. Simon Wallace claims clinicians use patient documents 50 percent of their time because they are highly depressed because of medical work demand, managerial employment, and not free time. They usually invest as much time organizing medical records as they do communicate personally with patients. To solve such challenges, medical voice and audio processing offer modern means such as communication interfaces that provide fewer resources, automated patient debate recording, and medical evidence production.

Secure, Private, and Robust ML for Healthcare Challenges

The protection and robustness of ML/DL in health conditions and other associated challenges [12] are presented in this section. Also, three key phases of the progression of the ML model along with numerous possible weakness sources are defined which pose major challenges in every step of the ML pipeline.

Vulnerabilities in data collection – The preparation of ML/DL models for medical assessment support needs a group of a large quantity of data which is normally time-consuming and needs major human effort. Even though in practice, clinical data are mainly collected to make sure the efficiency of the disease. Still, there are so many causes for vulnerabilities that can influence the proper utility of the fundamental ML/DL structures. The composed statistics generally include a lot of artifacts that arise because of two instrumental and environmental instabilities. This modality is extremely sensitive to movements, and even a small movement of the subject's head or respiration may lead to unwanted artifacts in the secondary image, thereby raising the risk of misdiagnosis. A healthcare ecosystem is very interdisciplinary and contains technical and non-technical human resources and a lack of skilled workers that can expand and sustain ML/DL systems. As for the well-organized function of data-driven healthcare, employees with strong theoretical and computational knowledge are needed, for instance, engineers and data scientists. On the other hand, the medical usability of ML/DL foundation systems is essential. Taking into consideration this feature, hospitals tend to depend only on physician-researchers who do not have computational knowledge to expand such systems.

Vulnerabilities due to data annotation – Most of the functions of ML/DL in healthcare systems are mainly supervised ML jobs that need plenty of labeled information. The method of assigning labels to all data models is called data annotation. Preferably, this assignment will be executed by qualified doctors to plan domain-enriched datasets that are essential for the growth of ML/DL models in healthcare systems. This document has exposed the preparation of ML/DL models with no sound grip of the field could be unsuccessful. Doctors, such as expert radiologists, have a limited number of professionals and are difficult to hire for secondary jobs such as data annotation. Thus, apprentice staff with slight domain knowledge are generally employed during data labeling, which generally leads to several troubles, for instance, coarse-grained labels, class inequality, label outflow, and disarrangements. Several exact data annotation-based vulnerabilities are being discussed. The first is Ambiguous Ground Truth in clinical datasets; the truth is often ambiguous and even specialist doctors oppose well-defined problem-solving tasks. This trouble becomes more difficult with the existence of malicious persons who want to disturb data, making the analysis tricky and causing troubles in finding its influence on an individual specialist assessment.

- **Small and unbalanced databases** – The number of datasets included in the production of ML/DL systems is insufficient at the core stage. The deficit in large-scale data sets, because health facts are normally smaller, constitutes a downside to the well-organized functions of DL access. The bulk of life-threatening health problems in most individuals are uncommon and identified once. Consequently, particularly ML/DL algorithms cannot be trained and advanced professionally for such a life-fearing healthcare task.
- **Class disparity and prejudice** – Class imbalance is so far an additional issue in the supervised ML/DL related to data that is of contradictory sampling allocation between groups. If a class imbalanced dataset were used to lead the method, the effects of the model would replicate in terms of community bias. Healthcare sector forecasts can have significant complications and therefore need to be mitigated. Various approaches to solve class inequity issues were projected in the report.
- **Scarcity** – Data scarcity is nothing more than evidence that has been lost due to numerous logics that exist in the real world. The performance of the ML/DL method is impaired considerably by the lack of data and remarks.

Model training vulnerabilities – Model training vulnerabilities involve unsuitable, imperfect training, infringement of privacy, corruption of processes, and piracy. Improper or imperfect conditional preparation where the ML/DL method has improper credentials. Furthermore, ML/DL is specifically defined in danger of numerous protection and privacy risks, such as adverse attacks, device attacks, and attacks on data corruption. The strain of ML/DL procedures maintains its technical use for security-critical activities and important applications in addition to existence. The assurance of the protection and efficiency of the ML/DL methods for such critical applications is therefore of utmost importance.

Implementation vulnerabilities – ML/DL use in the medical community essentially requires a human-centered view. In the implementation stage, it is therefore important to maintain the strength of the framework in the context of justice and transparency. The next weakness can be removed during the ML/DL implementation process.

- **Distribution changes** – In critical healthcare environments distribution shifts are immensely predicted, for example, dissimilar imaging centers, and later DL systems eligible for pictures of one area are used on multiple field images. The fundamental DL device is significantly degraded in these conditions. In comparison, predictive ML programs are built from previous patient data and usually experience the utility of the ML provision in new patients. Such a disparity may also be demoralized for adversarial development.
- **Incomplete data** – Facts composed for the patient's interest can contain missed remarks or variables in realistic environments. The usage of the missing ML/DL method values on the other hand contributes to two established issues, namely false positives, and false negatives. In actual healthcare environments, both issues would have significant implications. Therefore, the clinical details should be complete and compressed to allow correct outcome forecasts.

Measuring process vulnerability – Testing phase vulnerability affects the analysis of the initial ML/DL system result:

- **False-positive and false-negative outcomes, misinterpretation** – Improper systems training or partly completed data fed in the deduction listed in the preceding segment is the cause for false positive and false negative outcomes, finally, not just emphasizing the careful position of analytical procedures, but also spinning a crank over the exact nature of ML-empowered healthcare.

The protection of ML – A general concept here provides a general idea of ML safety from a healthcare viewpoint, and with the use of the ML system, in Figure 8.7 [13], various related safety problems arise.

Adversarial machine learning – Present attempts to find flaws in the planning and recommendations of ML/DL approaches are affected by adverse assaults. The principal protection risks to ML/DL approaches are adverse assaults. In opponent assaults, an opponent's key function is to generate opponent models by integrating minute techniques into the main input models to prevent the reliability of the ML/DL methods. Two main enemy assaults, listed below, are widely mentioned.

- **Poisoning attacks:** Adverse attacks that disrupt the preparation of the machine. In other terms, it is called poisoning attacks to manipulate training information to have an incorrect understanding of the awareness of ML/DL.
- **Evasion attacks:** Adverse assaults on the final stage of the techniques are regarded as attacks of escape. An adversary affects test statistics to jeopardize the ML/DL method's reliability in risky inputs. In the health sector, poisoning

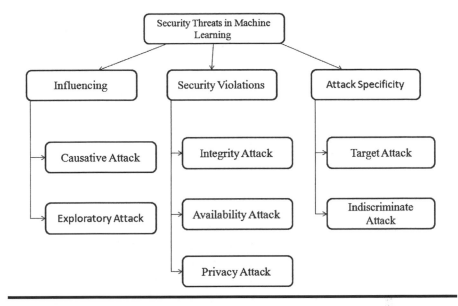

Figure 8.7 Security over healthcare.

attacks are especially appropriate and, in a few situations, it is challenging or sometimes unlikely to distort the evidence explicitly. It may be comparatively quick to accumulate new models; nevertheless, these effects slow ML/DL processes. The discovery of harmful attacks is also hazardous in healthcare environments with the safe usage of ML/DL. For example, besides popular ML methods implemented for hypothyroid research, logical poisoning attacks. The enemy's primary purpose was to avoid analyses of hypothyroid. Also, in healthcare settings, a few analysts reported the possibility of ML/DL assaults.

In comparison, the concept of adversarial patients for health systems is addressed to the adverse trends generated to escape ML/DL approaches. The cautionary can refer to unintended adversarial patients, who can be aimed at serious moral problems instead of deliberate adversarial models. A scientific assessment is made of the risk of massively different healing outcomes for patients with similar analytical parameters and the identification of the hostile patient subgroup. In this analysis, three medical techniques, including fundoscopy, copy of the dermal, and the upper-body X-ray, were targeted in the white box adversarial. In addition to numerous potential motivations to target opponents in medical exams that could be enhanced by the growing usage of ML methods in future strategies, particularly with the existence of computer-aided research and evaluation-support systems.

ML for Healthcare Challenges

This segment discusses the different problems that hinder the applicability of ML/DL systems in practical healthcare functions [14].

- **Safety challenges** – A brilliant accomplishment in a controlled laboratory environment isn't the same as safety assistance. The safety of ML/DL procedures assures proper care of patients in the ML/DL process. The protection during the ML/DL lifecycle should be stable. The schedule of the general job of the doctor is normal and the patients have familiar states of health. Their duty is to identify rare, vulnerable, and mysterious disorders of health, which arise every million years. ML/DL deployment to ensure the protection of current AI networks in unforeseen strata, outliers, boundaries, and vulnerable situations.

- **Privacy challenges** – The security of patient records in the ML/DL networks for creating predictions is the key problem of data-driven healthcare. Patients imagine they obey critical protection protocols through their health regulators, to preserve their natural rights to privacy, such as age, sex, date of birth, and health information. Potential privacy risks may be in two types: exposing sensitive details and cruel usage of data. Privacy relies on the precise context and nature of the facts, the climate, and the profiles of consumers. Improved privacy abuses using acceptable methods are also risky since such violations will damage the consumer directly. To deter infringement of privacy, such as re-identification of people, privacy should be investigated. Also, it is important to consider privacy issues at all levels of data collection and to ensure that data are re-allocated between various units within a hospital in a protected circumstance.

- **Ethical challenges** – It is important to ensure moral usage of the evidence of user-centered functions of the ML method such as healthcare. Before gathering facts on the structuring of ML structures, specific measures need to be taken to identify aim patients and their sociological phases. Also, it is the main consideration to agree that the gathering of evidence will affect the well-being and self-esteem of a patient. If moral problems are not reported, it is difficult to find findings in the functions of ML methods in operation. Also, it is important to provide a good visual view of the AI mechanism in unpredictable and complicated circumstances to guarantee the equal and moral function of robotic systems.

- **Causality is challenging** – Causality is the most significant element in health treatment since most critical health conditions involve basic thinking. Traditional learning algorithms cannot manipulate such problems and must analyze the evidence from causal contacts to respond to them. Awareness, which is mostly focused on inspection facts, is often quite difficult in healthcare because it needs the creation of causal models to address basic questions. DL structures need fundamental assumptions, and these models operate basically without a fundamental connection by leveraging samples and correlations. In certain conditions, this cannot be treated as an illness, because prediction involves no basic relationship. In healthcare, the lack of a simple partnership will pose issues with the outcomes of DL models. Decision-making will then be obligatory through interaction via causal analysis. It is necessary to estimate the causal impact of a few data on the goal production to maintain fair predictions [15].

- **Regulatory and policy challenges** – The complete potential of ML/DL networks to cope with legislative and policy problems in typical health conditions may be understood. Both the ML/DL therapeutic approach and its introduction into standard medical settings require this legislative guidance. In the usual medical setting, the integration of AI-enabled ML/DL systems should also be following Government and regulatory guides and regulations. The available regulations are inadequate for certifying ever-changing mechanisms, such as approved ML/DL systems since another big problem with the usage of medical ML/DL algorithms is how those systems can be run and controlled because these systems implement new user data learning. Furthermore, it is necessary to maintain a clear, effective, and stable protocol for the medical examination of the ML/DL mechanism in medical conditions, which does not affect the patient in any way. In hospitals, data scientists and AI engineers can regularly review the methods of AI to ensure its protection, pertinence, and functionality.

- **Availability of good quality data** – Because, in comparison to heterogeneous collections of vast multi-systems, the amount of information accessible to the examined population is very limited and competent; the supply of high-quality evidence is a serious health concern. Different small and big health organizations generate medical records daily. The growth of high-quality facts, analogous to medical conditions, is incredibly difficult and needs to be coordinated and secured. The accessibility of high-quality facts will support the potential function of epidemic detection and preparing decision-making effectively. The data compiled suffer from various problems including subjectivity, redundancy, and discrimination. As ML/DL models will deduce from the secret variables of the data they are eligible for. Therefore, the effects of the algorithm would be imitated by the data produced by the undesirable previous experience in hospitals. Many individuals lacking healthcare are refused emergency facilities, for example, and if AI knows about this, it can do so likewise. By generating inaccurate results for various sub-populations, the machine could explain racial prejudice, and it can also create its issues with modeling.

- **Lack of data standardization and exchange** – The ML/DL framework will help to develop a deep understanding of simple sanitary duties through the usage of other consumer details. Radiology, for example, does not cover imaging techniques. For radiologists, another EMR fact is necessary if an imaging analysis is to achieve an exact conclusion. This includes convergence and sharing of data across all medical methods. Noting that the following criteria of IT health services, typically affecting the excellence and efficacy of healthcare facts, have been commonly ignored, amid studies into general concepts of data sharing on public health. There are multiple health procedure protocols such as imaging trials that maintain the medical impact of the evidence. Present IT programs for healthcare ignore primarily values and physicians are not adopting well-known guidance. Data incorporation and the sharing of efforts through diverse fields and cultures then struggle. Data addition to the health records of multiple users is essential to the treatment of patients. The insufficiency of enthusiasm in the implementation of data-trading concepts in the larger health sector delays the efficacy of ML/DL as multi-modal data are crucial to ensure the deep comprehension of algorithms and to enhance the doctors' success in making clinical decisions utilizing data-driven insights.

- **Distribution shifts** – Another big obstacle and probably the most daunting issue to tackle is the complexity of data sharing. Distributions of evidence may be omitted for different purposes of medical practice and teaching and research. Due to this challenge, ML/DL programs built utilizing public datasets in actual health conditions do not produce expected results. In a clinical area, clinical imagination, where dissimilar protocols and limitations can influence images of drastically different distributions is commonplace distribution shifts [15]. ML systems are eligible mainly by the empirical risk minimization theory which provides good limits for their learning and guarantees if their declarations are met. For example, one of the key and powerful claims is that the preparation and inquiry data sets come from a parallel sector. However, this declaration is not sufficient, and systems educated under such a declaration should not generalize additional domains. Medical applications need a stable and secure function of ML/DL devices in a sensitive setting.

- **Updating hospital infrastructure is difficult** – Healthcare IT structures are largely proprietary and run in silos, contributing to cost and time-consumption reconsideration, adaptation, and modernization of software. In 2019, major hospitals using the global disease scheme classification, despite the details which had already been published in an updated version in 1990, were started on paper. With the application of recent tools, including ML/DL systems, the difficulty of improving hospital information technology will increase greatly.

Conclusions

In clinical applications, the use of ML/DL models will transform traditional health benefits. In every event, a special protection and welfare task should be targeted to ensure the safe and vigorous use of such models in clinical environments. In this segment, the concept of the ML pipeline in medical treatment and the identification of distinctive sources of weaknesses is provided as an overview of such challenges. Discussed practicable steps to deliver healthy and stable ML for applications like healthcare which are essential for protection. Finally, distinguishing transparent inquiries of problems needing scrutiny were seen.

References

[1] Alleghany, Mohamed, Thar Baker, Dhiya Al-Jumeily, Abir Hussain, Jamila Mustafina, and Ahmed J. Aljaaf. "Prospects of the machine and deep learning in analysis of vital signs for the improvement of healthcare services." In *Nature-Inspired Computation in Data Mining and Machine Learning*, pp. 113–136. Springer, Cham, 2020.

[2] Mittal, Shubham, and Yasha Hasija. "Applications of Deep Learning in Healthcare and Biomedicine." In *Deep Learning Techniques for Biomedical and Health Informatics*, pp. 57–77. Springer, Cham, 2020.

[3] Priyadarshini, Rojalina, Rabindra K. Barik, Chhabi Panigrahi, Harishchandra Dubey, and Brojo Kishore Mishra. "An investigation into the efficacy of deep learning tools for big data analysis in health care." In *Deep Learning and Neural Networks: Concepts, Methodologies, Tools, and Applications*, pp. 654–666. IGI Global, 2020.

[4] Liu, Minjie, Mingming Zhou, Tao Zhang, and Naixue Xiong. "Semi-supervised learning quantization algorithm with deep features for motor imagery EEG Recognition in smart healthcare application." *Applied Soft Computing* 89 (2020): 106071.

[5] Srivastava, Meenakshi. "A Surrogate data-based approach for validating deep learning model used in healthcare." In *Applications of Deep Learning and Big IoT on Personalized Healthcare Services*, pp. 132–146. IGI Global, 2020.

[6] Zerka, Fadila, Samir Barakat, Sean Walsh, Marta Bogowicz, Ralph T.H. Leijenaar, Arthur Jochems, Benjamin Miraglio, David Townend, and Philippe Lambin. "Systematic review of privacy-preserving distributed machine learning from federated databases in health care." *JCO Clinical Cancer Informatics* 4 (2020): 184–200.

[7] Tuli, Shreshth, Nipam Basumatary, Sukhpal Singh Gill, Mohsen Kahani, Rajesh Chand Arya, Gurpreet Singh Wander, and Rajkumar Buyya. "Healthfog: An ensemble deep learning based smart healthcare system for automatic diagnosis of heart diseases in integrated IoT and fog computing environments." *Future Generation Computer Systems* 104 (2020): 187–200.

[8] Sujitha, R., and V. Seenivasagam. "Classification of lung cancer stages with machine learning over big data healthcare framework."

[9] Ahmed, Zeeshan, Khalid Mohamed, Saman Zeeshan, and Xin Qi Dong. "Artificial intelligence with multi-functional machine learning platform development for better healthcare and precision medicine." *Database* 2020 (2020): 1–35.

[10] Teng, Fei, Zheng Ma, Jie Chen, Ming Xiao, and Lufei Huang. "Automatic medical code assignment via deep learning approach for intelligent healthcare." *IEEE Journal of Biomedical and Health Informatics* 24, no. (9) (2020): 2506–2515.

[11] Qayyum, Adnan, Junaid Qadir, Muhammad Bilal, and Ala Al-Fuqaha. "Secure and robust machine learning for healthcare: A survey." *arXiv preprint arXiv:2001.08103* (2020).

[12] Durga, S., Rishabh Nag, and Esther Daniel. "Survey on machine learning and deep learning algorithms used in internet of things (IoT) healthcare." In *2019 3rd International Conference on Computing Methodologies and Communication (ICCMC)*, pp. 1018–1022. IEEE, 2019.

[13] Ngiam, Kee Yuan, and Wei Khor. "Big data and machine learning algorithms for health-care delivery." *The Lancet Oncology* 20, no. 5 (2019): e262–e273.

[14] Alloghani, Mohamed, Thar Baker, Dhiya Al-Jumeily, Abir Hussain, Jamila Mustafina, and Ahmed J. Aljaaf. "Prospects of machine and deep learning in analysis of vital signs for the improvement of healthcare services." In *Nature-Inspired Computation in Data Mining and Machine Learning*, pp. 113–136. Springer, Cham, 2020.

[15] Yu, Marco, Yih-Chung Tham, Tyler H. Rim, Daniel S.W. Ting, Tien Y. Wong, and Ching-Yu Cheng. "Reporting on deep learning algorithms in health care." *The Lancet Digital Health* 1, no. 7 (2019): e328–e329.

Chapter 9

A Review of Neuromorphic Computing: A Promising Approach for the IoT-Based Smart Manufacturing

R. Joshua Arul Kumar
Rane Polytechnic Technical Campus, Trichy, India

S. Titus
K. Ramakrishnan College of Engineering, Trichy, India

B. Janet
National Institute of Technology, Trichy, India

Contents

DOI: 10.1201/9781003119784-9

Introduction

In recent times, the impact of Covid-19 has bought in greater uncertainty in terms of the functioning of the manufacturing industry. Hence, a paradigm shift towards smart manufacturing, involving more computer-based system usage and adaptation to a virtual environment is the need of the hour for better survival. The Internet of Things (IoT) acts as a bridge in bringing together the manufacturing industry and computation systems for the benefit of both. The necessity of smart deep learning algorithms for market analysis and course correction adds value and provides ways of making manufacturing systems smarter and manless factories feasible due to the predictive maintenance provided by the artificial intelligence systems. Hence, the combination of computational intelligence with automation based on the IoT is the best possible solution to revive the manufacturing sector in this time of bio-warfare across the globe. The development of better deep learning systems was a real challenge. Even though brain-inspired computing was developing with the support of neural networks for more than six decades, recent development in the past decade has driven the neuromorphic system as the most promising solution for the development of intelligent systems to help with data-driven decision-making. In this chapter, we will have a quick overview of the neuromorphic systems and the developments that happened in the last decade, which puts into context intelligent IoT systems in a wider perspective.

The Paradigm Shift in Computing Technology

Computing technology is explosively evolving in different dimensions due to the technological advancements and saturation that are encountered by the existing systems. There is a change in the use of computing devices, for example, from computers to handheld mobiles to wearables. Low power consumption has become the key for design, as the applications moved from computers to sensors in recent years. This led to the search for different alternatives in place of the Von Neumann architecture. Moore's law, the primary driver of integrated circuit technology has also taken a backseat in recent years [28]. The primary reason is the alterations in the way computing is looked over in terms of its performance. Moore's law addresses the increase in integration density by device size reduction, increasing chip area and device and circuit cleverness [105], all of which are dependent on technology. Nowadays, functionality has priority overclock speed or device feature size, with more focus on performance improvement rather than technology. There was a sudden paradigm shift from the GHz war between manufacturers since 2004, as Dennard's scaling rules became unsustainable. It also had a paradigm shift from looking at computations with Floating-Point Operations Per Second (FLOPS) as a benchmark to FLOPS per watt emphasising energy efficiency. The merging of logic and memory is attributed as a solution, to bring the processing of information closer to where it is stored, thereby addressing the Von Neumann's bottleneck as well as power efficiency.

Cellular Automata (CA) with its high degree of fine-grained parallelism evolved as a new model. It is extremely regular, brain-inspired computing and tends to rely more on random connectivity. CAs are Delay-Insensitive (DI) and their functionality is determined by their transition rules. Cell complexity depends on the number of states a cell can assume and the number of transition rules. However, CA could not emerge as a promising solution owing to the following challenges: (i) Low functional density makes it necessary to store transition rules in each cell leading to increased overhead, (ii) it is hard to find materials in nature that implement CA and (iii) there is a requirement of energy to be fed in order to sustain computation.

As a result, researchers started shifting their attention to brain-inspired computing. Neurons form a complex network in the brain that comes with remarkable abilities. If we extrapolate Moore's law, the number of neurons in the human brain (100 billion) will be equivalent to the number of transistors in a chip only by 2026 [56], although this has nothing in comparison to the performance of the human brain.

There exists a vast asymmetry between the working pattern of traditional computers and the human brain. Traditional computers can play with numbers at an unprecedented rate, is reliable, not fatigued and unbiased whereas the human brain on the other side can think "out of the box", detect patterns at a faster rate, and is not necessary to be programmed often, as it is good at learning [8]. All these can be done with a power of less than 20 watts. Creativity and imagination cannot be accomplished with traditional computers. These limitations faced by traditional computing led to the development of neuromorphic computing. They can solve challenging machine learning problems and work on a small footprint[1] to perform complex calculations faster with greater power efficiency. They use dynamic event-driven processing, exponentially memorize and can adapt fast with strong ability. They outplay the traditional computers in terms of calculability, complexity and regularisation theory [104].

The evolution of customisable hardware like Field Programmable Gate Arrays (FPGAs) accelerated the work on evolving a variety of brain-inspired network topologies, algorithms and models for neuromorphic computing. There has been a collective contribution by researchers from different fields like neuroscience, who studied the computational sense of the brain, electrical and electronics engineers, who transformed the studies to electrical models, the material scientists, who were instrumental in fabricating and characterising new materials and computer engineers, who developed network models, algorithms and support software. All these helped in the development of neuromorphic computing to a greater extent, particularly in the last decade. A mindmap created using an open-source Wisemap software [103] gives a visual organisation of the various aspects of neuromorphic computing along with the references to act as a quick guide. Figure 9.1 presents an overview of neuromorphic computing.

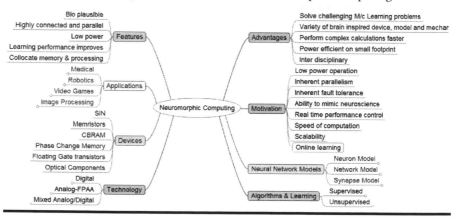

Figure 9.1 Overview of neuromorphic computing.

Motivation

Brain-inspired computing is as old as computer science itself. The replication of biological neural systems in computers has led to key discoveries in the field of artificial intelligence, machine learning and specifically Deep Learning. There has been tremendous interest shown in neuromorphic computing especially in the last decade as we can find more than 1000 research papers reported since the year 2015, compared to an equal amount in the three decades before [116]. The key motivators for neuromorphic systems are low power operation [81], inherent parallelism [113], inherent fault tolerance [7], ability to mimic neuroscience by creating devices with small footprints, real-time performance control [53], speed of computation [27], scalability and online learning [116], as seen in Figure 9.1.

Choice of Models

There seem to be many options in the choice of models. In some cases, a particular application area may drive the choice. For example, a pattern-classification problem may suggest a more bio-plausible[2] model whereas a pattern identification task may require a computationally driven model, owing to its high accuracy requirement. In other cases, the characteristics of a particular device or material may dominate the choice. There seems to be a variety of models that range from those predominantly bio-inspired,[3] to that of computation-driven. However, a neural network model, in general, defines the choice of components to make up the network, their operations and the interactions between them.

The various neural network models can be grouped under three categories: neuron models, synapse models and network models as shown in Figure 9.2.

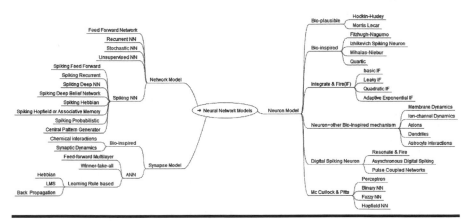

Figure 9.2   Neural network models.

Neuron Models

The behaviour of a biological neuron is to accumulate charges received from various synapses attached to it through a change in voltage potential across the neuron's cell membrane. Hence, these models have some concepts of charge accumulation and firing to affect other neurons. They can further be classified into the following.

Bio-Plausible Model

Here, the behaviour of the model is built as seen in a biological neural system.

- Hodgkin–Huxley model [3] which uses a 4D non-linear differential equation, tries to mimic the bio-neural system. Here, the implementation is carried out by using electric circuits made of resistors and capacitors, and model electro-chemical information transmission of natural neurons to some extent. This model involves a computational cost of 1200 floating-point computations (FLOPS) per 1 ms simulation.
- Morris–Lecar model [80], on the other hand, uses a simple 2D non-linear differential equation and involves a computational cost of one or several hundred FLOPS.

Biologically Inspired Model

This category mimics the behaviour of the biological neural system but not in the bio-plausible way. Rather, it considers the computational method also.

- Fitzhugh–Nagumo [71] and Hindmarsh–Rose [58] models: These are a simplified version of Hodgkin–Huxley model. They use simple computations and fewer parameters. It is easy to set and train as there are fewer parameters. It is simple to implement in a small footprint.
- Izhikevich spiking neuron model [70]: This model is popular due to its simple computation as well as the ability to reproduce bio-accurate behaviour. They exhibit bursting[4] and spiking[5] behaviour and are a good compromise between biophysical plausibility and computational cost (13 FLOPS).
- Mihalaş–Niebur neuron model [41]: This model also replicates bursting and spiking behaviour. It is defined by a set of linear differential equations and has neuromorphic implementations.
- Quartic model [50]: This model uses two non-linear differential equations and is implementable in the neuromorphic system.

Neuron Model with Additional Bio-inspired Mechanism

A few other models have been developed, which include modelling of neurons with other additional components like dendrites, axons, etc. Such models have added components like membrane dynamics [11], ion-channel dynamics [67], axons [95], dendrites [38] and glial cell or astrocyte interactions [54].

Integrate and Fire

These form the simple category of bio-inspired spiking neuron model. They are less biologically realistic, but produce enough complexity in behaviour. The variety of models include:

- Basic integrate and fire [2]: This model treats biological neurons as point dynamical systems and the spatial structure is neglected here. It maintains the current-charge level of the neurons. The shape of the action potentials is neglected and every spike is considered as a uniform event defined only by the time of its appearance.
- Leaky integrate and fire [123]: This is one of the most popular models in neuromorphic systems. It includes a leaky term to model, which causes the potential of the neuron to decay over time. It has the ability to reproduce neuro-computational properties and is limited to three different firing schemes that require only five FLOPS.
- Quadratic integrate and fire [16]: These are non-linear integrate and fire models and require around 10 FLOPS.
- Adaptive exponential integrate and fire [1]: It shares the features of Leaky integrate and fire and 2D integrate and fire models with excellent spike time predictions.

Digital Spiking Neuron

These models are characterised by cellular automaton theory as opposed to a set of non-linear or linear differential equations. They include resonate and fire [59], rotate and fire [60], asynchronous digital spiking neuron model [92] and pulse-coupled networks [129].

McCullock and Pitts Model

These are the primitive models used in Artificial Neural Networks (ANNs). They are derivatives of McCullock and Pitts neuron. The most basic model is the perceptron model. This model is commonly used in hardware implementations. They have simple thresholding where the weights are modified based on activation functions. The most basic activation functions employed are sigmoid function [73] and hyperbolic tangent function [15]. Later, many hardware-based activation functions like ramp-saturation function [14], linear [73], piecewise linear [57], multi-threshold [136], radial basis function, tangent sigmoid function [112] and periodic activation function [94] were involved. The other models which were developed from percep-tron are binary neural network neurons [34], fuzzy neural network neurons [131] and hopfield neural network neurons [61].

Synapse Models

Synapse models are evolved for neuromorphic systems since synapses are the most abundant elements occupying more chip area. Optimising them is essential for bet-ter hardware implementation. Synapse models are relatively simple and their com-plexity increases with bio-plausibility. However, the compelling reason to build complex synapse models is its plasticity mechanism, which has been found to be related to learning in the biological brain and causes the strength of neurons to change over time. Synapse models can be categorised as follows.

Biologically Inspired Synapse Implementation

In bio-inspired neuromorphic systems, synapse implementations model the chemi-cal interactions of synapses such as ion pumps or neurotransmitter interactions. Conductance-based synapse models [100] implement ion channels also. Spiking neuromorphic systems like Spike-Timing-Dependant Plasticity (STDP) exhibit plasticity and learning mechanisms inspired by potentiation and depression. Similarly, models based on synaptic dynamics focus on the shape of the outgoing spike from synapse or post-synaptic potential.

ANN Synapse Implementation

Non-bio-inspired synapse models are also developed. A few of them are feed-forward multilayer networks [93], winner-take-all [135] and convolutional neural networks [127]. ANN synapse implementations are also based on learning rules like Hebbian learning [83] which by modifying synaptic strengths lead to the reorganisation of connections within a neural network. Other implementations based on learning includes least mean-square (LMS) [120] and back-propagation learning rule [111].

Network Models

Network models primarily focus on the interconnection between different neurons and synapses and their way of interaction. A wide variety of network models are available for neuromorphic systems. The prime factors that govern the design of a network model are a) biological inspiration, b) topology of the network, c) feasibil-ity and applicability of training or learning algorithm and d) type of applications to be used.

Feed-Forward Network Model

The most popular network model in artificial neural networks is the feed-forward network model. The basic feed-forward network is characterised by multilayer perceptrons. A special case where the number of weights after a random assignment is never updated based on learning is extreme learning machines [134]. A few more variants of the feed-forward network model include multilayer perceptrons with delay, probabilistic neural networks which involve Bayesian calculations [6], single-layer feed-forward utilising radial basis functions as activation function [90] and convolutional neural networks [101].

Recurrent Neural Network (RNN) Model

These models allow for cycles in the network, thereby exhibiting dynamic temporal behaviour. The various models developed under RNN are non-spiking RNN [29], reservoir computing model where RNN is used as a reservoir and its output is fed into simple feed-forward network [78], winner-take-all which uses recurrent inhibitory connections [66], Hopfield network [130] and associative-memory-based models [49].

Stochastic Neural Network Models

These models introduce randomness into the processing of a network either in the activation function or weights which offer a better choice for optimisation problems. The best example of this type is the Boltzmann machine which was used in the early 1990s. But, now a modified version known as the restricted Boltzmann machine is used since the training time is significantly reduced and it also forms an integral part of the deep belief network [88].

Unsupervised Learning Models

These models are popular for implementations in neuromorphic systems beyond STDP. Hebbian learning mechanism [114] and self-organising maps [124] fall under this category.

Vision-Inspired Models

These models play a vital role in neuromorphic implementations pertaining to classification and deep learning. Cellular neural networks [96] were the earlier-used visual-system-inspired model whereas, in the early twentieth century, pulse-coupled neural networks [129] gained popularity. Other less-used network models include Cellular Automata [69], Fuzzy neural networks [79] and hierarchical temporal-memory-based models [68].

Spiking Neural Network (SNN) Model

The event-driven nature and improved energy efficiency are the two major factors that popularised the spiking neural network model. In a spiking neural model, the training is usually done in a traditional neural network and the resulting solutions are adapted to fit the spiking neuromorphic implementations. Hence, there are a variety of SNN models derived based on the traditional network implementations. The different SNN models include spiking feed-forward network [106] which is usually applied in low-level sensory systems, spiking recurrent networks [35], with its rich dynamics and high computational capacity used to study associative memory mapping, spiking deep neural networks [51], spiking deep belief networks [121], spiking Hebbian systems [21], spiking hopfield or associative memories [10], spiking winner-take-all network [102], spiking probabilistic network [63], spiking random neural networks [4], central pattern generators [37] which generate oscillatory motions and is therefore used in robotic motion.

Learning Algorithms

Learning algorithms play a vital role in neuromorphic computing, which is absent in traditional computing systems. The accurate and faster the learning, the faster the speed of the system arriving at the solution. The best learning algorithm takes into consideration the network topology, model and characteristics of the network. Its choice also depends on whether the training or learning is off-chip or on-chip and also whether the algorithm is online unsupervised or offline supervised or both. Most of the learning algorithms are grouped under two categories, supervised and unsupervised, as in Figure 9.3.

Supervised Learning Algorithms

The most primitive supervised algorithm is the back propagation. It can be applied to various network models like feed-forward, RNN, SNN and convolutional neural networks. There are various approaches available for back-propagation-based

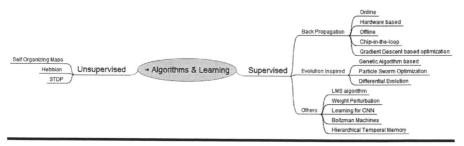

Figure 9.3   Learning algorithms.

learning. They are offline [55], online [77], hardware-based [126], gradient-descent-based optimisation [97] and chip in the loop [133]. The two major challenges faced by back-propagation algorithms are the restriction on the type of neuron model and network topologies and the higher cost involved in implementing with hardware. Hence, various other models were developed. A few of the popular models include the LMS algorithm [128], weight perturbation [89], learning mechanisms developed for convolutional neural networks (CNN) [40], Boltzmann machines [118] and hierarchical temporal memory [68]. Another category of supervised learning includes evolution-inspired algorithms. They don't rely on a particular characteristic or a model and optimise within characteristics of a particular hardware. They can be either on-chip or off-chip, based on the principles of genetic algorithm [98], particle swarm optimisation [20] and differential evolution [24].

Unsupervised Learning Algorithms

The unsupervised learning algorithms are necessary to extract the full potential of neuromorphic systems. They can be implemented on-chip and online. A few early implementations were based on self-organising rules or self-organising maps [91]. On the other hand, Hebbian-type learning rules [109] are very popular as online mechanisms for neuromorphic systems. There are variations in the Hebbian implementations. However, the most popular one is the STDP which is more biologically inspired. STDP also has custom circuits for potentiation and depression [75] in synapses. A lot of work needs to be carried out to develop algorithms for neuromorphic systems as learning is one which differentiates this, uniquely from that of Von-Neumann-based computing. Even algorithms like back propagation and associated memory models were developed with the Von Neumann architecture in mind. Hence, the factors to be considered for the choice of algorithms for neuromorphic implementations are (i) the chosen hardware, (ii) the chosen model, (iii) whether learning should be online or on-chip or both, (iv) arrival speed vs accuracy of results and (v) bio-plausible or bio-inspired learning.

Devices for Neuromorphic Computing

Carver Mead first noted that CMOS transistors operating in current mode below the threshold of the transistor gate voltage have highly similar sigmoidal current–voltage relationships as do neuronal ion channels and consume less power. This led to the development of neuromorphic silicon neurons (SiN) which is analogous to a neuronal function. It offers an intermediate between biological neurons and digital computers with respect to power and space efficiencies. It is also faster than real neurons in terms of computing speed. Further, the computational delay is independent of network size. Already a number of dedicated processes for manufacturing low-power sub-threshold SoC circuits are available.

However, SiN are facing the following challenges: (i) highly susceptible to mismatch in transistor threshold voltage, (ii) variability in intrinsic VLSI process, limiting the scalability, (iii) limitation in input voltage dynamic range in traditional sub-threshold current-mode differential pair that compounds the mismatch errors as size increases, (iv) these models are non-mechanistic, making the adjustment of parameters post fabrication or during computation difficult. Addressing these challenges led to the advent of Tri-Gate process which adds a new dimension to VLSI device scaling. Other approaches use nanotechnologies such as nanowires, memristors, etc. Still, they face problems like non-robustness and less efficiency in terms of yield. Hence, neuromorphic modelling should shift the focus to developing devices taking into account their degree of biological realism and robustness, along with integration density and computation and/or power efficiency [107].

As devices for neuromorphic computing started evolving, the key factors that helped in the development of circuit-level components are memory technology and optical components. The various device-level advancements for neuromorphic computing can be listed as follows.

Memristors

They are also known as "Memory Resistors" and were developed by HP in 2008. Memristors became popular as they exhibit STDP-like behaviour and are energy-efficient [122].

Conductive-Bridging RAM (CBRAM)

These are non-volatile memory technology and uses electrochemical properties to form and dissolve connections. They are used to implement synapses [25] and neurons [72].

Phase Change Memory

These can achieve high density than other devices. They are used to implement synaptic weight storage [26], synapses and neurons [125].

Floating Gate Transistors

These are used (i) as analogue memory cells for synaptic weights or parameter storage [42], (ii) to implement mechanisms like STDP [23], (iii) to implement dendrite model [22] and (iv) to design a neuron [13].

Optical Components

These are used because of inherent parallelism, speed of arriving at results and are less complex in programming. However, the major challenge of using optical components is storage [32] (Figure 9.4).

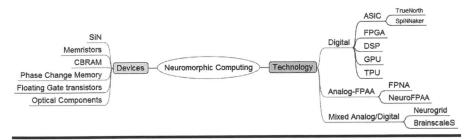

Figure 9.4   Devices and technology of neuromorphic systems.

Hardware Implementation Technologies

A broad spectrum of technologies is available for neuromorphic hardware, namely, CMOS with and without a combination of memristive or special devices, Digital Signal Processors (DSPs), Field Programmable Analogue Arrays (FPAAs), Graphics Processing Units (GPUs), FPGAs, accelerators and others. Hardware taxonomies for the implementation of neuromorphic systems at a higher level can be categorised into analogue, digital or mixed-signal implementations. The broad categories of digital systems include FPGAs which are most frequently used, owing to their ease of programmability [19]. It has more than 300 research papers published. Another category of digital systems, namely, Application-Specific Integrated Circuit (ASIC) designs, involve customised hardware chips like TrueNorth [64], SpiNNaker [76], having approximately 200 research publications. Analogue Systems also have a similar division: one focusing on Programmability ease, known as Field Programmable Analogue Arrays and the other on custom analogue implementations. A part of FPAA s are specially developed for neuromorphic systems like Field Programmable Neural Array [39] and NeuroFPAA [84] having inbuilt programmable components. Mixed analogue/digital systems owing to their natural similarity to biological systems are also very common. They are used to implement processing components of synapses and neurons. Because of the strong reliability to noise environment, usually the storage is made up of digital components in mixed systems. Programmability and learning also are carried out digitally and the rest is made of analogue components. Since the analogue circuitry that operates in sub-threshold mode is highly power-efficient, they play a greater role in mixed system design for the neuromorphic system. Two most popular neuromorphic implementations of mixed systems are Neurogrid [17] and BrainScaleS. While Neurogrid has a closer resemblance to the biological behaviour of neuromorphic systems, BrainScaleS operates at a much higher rate than Neurogrid [43].

FPGA happens to be the best choice of implementation in the case of neuromorphic systems at a small scale, owing to the relationship it has in implementing bio-plausible systems. Table 9.1 depicts the characteristics of FPGA and their relationship with bio-plausibility.

Table 9.1 Match of FPGA Characteristics with Bio-plausible Requirements

FPGA Features	Bio-plausible Requirements
Hardware cost	Inversely proportional to compactness
Scalability	Depends on the number of neurons and synapses
Performance	Simulation and evolution speed
Reliability	Robustness and fault tolerance
Design time, testing time and complexity	Inversely related to simplicity of algorithm

To select appropriate hardware, the following set of selection criteria needs to be analysed. They are cost, popularity and prevalence, Performance (speed), size and scalability, power consumption, dynamic reconfiguration, reconfiguration speed, data communication bandwidth, type of interface, validity checking, observability, reliability and ease of use.

Applications

Even though neuromorphic computing is at its early stage, there seems to be a staggering number of applications where it is employed. The variety of areas can be broadly grouped into data classification, control, anomaly detection, robotics, speech and image processing. The potential motivation is its usage of low power, smaller footprint and faster computation. The most popular applications involve "sensor"-based applications replicating various characteristics of biological visual [5], auditory [36] and touch-based systems [110]. Another class of applications is those which are implanted to interact with biological systems for medical monitoring or treatment [52]. Since spike-based models are bio-plausible, they have been used to develop pacemakers [31], retina implants [46], prosthetics [74] and fall detectors for elderly persons [119].

Robotics, in which neuromorphic systems are used prevalently include locomotion control [99], target following [45], learning a particular behaviour [132], social learning [30], autonomous navigation [9] and oscillatory motions using central pattern generators (CPG). Control tasks use neuromorphic systems because of the real-time performance requirements and the constraints in power, volume of elements and temporal processing component. Video games like Pong [12], PACMAN [44] and Flappy bird [115] also are examples of neuromorphic implementations. Imaging applications on the other hand include image compression [33], filtering [108],

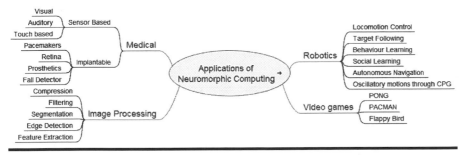

Figure 9.5 Applications of neuromorphic computing.

segmentation [18], edge-detection [82] and feature extraction [117]. Availability of popular data sets like MNIST data set, iris, gene, lymphography [86], mushroom [85], phoneme [48], Pima Indian diabetes [47], thyroid [87], Winconsin breast cancer [65] helps in making learning fast and easy for neuromorphic systems. Simple testing tasks help in evaluating system behaviours at the development phase. Availability of basic function approximation, temporal pattern classification, XOR logic gate implementation motivate researchers to develop such a variety of applications. Non-neural network applications like Graph algorithms also use neuromorphic systems which employ algorithms like maximum cut, minimum graph colouring, travelling salesman, shortest path and optimisation problems. The variety of applications of neuromorphic computing is listed in Figure 9.5.

Conclusion

The neuromorphic system has gained more importance in recent years as a suitable alternative to Von Neumann architecture, as the scalable future of Moore's law has come to a saturation level. Non-silicon approaches to material science face theoretical limits and are only slightly better than CMOS. Neural computing, on the other hand, has become a promising solution since it is based on algorithms and architectural change added with deep learning and the availability of humongous data sets. As it is more data- or application-driven than technology-driven, standardising will be a challenge, as each system is dependent on the type of application. However, taking the advantage of being biologically inspired and plausible, a considerable amount of progress of research is possible, as we have understood only a small portion of the brain activity. Hence, we conclude that neuromorphic systems are set to change the entire way the computing industry is working, to a better way with a paradigm shift from its focus on processing speed towards intelligence and decision-making. It is about to play an important role in the implementation of data science and Big Data analytics [62], where the use of neuromorphic systems is still nascent.

The manufacturing sector today is looking for emerging large-scale service-oriented automation with systems that are typically heterogeneous, dynamic and capable of handling multiple data types. This requires highly intelligent modules to be generated and as discussed, the neuromorphic system provides the best possible solutions with its quick learning capabilities, fast adaptation to the environmental changes and the ease of arriving at optimised results. The uniqueness of neuromorphic systems in a) scalability, b) time-sensitive processing, c) ability to handle a variety of data types and d) detecting and correcting inconsistent data provides enormous opportunity to be used in IoT-based systems for smart manufacturing.

Notes

1 Footprint refers to the runtime memory required while executing a program.
2 Bio-plausible refers to the use of technology to the extent that it adheres to the biological reality.
3 Bio-inspired refers to creating intelligent systems inspired by processes seen in nature, it includes bio-plausible systems also.
4 Discrete signal at non-periodic interval.
5 Refer to the transmission of information from the neuron after its membrane potential reaches a threshold, thus enabling a spike at discrete interval unlike continuous in ANN.

References

[1] Abbas, S Syed Ameer and Muthulakshmi, C. *Neuromorphic implementation of adaptive exponential integrate and fire neuron. Communication and Network Technologies (ICCNT), 2014 International Conference on*, pages 233–237, 2014. IEEE.
[2] Abbott, Larry F, Lapicque's introduction of the integrate-and-fire model neuron (1907). *Brain Research Bulletin*, 50(5):303–304, 1999.
[3] Abbott, Larry F and Kepler, Thomas B. Model neurons: from Hodgkin–Huxley to hopfield. *Statistical Mechanics of Neural Networks*, pages 5–18. Springer, 1990.
[4] Abdelbaki, Hossam and Gelenbe, Erol and El-Khamy, Said E. Analog hardware implementation of the random neural network model. *Neural Networks, 2000. IJCNN 2000, Proceedings of the IEEE-INNS-ENNS International Joint Conference on*, pages 197–201, 2000. IEEE.
[5] Adams, Samantha V, Rast, Alexander D, Patterson, Cameron, Galluppi, Francesco, Brohan, Kevin, Pérez-Carrasco, José-Antonio, Wennekers, Thomas, Furber, Steve, Cangelosi, Angelo. Towards real-world neurorobotics: Integrated neuromorphic visual attention. *International Conference on Neural Information Processing*, pages 563–570, 2014. Springer.
[6] Aibe, Noriyuki and Yasunaga, Moritoshi and Yoshihara, Ikuo and Kim, Jung H. A probabilistic neural network hardware system using a learning-parameter parallel architecture. *Neural Networks, 2002. IJCNN'02. Proceedings of the 2002 International Joint Conference on*, pages 2270–2275, 2002. IEEE.

[7] Akers, Lex, Walker, Mark, Ferry, David, Grondin, Robert. *A limited-interconnect, highly layered synthetic neural architecture. VLSI for Artificial Intelligence*, pages 218–226. Springer, 1989.

[8] Nayef Al-Rodhan. *Neuromorphic Computers: What will they Change?* 2016 (accessed August 21, 2017). http://www.globalpolicyjournal.com/blog/18/02/2016/neuromorphic-computers-what-will-they-change.

[9] Ames, Heather, Versace, Massimiliano, Gorchetchnikov, Anatoli, Chandler, Benjamin, Livitz, Gennady, Léveillé, Jasmin, Mingolla, Ennio, Carter, Dick, Abdalla, Hisham, Snider, Greg. Persuading Computers to Act More Like Brains. *Advances in Neuromorphic Memristor Science and Applications*, pages 37–61. Springer, 2012.

[10] Ang, Chong H, Jin, Craig, Leong, Philip HW, van Schaik, Andre. Spiking neural network-based auto-associative memory using FPGA interconnect delays. *Field-Programmable Technology (FPT), 2011 International Conference on*, pages 1–4, 2011. IEEE.

[11] Arthur, John V, Boahen, Kwabena A. Silicon-neuron design: A dynamical systems approach. *IEEE Transactions on Circuits and Systems I: Regular Papers*, 58(5):1034–1043, 2011.

[12] Arthur, John V, Merolla, Paul A, Akopyan, Filipp, Alvarez, Rodrigo, Cassidy, Andrew, Chandra, Shyamal, Esser, Steven K, Imam, Nabil, Risk, William, Rubin, Daniel BD and others. Building block of a programmable neuromorphic substrate: A digital neurosynaptic core. *Neural Networks (IJCNN), The 2012 International Joint Conference on*, pages 1–8, 2012. IEEE.

[13] Aunet, Snorre, Hartmann, Morten. Real-time reconfigurable linear threshold elements and some applications to neural hardware. *Evolvable Systems: From Biology to Hardware*, 227–239, 2003.

[14] Bañuelos-Saucedo, MA and Castillo-Hernández, J and Quintana-Thierry, S and Damián-Zamacona, R and Valeriano-Assem, J and Cervantes, RE and Fuentes-González, R and Calva-Olmos, G and Pérez-Silva, JL. Implementation of a neuron model using FPGAS. *Journal of Applied Research and Technology*, 1(3):248–255, 2003.

[15] Baptista, Darío, Morgado-Dias, Fernando. Low-resource hardware implementation of the hyperbolic tangent for artificial neural networks. *Neural Computing and Applications*, 23(3–4):601–607, 2013.

[16] Basham, Eric J, Parent, David W. An analog circuit implementation of a quadratic integrate and fire neuron. *Engineering in Medicine and Biology Society, 2009. EMBC 2009. Annual International Conference of the IEEE*, pages 741–744, 2009. IEEE.

[17] Benjamin, Ben Varkey, Gao, Peiran, McQuinn, Emmett, Choudhary, Swadesh, Chandrasekaran, Anand R, Bussat, Jean-Marie, Alvarez-Icaza, Rodrigo, Arthur, John V, Merolla, Paul A and Boahen, Kwabena. Neurogrid: A mixed-analog-digital multichip system for large-scale neural simulations. *Proceedings of the IEEE*, 102(5):699–716, 2014.

[18] Bernhard, Fabrice, Keriven, Renaud. *Spiking neurons on GPUs. Computational Science–ICCS 2006*, 236–243, 2006.

[19] Berzish, Murphy, Eliasmith, Chris, Tripp, Bryan. Real-time FPGA simulation of Surrogate models of large spiking networks. *International Conference on Artificial Neural Networks*, pages 349–356, 2016. Springer.

[20] Bezborah, Anshuman. A hardware architecture for training of artificial neural networks using particle swarm optimization. *Intelligent Systems, Modelling and Simulation (ISMS), 2012 Third International Conference on*, pages 67–70, 2012. IEEE.

[21] Bofill, Adria, Thompson, DP, Murray, Alan F. Citcuits for VLSI implementation of temporally asymmetric Hebbian learning. *Advances in Neural Information Processing Systems*, pages 1091–1098, 2002.

[22] Brink, Stephen, Koziol, Scott, Ramakrishnan, Shubha, Hasler, Paul. A biophysically based dendrite model using programmable floating-gate devices. *Circuits and Systems, 2008. ISCAS 2008. IEEE International Symposium on*, pages 432–435, 2008. IEEE.

[23] Brink, Stephen, Nease, Stephen, Hasler, P. Computing with networks of spiking neurons on a biophysically motivated floating-gate based neuromorphic integrated circuit. *Neural Networks*, 45:39–49, 2013.

[24] Buhry, Laure, Saïghi, Sylvain, Salem, Wajdi Ben, Renaud, Sylvie. Adjusting neuron models in neuromimetic ICs using the Differential Evolution algorithm. *Neural Engineering, 2009. NER'09. 4th International IEEE/EMBS Conference on*, pages 681–684, 2009. IEEE.

[25] Burr, Geoffrey W, Shelby, Robert M, Sebastian, Abu, Kim, Sangbum, Kim, Seyoung, Sidler, Severin, Virwani, Kumar, Ishii, Masatoshi, Narayanan, Pritish, Fumarola, Alessandro and others. Neuromorphic computing using non-volatile memory. *Advances in Physics: X*, 2(1):89–124, 2017.

[26] Burr, Geoffrey W, Shelby, Robert M, Sidler, Severin, Di Nolfo, Carmelo, Jang, Junwoo, Boybat, Irem, Shenoy, Rohit S, Narayanan, Pritish, Virwani, Kumar, Giacometti, Emanuele U and others. Experimental demonstration and tolerancing of a large-scale neural network (165 000 synapses) using phase-change memory as the synaptic weight element. *IEEE Transactions on Electron Devices*, 62(11):3498–3507, 2015.

[27] Burr, James B. Digital neural network implementations. *Neural Networks, Concepts, Applications, and Implementations*, 3:237–285, 1991.

[28] Calimera, Andrea, Macii, Enrico, Poncino, Massimo. The human brain project and neuromorphic computing. *Functional Neurology*, 28(3):191, 2013.

[29] Cauwenberghs, Gert. A learning analog neural network chip with continuous-time recurrent dynamics. *Advances in Neural Information Processing Systems, pages* 858–865, 1994.

[30] Cingolani, Roberto, Metta, Giorgio. Nanotechnology for Humans and Humanoids A vision of the use of nanotechnology in future robotics. *Nanotechnology (IEEE-NANO), 2015 IEEE 15th International Conference on*, pages 600–603, 2015. IEEE.

[31] Coggins, Richard, Jabri, Marwan. Wattle: A trainable gain analogue VLSI neural network. *Advances in Neural Information Processing Systems*, pages 874–881, 1994.

[32] Collins, Dean R, Penz, P Andrew. Considerations for neural network hardware implementations. *Circuits and Systems, 1989., IEEE International Symposium on*, pages 834–836, 1989. IEEE.

[33] Corinto, Fernando, Ascoli, Alon, Kim, Young-Su, Min, Kyeong-Sik. Cellular nonlinear networks with memristor synapses. *Memristor Networks*, pages 267–291. Springer, 2014.

[34] Deshmukh, Amol, Morghade, Jayant, Khera, Akashdeep, Bajaj, Preeti. Binary neural networks–a CMOS design approach. *Knowledge-Based Intelligent Information and Engineering Systems*, pages 153–153, 2005. Springer.

[35] Diehl, Peter U, Zarrella, Guido, Cassidy, Andrew, Pedroni, Bruno U, Neftci, Emre. Conversion of artificial recurrent neural networks to spiking neural networks for low-power neuromorphic hardware. *Rebooting Computing (ICRC), IEEE International Conference on*, pages 1–8, 2016. IEEE.

[36] Dominguez-Morales, Juan Pedro, Jimenez-Fernandez, Angel, Rios-Navarro, Antonio, Cerezuela-Escudero, Elena, Gutierrez-Galan, Daniel, Dominguez-Morales, Manuel J, Jimenez-Moreno, Gabriel. Multilayer spiking neural network for audio samples classification using SpiNNaker. *International Conference on Artificial Neural Networks*, pages 45–53, 2016. Springer.

[37] Donati, Elisa and Corradi, Federico and Stefanini, Cesare and Indiveri, Giacomo. A spiking implementation of the lamprey's Central Pattern Generator in neuromorphic VLSI. *Biomedical Circuits and Systems Conference (BioCAS), 2014 IEEE*, pages 512–515, 2014. IEEE.

[38] Elias, John G, Chu, H-H, Meshreki, Samer M. Silicon implementation of an artificial dendritic tree. *Neural Networks, 1992. IJCNN, International Joint Conference on*, pages 154–159, 1992. IEEE.

[39] Farquhar, Ethan, Gordon, Christal, Hasler, Paul. A field programmable neural array. *Circuits and Systems, 2006. ISCAS 2006. Proceedings. 2006 IEEE International Symposium on*, pages 4–pp, 2006. IEEE.

[40] Fieres, Johannes, Schemmel, Johannes, Meier, Karlheinz. Training convolutional networks of threshold neurons suited for low-power hardware implementation. *Neural Networks, 2006. IJCNN'06. International Joint Conference on*, pages 21–28, 2006. IEEE.

[41] Folowosele, Fopefolu, Hamilton, Tara Julia, Etienne-Cummings, Ralph. Silicon Modeling of the Mihalaş–Niebur Neuron. *IEEE Transactions on Neural Networks*, 22(12):1915–1927, 2011.

[42] Fujita, Osamu and Amemiya, Yoshihito. A floating-gate analog memory device for neural networks. *IEEE Transactions on Electron Devices*, 40(11):2029–2035, 1993.

[43] Furber, Steve. Large-scale neuromorphic computing systems. *Journal of Neural Engineering*, 13(5):051001, 2016.

[44] Galluppi, Francesco, Davies, Sergio, Furber, Steve, Stewart, Terry and Eliasmith, Chris. *Real time on-chip implementation of dynamical systems with spiking neurons. Neural Networks (IJCNN), The 2012 International Joint Conference on*, pages 1–8, 2012. IEEE.

[45] Galluppi, Francesco, Denk, Christian, Meiner, Matthias C, Stewart, Terrence C, Plana, Luis A, Eliasmith, Chris and Furber, Steve and Conradt, Jörg. *Event-based neural computing on an autonomous mobile platform. Robotics and Automation (ICRA), 2014 IEEE International Conference on*, pages 2862–2867, 2014. IEEE.

[46] Gaspar, Nora and Sondhi, Anish and Evans, Benjamin and Nikolic, Konstantin. *Live demonstration: A low-power neuromorphic system for retinal implants and sensory substitution. Biomedical Circuits and Systems Conference (BioCAS), 2015 IEEE*, pages 1–1, 2015. IEEE.

[47] Girau, Bernard. FPNA: applications and implementations. *FPGA Implementations of Neural Networks*, 103–136, 2006.

[48] Gironés, Rafael Gadea and Palero, Ricardo Colom and Boluda, Joaqufn Cerdá and Cortés, Angel Sebastia. FPGA implementation of a pipelined on-line backpropagation. *Journal of VLSI Signal Processing Systems for Signal, Image and Video Technology*, 40(2):189–213, 2005.

[49] Graf, H and De Vegvar, P. *A CMOS associative memory chip based on neural networks. Solid-State Circuits Conference. Digest of Technical Papers. 1987 IEEE International*, pages 304–305, 1987. IEEE.

[50] Grassia, Filippo and Levi, Timothée and Kohno, Takashi and Saïghi, Sylvain. Silicon neuron: digital hardware implementation of the quartic model. *Artificial Life and Robotics*, 19(3):215–219, 2014.

[51] Han, Bing and Sengupta, Abhronil and Roy, Kaushik. *On the energy benefits of spiking deep neural networks: A case study. Neural Networks (IJCNN), 2016 International Joint Conference on*, pages 971–976, 2016. IEEE.

[52] Harrer, Stefan and Kiral-Kornek, Isabell and Kerr, Robert and Mashford, Benjamin S and Tang, Jianbin and Yepes, A Jimeno and Deligianni, H. From Wearables to Thinkables-Deep Learning, Nanobiosensors and the Next Generation of Mobile Devices. *White Paper, ICONN*, 2016.

[53] Hasler, P and Akers, LA. VLSI neural systems and circuits. *Computers and Communications, 1990. Conference Proceedings, Ninth Annual International Phoenix Conference on*, pages 31–37, 1990. IEEE.

[54] Hayati, Mohsen and Nouri, Moslem and Haghiri, Saeed and Abbott, Derek. A digital realization of astrocyte and neural glial interactions. *IEEE Transactions on Biomedical Circuits and Systems*, 10(2):518–529, 2016.

[55] Haykin, Simon. Network neural: A comprehensive foundation. *Neural Networks*, 2(2004):41, 2004.

[56] Henderson, R. *Intel claims that by 2026 processors will have as many transistors as there are neurons in a brain*. 2014 (accessed August 21, 2017). http://www.pocket-lint.com/news/126289-intel-claims-that-by-2026-processors-will-have-as-many-transistors-as-there-ar

[57] Hikawa, Hiroomi. A digital hardware pulse-mode neuron with piecewise linear activation function. *IEEE Transactions on Neural Networks*, 14(5):1028–1037, 2003.

[58] Hindmarsh, Jim and Cornelius, Philip. *The development of the Hindmarsh-Rose model for bursting. Bursting: The Genesis of Rhythm in the Nervous System*, pages 3–18. World Scientific, 2005.

[59] Hishiki, Tetsuya and Torikai, Hiroyuki. *Bifurcation analysis of a resonate-and-fire-type digital spiking neuron. Neural Information Processing*, pages 392–400, Springer, 2009.

[60] Hishiki, Tetsuya and Torikai, Hiroyuki. *Neural behaviors and nonlinear dynamics of a rotate-and-fire digital spiking neuron. Neural Networks (IJCNN), The 2010 International Joint Conference on*, pages 1–8, 2010. IEEE.

[61] Hollis, Paul Wand Paulos, John J. An Analog BiCMOS Hopfield Neuron. *Analog Integrated Circuits and Signal Processing*, 2(4):273–279, 1992.

[62] Hordri, NF and Samar, A and Yuhaniz, SS and Shamsuddin, SM. A systematic literature review on features of deep learning in big data analytics. *International Journal of Advances in Soft Computing & Its Applications*, 9(1), 2017.

[63] Hsieh, Hung-Yi and Tang, Kea-Tiong. Hardware friendly probabilistic spiking neural network with long-term and short-term plasticity. *IEEE Transactions on Neural Networks and Learning Systems*, 24(12):2063–2074, 2013.

[64] Hsu, Jeremy. Ibm's new brain [news]. *IEEE Spectrum*, 51(10):17–19, 2014.

[65] Hussain, Shaista and Liu, Shih-Chii and Basu, Arindam. Hardware-amenable structural learning for spike-based pattern classification using a simple model of active dendrites. *Neural Computation*, 2015.

[66] Hylander, Paul and Meader, J and Frie, Eddie. *VLSI implementation of pulse coded winner take all networks. Circuits and Systems, 1993, Proceedings of the 36th Midwest Symposium on*, pages 758–761, 1993. IEEE.

[67] Hynna, Kai M and Boahen, Kwabena. *Neuronal ion-channel dynamics in silicon. Circuits and Systems, 2006. ISCAS 2006. Proceedings. 2006 IEEE International Symposium on*, pages 4, 2006. IEEE.

[68] Ibrayev, Timur and James, Alex Pappachen and Merkel, Cory and Kudithipudi, Dhireesha. *A design of HTM spatial pooler for face recognition using Memristor-CMOS hybrid circuits. Circuits and Systems (ISCAS), 2016 IEEE International Symposium on*, pages 1254–1257, 2016. IEEE.

[69] Isobe, Kanata and Torikai, Hiroyuki. A novel hardware-efficient asynchronous cellular automaton model of spike-timing-dependent synaptic plasticity. *IEEE Transactions on Circuits and Systems II: Express Briefs*, 63(6):603–607, 2016.

[70] Izhikevich, Eugene M. Simple model of spiking neurons. *IEEE Transactions on Neural Networks*, 14(6):1569–1572, 2003.

[71] Izhikevich, Eugene M and Fitz Hugh, Richard. Fitzhugh-nagumo model. *Scholarpedia*, 1(9):1349, 2006.

[72] Jang, Jun-Woo and Attarimashalkoubeh, Behnoush and Prakash, Amit and Hwang, Hyunsang and Jeong, Yoon-Ha. Scalable neuron circuit using conductive-bridge RAM for pattern reconstructions. *IEEE Transactions on Electron Devices*, 63(6):2610–2613, 2016.

[73] Jeyanthi, S and Subadra, M. *Implementation of single neuron using various activation functions with FPGA. Advanced Communication Control and Computing Technologies (ICACCCT), 2014 International Conference on*, pages 1126–1131, 2014. IEEE.

[74] Joshi, Jonathan and Zhang, Jialu and Wang, Chuan and Hsu, Chih-Chieh and Parker, Alice C and Zhou, Chongwu and Ravishankar, Udhay. *A biomimetic fabricated carbon nanotube synapse for prosthetic applications. Life Science Systems and Applications Workshop (LiSSA), 2011 IEEE/NIH*, pages 139–142, 2011. IEEE.

[75] Kanazawa, Yusuke and Asai, Tetsuya and Amemiya, Yoshihito. *A hardware depressing synapse and its application to contrast-invariant pattern recognition. SICE 2003 Annual Conference*, pages 1558–1563, 2003. IEEE.

[76] Khan, Muhammad Mukaram and Lester, David R and Plana, Luis A and Rast, A and Jin, Xin and Painkras, Eustace and Furber, Stephen B. *SpiNNaker: mapping neural networks onto a massively-parallel chip multiprocessor. Neural Networks, 2008. IJCNN 2008.(IEEE World Congress on Computational Intelligence). IEEE International Joint Conference on*, pages 2849–2856, 2008. IEEE.

[77] Krid, Mohamed and Dammak, Alima and Masmoudi, Dorra Sellami. *FPGA implementation of programmable pulse mode neural network with on chip learning for signature application. Electronics, Circuits and Systems, 2006. ICECS'06. 13th IEEE International Conference on*, pages 942–945, 2006. IEEE.

[78] Kudithipudi, Dhireesha and Saleh, Qutaiba and Merkel, Cory and Thesing, James and Wysocki, Bryant. Design and analysis of a neuromemristive reservoir computing architecture for biosignal processing. *Frontiers in Neuroscience*, 9, 2015.

[79] Kuo, Y-H and Kao, C-I and Chen, J-J. A fuzzy neural network model and its hardware implementation. *IEEE Transactions on Fuzzy Systems*, 1(3):171–183, 1993.

[80] Lecar, Harold. Morris-lecar model. *Scholarpedia*, 2(10):1333, 2007.

[81] Leong, Philip HW and Jabri, Marwan A. *A VLSI neural network for morphology classification. Neural Networks, 1992. IJCNN, International Joint Conference on*, pages 678–683, 1992. IEEE.

[82] Li, Shaobai and Dasmahapatra, Srinandan and Maharatna, Koushik. Dynamical system approach for edge detection using coupled Fitz Hugh–Nagumo neurons. *IEEE Transactions on Image Processing*, 24(12):5206–5219, 2015.

[83] Lisman, John. A mechanism for the Hebb and the anti-Hebb processes underlying learning and memory. *Proceedings of the National Academy of Sciences*, 86(23):9574–9578, 1989.

[84] Liu, Ming and Yu, Hua and Wang, Wei. *FPAA based on integration of CMOS and nanojunction devices for neuromorphic applications. International Conference on Nano-Networks*, pages 44–48, Springer, 2008.

[85] Liu, Xiaoxiao and Mao, Mengjie and Li, Hai and Chen, Yiran and Jiang, Hao and Yang, J Joshua and Wu, Qing and Barnell, Mark. *A heterogeneous computing system with memristor-based neuromorphic accelerators. High Performance Extreme Computing Conference (HPEC), 2014 IEEE*, pages 1–6, 2014. IEEE.

[86] Liu, Xiaoxiao and Mao, Mengjie and Liu, Beiye and Li, Boxun and Wang, Yu and Jiang, Hao and Barnell, Mark and Wu, Qing and Yang, Jianhua and Li, Hai and others. *Harmonica: A framework of heterogeneous computing systems with memristor-based neuromorphic computing accelerators. IEEE Transactions on Circuits and Systems I: Regular Papers*, 63(5):617–628, 2016.

[87] Liu, Xiaoxiao and Mao, Mengjie and Liu, Beiye and Li, Hai and Chen, Yiran and Li, Boxun and Wang, Yu and Jiang, Hao and Barnell, Mark and Wu, Qing and others. *RENO: A high-efficient reconfigurable neuromorphic computing accelerator design. Design Automation Conference (DAC), 2015 52nd ACM/EDAC/IEEE*, pages 1–6, 2015. IEEE.

[88] Lu, CC and Hong, CY and Chen, H. *A scalable and programmable architecture for the continuous restricted Boltzmann machine in VLSI. Circuits and Systems, 2007. ISCAS 2007. IEEE International Symposium on*, pages 1297–1300, 2007. IEEE.

[89] Maeda, Yutaka and Tada, Toshiki. FPGA implementation of a pulse density neural network with learning ability using simultaneous perturbation. *IEEE Transactions on Neural Networks*, 14(3):688–695, 2003.

[90] Maffezzoni, P and Gubian, P. *VLSI design of radial functions hardware generator for neural computations. Microelectronics for Neural Networks and Fuzzy Systems, 1994., Proceedings of the Fourth International Conference on*, pages 252–259, 1994. IEEE.

[91] Mann, James R and Gilbert, Sheldon. *An analog self-organizing neural network chip. Advances in Neural Information Processing Systems*, pages 739–747, 1989.

[92] Matsubara, Takashi and Torikai, Hiroyuki. *Dynamic response behaviors of a generalized asynchronous digital spiking neuron model. Neural Information Processing*, pages 395–404, 2011. Springer.

[93] McGinnity, TM and Roche, B and Maguire, LP and McDaid, LJ. Novel architecture and synapse design for hardware implementations of neural networks. *Computers & Electrical Engineering*, 24(1):75–87, 1998.

[94] Merkel, Cory and Kudithipudi, Dhireesha and Sereni, Nick. *Periodic activation functions in memristor-based analog neural networks. Neural Networks (IJCNN), The 2013 International Joint Conference on*, pages 1–7, 2013. IEEE.

[95] Minch, Bradley A and Hasler, Paul E and Diorio, Chris and Mead, Carver. *A silicon axon. Advances in Neural Information Processing Systems*, pages 739–746, 1995.

[96] Mosa, Ahmad Haj and Kyamakya, Kyandoghere and Ali, Mouhannad and Al, Fadi. Neuro-computing based Matrix Inversion Concept Involving Cellular Neural Networks Black-box Training Concept.

[97] Nair, Manu V, Dudek, Piotr. *Gradient-descent-based learning in memristive crossbar arrays. Neural Networks (IJCNN), 2015 International Joint Conference on*, pages 1–7, 2015. IEEE.

[98] Nirmala Devi, M, Mohankumar, N, Arumugam, S. Modeling and analysis of neuro–genetic hybrid system on FPGA. *Elektronika ir Elektrotechnika*, 96(8):43–46, 2009.

[99] Niu, Chuanxin M, Jalaleddini, Kian, Sohn, Won Joon, Rocamora, John, Sanger, Terence D, Valero-Cuevas, Francisco J. Neuromorphic meets neuromechanics, part I: the methodology and implementation. *Journal of Neural Engineering*, 14(2):025001, 2017.

[100] Noack, Marko, Krause, Markus, Mayr, Christian, Partzsch, Johannes, Schuffny, Rene. *VLSI implementation of a conductance-based multi-synapse using switched-capacitor circuits. Circuits and Systems (ISCAS), 2014 IEEE International Symposium on*, pages 850–853, 2014. IEEE.

[101] Nomura, Osamu, Morie, Takashi, Korekado, Keisuke, Matsugu, Masakazu, Iwata, Atsushi. *A convolutional neural network VLSI architecture using thresholding and weight decomposition. International Conference on Knowledge-Based and Intelligent Information and Engineering Systems*, pages 995–1001, 2004. Springer.

[102] Oster, Matthias, Wang, Yingxue, Douglas, Rodney, Liu, Shih-Chii. Quantification of a spike-based winner-take-all VLSI network. *IEEE Transactions on Circuits and Systems I: Regular Papers*, 55(10):3160–3169, 2008.

[103] Pablo N. Luna. Wise Mapping. URL: http://www.wisemapping.com

[104] Paugam-Moisy, Hélene. Spiking neuron networks a survey. Technical report, IDIAP, 2006.

[105] Peper, Ferdinand. The End of Moore's Law: Opportunities for Natural Computing? *New Generation Computing*, 35(3):253–269, 2017.

[106] Ponulak, Filip, Kasinski, Andrzej. Introduction to spiking neural networks: Information processing, learning and applications. *Acta Neurobiologiae Experimentalis*, 4(71), 2011.

[107] Poon, Chi-Sang, Zhou, Kuan. Neuromorphic silicon neurons and large-scale neural networks: challenges and opportunities. *Frontiers in Neuroscience*, 5, 2011.

[108] Querlioz, Damien, Bichler, Olivier, Vincent, Adrien F, Gamrat, Christian. *Theoretical Analysis of Spike-Timing-Dependent Plasticity Learning with Memristive Devices. Advances in Neuromorphic Hardware Exploiting Emerging Nanoscale Devices*, pages 197–210. Springer, 2017.

[109] Rachmuth, G, Poon, Chi-Sang. *Design of a neuromorphic Hebbian synapse using analog VLSI. Neural Engineering, 2003. Conference Proceedings. First International IEEE EMBS Conference on*, pages 221–224, 2003. IEEE.

[110] Rongala, Udaya Bhaskar, Mazzoni, Alberto, Oddo, Calogero Maria. Neuromorphic artificial touch for categorization of naturalistic textures. *IEEE Transactions on Neural Networks and Learning Systems*, 28(4):819–829, 2017.

[111] Rumelhart, David E, Hinton, Geoffrey E, Williams, Ronald J, others. Learning representations by back-propagating errors. *Cognitive Modeling*, 5(3):1, 1988.

[112] Sahin, I, Koyuncu, I. Design and implementation of neural networks neurons with RadBas, LogSig, and TanSig activation functions on FPGA. *Elektronika ir Elektrotechnika*, 120(4):51–54, 2012.

[113] Salam, Fathi MA. *A model of neural circuits for programmable VLSI implementation. Circuits and Systems, 1989, IEEE International Symposium on*, pages 849–851, 1989. IEEE.

[114] Schneider, Christian, Card, Howard. *CMOS implementation of analog Hebbian synaptic learning circuits. Neural Networks, 1991, IJCNN-91-Seattle International Joint Conference on*, pages 437–442, 1991. IEEE.

[115] Schuman, Catherine D, Disney, Adam, Singh, Susheela P, Bruer, Grant, Mitchell, J Parker, Klibisz, Aleksander, Plank, James S. *Parallel evolutionary optimization for neuromorphic network training. Machine Learning in HPC Environments (MLHPC), Workshop on*, pages 36–46, 2016. IEEE.

[116] Schuman, Catherine D, Potok, Thomas E, Patton, Robert M, Birdwell, J Douglas, Dean, Mark E, Rose, Garrett S, Plank, James S. A Survey of Neuromorphic Computing and Neural Networks in Hardware. *arXiv preprint arXiv:1705.06963*, 2017.

[117] Serrano-Gotarredona, Teresa, Masquelier, Timothée, Prodromakis, Themistoklis, Indiveri, Giacomo, Linares-Barranco, Bernabe. STDP and STDP variations with memristors for spiking neuromorphic learning systems. *Frontiers in Neuroscience*, 7:2, 2013.

[118] Sheri, Ahmad Muqeem, Rafique, Aasim, Pedrycz, Witold, Jeon, Moongu. Contrastive divergence for memristor-based restricted Boltzmann machine. *Engineering Applications of Artificial Intelligence*, 37:336–342, 2015.

[119] Škoda, Peter, Lipić, Tomislav, Srp, Ágoston, Rogina, B Medved, Skala, Karolj, Vajda, Ferenc. *Implementation framework for artificial neural networks on fpga. MIPRO, 2011 Proceedings of the 34th International Convention*, pages 274–278, 2011. IEEE.

[120] Srinivasan, Venkatesh, Dugger, Jeff, Hasler, Paul. An adaptive analog synapse circuit that implements the least-mean-square learning rule. *Circuits and Systems, 2005. ISCAS 2005. IEEE International Symposium on*, pages 4441–4444, 2005. IEEE.

[121] Stromatias, Evangelos, Neil, Daniel, Pfeiffer, Michael, Galluppi, Francesco, Furber, Steve B, Liu, Shih-Chii. Robustness of spiking deep belief networks to noise and reduced bit precision of neuro-inspired hardware platforms. *Frontiers in Neuroscience*, 9, 2015.

[122] Strukov, Dmitri B, Snider, Gregory S, Stewart, Duncan R, Williams, R Stanley. The missing memristor found. *Nature*, 453(7191):80, 2008.

[123] Tal, Doron, Schwartz, Eric L. Computing with the leaky integrate-and-fire neuron: logarithmic computation and multiplication. *Computing*, 9(2), 2006.

[124] Tamukoh, Hakaru, Sekine, Masatoshi. A dynamically reconfigurable platform for self-organizing neural network hardware. *Neural Information Processing. Models and Applications*, 439–446, 2010.

[125] Tuma, Tomas and Le Gallo, Manuel and Sebastian, Abu and Eleftheriou, Evangelos. Detecting Correlations Using Phase-Change Neurons and Synapses. *IEEE Electron Device Letters*, 37(9):1238–1241, 2016.

[126] Ueda, Michihito, Nishitani, Yu, Kaneko, Yukihiro, Omote, Atsushi. Back-Propagation Operation for Analog Neural Network Hardware with Synapse Components Having Hysteresis Characteristics. *PloS one*, 9(11):e112659, 2014.

[127] Vianello, E and Garbin, D and Bichler, O and Piccolboni, G and Molas, G and De Salvo, B and Perniola, L. *Multiple Binary OxRAMs as Synapses for Convolutional Neural Networks. Advances in Neuromorphic Hardware Exploiting Emerging Nanoscale Devices*, pages 109–127. Springer, 2017.

[128] Walker, MR and Akers, LA. *A neuromorphic approach to adaptive digital circuitry. Computers and Communications, 1988. Conference Proceedings, Seventh Annual International Phoenix Conference on*, pages 19–23, 1988. IEEE.

[129] Wang, Zhaobin, Ma, Yide, Cheng, Feiyan, Yang, Lizhen. Review of pulse-coupled neural networks. *Image and Vision Computing*, 28(1):5–13, 2010.

[130] Weinfeld, Michel. *6.2 A Fully Digital Integrated Cmos Hopfield Network Including The Learning Algorithm. The Kluwer International Series In Engineering And Computer Science Vlsi, Computer Architecture And Digital Signal Processing*, 169, 1989.

[131] Yamakawa, Takeshi. Silicon implementation of a fuzzy neuron. *IEEE Transactions on Fuzzy Systems*, 4(4):488–501, 1996.

[132] Yamazaki, Tadashi and Igarashi, Jun. Realtime cerebellum: A large-scale spiking network model of the cerebellum that runs in realtime using a graphics processing unit. *Neural Networks*, 47:103–111, 2013.

[133] Yang, Jinming and Ahmadi, Majid and Jullien, Graham A and Miller, William C. *An in-the-loop training method for VLSI neural networks. Circuits and Systems, 1999. ISCAS'99. Proceedings of the 1999 IEEE International Symposium on*, pages 619–622, 1999. IEEE.

[134] Yao, Enyi and Hussain, Shaista and Basu, Arindam and Huang, Guang-Bin. *Computation using mismatch: Neuromorphic extreme learning machines. Biomedical Circuits and Systems Conference (BioCAS), 2013 IEEE*, pages 294–297, 2013. IEEE.

[135] Yuille, Alan L and Grzywacz, Norberto M. A winner-take-all mechanism based on presynaptic inhibition feedback. *Neural Computation*, 1(3):334–347, 1989.

[136] Zhu, Xiaolei and Shen, Jizhong and Chi, Baoyong and Wang, Zhihua. *Circuit implementation of multi-thresholded neuron (MTN) using BiCMOS technology. Neural Networks, 2005. IJCNN'05. Proceedings. 2005 IEEE International Joint Conference on*, pages 627–632, 2005. IEEE.

Chapter 10

Text Summarization for Automatic Grading of Descriptive Assignments: A Hybrid Approach

Rachel Royan and Christina Jayakumaran
Loyola-ICAM College of Engineering and Technology, Chennai, India

Thompson Stephan
M. S. Ramaiah University of Applied Sciences, Bangalore, India

Contents

DOI: 10.1201/9781003119784-10

Introduction

Natural Language Processing (NLP) uses algorithms for human language interpretation and manipulation. One of the most commonly used machine learning fields is this application apart from other vital applications related to healthcare [1], the Internet of Things [2], communication systems [3], security [4], etc. If artificial intelligence [5] continues to grow, specialized specialists will need to develop models that examine speech and vocabulary, discover contextual trends, and create text and audio insights.

Assignment and class assessment form an integral part of the formative assessment of the students. With a growing spike in the online learning system, it is imperative to conduct small assessments and assignments to actively engage the students in learning. Manual grading of all the assignments by faculty members is time-consuming, tedious, and also liable to error. At times, the results may also vary based on differential reasoning. In the present day scenario, numerous research works are done in evaluating and grading programming-based assignments automatically. However, there are not many proposals for grading descriptive paragraph writing assignments which could be domain-independent and there is a growing demand to address this issue. In this paper, automatic grading of descriptive assignments is done based on the text-summarization techniques of NLP.

This chapter details the various extractive text-summarization techniques [6] and proposes a novel way for autoassessing descriptive assignments.

To grade the descriptive assignments, a combination of Rapid Automatic Keyword Extraction (RAKE) algorithm and Recall-Oriented Understudy for Gisting Evaluation (ROUGE) algorithm (in short, RAKE-ROUGE algorithm) is used in this work to extract the key phrases from the document and automatically grade the assignments. The RAKE algorithm [7] calculates a score at the document level and term level based on the number of key phrases generated and the score for each key phrase in that document. The subset of the output of the RAKE algorithm is fed into the ROUGE algorithm [8] for finding the correlation between the baseline reference and the students' answers. The weighted average of RAKE and ROUGE scores is used in finalizing the overall score for the assignment.

As a value addition to the project, we have also explained two other modules, namely, the plagiarism checker and the peer-review module. When an assignment is given to the students, there is a probability that students copy each other's assignments [9]. This doesn't do any good for the students. The faculty would find it difficult to determine such plagiarism if the count of students in the class is high. Hence, we use various text similarity measures to determine plagiarism between the assignments. In our plagiarism module, we calculate a weighted average of Cosine distance, Jaccard distance, and Pearson Correlation coefficient by giving more weight to the cosine distance.

The second additional module called the peer-review module allows us to randomly allocate student assignments to our peers [10]. As a part of the peer-review module, the assignments are evaluated by the peers and the score is marked into the interface. This module also serves us to validate the scores generated by the hybrid the RAKE-ROUGE method against the human evaluation. The rest of this chapter is organized as follows. In Section "Literature Survey", the literature survey is presented. The Section "Adaptation of a New Technique for Autograding Descriptive Assignments" discusses the adaptation of NLP techniques for autograding descriptive assignments. In the Section "Results and Discussion", we have presented some output screenshots and discussed the results and the concluding remarks mentioned in the Section "Conclusion".

Literature Survey

Shehab et al. [11] had proposed a system that evaluated essays from college students' essays at Mansoura University. The system contained two key components that complement each other's output. The first is the neural-network-based grading Engine that relies on a dataset of pre-graded essays and it assigns a grade to the essay under evaluation by comparing it against the pre-graded essays. The second component consists of a suite of evaluation functionalities that determines grammatical errors, usage of right words, and its mechanics using tools that are enabled by NLP. Also, Qiu et al. [12] proposed a novel approach for grading essay answers. Their work had datasets of questions and answers with each question belonging to a subject domain having multiple answer sets corresponding to the question. The system uses semantic-based similarity measures for filtering the structured data from unstructured data. But these techniques cannot be used in all the domains due to the unavailability of appropriate datasets. Hence, we decided on using keyword extraction and summarization techniques for our approach.

But before evaluating the assignments, it is imperative to perform preemptive processes such as stemming, tokenization, punctuations, and stop-word removal. Hasanah et al. [13] have shown how preprocessing of text improves the automated evaluation of short answers. Removal of stop words during the preprocessing phase helps in improving the efficiency of the algorithms calculating the similarity. It has been determined as part of an earlier research (Patel et al. [14]) that the criticality of eliminating stop words in metasearch engines is prerogative for results of better precision. The output from such proposed metasearch engine with and without stop words were being compared. The output from such a metasearch engine with and without stop words were being compared and it was found that those stop words can be filtered from an index because those are rarely being used in user searches. Similarly, Manalu et al. [15] have also shown that the usage of stop-word removal can be impactful in determining the result of review summarization. Once the preprocessing is done, we move on to extracting keywords and summarizing the assignments.

Dalal et al., in their paper [6], have performed a survey on two different approaches to summarization. Extractive summarization involves two steps: First, extracting the key textual elements, like sentences or paragraphs using statistical and linguistic analyses. Second, the extracted text is then used as a summary or "extract". Another approach is the abstractive summarization where the text is understood and re-told in fewer words. In our system, we have used extractive summarization techniques.

Ganiger et al. [16] have compared various keyword-extraction algorithms for single extractive documents such as RAKE algorithm, term frequency – inverse document frequency (TF-IDF), and TextRank algorithm and have proposed that the RAKE algorithm in comparison to TF-IDF and TextRank generates more prominent and weighted keywords. Large-scale text analysis and summarization have different impacts on the algorithms. Hernández et al. [17] have shown different extraction methods and how TF-IDF works well on large corpus and RAKE, alchemy API, and works well in extracting keywords from single documents. Rose et al. [7] have explained how the RAKE algorithm works. The various steps involved starting from determining the candidate keywords, then scoring them, and combining them to determine the possible key phrases have been elaborated and its effectiveness was demonstrated using precision and recall as the performance metric. Ghosh et al. [18] discussed how the local Indian languages influence English essays and they have proposed a new framework to overcome that.

Cristobal Romero et al. [19] deals with the techniques of data mining involving an educational environment where he considers the variety of user – groups and determines the most common task in such an environment that can be resolved through data-mining techniques.

Liu et al. [8], in their paper, describe that the ROUGE metric is very efficient, by calculating the correlation between assessment of essays by a variety of humans and ROUGE. It has also been compared to various other evaluation metrics to show that it is more efficient than other algorithms. He et al. [20] have designed ROUGE-C, an extension of ROUGE. The difference in the methodology of determining "test reference data" between ROUGE and ROUGE-C is that the former takes reference summaries as model and peer summaries as a test while the latter takes them the other way round.

Magara et al. [21], in their work, have compared the various text similarity measures such as Jaccard distance, Euclidean distance, cosine distance, and Pearson correlation coefficient and proposes that the cosine distance is efficient for calculating the similarity. Weighted cosine coefficient similar to the cosine coefficient proposed by Pribadi et al. [22] could be used in the Automated-Short-Answer-Scoring (ASAS) system. An evaluator, while evaluating a student's answer, usually looks for the significant words from the reference key and based on the relevancy and the closeness, the scoring is assigned, wherein every keyword carries different weights. This is combined with cosine similarity to give the weighted cosine similarity. Sheugh et al. [23] have discussed how the Pearson correlation coefficient is an efficient similarity measure. They have also proposed an extension of the Pearson correlation coefficient using reduced NAN result (a metric used in Matlab software) in similarity measure for all of the items having the same ratings, and the mean of ratings is equal with a common rating. Collaborative Filtering (CF) algorithms use correlation coefficient techniques such as Pearson, Cosine, and Jaccard for measuring the similarity between the user and reference items. Ayub et al. [24] had used an approach similar to Jaccard similarity and found that Jaccard similarity and cosine similarities perform well. Lahitani et al., in their paper, have deliberated on similarity techniques combining TF-IDF and cosine similarity [25] for automating the scoring for essays.

Tsoni et al., in their paper [9], have discussed the impact of plagiarism and how it affects the quality of the educational environment. It was also found that only a small percentage of academic institutions used plagiarism-detection software even though all of them had encountered plagiarism and cheating incidents. Therefore, we have also added a plagiarism-detection module. This uses various text similarity measures.

The random peer evaluation scheme implemented to validate the score as a part of this proposal was found to have been deliberated in the research by Sun [26]. The scores and feedback collected from their peers helped students to improve their programming skills. This experiment also showed that students got a better understanding of the concepts. The same is discussed much in detail in [10]. Bots et al. [10] designed a peer-review cum assessment tool abbreviated as PrESTO. The review and the assessment workflow enabled by the software, guide the users through the activities in a step-by-step process iteratively in the following order: review–feedback–assess–improve–extend.

Adaptation of a New Technique for Autograding Descriptive Assignments

The illustration of the system architecture is given in Figure 10.1. The sequence of the workflow is as follows:

- Text Preprocessing Module
- Assignment Correction Module
- Plagiarism-Detection Module
- Peer-Review Module

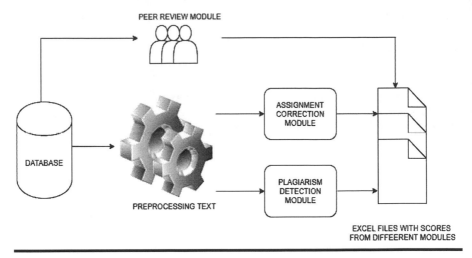

Figure 10.1   System architecture.

The database in Figure 10.1 stores the reference key designed by the faculty and the assignments submitted by the students. As illustrated in the right-most block, the scores obtained from various modules are being output in the form of an Excel sheet for analysis by the staff.

Text Preprocessing Module

It is imperative to do preprocessing of the text before passing it to any NLP-based text-summarization algorithm to make it in a more digestible form to enhance the efficiency of the algorithm (Figure 10.2).

Tokenization: The preprocessing module begins with the tokenization process which reads the text into words or tokens.

Removing punctuations: The documents may contain punctuations such as commas and full stops. These are unnecessary for the evaluation. Hence, punctuations are removed from the document.

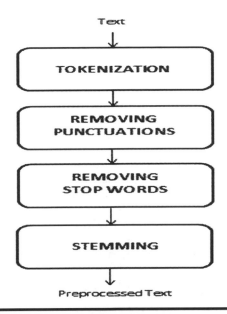

Figure 10.2   Flow of preprocessing module.

Removing stop words: After the removal of punctuations, stop words are removed and then stemming is performed. Stop words are considered as unwanted noise in a sentence. These words do not have any importance in the sentence, for example, "the", "a", "an", "in", etc.

Stemming: Stemming is the methodology of reducing a word to its root form from which it originated. A stemming algorithm might also reduce the words liking, liked, and likes to the stem "like".

Assignment Correction Module Using Hybrid RAKE-ROUGE Algorithm

The assignment correction module is the key component of our work wherein we propose a hybrid method of using the RAKE-ROUGE algorithm to perform semantic-based keyword extraction and autoscoring of assignments.

Hybrid RAKE-ROUGE Algorithm

In our manuscript, for the assessment of descriptive assignments, a combination of the RAKE-ROUGE algorithm is applied to extract key phrases and automatically score the assignments.

Input: *Set of assignment, Answer key*
Output: *Score for each assignment submitted*

```
        1. Apply tokenization, removal of stop words and
punctuations.
        2. Generate a set of candidate words,
C = {C₁, C₂, C₃, …, Cₙ} from the assignment.
        3. For each word in the candidate set C, calculate
                word_scores[Cₙ]←word_degree[Cₙ]/
word_frequency[Cₙ]
        4. Generate a phrase set P = {P₁, P₂, P₃, …, Pₙ} from the
set C by looping over the word scores combining them with the
other words scores;
                phrase_score[Pₙ]←Σ₁ⁿ word_score[Cₙ]
                phrase_scores["".join(phrase)]←phrase_score
        5. Calculate a cumulative score CS at the document
level by combining all the phrases' rake_score
        6. Compare the keywords extracted from step 3 with the
reference answer's keywords using the ROUGE metric and obtain
the ROUGE score RS.
        7. Final_Score of the assignment is calculated based on
the maximum score allocated by the teacher using the following
formula:
                Rake_weight = maximum score*0.6
                Rouge_weight = maximum score*0.4
                Final_score = (CS*Rake_weight) +
(RS*Rouge_weight)
```

The step-wise description of how the candidate set of words and phrases are generated and the calculation of the weighted scores at both phrase level and document level is illustrated in the Section "Keyword Extraction Using RAKE Algorithm". Step 6 of the algorithm is illustrated in detail in the Section "Keyword Comparison using ROUGE – Metric". The final grade for the assignment is obtained as a weighted average of the scores generated by the above two methods. We have allocated 60% weightage for the RAKE score and 40% weightage for the ROUGE score as this proportion of weights gave a maximum likelihood with the results from the human score (Figure 10.3).

Keyword Extraction Using RAKE Algorithm

RAKE algorithm is an extraction algorithm based on keywords that extracts key phrases from the assignment by inspecting the number of occurrences in the assignment and its co-occurrence with other words in the assignment.

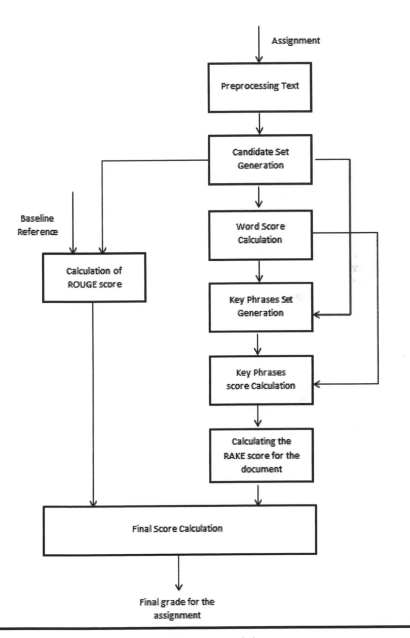

Figure 10.3 Flow of assignment correction module.

This algorithm works in three major steps:

1. **Candidate selection:** Here, we find all possible words, phrases, terms, or concepts (depending on the task) that can be candidate keywords from the assignment.
2. **Word score calculation:** The words are scored not only with respect to their frequency but also based on the length of the phrase in which they belong (Table 10.1). For each candidate, we calculate the word score by using the following formula:

$$word\_scores = word\_degree \,/\, word\_frequency \qquad (10.1)$$

The *word_degree* represents the frequency of its co-occurrence with other words in the candidate keywords and the frequency refers to the number of occurrences of the word in the assignment.

3. **Scoring phrases:** Now, using the word score phrases, scores are generated which may be the potential keywords. This is done by looping over the word scores combining them with the other words scores. If the combined score is more than a certain value, then the phrase is a potential keyword. This phrase along with its score is stored and a cumulative score is calculated for the document using these scores.

$$phrase\_score + = word\_scores \qquad (10.2)$$

$$phrase\_scores\big[""\,.join(\,phrase)\big] = phrase\_score \qquad (10.3)$$

Let's understand the various steps of the algorithm using an example.

Consider the following text:

"You can't laugh at the same joke over and over. So why are you always crying about the same problem?"

In the first step, preprocessing of the text is done and the candidate keywords are selected: ["You", "laugh", "joke"]

Table 10.1 Frequency and Word-Degree

Word	Frequency	Degree
Laugh	1	1
Joke	1	1
Always	1	2
Crying	1	2
Problem	1	1

["So", "always", "crying", "problem"]
Now, we calculate the frequency of all the words
Word-degree is similar to the degree of a node in a graph.

word_score[W] = degree[W]/frequency[W] Therefore, calculating word scores for the candidate keywords,

word_score['laugh'] = 1/1 = 1
word_score['joke'] = 1/1 = 1
word_score['always'] = 2/1 = 2
word_score['crying'] = 2/1 = 2
word_score['laugh'] = 1/1 = 1

Now, we can see that the keywords having maximum scores are "always" and "crying" with word score 2. Now when we loop over these keywords, we obtain the key phrase "always crying".

Word_score['always'] + word_score['crying'] = 2 + 2 = 4. The key phrase "always crying" has a combined score of 4.

Keyword Comparison Using ROUGE Metric

ROUGE is a metric and a software enabling the evaluation of automatic summarization in NLP by calculating how much the summary has recalled words from the text.

For assignment correction, we are calculating the ROUGE-n metric. Given the reference text, we calculate the ROUGE metric to check if all the necessary keywords are recalled in students' assignments or not.

ROUGE-N: Intersection of N-grams between the sample sentence or answer and reference sentence or answer.

■ **ROUGE-1** refers to the intersection or convergence of **unigram** among the reference and the sample sentence.

Reference sentence: the dog was found under the table
Sample sentence: the dog was under the table

$$ROUGE-1 = \frac{Number\ of\ Overlapping\ words}{Total\ number\ of\ words\ in\ the\ refernce\ asnwer} \quad (10.4)$$

In our example, there are 6 overlapping words and the total number of words in our reference sentence is 7. Therefore, the ROUGE-1 score is 6/7, i.e., 0.85

■ **ROUGE-2** refers to the intersection or convergence of **bigram** among the reference and the sample sentence (Table 10.2).

Table 10.2 Bigrams from the Reference and Sample Sentence

Reference Sentence	Sample Sentence
the dog	the dog
dog was	dog was
was found	was under
found under	under the
under the	the table
the table	

Reference sentence: the dog was found under the table
Sample sentence: the dog was under the table

$$ROUGE - 2 = \frac{Number\ of\ Overlapping\ bigrams}{Total\ number\ of\ bigrams\ in\ the\ refernce\ answer} \qquad (10.5)$$

In our example, there are 4 overlapping bigrams and the total number of words in our reference sentence is 5. Therefore, the ROUGE-1 score is 4/5, i.e., 0.8.

These ROUGE scores are used to determine how much the student has recalled the key points from the teacher's key. In python, there is a ROUGE package that calculates the different ROUGE scores.

```
        Recall, precision, rouge = rouge_n_sentence_
    level(reference sentence, sample sentence, 1)
            recall, precision, rouge = rouge_n_sentence_
    level(reference sentence, sample sentence,2)
```

ROUGE-C: In ROUGE-C, the content of the input information is decided by different types of summarization tasks. For single document summarization, the test is the source document; for multi-document summarization, the test is the source documents set, all source documents for a topic are treated as a single "document"; and for query-focused multi-document summarization, the test is the source document set and the query-related information (e.g., questions, viewpoints, and task descriptions in a topic). From [9], we have:

$$ROUGE - C = \frac{Number\ of\ Overlapping\ words}{Total\ Number\ of\ words\ in\ Sample\ Sentence} \qquad (10.6)$$

Plagiarism-Detection Module

The plagiarism module makes use of three text similarity metrics:

- Cosine similarity
- Jaccard similarity
- Pearson correlation coefficient.

The weighted sum average of all the three scores is calculated offering more weight to cosine similarity. Figure 10.4 represents the flow of a plagiarism-detection module. The assignments are preprocessed and the three different similarity measures are calculated. The final score is given by calculating a weighted average of all three.

Cosine Similarity

Cosine similarity converts each assignment into a vector and calculates the cosine product of these vectors. The vector conversion is done using a fit transformer and TF-IDF transformer functions.

$$SIM_C\left(\overrightarrow{t_a}, \overrightarrow{t_b}\right) = \frac{\overrightarrow{t_a}.\overrightarrow{t_b}}{\left|\overrightarrow{t_a}\right| + \left|\overrightarrow{t_b}\right|} \tag{10.7}$$

$\overrightarrow{t_a}, \overrightarrow{t_b}$ are the vectors of the two assignments being compared.

TF-IDF reflects how vital the word is to the assignment in an assortment or corpus. Though, the value of TF-IDF proportionately increases depending on the number of occurrences of the word within an assignment. However, it is also balanced by the frequency of the word within the corpus that helps to simply accept the very fact that some words seem to appear a lot generally.

After removing the stop words, the TF-IDF value is calculated for each word in the corpus:

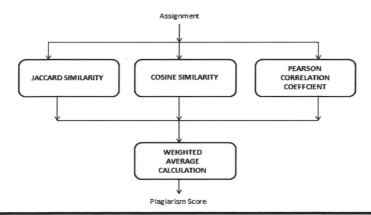

Figure 10.4   Flow of plagiarism-detection module.

Term Frequency:
The number of times a term occurs in the assignment is called its term frequency (TF).

$$TF_{t,d} = \frac{f_{t,d}}{\max_K f_{t,d}} \tag{10.8}$$

$f_{t,d}$ indicates the number of times the term t occurs in the document d and is called the *raw frequency.*

Inverse Document Frequency:
The IDF is a statistical indicator of the measure of how much information the word provides with respect to a single document or the set of documents within the corpus. The IDF diminishes the weight parameter for the frequently occurring terms in the assignment set and increases the weight parameter for the rarely occurring terms in the set. It is a logarithmic function of the quotient calculated by dividing the count of the number of assignments in the database by the number of assignments where the term t appears.

$$idf(t,D) = \log_2 \frac{N}{|\{d \in D : t \in d\}|} \tag{10.9}$$

N: total number of assignments in the database N = |D|
$|\{d \in D : t \in d\}|$:Number of assignments where the term t appears

Term Frequency – Inverse Document Frequency:
TF-IDF is calculated as:

$$tfidf(t,d,D) = tf(t,d) \times idf(t,D) \tag{10.10}$$

A TF-IDF parameter assigns weight that has a positive correlation to a high term frequency of the word within the assignment and has a smaller document frequency of the term with respect to the set of all assignments in the database.

Jaccard Similarity

Jaccard similarity is calculated by finding the number of words intersecting or overlapping between the two assignments and dividing by the union of the two assignments.

$$SIM_J(\vec{t}_a, \vec{t}_b) = \frac{\vec{t}_a \vec{t}_b}{|\vec{t}_a|^2 + |\vec{t}_b|^2 - \vec{t}_a \vec{t}_b} \tag{10.11}$$

$\vec{t}_a, \vec{t}_b$ are the vectors of the two assignments being compared.

Pearson Correlation Coefficient

The Pearson correlation coefficient, also referred to as the Pearson product-moment correlation coefficient or the bivariate correlation, is used to calculate the linear correlation between two variables X and Y.

$$SIM_P\left(\vec{t}_a,\vec{t}_b\right) = \frac{m\sum_{t=1}^{m} w_{t,a} * w_{t,a} - TF_a * TF_b}{\sqrt{\left[m\sum_{t=1}^{m} w_{t,a}^2 - TF_a^2\right]\left[\sqrt{m\sum_{t=1}^{m} w_{t,b}^2 - TF_b^2}\right]}} \quad (10.12)$$

where $TF_a = \sum_{t=1}^{m} w_{t,a}$ and $TF_a = \sum_{t=1}^{m} w_{t,b}$;

$w_{t,a}$ represents the TF-IDF value of term t in document a and $w_{t,b}$ represents the TF-IDF value of term t in document b.

Peer-Review Module

The peer-review module has two major parts:

- The first part, allocation of assignments to students is done in such a way that they do not receive their assignments for correction and also make sure that the same assignment is not assigned to different individuals for correction.
- In the second part, the assignments are mailed to the appropriate student for correction. Finally, an interface is provided for the students' to upload the mark of the assignments they evaluated.

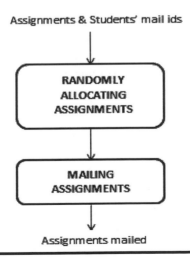

Figure 10.5   Flow of peer-review module.

Results and Discussion

In this section, we have presented some of the screenshots of the output obtained from the system.

- Figure 10.6 represents the main page where the student and the teacher can sign in to access the various functionalities of the system.
- Figure 10.7 represents the various functionalities available for the teacher to perform.
- Figure 10.8 represents various functionalities for the student to perform.
- Figure 10.9 represents the output of the assignment correction module. The assignments have been score out of 10.
- Figure 10.10 represents the output of the plagiarism-detection module. The first column shows the two assignments that are being compared; the next column represents the plagiarism score which is out of 100.
- Figure 10.11 shows the interface where the student can upload the marks for their peer's assignment.

To evaluate the performance of our system, we have calculated the correlation between the scores given by the system and scores given by two faculties who evaluated the same set of assignments (Table 10.3).

The score generated by the system and the score given by the two faculty members by manual evaluation is compared using correlation measure. In statistics, correlation or dependence is any statistical relationship, whether causal or not, between two random variables or bivariate data. It is calculated using the following formula:

$$Correlation(X,Y) = \frac{n\sum XY - \sum X \sum Y}{\sqrt{\left[n\sum X^2 - (\sum X)^2\right]\left[n\sum Y^2 - (\sum Y)^2\right]}} \tag{10.13}$$

The score generated by the system and the score given by two faculty members by manual evaluation is compared using correlation measure. The correlation measure is shown in Table 10.4 and that our system is 0.87 positively correlated to Faculty 1's evaluation and 0.97 positively correlated to Faculty 2's evaluation.

Figures 10.12–10.14 give us a visual representation of how much similar the evaluation is among the faculty, peer, and the system. The X-axis represents the students' assignment numbers and the Y-axis represents the marks obtained. We can see a positive correlation between the scores given. As the score given by the faculty increases so does the score given by the algorithm, and as a decrease in the score given by the faculty is seen, the score given by the algorithm also goes down.

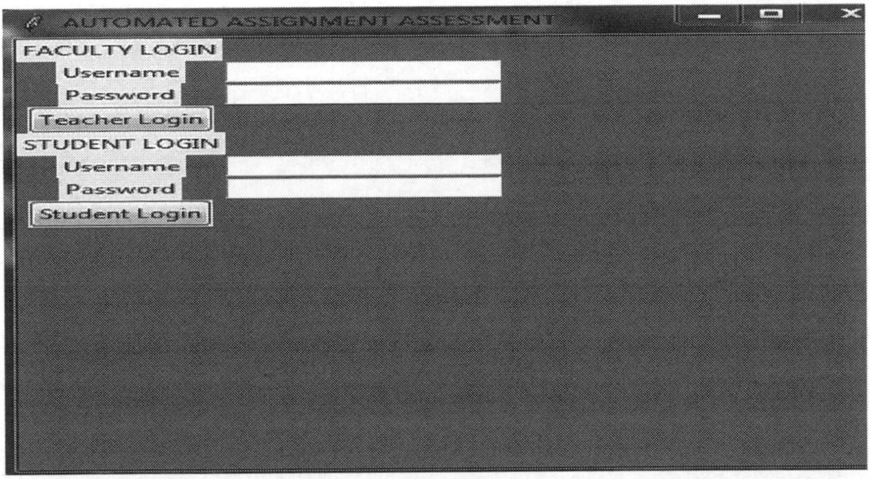

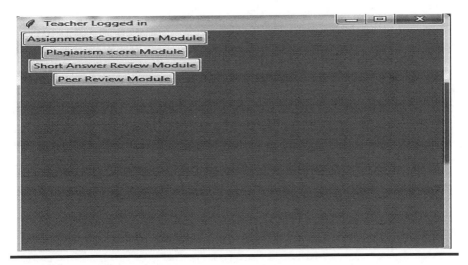

Figure 10.6   Main page.

Figure 10.7   Teacher's interface.

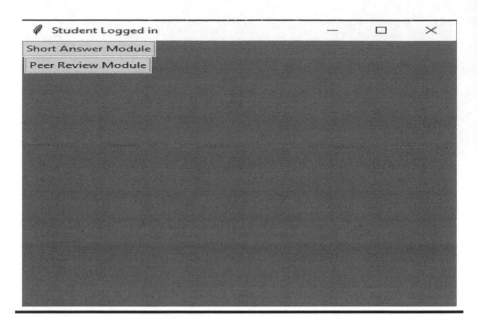

Figure 10.8   Student's Interface.

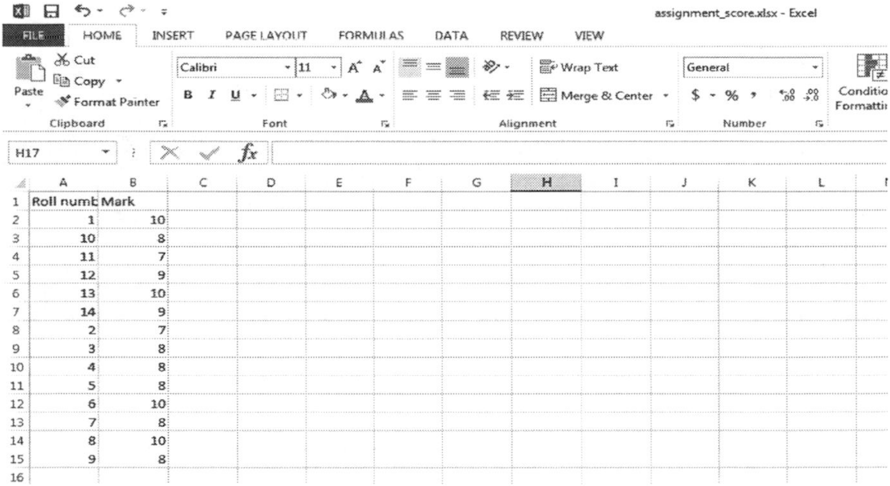

Figure 10.9   Assignment score.

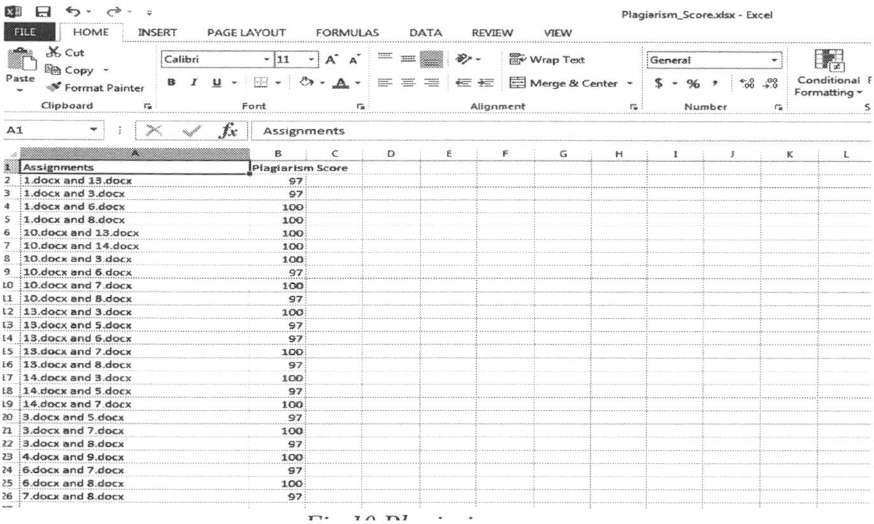

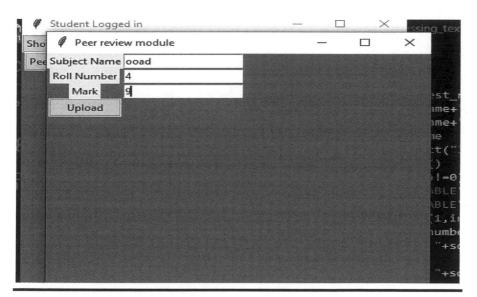

Figure 10.10   Plagiarism score.

Figure 10.11   Peer-review module.

Table 10.3 Scores Given by Two Faculties and Peer

Assignment Number	Score	Faculty 1 Score	Faculty 2 Score	Peer Score
1	10	10	10	10
2	7	7	6	8
3	8	8	7	8
4	8	7	8	9
5	8	7	7	8
6	10	9	10	10
7	8	8	7	8
8	10	9	10	10
9	8	7	7	8
10	8	8	7	9

Table 10.4 Correlation between the Scores Given by the Faculties and the Module Score

Correlation of assignment scores calculated with those given by Faculty 1	0.87831
Correlation of assignment scores calculated with those given by Faculty 2	0.978814
Correlation of assignment scores calculated with those given by peer	0.895547

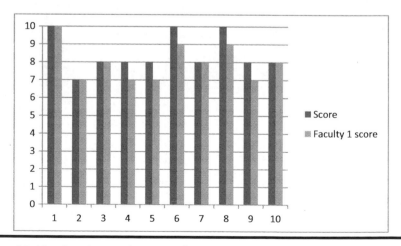

Figure 10.12 Consistency between the system score and Faculty 1 score.

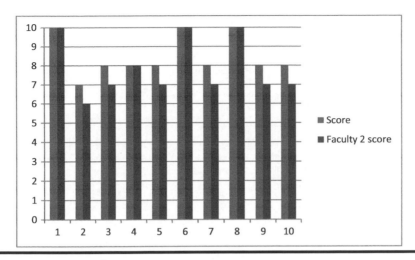

Figure 10.13   Consistency between the system score and Faculty 2 score.

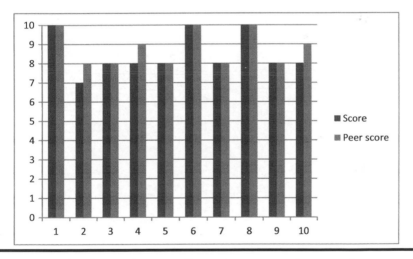

Figure 10.14   Consistency between the system score and peer-review score.

Conclusion

In line with the proposal objective, the methodology developed has automated the process of assessing and grading a descriptive assignment using semantic analysis. The primary contribution of this work is the assignment review module which uses the hybrid of the RAKE and ROUGE algorithm to extract the keywords from the students' assignments and automates the process of grading, based on the reference key. As a value addition to the project, it also included a plagiarism-detection module which tells how much the student has copied from other's assignment(s).

The accuracy of the score generated by the system is compared with the evaluation by the faculty and is found to have a correlation of around 90%. The future scope of the system is to identify the gaps and increase the accuracy and also to verify images and use image processing to evaluate the handwritten assignment.

References

[1] Al-Turjman, F., & Stephan, T. (2021). "An automated breast cancer diagnosis using feature selection and parameter optimization," *ANN Computers & Electrical Engineering*, 90, 106958. https://doi.org/10.1016/j.compeleceng.2020.106958

[2] Chithaluru, P., Al-Turjman, F., Kumar, M., & Stephan, T. (2020). "1-AREOR: An Energy-balanced Clustering Protocol for implementing Green IoT in smart cities," *Sustainable Cities and Society*, 102254. https://doi.org/10.1016/j.scs.2020.102254

[3] Stephan, T., Al-Turjman, F., & Balusamy, B. (2020). "*Energy and spectrum aware unequal clustering with deep learning based primary user classification in cognitive radio sensor networks*," *International Journal of Machine Learning and Cybernetics*. https://doi.org/10.1007/sl3042-020-01154-y

[4] Bhardwaj, A., Al-Turjman, F., Kumar, M., Stephan, T., & Mostarda, L. (2020). "*Capturing-the-Invisible (CTI): Behavior- based Attacks Recognition in IoT-oriented Industrial Control Systems*," *IEEE Access*, https://doi.org/10.1109/ACCESS.2020.2998983

[5] Stephan, T., Al-Turjrnan, F., Joseph, K. S., Balusamy, B., & Srivastava, S. (2020). "Artificial intelligence inspired energy and spectrum aware cluster based routing protocol for cognitive radio sensor networks," *Journal of Parallel and Distributed Computing*. https://doi.org/10.1016/j.jpdc.2020.04.007

[6] Dalal, V., & Malik, L. "*A survey of extractive and abstractive text summarization techniques*," *2013 6th International Conference on Emerging Trends in Engineering and Technology*, Nagpur, 2013, pp. 109–110. doi:10.1109/ICETET.2013.31

[7] Rose, S., Engel, D., Cramer, N., & Cowley, W. "Automatic keyword extraction from individual documents," in Berry, M. & Kogan, J. (eds) *Text Mining: Applications and Theory*, 1–20, 2010. https://doi.org/10.1002/9780470689646.ch1.

[8] Liu, F., & Liu, Y. "Exploring correlation between ROUGE and human evaluation on meeting summaries," *IEEE Transactions on Audio, Speech, and Language Processing*, vol. 18, no. 1, pp. 187–196, 2010, doi:10.1109/TASL.2009.2025096

[9] Tsoni, R., & Lionarakis, A., "*Plagiarism in higher education: The academics' perceptions*," *2014 International Conference on Interactive Mobile Communication Technologies and Learning (IMCL2014)*, Thessaloniki, 2014, pp. 296–300, doi:10.1109/IMCTL.2014.7011151.

[10] Bots, P., van Daalen, C. E., Dopper, S., & Westink, J. "*PrESTO: A Peer Review and Peer Assessment System with Incentives for High Quality Learning*," *18th International Conference on Information Technology Based Higher Education and Training (ITHET)*, Magdeburg, Germany, 2019, pp. 1–5, doi:10.1109/ITHET46829.2019.8937379.

[11] Shehab, A., Elhoseny, M., Hassanien, A. E. "*A hybrid key scheme for Automated Essay Grading based on LVQ and NLP techniques*," *2016 12th International Computer Engineering Conference*, pp. 65–70, 2016.

[12] Qiu, L., Ru, D., Long, Q., Zhang, W., & Yu, Y. "QA4IE: A question answering based system for document-level general information extraction," *IEEE Access*, vol. 8, pp. 29677–29689, 2020. doi:10.1109/ACCESS.2020.2970119.

[13] Hasanah, U., Astuti, T., Wahyudi, R., Rifai, Z., & Pambudi, R. A. *"An experimental study of text preprocessing techniques for automatic short answer grading in Indonesian,"* 2018 *3rd International Conference on Information Technology, Information System and Electrical Engineering (ICITISEE)*, Yogyakarta, Indonesia, 2018, pp. 230–234. doi:10.1109/ICITISEE.2018.8720957.

[14] Patel, B., & Shah, D. *"Significance of stop word elimination in meta search engine,"* 2013 *International Conference on Intelligent Systems and Signal Processing (ISSP)*, Gujarat, 2013, pp. 52–55. doi:10.1109/ISSP.2013.6526873.

[15] Manalu, S. R. *"Stop words in review summarization using TextRank,"* 2017 *14th International Conference on Electrical Engineering/Electronics, Computer, Telecommunications and Information Technology (ECTI-CON)*, Phuket, 2017, pp. 846–849. doi:10.1109/ECTICon.2017.8096371.

[16] Ganiger, S., & Rajashekharaiah, K. M. M. *"Comparative Study on Keyword Extraction Algorithms for Single Extractive Document,"* 2018 *Second International Conference on Intelligent Computing and Control Systems (ICICCS)*, Madurai, India, 2018, pp. 1284–1287. doi:10.1109/ICCONS.2018.8663040.

[17] Hernández-Castañeda, Á., García-Hernández, R. A., Ledeneva, Y., & Millán-Hernández, C. E. "Extractive automatic text summarization based on lexical-semantic keywords," *IEEE Access*, vol. 8, pp. 49896–49907, 2020, doi:10.1109/ACCESS.2020.2980226

[18] Ghosh, S., & Fatima, S. S. "Design of an Automatic Essay Grading (AEG) system," *Indian Context in Journal of Educational Technology*, vol. 4, no. 3, pp. 19–26, 2007.

[19] Romero, C., & Ventura, S. "Educational data mining: A review of the state of the art," *IEEE Transactions on Systems, Man, and Cybernetics, Part C (Applications and Reviews)*, vol. 40, no. 6, pp. 601–618, 2010. doi:10.1109/TSMCC.2010.2053532.000

[20] He, T. et al., *"ROUGE-C: A fully automated evaluation method for multi-document summarization,"* *IEEE International Conference on Granular Computing*, Hangzhou, 2008, pp. 269–274, doi: 10.1109/GRC.2008.4664680.

[21] Benard Magara, M., Ojo, S. O., & Zuva, T. *"A comparative analysis of text similarity measures and algorithms in research paper recommender systems,"* 2018 *Conference on Information Communications Technology and Society (ICTAS)*, Durban, 2018, pp. 1–5. doi:10.1109/ICTAS.2018.8368766.

[22] Pribadi, F. S., Adji, T. B., & Permanasari, A. E. "Automated Short Answer Scoring using Weighted Cosine Coefficient," 2016 *IEEE Conference on e-Learning, e-Management and e-Services (IC3e)*, Langkawi, 2016, pp. 70–74, doi:10.1109/IC3e.2016.8009042

[23] Sheugh, L., & Alizadeh, S. H. *"A note on pearson correlation coefficient as a metric of similarity in recommender system,"* 2015 *AI & Robotics (IRANOPEN)*, Qazvin, 2015, pp. 1–6. doi:10.1109/RIOS.2015.7270736

[24] Ayub, M., Ghazanfar, M. A., Maqsood, M., & Saleem, A. (2018). *"A Jaccard base similarity measure to improve performance of CF based recommender systems,"* 2018 *International Conference on Information Networking (ICOIN)*, pp. 1–6.

[25] Lahitani, A. R., Permanasari, A. E., & Setiawan, N. A. (2016). *"Cosine similarity to determine similarity measure: Study case in online essay assessment,"* 2016 *4th International Conference on Cyber and IT Service Management*.

[26] Sun, Q., Wu, J., Rong, W., & Liu, W. "Formative assessment of programming language learning based on peer code review: Implementation and experience report," *Tsinghua Science and Technology*, vol. 24, no. 4, pp. 423–434, 2019, doi:10.26599/TST.2018.9010109.

Chapter 11

Building Autonomous IIoT Networks Using Energy Harvesters

Rathishchandra R. Gatti, Shruthi H. Shetty, and Ashwath Rao

Sahyadri College of Engineering & Management, Mangalore, India

Contents

Introduction

Sensors have evolved right from being just simple display elements of the sensed data as we find in dial gauges back in the 1880s to the modern complex Industrial Internet of Things (IIoT) sensors that are not only wireless but also have micro-computational power built within them with built-in ultralow-power (ULP) micro-controllers. On the one hand, new components are integrated into the sensors to give additional functionalities other than the primary function of sensing the

DOI: 10.1201/9781003119784-11

measurand such as signal processing, edge computing, wireless data transmission, sensor fusion, and finally being autonomous by means of energy harvesting.

One can argue that due to advances in MEMS/NEMS technologies, the sensors are shrinking in their size and there is growth in ULP electronics as well, thus decreasing the power consumption of IIoT sensors. However, these two major trends in sensors cannot offset the ever-increasing reliance of the IIoT sensors on power consumption for their operations. For example, even if a particular IIoT sensor may consist of an array of only passive sensors with ULP microcontrollers, it may still require power for its own edge computing or at the least for wireless transmission of sensed data to the router or central server. This need for the power of IIoT edge devices has necessitated the growth of energy harvesting.

Energy Harvesting is the process of converting the available ambient energy in the vicinity of the IoT edge devices (IoT sensor, actuator, router, etc.) into useful forms of energy (usually electrical energy) as required by the IoT edge devices (sensor/actuator/transceiver/computing device). Currently, the reported state-of-the-art energy harvesters generate energy from 10 μW to 1 W (max) and are thus limited to powering only IoT sensors. The other IoT edge devices consume more power, from 1 to 5 W for small actuators to several KWs for data centers/servers. Only large renewable systems can be utilized to power such power-expensive IoT edge devices for autonomous operations. The scope of this chapter is limited to the powering of IIoT edge sensors that come within the purview of energy-harvestable edge devices.

Concept of Energy Harvesting Explained

To understand the concept of energy harvesting, one needs to have a basic understanding of the IoT smart sensor and its power requirements. A typical IoT smart sensor is shown in Figure 11.1(a). It consists of a sensor or a sensor array of multiple sensors, a wireless transceiver, a microcontroller (μC), a power-management circuit (PMC) and a battery. However, such an IoT sensor configuration that solely relies on the battery as the power source has serious reliability concerns and is expensive to maintain. Hence, one can replace the battery with battery–energy harvester combo or energy harvester, as shown in Figure 11.1(b) and (c), respectively. The transition of the battery-based IoT sensor to a completely battery-less IoT sensor is the current evolution needed for the ubiquitous deployment of IoT sensors. As of now, the transition is achieved till what is shown in Figure 11.1(b) as there is still a need for an energy buffer between the energy consumption of the sensors and the energy generation of the energy harvesters. However, recently, the trend to adopt neutral design policies toward completely battery-less IoT operation for complete autonomy is trending in the wireless sensor network research [1], as shown in Figure 11.1(c).

An energy harvester can thus be defined as a transducer that converts the available ambient energy into electrical energy in the order of microwatts to milli-watts that is sufficient to power the IoT sensors. One can consider energy harvesters as

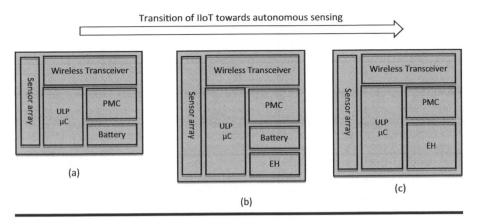

Figure 11.1 **(a) IoT smart wireless sensor, (b) IoT smart wireless sensor with battery – EH combo and (c) IoT smart wireless sensor with only EH.**

powering devices that need to be embedded into each IoT edge device to enable autonomous control of the WSN network. Energy harvesters can work either in tandem with the battery pack or independently to power all the activities in electronic components of the IoT sensor.

Energy harvesters are usually classified based on the energy source they scavenge and based on the energy transduction physics they use for energy scavenging. Based on the ambient power source being scavenged, energy harvesters are classified as – Kinetic Energy Harvesters (KEHs) [2], Vibration Energy Harvesters (VEHs) [3], Thermal Energy Harvesters (TEHs) [4], Light Energy Harvesters (LEHs) [5], Chemical Energy Harvesters (CEHs) [6], Triboelectric Energy Harvesters (TEEHs) [7] and Radio-Frequency Energy Harvesters (RFEHs) [8], as shown in Table 11.1. The sub-classifications of each major type of energy harvester are based on the energy transduction physics used. For example, VEHs are further classified as Electromagnetic Vibration Energy Harvesters (EMVEHs) [9], Piezoelectric Vibration Energy Harvesters (PZVEHs) [10], Magnetostrictive Vibration Energy Harvesters (MVEHs) [11] and Electrostatic Vibration Energy Harvesters (ESVEHs) [12] based on the known energy transduction physical phenomena that convert vibrations to electrical energy.

KEHs are transducers that convert ambient mechanical motion into electrical energy. The types of mechanical motion that can be harvested are straight-line motion, curvilinear motion and repetitive (straight-line or curvilinear) motion. Electrodynamic energy harvesters such as microhydraulic rotary generators and micropendulum generators can convert the non-repetitive kinetic motion to electric energy but a majority of the KEHs are VEHs that involve repetitive motion. The other option that is usually designed is the conversion of non-repetitive motion into repetitive motion such as vibrations so that it can be harnessed by VEHs.

VEHs constitute a major part of KEHs due to the presence of ambient vibrations in most of the targeted sensor locations in the industrial sector, especially machines and structures. One good example is the use of VEHs to power the GE

Table 11.1 Classification of Energy Harvesters

Sl.no	Ambient Energy to Be Harvested	Major Classification	Energy Transduction Principle	Sub-classification
1	Ambient vibrations or random kinetic motion convertible to repeated motion such as vibration	Kinetic Energy Harvesters (KEHs) out of which Vibration Energy Harvesters (VEHs) are the major part of KEHs.	Electromagnetic induction	Electromagnetic Vibration Energy Harvesters (EMVEHs)
			Piezoelectric effect	Piezoelectric Vibration Energy Harvesters (PZVEHs)
			Reverse magnetostrictive effect	Magnetostrictive Vibration Energy Harvesters (MVEHs)
			Capacitive effect	Electrostatic Vibration Energy Harvesters (ESVEHs)
2	Ambient heat or temperature difference	Thermal Energy Harvesters (TEHs)	Thermo-electric or Seeback effect	Thermoelectric Energy Harvesters (TETEHs)
			Pyroelectric effect (for time-varying continuous temperature)	Pyroelectric Energy Harvesters (PEHs)
3	Ambient Light	Light Energy Harvesters (LEHs)	Photoelectric effect	Photovoltaic Energy Harvesters (PVEHs)

4	Ambient chemicals that can be used as electrolyte or electrode	Chemical Energy Harvesters (CEHs)	Electrolysis	Electrochemical Energy Harvesters (ECEHs)
5	Ambient Frictional energy	Triboelectric Energy Harvesters (TEEHs)	Tribo-electric effect	TEEHs
6	Ambient RF waves	Radio-Frequency Energy Harvesters (RFEHs)	RF to electrical energy	RFEHs
7	Same ambient energy sources	Homogenous Hybrid Energy Harvesters (Homo-HEHs/ HoHEHs)	Multiple energy transduction principles	HoHEHs
8	Multiple ambient energy sources	Heterogeneous Hybrid Energy Harvesters (Hetero-HEHs HoHEHs)	Multiple energy transduction principles	HeHEHs

Insight mesh WSN that was deployed in the Shell's Nevada plant [13]. The VEH transduction mechanisms currently employed include piezoelectric effect [10b], electromagnetic induction [3], magnetostriction effect [11] and electrostatic effect [12]. Among VEHs, the inertial-based VEH types are PZVEHs and EMVEHs and constitute a major portion of the VEH state-of-the-art developments [2].

PZVEHs are based on the piezoelectric effect shown by a class of special piezo-electric materials such as lead titanate ($PbTiO_2$, quartz crystals, lead zirconate titanate (PZT), etc.) [14]. When these materials are subject to stresses induced due to ambient vibration, they generate an electric charge. PZVEHs are preferred in most of the IIoT sensors because they produce a good amount of voltage and power even for low strain variations. A typical PZVEH usually contains an inertial mass element suspended on a beam layered with piezoelectric materials on the surfaces perpendicular to the direction of vibration. When repeated pressure is applied to the piezoelectric beam, an EMF is produced.

EMVEHs are inertia-based VEHs wherein the inertial mass elements which are inductive in nature, like coil or magnet, are used. These are based on Faraday's electromagnetic induction coupling principle which states that EMF is produced between a coil and a magnet when there is relative motion between them. This necessitates three coil–magnet configurations: (a) stationary coil–moving magnet, (b) stationary magnet–moving coil and (c) moving coil–moving magnet with relative motion. The rate of change flux with respect to time and the amount of magnetic flux will decide the generated EMF of EMVEH. EMVEHs are employed for high-power, high-current, low-voltage applications [3].

MVEHs are transducers made of magnetostrictive materials such as Galfenol, Terfenol, etc., where the energy transduction is the Weidemann effect or the Matteuci effect [15]. When the ambient vibrations induce strains on the magnetostrictive material, the magnetic shape changes, inducing an EMF. Magnetostrictive materials have high energy density and their bidirectional coupling provides a good coupling factor [11], thus enhancing the energy transduction capability of the MVEHs.

ESVEHs employ a capacitive effect for energy transduction wherein mechanical vibrations cause relative motion between two parallel metallic plates that are subjected to supply voltage [12]. This requirement of supply voltage makes them a passive energy transducer, unlike other VEHs that do not require input voltage. However, similar to PZVEHs, ESVEHs are relatively easy to scale to MEMS/NEMS structures [16] and hence have widespread applications in IIoT sensors.

In TEHs, thermal energy in the form of heat or temperature difference is transduced into electrical energy by using the thermoelectric effect [17]. The most commonly used technology is the thermoelectric generator.

TEHs are also very common in the IIoT networks due to the abundance and omnipresence of heat in most industrial systems that require sensor monitoring. Heat is the most usual form of wasted energy. TEHs have low maintenance, are lightweight and durable in extreme conditions. TEHs are widely used in Wireless Body Area Networks (WBANs).

LEHs convert light energy into electrical energy by means of the photovoltaic (PV) effect. When photons are incident on a PV material, it knocks off the electrons of the outermost orbit that flows across the material causing electric current. Traditionally, monocrystalline, polycrystalline Silicon and Gallium Arsenide were used as PV materials but now the trend is toward mesoscopic PV cells such as dye-sensitized PV cells and perovskite PV cells [18]. In PVEHs, there are two major subdivisions, namely, indoor PVEHs and outdoor PVEHs. The indoor PVEHs have efficiencies in the range of 46–67% for indoor lights [19]. By using maximum power point tracking, the efficiency can shoot up to 76% [5, 20].

In CEHs, the chemical energy is converted to electrical energy by means of electrolysis in a microfabricated electrochemical cell [21]. One example of a state-of-the-art CEH is a flexible parylene-film-based microfabricated electrochemical cell that was used as a gastric battery. This CEH used gastric juice as the electrolyte, Zinc as anode and Palladium as cathode and was able to generate 1.25 mW of power for its surface area of 15 mm^2, just sufficient enough for powering the camera of endoscopic applications [22]. Such CEHs can also be used for medical implants and in other applications where the chemicals can be used either as the electrolyte or the sacrificial electrode. Although the consumption is non-renewable, due to the amount of consumption in microquantities, these CEHs can still be considered for self-sustaining IIoT applications.

TEEHs [7] are based on the contact electrification process wherein the electric charge is produced when two different materials of different polarities when contacted with each other and then separated by a small distance. TEEHs have high energy density compared to PZVEHs and EMVEHs and are simple, cost-effective to fabricate and can use natural eco-friendly materials. TEEHs also are reported to be very energy efficient with minimum energy losses and are extremely reliable because of their construction.

Energies from the far-field radio-frequency (RF) waves can be converted into electrical DC power by means of RFEHs [8]. RFEHs are typically rectennas attached to suitable PMCs. Each rectenna has an RF antenna and non-linear ultrafast diode by means of which it can transduce RF waves into DC power. The available RF energy ranges from 0.1 to 100 μW. RFEHs are becoming prominent due to the abundant availability of RF waves (energy source) in the ambient atmosphere.

The reliability of an energy-harvesting system increases when there is a continuous supply of ambient energy for the required power characteristics in its vicinity. This is often not possible if only one form of energy is considered. To increase the probability of energy supply and make the system more reliable, energy-harvesting researchers are exploring the possibilities of hybrid energy harvesting. Hybrid

Energy Harvesters (HEHs) are EH systems capable of harvesting more than one type of energy source [23].

Another enabler toward the need for HEHs is that ambient energy is always found as an amalgamation of different energy forms. One example is rotating machinery and, for that matter, any machinery involving components having relative motion to each other. In this case, there is always vibration and heat that exist as ambient energy losses. Hence, employing a thermal vibration HEH [24] will harness most of the ambient energy in the vicinity of machine parts. There may also be a possibility that a particular machinery or its subsystem can have both high frequency–low amplitude vibrations and low frequency–high amplitude vibrations to coexist. In such a scenario, one can employ PZVEHs in tandem with EMVEHs [25]. Hence, HEHs can further be sub-classified as Homogenous HEHs and Heterogeneous HEHs. Homogenous HEHs form when two or more types of energy harvesters of different energy transduction physics but harvest the same ambient energy source are combined. Heterogeneous HEHs form when two or more types of energy harvesters scavenging from different ambient energy sources are combined. As mentioned above, a thermal—vibration HEH is a Heterogeneous HEH and piezo-electromagnetic HEH will be a homogenous HEH because both harvest the same source, namely, vibration. The solar-vibration HEH consisting of nanopillar photovoltaic cells with PVDF-based piezoelectric nanogenerator was reported by [26]. These nanopillars were plasma-etched and annealed to fabricate to a size of a few hundred nanometers with a solar cell efficiency of about 3.29%. The PVDF components were able to produce 0.8 V for 100 dB sound vibration. [27] demonstrated a flexible HEH that could simultaneously scavenge solar, thermal and vibrational energies by employing photovoltaic, pyroelectric and piezoelectric transduction principles. This HEH used poly(vinylidene fluoride) (PVDF) nanofilms that demonstrated both pyroelectric and piezoelectric properties in conjunction with ZnO–poly(3-hexylthiophene) (P3HT) heterojunction solar cell for hybrid energy-harvesting. [28] demonstrated a solar–thermal HEH for harnessing energy from indoor sunlight and temperature difference. This HEH was sufficient to power 1 mAh of thin battery for 20 min using solar energy, in 40 min using thermal energy and in eight hours using vibrational energy.

Energy Requirements of IIoT Sensors and Extent of Autonomy

There is no straightforward approach for understanding the power requirements of the IIoT network. Several energy generation-consumption models can be found in the literature with different perspectives. As discussed in [29], a very simplified model analogous to the bounded-buffer problem, the net energy required for an operation time (t) at an instant τ by the IIoT edge device can be given by

$$E_{DEV}(t) \geq E_{buf}^{(t=0)} + E_{scv} \qquad (11.1)$$

where $E_{DEV}(t) = \int_{\tau=0}^{t} P_{DEV}(\tau)d\tau$ = energy required by the IoT edge device, $E_{SCV} = \int_{\tau=0}^{t} P_{scv}(\tau)d\tau$ = energy harvested or scavenged, $E_{buf}^{(t=0)}$ is the buffer or stored energy, P_{DEV} = power required by the device and P_{SCV} = scavenged or harvested power. However, the recent developments focus on neutral designs with reducing the $E_{buf}^{(t=0)}$ to almost zero when the network is up and running. This is triggered by the fact that batteries are highly unreliable and those IoT networks that run without batteries can run for a long time without much human maintenance interventions, thus approaching a complete autonomous state as described in Figure 11.1(c).

The P_{DEV} can be calculated as

$$P_{DEV}(t) = P_{NET} + P_{ACQ} + P_{PRC} + P_{SYS} \qquad (11.2)$$

where P_{NET} = power for networking or data communication, P_{ACQ} = power for data acquisition, P_{PRC} = power for data processing and P_{SYS} = power for system operations like RTOS and wake-ups.

The power for networking or data communication is given by

$$P_{NET} = \sum_{i=0}^{N_{MSG}} \frac{N_R h(N_{SF}, E_{MSG})}{T_{MSG}(i)} \qquad (11.3)$$

where N_R = number of retransmissions, $h(N_{SF}, E_{MSG})$ is an energy-transmission function which depends on the spreading factor N_{SF} and the energy required for transmission E_{MSG}. The time between the consecutive messages $T_{MSG}(i)$ can be approximated to the expected value of the time $E(T_{MSG})$ for long-term averaging of probability distribution models of sensor data transmission. As it can be seen in equation (11.3), the selection of the spreading factor becomes critical for energy consumption. Usually, there is a tradeoff between the energy consumption for data transmission and the quality of the signals as higher N_{SF} corresponds to improved quality at the expense of energy.

The P_{ACQ} component depends on the sampling rate or the number of samples (N_s) to be acquired by the sensors for a fixed interval and the energy consumption (E_{smp}) for acquiring one such data sample. It is given as

$$P_{ACQ} = N_s E_{smp} / T_s \qquad (11.4)$$

for regular sensing intervals and

$$P_{ACQ} = P(X)N_s'E_{smp} / T_s \qquad (11.5)$$

for an event X with a probability of occurrence $P(X)$ within the sensing interval T_s and number of event samples N_s'.

The P_{PRC} and the P_{SYS} components depend primarily on two things, namely, (a) IIoT hardware configuration and its processing components, namely, the microcontroller and signal conditioners and (b) the time for built-in processing algorithms. It is hard to mathematically model this power component but can be accurately measured or approximately simulated.

Due to advancements in ULP electronics, transducer material fabrication processes and sensor fusion with PULP architecture, sensors have been miniaturized, thus reducing their power requirements enabling the IIoT energy management. The typical power requirements of the sensor elements used in the IIoT sensors are given in Table 11.2. Most of these sensor elements are digital sensors with digital output.

According to EEBMC benchmarking [30], the recent best-performing (in terms of processing speeds) ULP microcontrollers are summarized in Table 11.3 with the legacy ULP product MSP430. It can be observed that even the best-performing ULP LP5100 from Nanjing has a maximum power consumption rating of about 6 mW and can be used for ULP applications such as neurological implants. The typical voltage ratings of most of the ULPs were designed for voltage ratings in the order of 3–5 V.

Table 11.2 Power Requirements of Commonly Used ULP Sensor Elements

Sl. no	ULP Sensor Element	Typical Power Requirements (mW)
1	RFID Sensor	0.88–10 µW
2	IR sensor	175 µW
3	pH sensor	2.9 mW
4	Temperature sensor	max 648 µW
5	Accelerometer	max 12 µW
6	Acoustic sensor	25–30 mW
7	Fused sensor arrays using PULP platform	165 mW
8	Wireless sensor node	48–66 mW

Table 11.3 Power Requirements of Best-Performing ULP Microcontrollers*

	ULP Microcontroller	*Make*	*Year*	*Maximum Power**
1	LP5100 Rev.1	Nanjing Low Power ICTICL	2020	6 mW
2	R7F0E01182CFP	Renesas Electronics	2020	140 μW
3	RL78/I1D	Renesas Electronics	2019	209 μW
4	STM32WB3x/5x	STMicroelectronics	2019	190 μW
5	ATSAML10E16A	Microchip Technology	2019	90 μW
6	ATSAML11E16A	Microchip Technology	2019	90 μW
7	STM32L412	STMicroelectronics	2018	284 μW
8	STM32L552	STMicroelectronics	2018	382 μW
9	ADuCM4050	Analog Devices	2018	1.4 mW
10	MSP430	Texas Instruments	1992	506–828 μW

* Calculated based on maximum current and maximum voltage as specified in the respective datasheets

The other IIoT components are the transceivers for low-power wireless transmissions that can also be designed for ULP capacities, thus aiding the autonomous feasibility of IIoT networks. One such ULP transceiver was developed for WBAN in the frequency range of 2.36–2.48 GHz range and consumes about 0.715 mW to transmit about 1 Mbps data and 2.59 mW with on-off keying modulations [31]. Another ULP transceiver was developed as a 28-nm CMOS single-chip that had a power consumption capacity of 2.75 mW and 3.6 mW for receiving and transmitting, respectively, using BLE communication [32].

State of the Art and Possible Autonomous IIoT in Major Industries

According to markets and markets research, the IIoT is rapidly growing at a compound annual rate of about 7.4%. This may be due to enabling complementary technologies such as AI/ML and faster ULP processors. In 2020, the market size of IIoT was about USD 73 billion and is expected to be USD 110 billion in 2025.

The market share of different industrial sectors majorly includes manufacturing followed by energy, oil & gas, mining, healthcare, retail logistics, transport and agriculture. However, the reported energy-harvesting-based IIoT networks are used in some of these industrial sectors.

- **Manufacturing and Industrial plants** – About 30% of the IIoT is expected to be in smart manufacturing. The main thrust areas of importance for IIoT in manufacturing include optimizing the product lines, increasing machine life expectancy, effective resource utilization by reducing wastage of resources, remote access to manufacturing facilities and AI-driven factory automation with machine-to-machine (M2M) communication or even component-to-component communication (if the machine is large and needs wireless connectivity of its sensor network). The optimization of the product lines involves reducing the in-process manufacturing processes to reduce lead time as well as their associated costs and time. This is possible by having RFID tags on the produced products and then tracking them using IIoT sensors and networks [33], which can be made autonomous by powering them with RFEHs. One such technology that can be used is the Wattup® from Energous Corp. which has a wireless transmitter and receiver. RFEH must be coupled to the Wattup® transmitter and the Wattup® receiver to the wireless sensor node. Another application of IIoT sensors is in predictive condition monitoring of machinery for preventive maintenance to increase the useful life of the machines [34]. Typically, this involves condition monitoring sensors or an array of sensors with a predefined sensor fusion technology that is connected to the IIoT network. These IIoT sensors can be powered by VEHs, particularly Piezoelectric VEHs and TEHs or hybrid thermal vibration EHs. The commercially available TEG-based thermal EH from Perpetua was used industrial condition monitoring WSN of rotating machinery [35].
- **Energy** – Most often, energy is wasted in the form of heat. This is especially true when energy generation and distribution is on the scale of MW to GW. Heat dissipation needs to be critically controlled which otherwise may lead to dangerous accidents. This has necessitated the development of autonomous WSNs by means of employing TEHs and using the available heat losses as a source of energy [36]. VEHs can be utilized in tandem with WSNs which are involved in condition monitoring of vibrating machinery such as motors, generators, compressors and engines [37]. These rotary machines are prevalent in almost every type of energy plant such as solar-thermal plant, thermal power plant, wind energy plant, etc.
- **Healthcare** – The main use of the IoT in healthcare is in remote health monitoring of patients by the physicians, hospitals and insurance companies by using secured gateways. The patient-monitoring sensors can be in-vitro and/or in-vivo wireless sensors using the WBANs. The lifespan of the WBAN can be increased by using TEHs such as the TEG producing about 1.39 mJ

to transmit five words of 12-bit data. A PVEH-powered wireless sensor was tested by applying the PVEH subcutaneously. The experimental simulation was performed by placing the under a porcine flap of 3-mm thickness to power the implant [38]. Although such implantable energy-harvesting is feasible, it demands further risk and safety assessments to meet the stringent healthcare product clearances. For both in-vivo and in-vitro WBANs, embedding energy harvesters and making them autonomous is essential for making data mining hassle-free and intrusion-free. For example, a wired gastrointestinal endoscopy may be very intrusive and uncomfortable for the patient and may also be difficult to sense hard-to-reach locations. This can be replaced by capsule endoscopy wherein the camera sensors and a battery are sent in the form of a capsule. What would still be better is having an energy harvester integrated into the capsule. This was done by [22] wherein an electrochemical EH was used to utilize digestive juice as an electrolyte to generate electrical energy and hence charge the capsule batteries. In this case, zinc and palladium are used as electrodes and gastric juice is used as an electrolyte.

- **Agriculture** – Precision agriculture requires IIoT sensors for sensing soil, water, fertility, pH and climatic conditions for crop cultivation [39]. The IIoT is also required for livestock monitoring using RFID tags and pest and insect control using cameras and image processing. Nevertheless, IIoT sensors such as accelerometers are also required for condition monitoring of agricultural equipment and vehicles which are generally subject to high torque and wear conditions.

- **Infrastructure** – WinShine LD-MC wireless magnet contact is self-powered by embedding a PVEH, thus enabling the device to run for several days without the hassle of battery replacement. The size of the housing is very small ($90.5 \times 21.5 \times 13.5$ mm^3), thus making it convenient to install on aluminum, wood and other concrete materials. The radio technology used is Enocean 868 MHz with a transmission range of about 30 m within a building and 300 m free field, thus making it suited for infrastructure monitoring/smart buildings. ILLUMRA™ has come up with single rocker and double rocker self-powered light switches that can avoid wiring costs by making the switches wireless. These switches are self-powered by kinetic energy consumed from the switching action that is sufficient for them to control the lighting and other consumer appliances of residential and commercial buildings through ILLUMRA™ receivers (E3R-R12GP, E3R-R12-5IBBP). The datasheet claims that these self-powered switches run maintenance-free for about 20 years. Enocean™ manufactures a self-powered wireless occupancy sensor mountable on ceilings to control energy use based on occupancy in rooms. It is powered by indoor PV cells and works together with other RF-communication-enabled devices to perform building control operations such as switching off lights, room temperature devices and other electrical appliances when the room is unoccupied and on when occupied. Enocean™ also manufactures ETHSx, a self-powered wireless temperature and humidity sensor for smart homes that is powered by indoor PVEHs. In dark areas where light energy-harvesting is not feasible, this sensor node also can run by coin battery. Most smart homes use remote control units for different appliances or one universal remote control for multiple appliances other than mobile phone control. In such cases, the remote can be powered by the kinetic energy of key motion using PZVEH microgenerators sufficient to power the IR communication as manufactured by Arveni [40].

Future Scope of Expansion of Autonomous IIoT Deployment

It can thus be observed that several key factors will lead to the rapid development of autonomous IIoT technologies and their deployment. The scalability of sensors and energy harvesters to MEMS/NEMS will enable the deployment of sensors in hard-to-reach locations such as within the human body (WBANs), nuclear reactors, etc. The trend toward HEHs will increase the reliability of the self-powering of IIoT sensors, thus enabling the rapid deployment of autonomous IIoT. The development of ULP technologies is leading towards decreasing the power consumption and increasing the performance of the components of IIoT smart sensors, thus making way for autonomous IIoT deployment. By making the IIoT edge devices more autonomous with due considerations for the reliability of power sources, the IIoT is likely to substantially increase and cascade to new unexplored application domains.

References

[1] N. Bui and M. Rossi, "Staying alive: System design for self-sufficient sensor networks," *ACM Transactions on Sensor Networks (TOSN)*, vol. 11, no. 3, pp. 1–42, 2015.

[2] A. Khaligh, P. Zeng, and C. Zheng, "Kinetic energy harvesting using piezoelectric and electromagnetic technologies—state of the art," *IEEE Transactions on Industrial Electronics*, vol. 57, no. 3, pp. 850–860, 2009.

[3] R. R. Gatti, "Spatially-varying multi-degree-of-freedom electromagnetic energy harvesting," Curtin University, 2013.

[4] *Thermal energy harvesting for WSNs*: IEEE, 2010.

[5] D. Brunelli, L. Benini, C. Moser, and L. Thiele, "An Efficient Solar Energy Harvester for Wireless Sensor Nodes," in *2008 Design, Automation and Test in Europe*, 2008.

[6] H. Im *et al.*, "High-efficiency electrochemical thermal energy harvester using carbon nanotube aerogel sheet electrodes," *Nature Communications*, vol. 7, no. 1, pp. 1–9, 2016.

[7] A. Ibrahim, M. Jain, E. Salman, R. Willing, and S. Towfighian, "A smart knee implant using triboelectric energy harvesters," *Smart Materials and Structures*, vol. 28, no. 2, p. 25040, 2019.

[8] *A fully-autonomous Integrated RF Energy Harvesting System for Wearable Applications*: IEEE, 2013.

[9] *Electromagnetic Energy Harvesting by Spatially Varying the Magnetic Field*: Springer, 2012.

[10] N. Sezer and M. Koç, "A Comprehensive Review on the State-of-the-Art of Piezoelectric Energy Harvesting," *Nano Energy*, p. 105567, 2020.

[11] H. Jafari, A. Ghodsi, S. Azizi, and M. R. Ghazavi, "Energy harvesting based on magnetostriction, for low frequency excitations," *Energy*, vol. 124, pp. 1–8, 2017.

[12] F. U. Khan and M. U. Qadir, "State-of-the-art in vibration-based electrostatic energy harvesting," *Journal of Micromechanics and Microengineering*, vol. 26, no. 10, p. 103001, 2016.

[13] G. E. Energy, *Essential Insight. mesh Wireless Condition Monitoring*.

[14] H. Roshani, S. Dessouky, A. Montoya, and A. T. Papagiannakis, "Energy harvesting from asphalt pavement roadways vehicle-induced stresses: A feasibility study," *Applied Energy*, vol. 182, pp. 210–218, 2016.

[15] L. Wang and F. G. Yuan, "Vibration energy harvesting by magnetostrictive material," *Smart Materials and Structures*, vol. 17, no. 4, p. 45009, 2008.

[16] C. P. Le and E. Halvorsen, "MEMS electrostatic energy harvesters with end-stop effects," *Journal of Micromechanics and Microengineering*, vol. 22, no. 7, p. 74013, 2012.

[17] S. J. Kim, J. H. We, and B. J. Cho, "A wearable thermoelectric generator fabricated on a glass fabric," *Energy Environmental Science*, vol. 7, no. 6, pp. 1959–1965, 2014.

[18] H. Yu, Q. Yue, J. Zhou, and W. Wang, "A hybrid indoor ambient light and vibration energy harvester for wireless sensor nodes," *Sensors (Basel, Switzerland)*, vol. 14, no. 5, pp. 8740–8755, 2014, doi: 10.3390/s140508740.

[19] Y. Aoki, "Photovoltaic performance of Organic Photovoltaics for indoor energy harvester," *Organic Electronics*, vol. 48, pp. 194–197, 2017, doi: 10.1016/j.orgel.2017.05.023.

[20] Y. Wang et al., "Storage-less and converter-less photovoltaic energy harvesting with maximum power point tracking for internet of things," *IEEE Transactions on Computer-Aided Design of Integrated Circuits and Systems*, vol. 35, no. 2, pp. 173–186, 2015.

[21] H. Wei et al., "Energy conversion technologies towards self-powered electrochemical energy storage systems: The state of the art and perspectives," *Journal of Materials Chemistry A*, vol. 5, no. 5, pp. 1873–1894, 2017.

[22] P. Mostafalu and S. Sonkusale, "Flexible and transparent gastric battery: Energy harvesting from gastric acid for endoscopy application," *Biosensors and Bioelectronics*, vol. 54, pp. 292–296, 2014.

[23] H. Ryu, H.-J. Yoon, and S.-W. Kim, "Hybrid energy harvesters: Toward sustainable energy harvesting," *Advanced Materials*, vol. 31, no. 34, p. 1802898, 2019.

[24] M. Goudarzi, K. Niazi, and M. K. Besharati, "Hybrid energy harvesting from vibration and temperature gradient by PZT and PMN-0.25 PT ceramics," *Materials Physics and Mechanics*, vol. 16, no. 1, pp. 55–65, 2013.

[25] R. Hamid and M. R. Yuce, "A wearable energy harvester unit using piezoelectric–electromagnetic hybrid technique," *Sensors and Actuators A: Physical*, vol. 257, pp. 198–207, 2017.

[26] D.-Y. Lee et al., "Hybrid energy harvester based on nanopillar solar cells and PVDF nanogenerator," *Nanotechnology*, vol. 24, no. 17, p. 175402, 2013.

[27] Y. Yang, H. Zhang, G. Zhu, S. Lee, Z.-H. Lin, and Z. L. Wang, "Flexible hybrid energy cell for simultaneously harvesting thermal, mechanical, and solar energies," *ACS Nano*, vol. 7, no. 1, pp. 785–790, 2013.

[28] Y. K. Tan and S. K. Panda, "Energy harvesting from hybrid indoor ambient light and thermal energy sources for enhanced performance of wireless sensor nodes," *IEEE Transactions on Industrial Electronics*, vol. 58, no. 9, pp. 4424–4435, 2010.

[29] B. Martinez, M. Monton, I. Vilajosana, and J. D. Prades, "The power of models: Modeling power consumption for IoT devices," *IEEE Sensors Journal*, vol. 15, no. 10, pp. 5777–5789, 2015.

[30] EEMBC, *Scores for ULPMark-CP and ULPMark-PP.* [Online]. Available: https://www.eembc.org/ulpmark/scores.php (accessed: January 14 2021).

[31] M. Vidojkovic et al., "A 2.4 GHz ULP OOK Single-Chip Transceiver for Healthcare Applications," *IEEE Transactions on Biomedical Circuits and Systems*, vol. 5, no. 6, pp. 523–534, 2011, doi: 10.1109/TBCAS.2011.2173340.

[32] F. Kuo et al., "A Bluetooth low-energy (BLE) transceiver with TX/RX switchable on-chip matching network, 2.75mW high-IF discrete-time receiver, and 3.6mW all-digital transmitter," in *2016 IEEE Symposium on VLSI Circuits (VLSI-Circuits)*, 2016, pp. 1–2.

[33] A. R. Neto, M. F. G. Ribeiro, G. G. Cunha, and L. Landau, "The industrial internet of things and technological innovation in its applications for resources optimisation," *International Journal of Simulation and Process Modelling*, vol. 12, no. 6, pp. 525–534, 2017.

[34] D. Ganga and V. Ramachandran, "IoT-Based Vibration Analytics of Electrical Machines," *IEEE Internet of Things Journal*, vol. 5, no. 6, pp. 4538–4549, 2018, doi: 10.1109/JIOT.2018.2835724.

[35] Thomas Kafka, "Industrial Application of Thermal Energy Harvesting," Accessed: January 14, 2021. [Online]. Available: https://perpetuapower.com/wp-content/uploads/2015/12/GE_IDTechEx_Presentation_Berlin_20140402.pdf

[36] L. Hou, S. Tan, Z. Zhang, and N. W. Bergmann, "Thermal Energy Harvesting WSNs Node for Temperature Monitoring in IIoT," *IEEE Access*, vol. 6, pp. 35243–35249, 2018, doi: 10.1109/ACCESS.2018.2851203.

[37] A. S. Weddell, D. Zhu, G. V. Merrett, S. P. Beeby, and B. M. Al-Hashimi, "A practical self-powered sensor system with a tunable vibration energy harvester," 2012.

[38] T. Wu, J.-M. Redouté, and M. R. Yuce, "A wireless implantable sensor design with sub-cutaneous energy harvesting for long-term IoT healthcare applications," *IEEE Access*, vol. 6, pp. 35801–35808, 2018.

[39] S. S. K. Pokala and A. A. Bini, "A low cost IoT enabled device for monitoring agriculture field and smart irrigation system," in *Inventive Communication and Computational Technologies*: Springer, 2021, pp. 923–932.

[40] J.-F. Martin, *Self-contained U or V shaped piezoelectric device for generating voltage, U.S. Patent 8,198,788*: USPTO.

Chapter 12

An Interactive TUDIG Application for Tumor Detection in MRI Brain Images Using Cascaded CNN with LBP Features

G. Dheepa and P. L. Chithra
University of Madras, Chennai, India

Contents

DOI: 10.1201/9781003119784-12

Introduction

A brain tumor is an abnormal development of anomalous cells inside the brain [1]. It is classified into two types, namely, Low-Grade Gliomas (LGG) or benign and High-Grade Gliomas (HGG) or malignant [2, 3]. The LGG tumor is very less aggressive with non-cancerous cells and the HGG tumor contains malignant or cancerous cells originating anywhere in the human body that spreads towards the brain [4]. This brain tumor has a complex tissue structure that is interconnected in a complicated manner [5]. Even under treatment, brain tumor patients are not surviving on an average of more than 14 months after diagnosis [6]. Magnetic Resonance Imaging (MRI) is a diagnostic technique used by neuroradiologists for capturing brain tissues, which gives a detailed and very deep structure of the brain without having to use ionization radiation [7, 8]. Each patient image from an MRI comprises four multi-model MRI sequences, i.e., FLAIR (Fluid-Attenuated Intervention Recovery), T1-weighted sequence (T1), T1 with a contrast-enhanced image (T1c), and a T2-weighted sequence (T2) [9]. These four multi-modal sequences are present in both LGG and HGG images [10]. The example images of four MRI sequences are shown in the below figure.

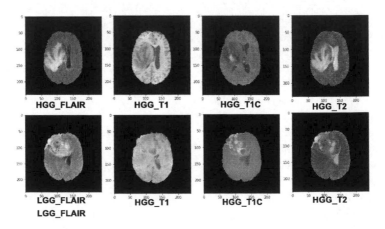

An accurate windows application of tumor detection has great practical importance in tumor diagnosis and treatment planning [11]. There are a huge number of works that have been done in MRI brain tumor identification. In earlier days, this task used to be performed manually by radiologists [12]. However, manual methods of tumor detection are time-consuming and their results often vary among neuroradiologists [13]. So, semi-automatic and automatic detection methods are used for research applications and clinical applications [14]. Existing semi-automatic detection techniques include Support Vector Machine (SVM) [15], K-means [16], Discrete Wavelet Transformation (DWT) [5, 17], Fuzzy-C-Means (FCM) [18], K-Nearest Neighbor [19], Continuous Wavelet Transformation (CWT), Conditional Random Field (CRF) [10], Random Forest (RF) [20] and Markov Random Field (MRF). These methods are less accurate, time-consuming and radiologist dependent process.

Now-a-days, there is a need for accurate tumor detection in the availability of medical data and the development in technology and science [21]. To avoid the limitations in semi-automated methods, automated neural network-based methods are used for finding a tumor in 3-dimensional MRI brain images [22]. These methods have been used to classify image features automatically [23]. Some of the currently available methods outperformed deep learning methods, like Feed Forward Artificial Neural Network (FFANN), U-Net, Fully Convolutional Neural Network (FCNN), Multi-Layer Perceptron (MLP) and Probabilistic Neural Network-based methods handles a single way of feature map [24]. In these methods, the image features alone to be processed in the network layers are for extracting and classifying image features automatically. Mostly, deep learning methods use a patch-based image classification technique to convert an input image into a group of patches [25]. These patch-based image classification techniques have very little accuracy compared to the image-based methods [26].

To overcome these limitations and to get more accuracy, a novel cascaded Convolutional Neural Network (CNN) has been implemented for handling multiple cascaded features [27]. In this method, features like patterns and textures are extracted in all brain images using LBP. The LBP texture descriptors are used to describe the patterns and texture of a given image which is mostly used for image classification, object detection and recognition algorithm [28]. This LBP feature extraction is to extract and represent the image attributes [2]. The extracted features have been convolved by three kernels of 3×3, 7×7 and 5×5 to produce different feature maps. These are cascaded to produce an efficient feature. Again, these feature maps have been processed into an upcoming two convolutional and two pooling layers. Then, this outcome is processed in the Fully Connected (FC) layer. Finally, the softmax classification is used for carrying out the pixel-wise prediction of classes. These predicted class labels have been compared with ground truth for performance calculation.

The whole architecture is tested by BRATS 2018 tumor dataset. Experimental results achieved an average of 97% accuracy, 94% specificity, 98% precision, 98%

F1-score and 99% sensitivity values for detecting normal and abnormal brain MRI images.

Thus, the proposed method is pristine in the following ways.

■ The detailed features like patterns and textures are extracted in all brain images using the LBP feature extraction technique.

■ The extracted LBP features of all brain images are processed using cascaded CNN for detecting tumor and non-tumor images.

■ This cascaded CNN architecture has an input of three different cascaded features from 3 × 3, 7 × 7 and 5 × 5 kernels which have comparatively greater accuracy than the existing methods.

■ The proposed method takes the whole image as an input for training the cascaded CNN architecture which has higher performance than the methods having an input of image patches.

■ This cascaded CNN works well with LBP features than the existing feature extraction techniques and it has 5% higher accuracy than the existing brain tumor detection technique. It demonstrates the efficiency of the proposed method for detecting normal and abnormal brain images.

■ The whole algorithm is converted to an interactive window-based application named TUDIG (TUmor DIAgnosis).

Related Works

The tumor is considered anomalous and intracranial cells in the central spinal canal or nucleus of the brain [29]. An accurate and automated tumor identification algorithm from MRI is essential for medical analysis, clinical assessments, interpretation and treatment [30]. There are many techniques are reported for MRI brain tumor detection [31]. Traditionally, the tumor detection technique is done manually by radiologists but this method has low accuracy, and high rater variability. Nowadays, some of the existing toolkits are available for brain tumor diagnosis [32]. Devatzitos et al. proposed a phenomics toolkit based on imageprocessing methods for diagnosing brain tumors [33]. BraTS toolkit is specifically designed for the segmentation process [34]. HemoSYS tool is also uses some image processing concepts for diagnosis [35]. Recently, semi-automated and automated detection methods are used for research applications and clinical applications. Conventionally, K-Means, random forest and FCM methods have been used for tumor identification. Madhukumar and Sathyakumari have proposed K-Means and FCM-based tumor diagnosis methods [36]. Parveen et al. [18] have developed a novel FCM algorithm for tumor detection. Rajagopal [37] has implemented a weighted random forest classifier for tumor diagnosis. In this algorithm, optimized ant colony-based features are extracted in all brain images and processed using a random forest classifier to perform tumor detection in brain images. FCM, random forest and K-Means methods are all semi-automatic; that is, they are radiologist-dependent and time-consuming.

Angulakshmi and Lakshmi Priya used a spectral clustering algorithm for tumor identification. In this, the superpixels are extracted in all brain images and tumor diagnosis is performed using spectral clustering [38]. Mohammadreza et al. also used a superpixel-based tumor-detection. algorithm. In this method, each image is split into a number of superpixels; when compared to the Gabor textons, intensity-based, image curvatures and fractal analysis are computed in each superpixel. Further, SVM and Extremely Randomized Trees (RT) are used for classing each superpixel image pixels into tumor or non-tumor [39]. These methods have very low performance in LGG tumor images. Nilesh et al. used Berkeley's Wavelet Transformation (BWT) and SVM-based methods as tumor-identification techniques [40]. Sandhya et al. have implemented 2D Daubechies DWT as a brain tumor classification technique [41]. In this, the foreground brain region alone is to be extracted using the Active Contour Model (ACM) and their features are extracted using DWT. The extracted feature dimension is reduced using Independent Component Analysis (ICA). Then, this reduced feature is classified using SVM. These methods are also radiologist-dependent processes because they requires programmer interaction for initializing parameters.

Noosan et al. have extracted statistical features like average contrast, skewness, mean, energy and entropy, kurtosis and some Gray Level Co-occurrence Matrix (GLCM) features like entropy, correlation, inertia, homogeneity, inverse difference, absolute value, maximum probability and energy (angular second movement). Then, these features are classified using a wavelet for tumor identification [42]. Jasmine and Thirumurugan have extracted statistical features like standard deviation and moment, Arithmetic Mean Feature (AMF) features and GLCM features like energy, contrast, inertia and moment inertia, correlation, and homogeneity from all brain images. The extracted features have been classified using the Co-active Adaptive Neuro-Fuzzy Inference System (CANFIS) to find if it is tumor or non-tumor [43]. Sivakumar and Ganeshkumar extracted Local Ternary Pattern (LTP) features and some GLCM features like contrast, angular second moment, entropy, homogeneity, mean, and correlation. The extracted features have been classified using the CANFIS algorithm for brain tumor identification [44]. These three algorithms can work well in defined features but it has low performance compared to the currently available automated tumor detection methods.

Belkacem et al. have implemented multi-segmentation-based brain-tumor detection. In this, an improved region growing method has been proposed which uses expectation-maximization and quasi-Monte Carlo algorithm for defining the class labels. Nowadays, Extreme Learning Machine (ELM) [45] and Ensemble Classifier (EC) have been used for the tumor-detection process. Parasuraman et al. have proposed EC for tumor diagnosis [46]. In this method, the GLCM features are extracted in all brain images and processed using ensemble classifiers. This ensemble classification technique is an efficient tumor-identification method having a combination of Feed-Forward Artificial Neural Network (FFANN), SVM and ELM methods. In this method, detailed information may be lost in poor illumination images. This method also needs interaction from the programmer to initialize parameters for classifying tumor images.

To overcome these limitations, an accurate and automated algorithm is necessary for tumor detection in MRI images. Advanced deep learning-based methods have been used to classify the image features automatically from the input data. Some of the currently available deep learning methods like Feed Forward Artificial Neural Network (FFANN), U-Net, FCNN, MLP and Probabilistic Neural Network are performing better in brain tumor diagnosis [47]. Kumar et al. have implemented FFANN for brain tumor diagnosis. In this, the GLCM features are extracted and processed using FFANN for detecting brain tumors [48]. FFANN algorithm works better in pattern-recognition and pattern classification techniques [49]. Saumya et al. also extracted GLCM and Principal Component Analysis (PCA) for training Neural Networks that achieved competitive performance than the traditional semi-automatic methods.

Mohmoud Khaled et al. used a two-phase diagnosis system in an automated manner. In this method, the brain region alone to be segmented and preprocessed using median filter. The preprocessed images are further processed using CNN to detect tumor and non-tumor images automatically from the input data [50]. Hema et al. have implemented CNN and particle swarm optimization (PSO) algorithm for an efficient brain tumor classification [51]. Some of the transfer learning-based deep learning models like Alex net and Google net are also used as efficient tumor identification methods [52]. The DWT feature extraction and CNN-based classification also perform better in the tumor diagnosis process [53]. Talwar et al. extracted DWT-based wavelet features and classified them using a probabilistic neural network for brain-tumor detection [54]. Adel et al. also implemented a deep CNN for automatic brain tumor identification in 3-dimensional MRI images [55]. Zeynettin et al. also implemented a patch-based CNN model for tumor detection. This algorithm has the drawback of patchreconstruction problem and also contains data-loss problem while reconstruction [56]. These automated methods are handles a single way of feature maps and patch-based tumor detection systems which has very less accuracy than the image-based tumor detection methods. To avoid these drawbacks, an interactive TUDIG application based on LBP features and cascaded CNN is proposed for the automatic identification of MRI tumor images.

Materials and Methods

In this research, an accurate and automated windows application based on cascaded CNN with LBP features is developed for tumor detection in brain MRI images. The proposed tumor detection method has the following main phases: first, database and workstations are defined to develop the project; then, the tumoral features are extracted using LBP; after that, the idea behind CNN is analyzed; the LBP features are processed using cascaded CNN; the processed output is then sent to the FC layer and the extracted features are classified using softmax; further, the loss function is calculated using Categorical Cross Entropy; the proposed algorithm is trained and their performance is calculated using Benchmark metrics; finally, this complete algorithm is converted to the interactive windows application named TUDIG. The main workflow of this proposed algorithm using LBP, cascaded CNN and TUDIG application are illustrated in the below figure.

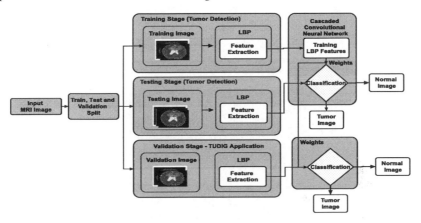

Database and Workstation

This experiment has been tested using BRATS-2018 dataset contains 210 patient images of HGG and 75 images of LGG. Each patient image comprises four multi-model MRI sequences, i.e., FLAIR, T1-weighted sequence (T1), T1 with a contrast-enhanced image (T1c), and T2-weighted sequence (T2). These sequences are annotated by experienced radiologists and also contain pre-processed image sequences. This dataset is scanned by various vendors at several different centers, namely Massachusetts General Hospital, Wang lab, Debrecen University, Computational Biomarker Imaging Group (CBIG), Bern University, Center for Neuroimaging in Psychiatry (CNIP) and Heidelberg University. The proposed algorithm is implemented using a version of Python 3.7 running on the Windows 7 operating system having Intel R-core (TM) i7-4500U 2.30 GHz speed, 12 GB RAM and 2 GB of Graphic Processor Unit (GPU). In Python 3.7, Keras and Tensorflow have been used to develop the cascaded CNN architecture and Tkinter packages are used to develop an interactive windows application of TUDIG (TUmor DIAgnosis).

Feature Extraction Using LBP

LBP is used for characterizing the pattern, texture and local representation of an image. The local representation is computed by comparing every pixel with the surrounding pixel values. The LBP is computed by using both mehotas and scikit-image packages in the python 3.7 version. Both these packages work well but scikit-image package is easier to use for implementing the LBP algorithm. In this algorithm, a neighborhood of 3 × 3 or 7 × 7 window size surrounding a center pixel is chosen for every pixel in the brain image. The simple 3 × 3 window is extremely fast and efficient, which requires a very simple thresholding method and quicker bit operations. In this, each pixel value is considered as a center pixel and compared with the surrounding pixels. If the surrounding pixels are greater than the center pixel, it means the corresponding pixel value is replaced by zero, else that corresponding pixel value is replaced by one. Then, the LBP value is calculated for the center pixel based on the surrounding pixel value position. The overall workflow of the LBP is depicted in below figures.

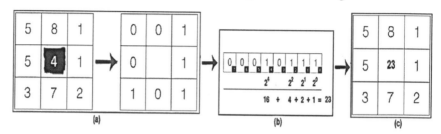

(a)   (b)   (c)

First, a standard window is moved over each pixel value. Here, each image pixel is considered as the center pixel that is compared with the surrounding pixels for calculating the threshold value. In the above figure (a), the window center pixel value (4) is compared with the surrounding window pixel values. The greater pixels are turned into one and lesser pixels are replaced by zero from every standard window. In eight window pixels, a total of 2^8 combinations of LBP codes are possible. The calculated LBP code for the center pixel based on the position of the surrounding pixel value is shown in the above figure (b). Here, the 8-bit neighborhood of the binary center pixel is converted into the decimal representation. The calculated LBP value is replaced into center pixel and is represented in the above figure (c). Likewise, the LBP value is calculated for every pixel value and stored as an output array having the same height and width as an original image. The examples of brain images in the first row and their corresponding LBP calculated image in the second row are presented in the below figure.

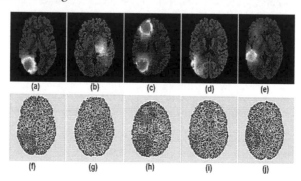

(a)   (b)   (c)   (d)   (e)

(f)   (g)   (h)   (i)   (j)

Convolutional Neural Network (CNN)

CNN is the deep learning algorithm that takes an input and assigns weights and bios to the image to differentiate the image. CNN is used to classify the input image based on some dimensionality-reduction techniques. CNN is able to extract the image features automatically from the input data. This architecture contains two major building blocks, namely the convolutional layer and the pooling layer. This pooling layer may be either max-pooling or average pooling. Each input image in the CNN architecture is processed by two convolutional layers and two pooling layers, followed by the FC layer. After that, softmax is applied for predicting the desired target. The basic architecture of the CNN illustrated in the below figure. This network has the rectangular grid of input patches which requires previous layer input also in the rectangular grid f neurons. First, each image x combined with weight w and bios b to be activated using non-linear transformation function to produce output feature map F_{out} is defined in equation (12.1).

$$F_{out} = f\left(\sum_{i=1}^{n} x_i w_i + b\right) \tag{12.1}$$

where i = 1,2 ... n and f is the activation function, which is used to transform an input into an output. There are various activation functionsavailable. In this, Sigmoid, ReLU, Leaky ReLU and tanh are mostly used. The sigmoid function turns all values between zeros to ones. The formula for the sigmoid activation function is defined in equation (12.2).

$$\sigma(x) = \frac{1}{1 + e^{-x}} \tag{12.2}$$

The formula for the tanh function is defined in equation (12.3).

$$\tanh = \tanh(x) \tag{12.3}$$

The range of x in the tanh function is between-1 and 1. The tanh function turns all values between −1 to 1 The formula for the ReLU activation function is defined in equation (12.4).

$$ReLU = \max(0,x) \tag{12.4}$$

$$f(i,j) = \begin{cases} 0 \ If \ (X) < 0 \\ X \ otherwise \end{cases}$$

The range of x from the ReLU activation function is zero to x. This activation function turns all features values from zero to x. The Leaky ReLU activation function is defined in equation (12.5).

$$Leaky\ ReLU = \max(0.01x,x) \tag{12.5}$$

$$f(i,j) = \begin{cases} 0.01\ If\ (X) < 0 \\ X\ otherwise \end{cases}$$

The range of x from the Leaky ReLU activation unction is 0.01 to x. This activation function turns all values in the range between 0.01 and x. Each input image is convolved using weight and bios to be non-linearly transformed using the activation function to produce a feature map of the first convolutional layer. Mostly, the ReLU activation function performs better in a CNN architecture. The size of the first output feature map has been computed using equation (12.6).

$$N_{out} = \left(\frac{N_{in} + 2p - k}{s}\right) + 1 \tag{12.6}$$

where N_{in} is considered as the number of input features, N_{out} is the output features, k is the kernel size, p is the padding size and s is stride size. The first convolutional layer output is processed in the pooling layer. It is used to reduce the dimension of the feature map and also to reduce the computational complexity. Suppose, if the pooling layer is not available on CNN, the computational load of the fully connected layer is increased. There are two basic pooling operations, namely max-pooling and average pooling. In max-pooling, the maximum value is only considered from every 2 × 2 grid from each input image for further process. In average pooling, only an average value is considered from every 2 × 2 grid from an input further process.

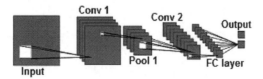

Consider the first convolution dimension width $w1$, height $h1$ and dimension $d1$ to be reduced as $w2$, $h2$ and $d2$, is given in equations (12.7), (12.8) and (12.9).

$$w2 = (w1 - f)/s + 1 \tag{12.7}$$

$$h2 = (h1 - f)/s + 1 \tag{12.8}$$

$$d2 = d1 \tag{12.9}$$

where f is the filter and s is the stride are the two hyperparameters used in every convolutional and pooling layer. Again, this reduced pooling output is processed using a second convolutional operation for extracting image features. Likewise, each input image is processed into several stacks of convolutional and pooling layers for image feature extraction and dimensionality reduction, respectively. Finally, this extracted feature dimension is converted to a single vector for predicting the pixel-wise probability of each input image. This single vector is processed in the fully connected layer which connects the neurons from the previous layer to the neurons from the next layer. This layer is also having the parameters of weight, bios and neurons. The convolution operation in a fully connected layer is used for classifying images from a different category of the class by training. At the end of the fully connected layer, a softmax or logistic function is used for predicting the desired classification. Softmax is used to predict multi-class and logistic functions used to predict binary class.

Classification Using Cascaded CNN

This method is an improved algorithm of CNN. In this algorithm, each and every input image is processed using a block of three different 3 × 3, 7 × 7 and 5 × 5 kernels to produce three different features from each convolutional block. Consider x is an input image to be combined with weight w and bios b from three kernels, namely 3 × 3, 7 × 7 and 5 ×5 to produce three outputs $C1$, $C2$ and $C3$ as given in equations (12.10), (12.11) and (12.12).

$$C1 = f\left(\sum_{i=1}^{n} x_i w_i + b \right) \tag{12.10}$$

$$C2 = f\left(\sum_{j=1}^{n} x_j w_j + b \right) \tag{12.11}$$

$$C3 = f\left(\sum_{k=1}^{n} x_k w_k + b \right) \tag{12.12}$$

These three convolutional layer outputs $C1$, $C2$ and $C3$ are cascaded to produce an output Y_{cas} is given in equation (12.13).

$$Y_{cas} = C1 + C2 + C3 \tag{12.13}$$

Then, this cascaded output Y_{cas} is processed using a convolutional layer with weight w and b to produce output feature map $C4$ is given in equation (12.14).

$$C4 = f\left(\sum_{i=1}^{n} x_i w_i + b \right) \tag{12.14}$$

This output feature map $C4$ is processed using max-pooling for dimensionality reduction. This will reduce the computational complexity of the convolutional operation. After this, the pooling output is processed using a convolutional layer to produce $C5$ output given in equation (12.15).

$$C5 = f\left(\sum_{i=1}^{n} x_i w_i + b\right) \tag{12.15}$$

The convolutional output feature map $C5$ is processed in the max-pooling layer for dimensionality reduction of features. Then, the pooling output is processed in the upcoming fully connected and softmax layers. In an FC and softmax layer, the downsampled pooling output is converted to a single dimension to predict pixel-wise probabilities of class labels. The overall architecture of the cascaded CNN is visualized in the below figure.

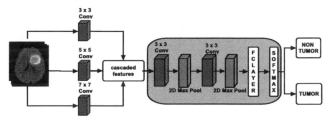

Fully Connected (FC) Layer

This layer takes an input from the previous layer and flattens them into a single dimension for predicting one-to-one pixel probabilities of class labels. The 1D convolution operation in a fully connected layer is used for classifying images from a different category of the class by training. This layer also has the parameters of weight, bios and neurons. Each input neurons from the FC layer is combined with weight and bios to produce a 1-dimensional feature vector as an output. At the end of the fully connected layer, softmax or logistic function is used for predicting the desired classification. An output feature vector from a fully connected layer is processed by logistic or softmax function for class labels prediction in each input image. Softmax is used to predict multi-class and logistic function is used to predict binary class. The schematic workflow representation of the FC layer is depicted in the below figure.

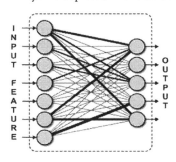

Softmax Classification

An output from the FC layer is for carrying out the pixel-wise prediction of classes. This classification technique is used for the probability computation of each class. It is the generalization of binary from logistic regression. The softmax takes row value as zero (0) for the first class and one (1) for the second class. This method takes an input x and maps it with class labels for predicting the tumor prediction. The layers configuration used in the proposed method is detailed in the below table.

Layers	Type	Stride Value	Filter Size	Filters	Activation	Normalization	FC Units	Input
Layer 1	Conv	1×1	3×3	64	ReLU	B-N	-	1×240×240
Layer 2	Conv	1×1	3×3	64	ReLU	B-N	-	1×240×240
Layer 3	Conv	1×1	7×7	64	ReLU	B-N	-	64×240×240
The feature maps from Layers 1, 2 and 3 are cascaded to be processed using upcoming layers								
Layer 4	Conv	1×1	3×3	128	ReLU	B-N	-	64×240×240
Layer 5	Max-pool	2×2	3×3	-	-	B-N	-	128×240×240
Layer 6	Conv	1×1	3×3	128	ReLU	B-N	-	128×120×120
Layer 7	Max-pool	2×2	3×3	-	-	B-N	-	128×120×120
Layer 8	-	-	-	-	-	-	256	115200 (128×30×30)
Layer 9	-	-	-	-	-	-	256	256
Layer 10	-	-	-	-	-	-	2	256

Loss Function

It is used for error identification and to identify similarities between predicted and targeted labels. There are several types of loss functions available are Mean-Squared Error (MSE), Cross-Entropy Loss (XE), Mean Absolute Error, Maximum Mean Discrepancy, Gaussian Log Likelihood, Squared Error loss, Smooth Absolute Loss Function, and Absolute Loss Function. Categorical Cross Entropy performs better in CNN-based applications for identifying errors between true $p(x)$ and predicted $q(x)$ distribution is defined in equations (12.16) and (12.17).

$$H(p,q) = -\sum_{i=1}^{n} p(x_i) \log(q(x_i)) \tag{12.16}$$

$$H(p,q) = -(p(x_1) \log(q(x_1)) \ldots p(x_n) \log(q(x_n)) \tag{12.17}$$

Training

All images from BRATS 2018 dataset are split into training, testing and validation. The whole cascaded CNN network is trained using the dataset images with parameters like weight, bios, filter size, padding, number of filters, activation function, batch normalization and some trainable parameters in a softmax and FC layer. First, the LBP features are extracted and classified using cascaded CNN with network parameters. This cascaded CNN is to extract features automatically from the input data. The last cascaded CNN layer feature is fed into the FC layer for converting the feature into a single dimension. Here, the softmax technique is used to predict the tumor images. These classified labels of all training images have been compared with original labels for calculating performance. If the performance is low, it means the network weight value is adjusted and it retrains the network up to the maximum accuracy. The final network weights and their models are stored in a system for future use. Next, testing images are processed using LBP features with cascaded CNN and tested using already stored trained weights to predicts whether this algorithm works well in new test images or not. Finally, the interactive windows application is developed in the name of TUDIG. In this, the brain MRI images are processed using LBP with cascaded CNN and validated using already stored trained weights to predicts whether the tumor is present in the validation images or not. Finally, this interactive application tells if the selected image is a tumor or non-tumor type.

Evaluation

The whole input cascaded architecture is trained with a batch of five images. After processing a batch, all remaining images from BRATS-2018 dataset have been processed simultaneously and the outcome of the extracted features is predicted to be labeled using class labels in the softmax layer. These predicted class labels are compared with original labels using some benchmark metrics like accuracy, specificity, precision, F1-score and sensitivity and are illustrated in equations (12.18) to (12.22).

$$Accuracy = (TP + TN) / (TP + FP + FN + TN) \tag{12.18}$$

$$Specificity = (TN) / (TN + FP) \tag{12.19}$$

$$Precision = (TP) / (TP + FP) \tag{12.20}$$

$$F1 - score = (2TP) / (2TP + FP + FN) \tag{12.21}$$

$$Sensitivity = (TP) / (TP + FN) \tag{12.22}$$

where TP is True Positive and TN is True Negative, FP is False Positive and FN is False Negative.

TUDIG Application

The TUDIG is an interactive windows application for detection. In this application, the Python Tkinter packages have been used to implement the windows design and also the images from BRATS 2018 dataset used for predicting non-tumor and images. This application contains parameters like the size of the window, number of frames, frame size, grids, buttons, text box, background and foreground color, font size and font color of the text, etc. Already, all input images from BRATS 2018 dataset are split into training, testing and validation. The validation images are used in this TUDIG application. First, the button named "select an input image" is clicked by the developer. This click will direct the image file from the system and the required brain image file is chosen by the user. Then, LBP features are extracted from the selected image file and processed using cascaded CNN with the help of already-stored trained weights to predict whether the tumor is present or not. These predicted results along with their image files are displayed in the TUDIG window. This interactive windows application is very efficient and very fast in predicting tumor and non-tumor images in MRI brain images.

Experimental Results and Discussion

Effectiveness of LBP

The LBP algorithm is to extract the patterns and textures of the image. All images from BRATS 2018 dataset have been processed using the LBP algorithm for extracting features of an image. This technique extracts the detailed information of the image. A standard 3 ×3 window is slid over the input image surrounding a center pixel chosen for every pixel in the brain image. If the surrounding pixels are greater than the center pixel, it means the corresponding pixel value is replaced by zero, else that corresponding pixel value is replaced by one. Then, the LBP value is calculated for the center pixel based on the position of the surrounding pixel value. For LBP value calculation, the positions of the one-value pixels are considered. The 2 power of pixel position is calculated for every window pixel and their values are added together to predict the LBP value. The calculated LBP value is placed in the window's center pixel in the original image. Likewise, the window is moved over all image pixels and their LBP value is replaced in all image pixels. The LBP-replaced image contains detailed information like patterns and textures of an input image. The LBP feature extraction technique is performs better in CNN-based applications than other feature extraction techniques like Color Histogram features, Histogram Of Gradient (HOG), Scale Invariant Feature Transform (SIFT) and Speeded Up Robust Features (SURF).

Effectiveness of Cascaded CNN

The cascaded CNN is to extract features automatically from the input data. In this, each input image from BRATS 2018 dataset is processed by three kernels, namely 3 ×3, 7 ×7 and 5×5 filters to produce separate features. These are cascaded to produce cascaded output features. Then, this outcome is processed in two convolutional and two max-pooling layers to produce the final extracted features. These are fed into the FC layer for converting the feature into a single dimension. In a fully connected layer, the softmax classification technique is used to predict if the tumor is present or not. Normally, the traditional CNN model does not have these cascaded features. In the traditional CNN model, all input images are directly processed in stacks of convolutional, pooling and softmax layers. This traditional CNN model has very little accuracy compared to the cascaded CNN. The performance of cascaded CNN is depicted in the below table.

Gliomas Type	Sequence Name	Accuracy	Specificity	Precision	F1-Score	Sensitivity
HGG	Flair	0.95	1.00	0.99	0.99	1.00
	T1	0.96	0.94	0.97	0.96	1.00
	T1C	0.94	0.93	0.97	0.96	0.99
	T2	0.98	1.00	1.00	1.00	1.00

Gliomas Type	Sequence Name	Accuracy	Specificity	Precision	F1-Score	Sensitivity
LGG	Flair	0.97	1.00	1.00	1.00	1.00
	T1	0.96	0.98	0.99	0.99	0.99
	T1C	0.96	0.98	0.99	0.99	1.00
	T2	0.94	0.97	0.99	0.99	1.00
Average (HGG, LGG)		0.96	0.97	0.98	0.98	0.99

The flair image in HGG has 95% accuracy, 99% precision and F1-score, 100% specificity and sensitivity values. But, the flair images in LGG have higher performance than the flair images in HGG images. The flair images in LGG have 97% accuracy, 100% precision, F1-score, specificity and sensitivity values. The T1 image in HGG has 96% accuracy, 97% precision, 96% F1-score, 94% specificity and 100% sensitivity values. But, the T1 images in LGG have higher performance than the T1 images in HGG. The T1 images in LGG have 96% accuracy, 99% precision, and F1-score, 98% specificity and 99% sensitivity values. The T1C image in HGG has 94% accuracy, 97% precision, 96% F1-score, 93% specificity and 99% sensitivity values. But, the T1C images in LGG have higher performance than the T1C images in HGG images. The T1C images in LGG have 96% accuracy, 99% precision, and F1-score, 98% specificity and 100% sensitivity values. The T2 image in HGG has 98% accuracy, 100% precision, F1-score, specificity and sensitivity values. But, the T1C images in LGG have lower performance than the T1C images in HGG images. The T1C images in LGG have 94% accuracy, 99% precision and F1-score, 97% specificity and 100% sensitivity values. Finally, the overall performance of the cascaded CNN has 96% accuracy, 97% specificity, 98% precision, 98% F1-score and 99% sensitivity values.

Tumor Detection Performance of Proposed Network Using BRATS-2018 Dataset

The extracted LBP features from BRATS 2018 dataset are processed using cascaded CNN. This cascaded CNN can extract image features automatically from the input data. In this, all input images from BRATS 2018 dataset are processed in the hierarchy convolutional, pooling and softmax layer for predicting normal and abnormal brain images. Thus, the proposed cascaded CNN with LBP features is performs better when compared to the traditional neural network-based approaches. The performance of LBP features with cascaded CNN using HGG and LGG images is illustrated in the below table and figures.

Gliomas Type	Sequence Name	Accuracy	Specificity	Precision	F1-Score	Sensitivity
HGG	Flair	0.99	0.91	0.96	0.96	1.00
	T1	0.95	0.90	0.96	0.96	1.00
	T1C	0.96	0.98	0.99	0.99	0.98
	T2	0.98	1.00	1.00	1.00	1.00
LGG	Flair	0.98	0.90	1.00	1.00	1.00
	T1	0.96	0.93	0.97	0.97	1.00
	T1C	0.99	0.96	0.98	0.98	1.00
	T2	0.95	0.97	0.99	0.99	1.00
Average (HGG and LGG)		0.97	0.94	0.98	0.98	0.99

The flair image in HGG has 99% accuracy, 96% precision, and F1-score, 91% specificity and 100% sensitivity values. But, the flair images in LGG have higher performance than the flair images in HGG images. The flair images in LGG have 98% accuracy, 100% precision, F1-score, 90% specificity and 100% sensitivity values. The T1 image in HGG has 95% accuracy, 96% precision and F1-score, 90% specificity and 100% sensitivity values. But, the T1 images in LGG have higher performance than the T1 images in HGG images. The T1 images in LGG have 96% accuracy, 97% precision and F1-score, 93% specificity and 100% sensitivity values. The T1C image in HGG has 96% accuracy, 99% precision and F1-score, 98% specificity and sensitivity values. But, the T1C images in LGG have higher performance than the T1C images in HGG images. The T1C images in LGG have 99% accuracy, 98% precision and F1-score, 96% specificity and 100% sensitivity values. The T2 image in HGG has 98% accuracy, 100% precision, F1-score, specificity and sensitivity values. But, the T1C images in LGG have lower performance than the T1C images in HGG images. The T1C images in LGG have 95% accuracy, 99% precision, and F1-score, 97% specificity and 100% sensitivity values. Finally, the overall performance of the cascaded CNN using LBP features has 97% accuracy, 94% specificity, 98% precision, 98% F1-score and 99% sensitivity values.

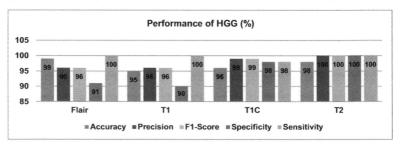

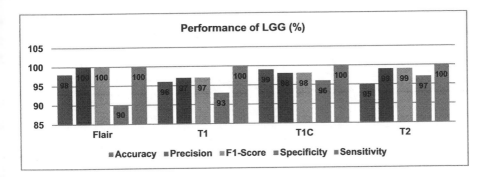

Performance Comparison of Proposed Network with Existing Methods Using BRATS-2018 Dataset

The cascaded CNN with LBP features algorithm performance are compared with existing algorithms for evaluating the performance. The proposed accuracy, precision, F1-score and sensitivity values are compared with FFANN, EC, ELM and SVM methods. These methods are used to learn tumoral features automatically from input MRI data. Kumar et al. have implemented FFANN for brain tumor diagnosis. In this, the GLCM features extracted are processed using FANN for detecting brain tumors [48]. The FFANN algorithm works better in pattern-recognition and pattern-classification techniques. Parasuraman et al. have proposed Ensemble Classifier (EC) for tumor diagnosis [46]. In this method, the GLCM features are extracted in all brain images and processed using ensemble classifiers. This ensemble classification technique is an efficient tumor-identification method having a combination of FFANN and SVM methods. In this method, detailed information may be lost in poor illumination images. The SVM and ELM are also semi-automatic methods used in the tumor detection process. These semi-automatic methods need interaction from the programmer to initialize parameters for classifying tumor images. To overcome these limitations, an accurate and automated windows application based on cascaded CNN with LBP features is proposed. The comparison of the proposed with state-of-the-art methods is depicted in the below table and figures.

Classification Technique	Accuracy (%)	Precision (%)	F1-Score (%)	Sensitivity (%)
FFANN	84.33	89.41	90.66	91.94
Ensemble Classifier (EC)	91.17	94.17	94.81	95.47
Support Vector Machine (SVM)	89.67	92.99	93.90	94.83

Classification Technique	Accuracy (%)	Precision (%)	F1-Score (%)	Sensitivity (%)
Extreme Learning Machine (ELM)	86.00	90.20	91.63	93.12
Proposed Method	**97.00**	**98.00**	**98.00**	**99.00**

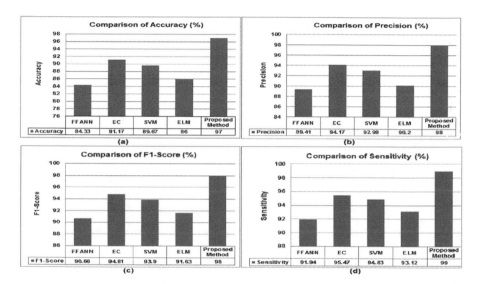

The FFANN method has 84.33% accuracy, 89.41% precision, 90.66% F1-score and 91.94% sensitivity. The FFANN method has lower performance than ELM and SVM methods. The SVM method has 84.67% accuracy, 92.99% precision, 93.90% F1-score and 94.87% of sensitivity values. The ELM method has 86.00% accuracy, 90.20% precision, 91.63% F1-score and 93.12% sensitivity values. The SVM and ELM methods have higher performance than the FFANN method. The EC method has 91.17% accuracy, 94.17% precision, 94.81% F1-score and 95.47% sensitivity values. This EC method has a competitively higher performance than the SVM, ELM and FFANN methods. These methods have limited performance in poor illumination images and need interaction from the programmer to initialize parameters for classifying tumor images. This FFANN method does not have cascaded features while training the network. In this FFANN method, all images from BRATS 2018 dataset are processed in the forwarded artificial neural network application. Thus, the proposed method works better in poor illumination images and does not need any programmer interaction for initializing parameters. The proposed cascaded CNN with the LBP feature extraction method has 97% accuracy, 94% specificity, 98% precision, 98% of F1-score and 99% sensitivity values. The performance values of our proposed tumor-identification method have comparatively higher performance than the existing SVM, EC, ELM and FFANN methods.

Performance of TUDIG Application

The TUDIG is an interactive windows application used to detect brain tumors. The TUDIG application is very fast processing and accurate for brain tumor identification. The application is developed by using Python Tkinter packages. The Python Tkinter packages are very effective for developing windows applications and also easy to implement windows applications. This package contains parameters like the size of the window, number of frames, frame size, grids, buttons, text box, background and foreground color, font size and font color of the text, etc. The above-mentioned parameters are more than enough to implement an interactive window-based application. In this application, "select an input image" button is clicked by the developer. This click will direct the image file from the system and the required brain image file is chosen by the user. Then, the LBP features are extracted and processed using cascaded CNN with the help of already stored trained weights to predict tumor or not. In this application, some of the images are trained previously by the programmer and their learnable weights have been stored. Then, the brain tumor present in the new untrained images is predicted easily by the usage of trained weights. So, the training time was reduced in every brain-tumor-detection process in the MRI images. The untrained images have been used in the TUDIG application. The proposed method works well and performs prediction effectively in untrained images. These predicted results along with their image files are displayed in the TUDIG window. The TUDIG application detects tumors very fast and accurately because the training time is reduced while detecting a brain tumor using cascaded CNN. The screenshots of the proposed TUDIG application is shown in the below figure (a) and (b).

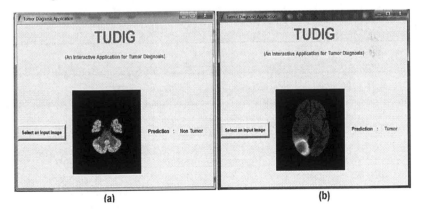

(a)   (b)

Conclusion

An accurate tumor detection algorithm from brain MRI is essential for medical analysis, clinical assessments, interpretation and treatment. In this research, an interactive and automated windows application using LBP features and cascaded

CNN is developed for tumor detection. The images from BRATS 2018 dataset have been used to develop this proposed method. In this, all images from this dataset are processed using LBP for extracting image features. These are again processed using cascaded CNN to detect brain tumors. Here, every input feature is convolved separately with 3×3, 7×7 and 5×5 filters to produce separate feature maps. These are cascaded to be processed by two convolutional and two max-pooling layers. This outcome is "flattened" as a single vector in the FC layer for predicting probabilities in each pixel. Here, the softmax function is used for pixel-wise prediction of class labels like tumor and non-tumor. The whole algorithm is trained and their learnable weights are stored. Then, the interactive TUDIG application is developed and the tumor present in the given input image is predicted by using the already stored trained weights. Thus, the proposed application achieves 97% accuracy, 94% specificity, 98% precision, 98% F1-score and 99% sensitivity values. The performance values of our proposed tumor-identification method have comparatively higher performance than the existing SVM, EC, ELM and FFANN methods.

References

[1] D. Haritha, "Brain Tumor Segmentation", *International Journal of Advanced Technology in Engineering and Sciences*, 2016, Vol. 3, No. 4, pp. 265–270. ISSN: 2348-7550

[2] Md. Abdur Rahim and H. Najmul, "Face Recognition using Local Binary Patterns (LBP)", *Global Journal of Computer Science and Technology Graphics & Vision*, 2013, Vol. 13, No. 4, pp. 1–9. ISSN: 0975-4350

[3] K. Damandeep and S. Surender, "Detection of Brain Tumor using Image Processing Techniques", *International Journal of Engineering and Advanced Technology (IJEAT)*, 2019, Vol. 5S3, No. 8, pp. 2249–8959.

[4] P.L. Chithra, G. Dheepa, "An analysis of segmenting and classifying tumor regions in MRI images using CNN", *International Journal of Pure and Applied Mathematics*, Vol. 24, No. 118, pp. 1–12.

[5] U. Khalid, R. Kashif, "Brain tumor classification from multi-modality MRI using wavelets and machine learning", 2017, No. 21, pp. 871–881.

[6] S. Pereira, V. Alves, "Brain tumor segmentation using convolutional neural network in MRI images", *IEEE Transactions on Medical Imaging*, 2017, No. 35, Vol. 5, pp. 1240–1251.

[7] J. Kleesiek and G. Urban, "Deep MRI brain extraction: A 3D convolutional neural network for skull stripping", *Neuro Image*, 2016, No. 129, pp. 460–469.

[8] S. Muhammad, A. Javaia, "Brain tumor detection based on extreme learning", *Neural Computing and Applications*, https://doi.org/10.1007/s00521-019-04679-8, pp. 1-13.

[9] P.L. Chithra and G. Dheepa, "Di-phase midway convolution and deconvolution network for brain tumor segmentation in MRI images", *International Journal of Imaging Systems and Technology*, 2020, No. 30, pp. 674–686, https://doi.org/10.1002/ima.22407.

[10] Z. Xiaomei, Y. Wu, "A deep learning model integrating FCNNs and CRFs for brain tumor segmentation", *Medical Image Analysis*, 2018, No. 43, pp. 98–111.

[11] W. Yao, W. Yang, "*Semi-automatic segmentation of brain tumors using population and individual information*", 2013, No. 26, pp. 786–796.

[12] A. Shenbagarajan and V. Ramalingam, "MRI brain image analysis for tumour diagnosis using hybrid MB-MLM pattern classification technique", *Biomedical Research*, 2016, Special Issue: S191-S203, 0970-938X.

[13] U. Devrim, E. Ahmet, "*Robustness of Local Binary Patterns in Brain MR Image Analysis*", *Proceedings of the 29th Annual International Conference of the IEEE EMBS Cité International*, Lyon, France, August 23–26, 2017, pp. 2098–2101.

[14] L. Jin and L. Min, "A survey of MRI-Based brain tumor segmentation methods", *TSINGHUA Science and Technology*, 2014, Vol. 19, No. 16, ISSN: 1007-0214.

[15] A. Marco, M. Salem, "An Automatic Classification of Brain Tumors through MRI Using Support Vector Machine", *Egyptian Computer Science Journal*, 2016, Vol. 4, No. 40, pp. 11–21. ISSN: 1110-2586

[16] V. Anitha, S. Murugavalli, "Brain tumour classification using two-tier classifier with adaptive segmentation Technique", *IET Computer Vision*, 2015, pp. 1–9. ISSN: 1751-9632

[17] N. Varuna Shree and T. N. R. Kumar, "Identification and classification of brain tumor MRI images with feature extraction using DWT and probabilistic neural network", *Brain Informatics*, 2018, No. 5, pp. 23–30.

[18] S. Amritpal Parveen, "*Detection of Brain Tumor in MRI Images, using Combination of Fuzzy C-Means and SVM*", *2015 2nd International Conference on Signal Processing and Integrated Networks (SPIN)*, 2015, 978-1-4799-5991-4/15/$31.00 ©2015 IEEE, 98–102.

[19] V. Nikitha, D. Jadhav, "Detection and Classification of Brain Tumors", *International Journal of Computer Applications*, 2016, Vol. 8, No. 112, pp. 48–53. ISSN: 0975-8887

[20] G.B. Praveen, "Multi stage classification and segmentation of brain tumor", IEEE, 2016, No. 9, pp. 1628–1632.

[21] A. Solmaz, T. Farshad, "Detection of Brain Tumor in 3D MRI Images using Local Binary Patterns and Histogram Orientation Gradient", *Neurocomputing*, 2016, pp. 1–23, http://dx.doi.org/10.1016/j.neucom.2016.09.051.

[22] S. Li and Z. Songtao, "*Multi-view 3D CNN with Dense CRF for Brain Tumor Segmentation and Survival Prediction*", *MICCAI BRATS 2018*, pp. 448–456.

[23] M. Havaei, A. Davy, "Brain tumor segmentation with deep neural network", *Medical Image Analysis*, 2017, No. 35, pp. 18–31.

[24] M. Heba, El. Sayed, "Semi Classification using deep learning neural networks for brain tumors", *Future Computing and Informatics Journal*, 2018, No. 3, pp. 68–71.

[25] C. Eric and Chang, "*Automatic Brain Tumor Segmentation Using a U-net Neural Network*", *MICCAI BRATS 2018*, pp. 63–73.

[26] A. Saumya, C. Siddhartha, "Brain Tumor Detection using PCA and NN with GLCM", *International Journal for Research in Applied Science & Engineering Technology (IJRASET)*, 2018, Vol. 6, No. 9, 170–177. ISSN: 2321-9653

[27] P.L. Chithra and G. Dheepa, "An Efficient Cascaded CNN Architecture for Brain Tumor Detection in MRI Images", *International Journal of Innovative Technology and Exploring Engineering*, 2020, Vol. 3, No. 9, pp. 1663–1668, ISSN: 2278-3075

[28] F. Petro Garcia, and E. Luisa Peixoto, "On the Application LBP Texture Descriptors and Its Variants for No-Reference Image Quality Assessment", *Journal of Imaging*, 2018, Vol. 4, No. 114, doi:10.3390/jimaging4100114.

[29] P. Gladis and S. Palani, "Brain Tumor Detection and Classification Using Deep Learning Classifier on MRI Images", *Research Journal of Applied Sciences, Engineering and Technology*, 2015, Vol. 2, No. 10, pp. 117–187.

[30] H. Dong and G. Ysng, "Automatic brain tumor detection and segmentation using U-net based fully convolutional network", *Springer*, 2017, Vol. 69, No. 3, pp. 1–12.

[31] H. Belkacem, C. Zouaoui, "Fully automatic multi segmentation approach for magnetic resonance imaging brain tumor detection using improved region-growing and quasi-Monte Carlo-expectation maximization algorithm", *International Journal of Imaging Systems and Technology*, Wiley Online Library, 2018, pp: 1–8, DOI: 10.1002/ima.22376.

[32] D. Walker and W. Hamilton, "Strategies to accelerate diagnosis of primary brain tumors at the primary–secondary care interface in children and adults", *Future CNS Oncology*, 2013, Vol. 2, No. 5, pp. 447–462.

[33] C. Davatzikos and S. Rathore, "Cancer imaging phenomics toolkit: quantitative imaging analytics for precision diagnostics and predictive modeling of clinical outcome", *Journal of Medical Imaging*, 2018, Vol. 5, No. 1, 011018, pp. 1–21.

[34] F. Kofler and C. Berger, "BraTS Toolkit: Translating BraTS Brain Tumor Segmentation Algorithms Into Clinical and Scientific Practice", *Frontiers in Neuroscience*, Vol. 14, No. 125, pp. 1–8.

[35] J. Senarathna, A. Prasad, "HemoSYS: A Toolkit for Imagebased Systems Biology of Tumor Hemodynamics", *Scientific Reports*, 2020, No. 10, p. 2372, https://doi.org/10.1038/s41598-020-58918-3.

[36] S. Madhukumar and N. Sathyakumari, "Evaluation of k-Means and fuzzy C-means segmentation on MR images of brain", *The Egyptian Journal of Radiology and Nuclear Medicine*, 2015, No. 46, pp. 475–479.

[37] R. Rajagopal, "Glioma brain tumor detection and segmentation using weighting random forest classifier with optimized ant colony features", *International Journal of Imaging Systems and Technology*, 2019, pp. 1–7, DOI: 10.1002/ima.22331.

[38] M. Angulakshmi, G. Lakshmi Priya, "Brain tumour segmentation from MRI using super-pixels based spectral clustering", *Journal of King Saud University – Computer and Information Sciences*, 2018, https://doi.org/10.1016/j.jksuci.2018.01.009.

[39] S. Mohammadreza and Y. Guang, "Automated brain tumour detection and segmentation usingsuperpixel-based extremely randomized trees in FLAIR MRI", *International Journal of CARS*, 2017, No. 12, pp. 183–203, DOI 10.1007/s11548-016-1483-3.

[40] B. Nilesh, R. Arun, "Image Analysis for MRI Based Brain Tumor Detection and Feature Extraction Using Biologically Inspired BWT and SVM", *International Journal of Biomedical Imaging*, https://doi.org/10.1155/2017/9749108, pp. 1–13.

[41] K. Sandhiya, "A novel approach for the detection of tumor in MR images of the brain and its classification via independent component analysis and kernel support vector machine", *Imaging Med*, 2017, Vol. 3, No. 9, pp. 33–44.

[42] R. Nooshin and K. Miroslav, "Brain tumors detection and segmentation in MR images: Gabor wavelet vs. statistical feature", *Computers and Electrical Engineering*, 2015, No. 45, pp. 286–301.

[43] Jasmine Hephzipah and P. Thirumurugan, "Computer aided automated detection and classification of braintumors using CANFIS classification method", *International Journal of Imaging Systems and Technology*, 2018, No. 30, pp. 1–8, DOI: 10.1002/ima.22318.

[44] P. Sivakumar and P. Ganeshkumar, "CANFIS based glioma brain tumor classification and retrievalsystem for tumor diagnosis", *International Journal of Imaging Systems and Technology*, 2016, pp. 1–9, DOI: 10.1002/ima.22215.

[45] Musatafa, A., Sabrina, T. (2017). "Extreme Learning Machine: A Review", *International Journal of Applied Engineering Research*, 2017, Vol. 12, No. 14, pp. 4610–4623. ISSN: 0973-4562

[46] K. Parasuraman, B. Vijayakumar, "Brain Tumor MRI Segmentation and Classification Using Ensemble Classifier", *International Journal of Recent Technology and Engineering (IJRTE)*, 2018, No. 8, pp. 224–252. ISSN: 2277-3878

[47] D. Zikic and Y. Ioannou, "*Segmentation of brain tumor tissues with convolutional neural net-works*", *Proceedings MICCAI BraTS (Brain Tumor Segmentation Challenge)*, 2014, pp. 36–39.

[48] P. Kumar, B. Vijayakumar, "An Efficient Brain Tumor MRI Segmentation and Classification Using GLCM Texture Features and Feed Forward Neural Networks", *World Journal of Medical Sciences*, 2016, No. 2, Vol. 13, pp. 85–92. ISSN: 1817-3055

[49] H. Murat, "A brief review of feed-forward neural networks", *Communications Faculty of Sciences University of Ankara Series A2-A3*, 2016, Vol. 1, No. 50, pp. 11–17.

[50] K.A. Mahmaud and I.A. Ali, "Two-phase multi-model automatic brain tumour diagnosis sys-tem from magnetic resonance images using convolutional neural Networks", *EURASIP Journal on Image and Video Processing*, 2018, No. 97, https://doi.org/10.1186/s13640-018-0332-4.

[51] R. Hema, "Brain tumor image classification and grading using convolutional neural network and particle swarm optimization algorithm", *International Journal of Engineering and Advanced Technology (IJEAT)*, 2017, Vol. 8, No. 35, pp. 42–48. ISSN: 2249-8958

[52] A. Jevaria, and S. Muhammad, "A New Approach for Brain Tumor Segmentation and Classification Based on Score Level Fusion Using Transfer Learning", *Journal of Medical Systems*, 2019, pp. 1–16, https://doi.org/10.1007/s10916-019-1453-8.

[53] Javaria. A., Muhammad. S. (2020). "Brain tumor classification based on DWT fusion of MRI sequences using convolutional neural network", *Pattern Recognition Letters*, 129, 115–122, https://doi.org/10.1016/j.patrec.2019.11.016.

[54] R. Talwar and I. Mohammed, "A Novel Approach to Brain Tumor Classification using Wavelet and Probabilistic Neural Network", *International Journal of Ethics in Engineering & Management Education*, 2017, Vol. 1, No. 11, pp. 2348–4748.

[55] K. Adel and M. Issam, "*Brain Tumor Segmentation in Multimodal 3D-MRI of BraTS'2018 Datasets using Deep Convolutional Neural Networks*" MICCAI BRATS 2018, pp. 252–262.

[56] Z. Akkus and A. Galimzianova, "Deep learning for brain MRI segmentation: state of the art and feature directions", *Journal of Digital Imaging*, No. 30, 2017, pp. 449–459.

Chapter 13

Virtual Reality in Medical Training, Patient Rehabilitation and Psychotherapy: Applications and Future Trends

M. Karthigha and Madhumathi Ramasamy

Sri Ramakrishna Engineering College, Coimbatore, India

Contents

DOI: 10.1201/9781003119784-13

Introduction

Virtual reality is a breakthrough computer technology, dominating the current technologies as it has the distinguishing feature of creating a simulated environment. The user can have an immersive experience as the computer spawned scenes and objects that appear to be real. They can intermingle with the 3D visual world by using a virtual reality headset with a brace of goggles. Basically, the VR components comprise hardware and software. The output devices encompass tools for vision, auditory and tactile movements. The hardware consists of sensors for tracking the motion of the users with input devices such as joysticks, tracking balls, wands and gloves [1]. There are three types of virtual reality. They are fully immersive, semi-immersive and non-immersive. At present, VR is shaping our future as various sectors are actively exploring and adopting VR. The following is the catalog of the industries utilizing VR:

- Automotive industry
- Healthcare
- Retail
- Tourism
- Real estate
- Architecture
- Learning and Development/Education
- Entertainment
- Sports
- Art and design
- Marketing

The Head-Mounted Display (HMD) is an important component of virtual reality. The widely renowned HMDs in 2021 are

- Oculus Quest 2
- Sony PlayStation VR
- HTC Vive Cosmos
- Valve Index
- HP Reverb G2

Lately, owing to its growth potential, VR has been used extensively in the medical field. Due to its positive outcomes, the growth of market share is increasing every year for the healthcare industry. Ref. [2] shows the predicted VR market size in 2025. Healthcare tops next to gaming with a market size of $5.1b.

In recent times, there have been countless exhilarating advancements taking place in healthcare. It created ineffaceable enhancement to people's health and lives. Patients who have medical conditions of chronic pain, psychological disorder and others have VR as their salvage. The following categories of health have been influenced the most by virtual reality [3]:

- Psychological therapy
- Neuroscience
- Physical therapy
- Occupational therapy
- Rehabilitation
- Medical training

Several healthcare organizations and doctors are exploring areas where VR shows better performance than conventional methodologies for a better life. This is confirmed by the fact that the world's most eminent companies started investing massive resources in the enhancement of VR devices and its applications in healthcare.

VR in Medical Training

From the last decade onward, VR has been employed in medical training. The American Board of Internal Medicine (ABIM) has recommended practitioners to be educated by simulation tools prior to attempting directly on patients so that it could be effective in their clinical trial performance [4]. VR medical training simulations provide a personalized learning experience and will be adapted to diverse learning

Figure 13.1 Surgical training with virtual reality [5].

styles that is not possible in conventional teaching. These enable autonomous learning let learners develop skills based on their abilities. They can practice critical skills any number of times without any risk.

VR medical simulation training increases the outcome of learning by reducing undesirable impacts with some conventional teaching practices. Various hardware and software are used for virtual reality training.

Surgical Training

The very first surgical simulator that makes use of VR technology was developed at NASA. It is one of the critical skills that poses numerous challenges like legal and ethical concerns for patient safety and related difficulties. Surgical training cannot be practiced by practitioners on live patients as it could be a risk to the patients [6]. The most widely used VR training surgical simulators are tabulated in Table 13.1.

The following are some of the surgical simulations that make it easy for practitioners to take training,

i) Dental Surgical Simulation

This surgical simulation involves the handling of tissues. Voxel-based simulation is used in dental surgeries. Voxel-based simulations are similar to medical image processing. Dental surgeries need strong haptic feedback which is provided effortlessly by virtual reality. Some of the well-known dental simulators are PeioSirm, VoxelMan, Dentsim, IDEA and Simodant. The features of these trainers are listed in Table 13.2.

ii) Otolaryngology Surgical Simulator

The temporal bone is the most complicated structure in otolaryngology. To cure otology disorders, the three-dimensional structure of the temporal bone is indispensable. Instead of dissection, virtual reality can be enabled to work with a virtual reality temporal bone simulator. This simulator includes software connected to a force feedback stylus and specialized eyeglasses that help in visualizing the 3D temporal bone and simulating dissection of it. Sinus surgery and Myringotomy surgical simulators are also available in the market. The available simulators are presented in Table 13.3.

iii) Eye Surgical Simulator

Eye surgery is more vulnerable as it involves microsurgical procedures. Hence Eye surgical simulators are boon to practitioners. The proposed eye surgery simulators in the literature are tabulated in Table 13.4.

iv) Minimally Invasive Surgery (MIS) Simulators

Minimally Invasive Surgery (MIS) includes laparoscopy, endovascular surgery and gastrointestinal endoscopy. The simulators available in the market are tabulated in Table 13.5.

Table 13.1 Commercial VR Trainers

Trainers	Type	Modules	Metrics
LapSim [7]	Virtual Reality Simulator	Modules include ■ Laparoscopy ■ Cholecystectomy ■ Appendicectomy ■ Suturing ■ Anastomosis ■ Gynecological procedures	■ Time ■ Instrument path length ■ Procedure-specific errors
LapMentor [8]	Virtual Reality Simulator	Modules include ■ Camera movement ■ Object translocation and suturing ■ Cholecystectomy ■ Hernia repair ■ Nephrectomy ■ Urologic procedures ■ Percutaneous interventions ■ Catheter interventions ■ Gastric bypass ■ 2-handed maneuvers ■ Endoscopy ■ Hand–eye coordination ■ Sigmoidectomy	■ Time ■ Economy of movement ■ safety ■ Electrosurgical dissection ■ Procedural errors
MIST-VR [9]	Virtual Reality Simulator	Modules include ■ Laparoscopy	■ Tool contact ■ Inappropriate target release ■ Inappropriate cautery application
LapVR [10]	Virtual Reality Simulator	Modules include ■ Camera navigation ■ Peg transfer ■ Cutting and clip application ■ Cholecystectomy	■ Time ■ Procedure-specific errors

(continued)

Table 13.1 *(continued)* **Commercial VR Trainers**

Trainers	Type	Modules	Metrics
SurgicalSim	Virtual Reality Simulator	Modules include ■ Tissue manipulation ■ Dissection ■ Suturing ■ Knot tying ■ Cholecystectomy	■ Time ■ Instrument path length ■ Procedure-specific errors
ProMIS Simulator [11]	Virtual Reality and Augmented Reality (Hybrid) Simulator	Modules include ■ Appendectomy ■ Colectomy	■ Full measurement ■ Feedback

Anatomy Teaching

Anatomy is associated with every medicine branch. Doctors and those who perform any procedure on patients, such as those who carry out emergency processes or those who do examination radiology, have to undergo anatomy training. The motive of having an anatomy-teaching simulator is to expedite the understanding of the complex anatomy of the human body. Three-dimensional models of the human body are an important aspect of anatomy. Virtual reality devices, virtual reality controllers and motion-tracking can be used for anatomy training for better training, as shown in Figure 13.2.

The interaction site of the virtual reality surgical simulator starts from single the site of interaction to the entire body, including the chest and abdomen, depicted in Figure 13.3.

Virtual Reality in Patient Rehabilitation

Virtual reality helps with patient rehabilitation for various kinds of impairments. Some of them are as follows.

Motor Skills Impairment Rehabilitation

Motor skills that include brain and body activity, which is responsible for every action that humans do in their day-to-day life. Motor impairment is the condition where they cannot perform a simple activity like grabbing an object. Virtual reality can improve their lives by giving positive learning experiences. This kind of virtual reality rehabilitation is quite engaging and at the same time motivating for

Table 13.2 VR Dental Surgical Simulator [12]

Trainers	Features	Simulation Exams
PeioSirm	■ Animated teeth are available ■ Left and right operation ■ Off-campus option is available	Available
VoxelMan	■ Feedback is available ■ Animated teeth are available ■ Off-campus option is available	Available
Dentsim	■ Ergonomic feature is available ■ Feedback is available ■ Left and right operation ■ Data can be accessed by mentors ■ Plastic teeth are used ■ Realistic	Available
IDEA	■ Feedback is available ■ Mentors can watch the activities ■ Left and right operation ■ Animated teeth are available ■ Off-campus option is available	Not Available
Simodant	■ Ergonomic feature is available ■ Feedback is available ■ Mentors can monitor realtime and can give feedbacks ■ Left and right operation ■ Animated teeth are available ■ Off-campus option is available ■ Realistic	Available

the patients. People with neuro disorders perform their actions using virtual reality. Virtual reality can be used for the rehabilitation of people who are suffering from

■ Cerebral palsy
■ Parkinson's disease
■ Stroke
■ Autism
■ Multiple sclerosis

Some of the rehabilitation techniques involve games. The hardware and software in VR rehabilitation designing is depicted in Figure 13.4.

Table 13.3 VR Otolaryngology Surgical Simulators [14]

Trainers	*Features*	*Networking*
Temporal bone surgical simulators		
Mediseus surgical drilling simulator SDS	■ Haptic device used ■ Image rendering is integrated ■ CT dataset is the image dataset	Available
VoxelMan	■ Haptic device used ■ Image rendering is integrated ■ CT dataset and image libraries are used as image dataset	Not Available
Ohio University	■ Haptic device used ■ NVIDIA Quadro FX4600 for image rendering ■ and image libraries with CT dataset are used as image dataset	Not Available
Stanford surgical simulator	■ Haptic device used ■ Cyberscope for image rendering ■ CT dataset is used as image dataset	Not Available
Sinus surgical simulator		
ES3	■ Haptic device used ■ SGI Octane workstation for image rendering ■ CT dataset is used as image dataset	Not Available
Dextroscope	■ Dextroscope workstation is used ■ Vizdexter 1.2 is used for image rendering	Not Available
Myringotomy		
3D VR Myringotomy simulator with Haptics	■ Haptic device used ■ OGRE 3D used for image rendering	Not Available
Myringotomy simulator	■ Optical tracker is used. ■ Open Dynamics Engine for image rendering ■ Computer-generated 3 D meshes	Not Available

Table 13.4 VR Eye Surgical Simulator

Simulator	Features
Retina laser photocoagulation Simulator	■ Monitor-based visual system ■ Haptics not available
Cataract extraction phacoemulsifier	■ Monitor-based visual system ■ Haptics are available ■ Tactile Feedback
Vitreoretinal surgery	■ Monitor-based visual system ■ High-speed graphics

Table 13.5 MIS VR Simulators [15]

Simulator	Exercises
Laparoscopy VR Simulators	
Laparoscopy VR/ProMIS	■ Cholecystectomy ■ Colectomy ■ Nissen fundoplication ■ Appendectomy ■ Ectopic pregnancy ■ Salpingo-oophorectomy
MIST VR Nephrectomy	■ Nephrectomy
LAP Mentor	■ Cholecystectomy ■ Hernia ■ Gastric bypass ■ Sigmoidectomy ■ Hysterectomy ■ Nephrectomy
LapSim	■ Cholecystectomy ■ Appendectomy ■ Salpingectomy ■ vaginal cuff opening
Endovascular Surgery VR Simulators	
CathLabVR	■ Carotid stenting ■ cardiac surgery

(*continued*)

Table 13.5 *(continued)*   **MIS VR Simulators [15]**

Simulator	Exercises
VIST/VIST-C and VIST-Lab	■ Neurocoil stenting ■ Angiography ■ carotid stenting
PRS	■ Carotid stenting ■ Cerebral thrombus removal
Gastrointestinal Endoscopy Surgery VR Simulators	
EndoscopyVR	■ Colonoscopy ■ Polypectomy ■ Biopsy ■ Sigmoidoscopy
GI-BRONCH	■ Colonoscopy ■ Gastroscopy ■ Sigmoidoscopy ■ Gastric bleeding

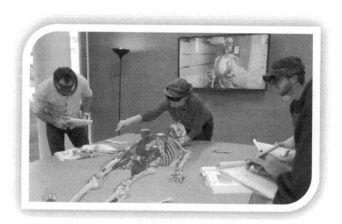

Figure 13.2   Virtual reality in anatomy training [16].

Autism Spectrum Disorder (ASD)

Autism Spectrum Disorder (ASD) is a disability in which the patients lack an understanding of their environment itself. So, they suffer from communication and social relationships. VR helps ASD persons overcome these difficulties and succeed in life, as shown in Figure 13.5.

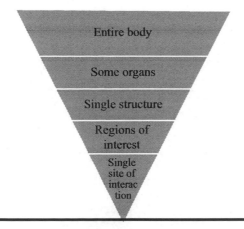

Figure 13.3   Order of interaction sites of the surgical simulator.

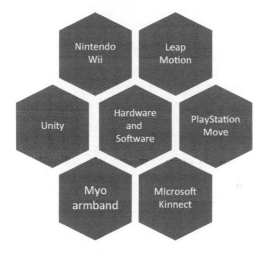

Figure 13.4   The hardware and software in VR rehabilitation.

The various simulators for the autism spectrum and its features are listed in Table 13.6 [13].

Stroke Rehabilitation

Stroke rehabilitation is difficult and it takes a long time to cure. The exercise for stroke patients can be given through virtual reality, which is more engaging and interesting. IREX, OmniVR, Jintronix, InMotion ARM, Armeo, HandTutor and Amadeo are some of the tools that use virtual environments [17]. Some of the VR systems for stroke rehabilitation are as follows.

Figure 13.5 VR in ASD.

Table 13.6 ASD VR Simulators

Simulator Environment	Type	Purpose
Virtual Cafe	Desktop VR	■ Communication ■ Social interaction
"I'm going to act as if…"	Desktop VR	■ Symbolic thinking ■ Imagination
StoryTable application	Touch-and-gesture projection VR	■ Communication ■ Social interaction
Collaborative virtual learning environment	Desktop VR	■ Communication ■ Social interaction
Virtual house	Desktop VR	■ Fire safety
Virtual school	Desktop VR	■ Fire safety ■ Tornado safety
Virtual street	Desktop VR	■ Street-crossing
Virtual fantasy land	Desktop VR	■ Attention
VR, virtual amusement park	Projection VR	■ Sensory ■ Integration
Virtual street, playground and school	Desktop VR	■ Engagement

Figure 13.6 VR-based treatment for the "Fear of Spider" [20].

- Wii board balance system (2016)
- Robotic assist gait training with VR (2017)
- Nintendo Wii balance training (2012)
- Treadmill-training-based real-world video recording (2014)
- Nintendo (2015)
- Robotic/virtually simulated, arm and finger rehabilitation activities (2015)
- Community-based virtual reality (2015)
- Virtual reality-based bilateral upper extremity training (2016)

Pediatric Motor Rehabilitation

VR helps to develop learning and enhance the performance of motor skills in children with neurological deficiencies. VR in pediatric rehabilitation involves several hardware, software devices and interfaces. The training could be given to the children in the form of VR games. The current VR simulators available in the market are listed [18].

DDR

- The equipment used in this simulator are PlayStation Wii, TV and DDR mat.
- Regular room with normal lighting is used as the environment.
- The children can interact with this system using sensors in the DDR mat which detect weight-bearing.
- The game has predetermined difficulty levels. Stimulus presentation and game duration are fixed.
- The minimum motor requirements for this system are independent standing postural control with dynamic balance.

- The maximum motor requirements are dynamic and reactive responses.
- The feedbacks are visual and auditory. Metrics is the game score. No multi-player capability is available.

Eye/EyeToy

- The equipment used in this simulator are PlayStation console, TV screen and camera.
- Regular room with normal lighting is used as the environment.
- The children can interact with this system by cameras which sense body movements.
- The game has predetermined difficulty levels. Stimulus presentation is predetermined and the game duration is fixed.
- The minimum motor requirements for this system are standing and sitting without any support.
- The maximum motor requirements are dynamic and reactive responses, active position changing of the body.
- The feedbacks are visual and auditory. Metrics is the game score. No multi-player capability is available.

IREX/GX

- The equipment used in this simulator are TV screen, camera, green backdrop, glove and computer system.
- A regular room with specific lighting is used as the environment.
- The children can interact with this system by using gloves which sense hand and body movements.
- The game has predetermined difficulty levels. Stimulus presentation is fixed and game duration is user-defined.
- The minimum motor requirements for this system are standing and sitting without any support.
- The maximum motor requirements are dynamic and reactive responses, active position changing of the body.
- The feedbacks are visual and auditory. Metrics are the joint angle accuracy and time.
- Multiplayer capability is available.

PITS

- The equipment used in this simulator are flat TV screen, glove and computer system.
- A small room with normal lighting is used as the environment.
- The children can interact with this system by using gloves which sense hand and body movements.

- The game has predetermined difficulty levels. The stimulus presentation is adjusted and the game duration is also adjusted.
- The minimum motor requirements for this system are sitting without any support.
- The maximum motor requirement is sitting independently.
- The feedbacks are visual and auditory. Metrics is the ability to capture different types of data.
- No multiplayer capability is available.

PlayStation 3-based sensor glove

- The equipment used in this simulator are computer systems with Linux environment, flat TV screen and DSL modem.
- A small room with normal lighting is used as the environment.
- The children can interact with this system by using gloves which sense hand and body movements.
- The game has predetermined difficulty levels. Stimulus presentation and game duration are fixed.
- The minimum motor requirement for this system is sitting without any support.
- The maximum motor requirement is sitting independently.
- The feedbacks are visual, auditory and haptics. Metrics are training time and walking distance.
- No Multiplayer capability is available.

Wii/WiiFit

- The equipment used in this simulator are Wii console, TV, Wii games and Wiimote.
- Regular room with normal lighting is used as the environment.
- The children can interact with this system by using Wiimote.
- The game has predetermined difficulty levels. Stimulus presentation and game duration are fixed.
- The minimum motor requirements for this system are standing and sitting without any support.
- The maximum motor requirements are dynamic and reactive responses.
- The feedbacks are visual, auditory and haptics. Metrics are game score and training time.
- No multiplayer capability is available.

VR in Lower-Limb Rehabilitation

The rehabilitation of lower limbs can be provided using VR. The movement imagination will improve the rehabilitation process. The VR techniques in the literature are tabulated in Table 13.7 [19].

Table 13.7 VR Techniques in Lower-Limb Rehabilitation

Author	Movement Visualization	Immersion	Robotic device	Motor Function
Aiello et al.	Indirect	Non	No	Gait
Cikajlo et al.	Indirect	Non	No	Balance
Fung et al.	Indirect	Semi	No	Gait
Kizony et al.	Indirect	Semi	No	Gait
Betker et al.	Abstract	Non	No	Balance
Mercier et al.	Abstract	Non	No	Gait
Deutsch et al.	Abstract	Non	Yes	Ankle
Cho et al.	Abstract	Game	No	Balance

VR in Psychotherapy

Psychotherapy is given to people who suffer from mental illnesses. Numerous treatments are available to uplift people from such kinds of illnesses. VR has been applied to the treatment of

- Phobias
- Anxiety
- Depression
- Stress

With the advent of technological improvement, VR devices have been sophisticated to meet the needs. HMDs like Oculus Rift, HTC Vive are widely used in psychotherapy. The challenge of applying VR in psychotherapy is the need for a skilled psychotherapist who could understand the VR technology. Some of the areas where VR could be employed are

- Social anxiety
- Exam-related anxiety
- Fear of flying
- Fear of heights (Acrophobia)
- Fear of animals
- Fear of driving
- Fear of public speaking
- Eating disorder

- Pain distraction
- Gambling disorder

Figure 13.6 depicts the psychotherapist giving treatments for the fear of spiders using VR technology.

There have been many researches in this field. Some of the works are as follows [21].

- Emmelkamp et al. (2011) proposed a VR-based treatment for Acrophobia: Cognitive-behavioral approach; 10 patients were used as the sample.
- Emmelkamp et al. (2001) compared VR-based treatment with exposure in vivo: Cognitive-behavioral approach; 33 patients were used as the sample.
- Garcia et al. (2002) proposed a VR treatment for spider phobia: Cognitive-behavioral approach; 23 patients were used as the sample.
- Maltby et al. (2002) proposed a VR treatment for fear of flying: Cognitive-behavioral approach; 45 patients were used as the sample.
- Riva et al. (2001) proposed a VR treatment for obesity stress: Experiential-cognitive behavioral approach; 20 patients were used as the sample.
- Vincelli et al. (2003) proposed a VR treatment for patients with agoraphobia: Experiential-cognitive behavioral approach; 12 patients were used as the sample.

Mobile applications to experience VR: Recently many mobile applications have been developed for experiencing virtual reality. Airway EX Virtual Surgery Simulator App, Anatomyou VR: 3D Human Anatomy App, Bacteria VR 3D, Bard VR, Precision Genomics VR, Touch Surgery, Surgical Simulator and InMind VR [22] are some of the mobile applications for medical training, rehabilitation and psychotherapy, available in the market, which can be accessed through smartphones.

Conclusion and future enhancement: Virtual reality in the medical field is growing at a tremendous rate. Medical training, rehabilitation and psychotherapy are immensely using virtual reality. Many people, both practitioners and patients, are benefitted by to the technology. Various VR simulators are available in the market and many researches are also happening in this domain so that people would be benefitted at lower costs.

Artificial intelligence with VR: In the future, artificial intelligence could be integrated into virtual reality. According to the user's learning abilities, the VR system could be trained. According to individual patients, the VR system could be customized. This will be a breakthrough combination which will eventually increase the performance of the virtual reality system.

References

[1] https://www.frontiersin.org/articles/10.3389/fpsyg.2018.02086/full
[2] https://www.statista.com/chart/4602/virtual-and-augmented-reality-software-revenue/
[3] https://getreferralmd.com/2019/09/9-ways-to-use-virtual-reality-in-healthcare/
[4] American Board of Internal Medicine. Procedures required for internal medicine [internet]. USA: ABIM; 2010 [Accessed May 2, 2010]. Available from: [http://www.abim.org/certification/policies/imss/im.aspx.]
[5] https://venturebeat.com/2019/10/30/fundamentalvr-raises-4-8-million-for-virtual-reality-medical-training/
[6] Haller G, Myles PS, Taffe P, Perneger TV, Wu CL. Rate of undesirable events at beginning of academic year: Retrospective cohort study. *Br Med J* 2019;339(1):3974
[7] Duffy AJ, Hogle NJ, McCarthy H, Lew JI, Egan A, Christos P, et al. Construct validity for the LAPSIM laparoscopic surgical simulator. *Surg Endosc* 2005;19(3):401–5.
[8] Zhang A, Hunerbein M, Dai Y, Schlag PM, Beller S. Construct validity testing of a laparoscopic surgery simulator (Lap Mentor): evaluation of surgical skill with a virtual laparoscopic training simulator. *Surg Endosc* 2008;22(6):1440–4.
[9] Kothari SN, Kaplan BJ, DeMaria EJ, Broderick TJ, Merrell RC. Training in laparoscopic suturing skills using a new computer-based virtual reality simulator (MIST-VR) provides results comparable to those with an established pelvic trainer system. *J Laparoendosc Adv Surg Tech* 2002;12(3):167–73.
[10] Iwata N, Fujiwara M, Kodera Y, Tanaka C, Ohashi N, Nakayama G, et al. Construct validity of the LapVR virtual-reality surgical simulator. *Surg Endosc* 2011;25(2):423–8.
[11] Broe D, Ridgway PF, Johnson S, Tierney S, Conlon KC. Construct validation of a novel hybrid surgical simulator. *Surg Endosc* 2006;20(6):900–4.
[12] Roy E, Bakr MM, George R. The need for virtual reality simulators in dental education: a review. *Saudi Dent J* 2017;29:41e7.
[13] Wang M, Anagnostou E Virtual reality as treatment tool for children with autism. In *Comprehensive Guideto Autism*; Springer: New York, NY, 2014; pp. 2125–2141.
[14] Arora A, Lau LY, Awad Z, Darzi A, Singh A, Tolley N. Virtual reality simulation training in otolaryngology. *Int J Surg* 2014;12:87–94. doi:10.1016/j.ijsu.2013.11.007
[15] Våpenstad C, Buzink SN. Procedural virtual reality simulation in minimally invasive surgery. *Surg Endosc* 2013;27(2):364–377.
[16] https://www.healthysimulation.com/virtual-anatomy/
[17] Fu MJ, Knutson JS, Chae J. Stroke rehabilitation using virtual environments. *Phys Med Rehabil Clin N Am.* 2015;26:747–57.
[18] Galvin J, Levac D. Facilitating clinical decision-making about the use of virtual reality within paediatric motor rehabilitation: describing and classifying virtual reality systems. *Dev Neurorehabil.* 2011;14(2):112–122.
[19] Ferreira Dos Santos L, Christ O, Mate K, Schmidt H, Krüger J, Dohle C. Movement visualization in virtual reality rehabilitation of the lower limb: a systematic review. *Biomed Eng* Online. 2016;15(Suppl 3):144.
[20] https://www.smartweek.it/virtual-reality-for-games-entertaining-and-psychotherapy/
[21] Riva, G. Virtual reality in psychotherapy: review. *CyberPsychol Behav* 2005;8:220–230.
[22] https://guides.dml.georgetown.edu/VirtualRealityMedicine/VRandSmartPhones

Chapter 14

Complexity Measures of Machine Learning Algorithms for Anticipating the Success Rate of IVF Process

A. Mercy Rani and A. Ranichitra

Sri S Ramasamy Naidu Memorial College, Sattur, India

Contents

DOI: 10.1201/9781003119784-14

Introduction

Infertility is one of the hottest research topics in today's medical field. The infertility issue is expanding radically because of heredity, adjustments in ways of life, food habits, and environmental factors. Infertility is also a disease in which a couple can't envisage a child. Specialists don't consider a couple to have infertility issues unless the couples have effectively attempted conceiving a child within a year, or if the woman is older than 35, for more than half a year. A few couples who experience intermittent miscarriages may likewise be viewed as infertile and should look for help from their doctor or a fertility master.

In-vitro fertilization (IVF) is a medical treatment for couples who have infertility problems. Robert Edwards and Patrick Steptoe are the pioneers of IVF and it has been used since the late 1970s. The baby, Louise Brown, was the first test-tube child born on 25th July 1978. The reasons for a couple undergoing an IVF treatment are low sperm count, problems with ovulation, problems with fallopian tubes if either of you have been sterilized, endometriosis, and to avoid inherited genetic disorders in children.

Infertility has customarily been an idea of a woman's concern. Be that as it may, Infertility in males is likewise as basic as female infertility. Infertility is essentially an equivalent open door condition and henceforth both women and men can be the wellspring of infertility. Around one out of each three instances of infertility is because of the man alone. Hence, this study concentrates on the various male infertility factors to identify the success rate of IVF treatment. Infertility in women may be because of elements such as age, body weight, hormonal irregularity, auto-immune issue, utilizing liquor or tobacco, fallopian tube issues, and so forth, and that of men incorporate age, smoking, overconsumption of liquor and medications, abundance stress, obesity, exposure to harmful substances, disease, and so forth.

Risk Factors and Tests for Predicting Infertility in Men

Risk factors for infertility in men include the following [1]:

- Age
- Being overweight or obesity
- Smoking
- Using certain illegitimate drugs
- Excessive use of alcohol
- Electronic devices
- Exposure to testosterone medications

- Direct contact to radiation
- Stress
- Frequent contact to excess temperatures
- Affect with ecological pollutants and pesticides
- Few past or present diseases
- Major abdominal or pelvic surgery
- Medication and surgery.

The full history and physical examination are considered for diagnosing male Infertility. The various diagnoses for predicting male fertility are listed as follows [2].

- Sperm analysis
- Hormone testing
- Genetic testing
- Testicular surgery
- Imaging test
- Test for sperm quality

Masculine Infertility Treatments

Masculine infertility may be treated with clinical, surgical, or Assisted Reproductive Technology (ART) depending upon the key explanation. Clinical and surgical medicines are typically regulated by a urologist who has viable involvement with barrenness. Infertility in males can be treated using ART which is utilized to help individuals in accomplishing a pregnancy. Depending upon the reason for infertility, the associated sorts of treatment may assist with defeating male infertility; ART covers a wide range of treatments [3].

- **In-vitro fertilization (IVF)** is the most efficient and universal form of ART in which the fertilization takes place outside the body.
- **Zygote intrafallopian transfer (ZIFT)** is analogous to IVF but fertilization happens in the laboratory and the embryo will be transferred into the fallopian tube.
- **Gamete intrafallopian transfer (GIFT)** is transmitting eggs and sperm into the woman's fallopian tube. Fertilization occurs in the woman's body.
- **Intracytoplasmic sperm injection (ICSI)** includes the immediate infusion of single sperm into each egg to accomplish preparation.

The IVF is the most notable treatment wherein female oocytes are prepared by sperms under research facility conditions that produce embryos. The embryos are moved to the uterus for implantation. Figure 14.1 shows the steps followed in the IVF process [4].

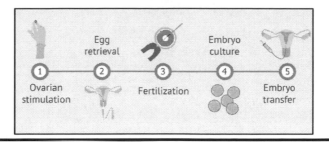

Figure 14.1   In-vitro fertilization process [5].

- **Stimulating ovaries** – Normally, a female fabricates an egg every month. Drugs are given to women to generate more eggs. Through this cycle, the women ought to have common transvaginal ultrasounds to look at the ovaries and blood tests to check hormone levels.
- **Egg repossession** – Eggs (oocytes) are retrieved from female patients using transvaginal aspiration directly from the ovarian follicles, about 36 hours after an injection of HCG (Human Chorionic Gonadotropin).
- **Fertilization** – To maximize the successful fertilization of eggs by the sperm, each complex is transferred to the insemination media which has a special solution for providing all the nutrients and substances. Naturally, fertilization usually occurs in the fallopian tube. In some cases, the ICSI method is used to reduce the probability of non-fertilization.
- **Embryo development** – The sperm fertilizes the egg and it is called an embryo. The embryos are put into a special incubator over 5–6 days where the growing conditions use a mix of amino acids like our body nurture the embryo. The embedding of undeveloped organisms on the blastocyst stage snared on the uterus helps the odds of a fruitful pregnancy.
- **Embryo transfer** – If the embryos are developed in the lab, it is ready to be transferred into a woman's womb. This process is a simple one; it takes only about 5 minutes. Multiple embryos might be set into the woman's womb all the while relying upon the parental age; it leads to twins, triplets, or more [6].
- **The final blood test** – After two weeks of embryo transfer, the doctor checks the levels of hormone HCG by taking a blood test.

Advantages of IVF

The main purpose of IVF is attaining a triumphant pregnancy and a hale and hearty child. People having the following problems may take an IVF treatment to have a healthy baby [7].

Blocked tubes – IVF is the best treatment for women who are having blocked or damaged fallopian tubes to conceive a baby with their eggs.

Patients with a low ovarian reserve – IVF provides the opportunity for the patients having an older and low ovarian reserve.

Male infertility – The couples having male infertility have an elevated possibility of conceiving with IVF than conceiving in nature.

Polycystic ovary disorder (PCOD) – It is a typical state where there is a hormone inequity prompting unpredictable menstrual cycles. In vitro preparation has been demonstrated to be exceptionally effective in patients with PCOD, who won't imagine with ovulation acceptance.

Endometriosis – IVF is fruitful in patients with endometriosis, in which the portion of the worm lining develops outside the worm.

Premature ovarian failure – IVF provides donor eggs for women with premature ovarian failure or menopause.

Though it was found that IVF is the most successful and assistive form of reproductive methodology, only 5% of couples with infertility will go for IVF, according to the American Society of Reproductive, due to less success rate, cost, and other side effects. To increase the number of couples who would take the IVF treatment without anxiety, the data for finding the success rate of IVF is essential for couples before going through the IVF treatment [8, 9]. Subsequently, this chapter aims to foresee the success rate depending on the male ripeness variables and it will be useful for the early distinguishing proof of original patients and the decision of semen giver's competitors utilizing the IVF richness dataset [10].

Hence, this chapter aims to predict the success rate based on the male fertility factors and it will be helpful for the early identification of seminal patients and the choice of semen donor candidates using the IVF fertility dataset [10]. Experiment results on the fertility diagnosis dataset have been studied using the machine learning (ML) classifiers k-Nearest Neighbor (kNN), Naive Bayes, Decision Tree, Random Forest (RF), and Neural Networks.

This chapter is structured as follows: The section "Literature Survey" discusses the various research findings carried out in this area; Then, various machine learning algorithms to estimate the success rate of the IVF process is analyzed, followed by the chapter conclusion.

Literature Survey

In medical research, Digital Image Processing plays a vital role to diagnose diseases in the human body based on scanned images. Diseases in the small parts of the human body such as skin [11] and nails [12, 13] can also be found using image-processing techniques and in [14], the MRI brain images are segmented using the Parallel Genetic Algorithm (PGA). Recently, machine learning algorithms have been used for predicting the statuses of diseases based on the history of medical data. Nowadays, infertility is a major problem for couples due to food habits and environmental factors. The member clinics of the Society for Assisted Reproductive Treatments (SART) [15] constitute 90% of the ART clinics in the US and it released a report in 2014. The SART has concentrated on the concept of a safe and healthy baby. They presented data on the percentage of women in categories of various age ranges. A high success rate of 54% was found when the parental age was below 35 years and a low success rate of 3.9–13.3% was found when the parental age was above 40. Another latest report was released by medical research centers like the Center for Disease Control (CDC) in 2017 [16]. It provides the data of 448 fertility clinics on 284,385 ART cycles carried out in 2017. According to this report, using ART, 1.7% of babies are born every year in the US. The results of the above report show that

- 68,908 live new conceived which conveyances of at least one living baby.
- Among 284,385 ART cycles, 87,535 eggs or embryos were predicted for the upcoming ART process, and 196,850 were predicted for pregnancy.

According to the above reports, the necessity of finding the success rate of IVF treatment has increased nowadays. Earlier, several studies have been made in finding the estimation of the success of IVF treatment using data mining and machine learning approaches. Hassan Rafiul et al. [17] proposed an algorithm that analyzes and finds the IVF status in pregnancy with better accuracy. The proposed algorithm was developed using machine learning techniques which are called an automatic classification of feature selection using the hill-climbing approach. The pregnancy success of IVF treatment was predicted by analyzing 25 attributes using five different machine learning algorithms: Classification and Regression Trees (CART), Support Vector Machines (SVM), Multilayer Perceptron (MLP), C4.5, and RF. The performance of the estimation of pregnancy was calculated using the metrics Accuracy, F-measure, and Area Under Curve (AUC). Nidhin Raju et al. [18] found the existence of Interstitial Lung Diseases (ILD) with the help of deep learning algorithms. In the anticipated work, multi-label classification was performed to identify the 17 different categories of ILD by analyzing High-Resolution Computed Tomography (HRCT) images. A Convolutional Neural Network (CNN) architecture called SmallerVGGNet was used to get the features of images and the results provided an average accuracy of 95%, which is greater than the accuracy of clinical history of 20%. Khosravi Pegah et al. [19] proposed an AI approach for predicting the quality of embryos with the help of thousands (about 50,000 images) of trained embryos using Deep Neural Networks (DNNs). They developed a framework called STORK using the GI model, and it estimates the excellence of the blastocyst by an AUC of above 0.98 and it performs better than discrete embryologists. A decision tree was created with the 2182 embryos in the clinical data to identify the pregnancy possibility states. The results show that the possibilities of pregnancy depend on age and it changes from 13.8% to 66.3% for individual embryos.

Guvenir H. et al. [20] developed a new method for finding the success proportion of the IVF process which is constructed from the RIMARC ranking algorithm called Success Estimation Using a Ranking Algorithm (SERA). The proposed algorithm is compared with the Naive Bayes Classifier and Random Forest using the metrics AUC and Accuracy. The outcome of the system showed that the SERA algorithm is effective in estimating the success of IVF treatment. This study also determined the attributes and their values which creates an impact on the result of the IVF process. The performance of the new algorithm is compared against Naive Bayes Classifier and Random Forest using the metrics Accuracy, Receiver Operating Characteristic (ROC) curve, and the time of execution. Bidgoli et al. [21] classified the semen samples using a genetic algorithm with an Artificial Neural Network. The proposed method used the bootstrap method to solve the unbalancing of the dataset. The accuracy of the proposed optimized MLP for predicting seminal quality algorithm is dependent on the lifestyle and status of the patient's health. J.L.Girela et al. [22] used MLP to analyze the connection between lifestyle and the quality of semen. The seminal parameters sperm concentration and motility are studied and they were used to identify the factors which further affect these two seminal parameters. Durairaj M. et al. [23] used data-mining techniques to identify influential tests that are utilized to define the success percentage of the IVF process. The proposed method helps to identify the reduced list of significant parameters needed to estimate the success rate of IVF. The fertility data analysis was done by applying a supervised algorithm for pre-processing and the parameters important for determining the success rate are selected with the help of a feature-selection algorithm. David Gi et al. [24] used three classification methods, Decision Trees (DT), MLP, and SVM, to analyze the accuracy of the estimation of the quality of the semen samples. Uyar Asli et al. [25] proposed an intelligent system to increase the success rate of pregnancy. In this system, the success was determined by the result of new embryos and the model was trained using past data by applying the SVM-based classification method. The embryo is represented using 17 features associated with the features of a patient, medical analysis, the way of treatment, and embryo structural values. The observed outcomes showed 82.7% prediction accuracy.

From the above literature, we observed that data-mining techniques and AI approach will guide the couple to decide on undergoing the IVF treatment. Hence, this chapter builds the machine learning model to estimate the success status IVF process using kNN, Naive Bayes (NB), Decision Tree (DT), RF, and Neural Network algorithms.

Study of Machine Learning Classification Algorithms

This study takes classification approaches kNN, Naive Bayes, Decision Tree, Random Forest, and Neural Network for analyzing the data and finally, the model is built using the best classifier. Figure 14.2 describes the architecture of the proposed model.

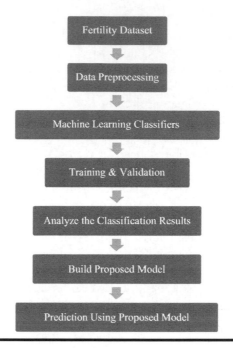

Figure 14.2 Proposed system architecture

Algorithm for the proposed model:

Step 1: Collect the data for analysis.

Step 2: Pre-process the data using the Synthetic Minority Oversampling Technique (SMOTE) to balance the class labels in the dataset.

Step 3: Use the Cross-Validation Method to divide the dataset as training data and testing data.

Step 4: Train the data by applying the Machine Learning Classifiers kNN, Naive Bayes, Decision Tree, Random Forest, and Neural Networks.

Step 5: Perform Steps a–c to test the trained models using the test dataset.

    (a) Calculate the evaluation results using AUC, Accuracy, F1-Score, Recall, and Precision.

    (b) Generate the Confusion Matrix to summarize the correct and incorrect predictions.

    (c) Choose the appropriate classifier based on the evaluation results and the confusion matrix.

Step 6: Build the proposed model using the classifier identified in Step 5.

Step 7: Predict the data using the proposed model.

Dataset

The fertility dataset [10] in the UCI machine learning repository is taken for data analysis. It contains infertility details of 100 male patient's semen sample whose age is between 18 and 36 years. Semen absorption is related to social and demographical facts, natural features, health conditions, and life behaviors with 10 features. Table 14.1 shows attribute, type, and values of categorical attributes; 5 out of the 10

Table 14.1 Fertility Dataset and Its Attributes

Attributes	Type	Values
Season (the period in which the study was carried out)	Numeric	Winter (–1) Spring (–0.33) Summer (0.33) Fall (1)
Age	Numeric	18–36 (0–1)
Childish illness (i.e., chickenpox, measles, mumps, polio)	Categorical	True (0) False (1)
Mishap or severe injury	Categorical	True (0) False (1)
Surgery happened	Categorical	True (0) False (1)
The high temperature in the previous year	Numeric	Fewer than three months ago (–1) Greater than three months ago (0) No fever (1)
Taking liquid courage	Numeric	Many times per day (0) Daily (0.2) Many times per week (0.6) One time per week (0.8) Not ever (1)
Smoking practice	Categorical	Not ever (–1) Rare (0) Every day (1)
Sitting hours per day	Numeric	0–1
Status of diagnosis (output)	Categorical	Normal (N) Altered (O)

attributes have numerical values while the remaining five attributes are categorical. The categorical attributes have binary values 0 or 1 or multiple values. The samples are identified with nine attributes and one attribute represents the quality of semen as Normal (N) or Altered (O).

The input attributes in the dataset are represented using a range of normalized values. The attributes which are having two independent values are denoted using binary numbers (0, 1). The attributes which have three autonomous attribute values, such as, "High temperatures in the previous year" and "Smoking practice" are represented using the triple values (–1, 0, 1). For example, feature –1 represents "not ever", 0 refers to "rare", and 1 represents "every day". The feature "Season" has four different values (–1, –0.33, 0.33, 1) in which –1 represents the winter season, –0.33 represents the spring season, 0.33 represents the summer season, and 1 represents the fall season.

Data Pre-Processing

Data pre-processing is a primary task in data analytics to prepare the dataset for further analysis by removing missing values, inappropriate features, and clean the dataset with values that are unnecessary for the analysis. The dataset considered in this research has no missing or incorrect values and hence the initial phase of the pre-processing task is eliminated. However, the dataset is not balanced as the class labels do not have an equal number of instances. The number of samples for the class label Altered (O) is very low when compared to the class label Normal (N). This unbalanced instance makes the machine learning algorithms find the maximum class data and ignores the minimum class data. As the minimum class instance, "Altered" will be considered as noise, the machine learning classifiers will produce biased and erroneous results with this unbalanced dataset. Most of the researchers do not concentrate on class distribution, rather they concentrate on improving the accuracy of their models [26, 27].

In Refs [28, 29], resampling methods are used to analyze unbalanced data in the pre-processing step. The main benefit of the sampling methods is that they are independent from the primary classification approach. Resampling methods are categorized into three categories: random undersampling techniques, which balance the class distributions of the dataset by randomly eradicating the majority class samples; random oversampling techniques which balance the class distributions of the dataset by repeating some samples of a minimum class or generating new samples of the minimum class with the current minority samples; finally, hybrid methods combining both undersampling and oversampling. Among these, the first two categories are the non-heuristic methods and the simplest methods. The major disadvantage of the first category is that it discards possibly useful data which is important for building the models. The sample selected by random undersampling may be unfair data and thereby produce inaccurate results. The main drawback of random oversampling is that the replication of minimum class samples increases the likelihood of overfitting. To overcome the disadvantages of the above-stated methods, SMOTE [30], the most significant sampling technique, can be used. The main task of SMOTE is in creating new minimum class samples by adding several duplicate minimum class samples for oversampling the training set.

Hence, the proposed work applies the resampling method SMOTE to balance the fertility dataset. SMOTE generates additional samples by adding numerous existing minimum samples. After applying SMOTE, the dataset generated is the balanced dataset with 176 samples of each class with 88 instances whereas the original dataset has 88 instances of Normal (N) and 12 instances of Altered (O).

Machine Learning Classifiers

■ **kNN** – It [31] is a supervised and easily understandable machine learning approach, and classification and regression problems can be solved using this algorithm. It works based on the similarity measures such as remoteness or closeness with nearly mathematical calculations. The Euclidean distance is the most widespread and common choice for distance calculation. The value of k is the number of most similar instances or neighbors. There is no fixed value of k; the appropriate value of k is chosen by running the dataset with varying values of k, and the most appropriate value is chosen, depending on the accuracy parameter.

■ **Naive Bayes** – Naive Bayes [32, 33] is also an easily usable algorithm to classify binary and multi-class categorical input values. It belongs to Bayesian decision theory and is named Naive Bayes since the computation of the probability of each hypothesis is simple and makes the calculation traceable. The structure of the classifier takes one parent node with more children nodes. The parent node is a class feature and the children are other features of a particular sample.

■ **Decision tree** – Decision tree [34] is one of the widely used machine learning algorithms for building a model since it can be used with both classification and regression. It is a tree-like structure and initially, it divides the samples with two or more than the same sets which depends on the most important features which make the discrete set of groups as possible. The decision tree algorithm built a prototype that finds the value of an output feature utilizing decision rules derived from the other features. In the decision tree, the topmost node is called the root and the tree has multiple levels, depending upon the data in the dataset. The internal nodes in the tree depict a test case for the input features. The leaf or terminal nodes represent the outcome of a particular decision. Traversing the tree down the path from each node will provide the decision rules to infer a particular outcome. This process is performed recursively and repeatedly for each sub-tree with new root nodes [35].

■ **Random forest** – Random forest [36] is used for classification though it supports both classifications as well as regression. Random forest is a simple and familiar algorithm it gives good results even when it has no hyper-parameter tuning. This algorithm creates a forest which is a group of decision trees and it uses the bagging method to train the data. When a decision tree is built, it searches and selects the best feature of the dataset along with the random subset of features.

■ **Neural Network** – Neural Network [37] is a machine learning algorithm that makes use of the architecture inspired by the neurons in the brain. In the human brain, the brain neuron gets input and outputs it to another neuron based on the input it received. In recent years, Neural Networks have become widespread and are used in many applications as it is used to build the machine learning model for classification, clustering, and prediction. The architecture of Neural Networks contains various layers and the layers are independent of one another. Each layer has an arbitrary number of nodes and it is called a bias node. In each layer, the yield of one node becomes an input for the other node. The nodes and edges have the weight which facilitates control of signal qualities of correspondence which can be intensified or else debilitated by the repetitive process. This method predicts the future data based on the training and the following changes incurred in matrices, node, and edge weights. Figure 14.3 shows the structure of the Neural Network of two concealed layers with its unified cluster of nodes [38].

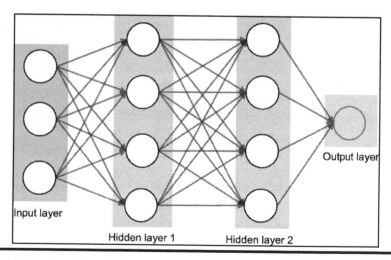

Figure 14.3 Sample architecture of the neural network (two concealed layers) [38].

Training and Validation

The performance of machine learning models is evaluated by statistical methods. Most of the researchers used the k-fold Cross-Validation statistical technique to estimate the efficiency of machine learning models since it is easy to implement and it works well on a limited data sample. This method is used to compare the different classifiers and choose the best classifier among them. Initially, the dataset is divided into k-folds; the model is trained by considering k1 folds employing training data, and the remaining part of the dataset is used for validating the model. In this work, 176 instances in the dataset are divided into 10 (k = 10) equal-sized folds. The stratified k-fold cross-validation ensures that the ratio of each class Normal (N) and Altered (O) is almost similar in the total dataset. For this cross-validation scheme, the task is repeated 10 times, and for each time, a different set of test data is considered.

Performance Analysis of the Classification Algorithms

In the proposed work, initially, the unbalanced class labels in the dataset are balanced using the SMOTE resampling technique. The model is trained using the k-fold Cross-Validation scheme (k = 10) with the machine learning algorithms kNN, Naive Bayes, Decision Tree, Random Forest, and Neural Network for classifying the seminal quality as Normal (N) and Altered (O) based on male's fertility factors. The evaluation metrics of the proposed model are compared against the results of the original dataset.

In classification approaches, the confusion matrix is one of the most widely used metrics for finding the correctness and accuracy of any classifier model in which the output can be of two or more types of classes. In this chapter, this matrix is used to categorize the male's seminal quality as Normal (N) or Altered (O). The result of the confusion matrix of the proposed work is shown in Table 14.2. It describes the number of instances correctly classified or incorrectly classified using binary classifiers. The total number of instances in the dataset is calculated by adding TP, FP, TN, and FN.

Table 14.2 Binary Classification – Confusion Matrix

Predicted result			
		Normal (N)	Altered (O)
Actual result	**Normal (N)**	TP	FP
	Altered (O)	FN	TN

- TP is the number of True Positives (TP), which implies that the classifier predicted the seminal quality as Normal-N (True) when the real output is also Normal-N (Positive).
- FP is the total number of False Positives (FP) which implies that the classifier predicted the seminal quality as Altered-O (False) when the actual outcome is Normal-N (Positive).
- FN is the number of False Negatives (FN) which implies that the classifier predicted the seminal quality as Normal-N (False) when the actual outcome is Altered-O (Positive).
- TN is the number of True Positives (TP) which implies that the classifier predicted the seminal quality as Altered-O (True) when the actual outcome is also Altered-O (Negative).

The Confusion Matrix of the fertility dataset for the classifiers kNN, Naive Bayes, Decision Tree, Random Forest, and Neural Network are shown in Table 14.3. The results are Normal or Altered, where Normal (N) indicates the good quality of the semen whereas Altered (O) indicates the bad quality of the semen.

Area-Under-ROC-Curve (AUC) – ROC curve is drawn between True Positive (TP) values and False Positive (FP) values. During the changes of threshold values from 0 to 1, the False Positive values and the True Positive values are plotted between the x- and y-axes. It plots the total accumulated area covered by the ROC curve. A good performance of the classifier is indicated by the AUC value close to 1; the value 0 indicates bad performance. The aggregate performance of all classification models can be calculated using the AUC.

Accuracy – It is a relation between the total numeral of predictions properly found to the total numeral of samples.

$$CA = (TP + TN) / (TP + TN + FP + FN)$$

Recall – It is a relation between the correctly predicted normal seminal quality as normal to the total numeral of normal seminal samples.

$$Recall = TP / (FN + TP)$$

Precision – It is a relation between the properly predicted normal seminal quality as normal.

$$Precision = TP / (FP + TP)$$

F1-Score – is a relation harmonic mean value of recall and precision.

$$F1 = 2 \times Precision \times Recall / (Precision + Recall)$$

Table 14.3 Confusion Matrix of the Considered Classifiers (Cross-Validation)

Actual	kNN Predicted			Naive Bayes Predicted			Tree Predicted			Random Forest Predicted			Neural Network Predicted		
	N	O	Σ	N	O	Σ	N	O	Σ	N	O	Σ	N	O	Σ
N	70	18	88	87	1	88	85	3	88	88	0	88	86	2	88
O	0	88	88	13	75	88	5	83	88	1	87	88	0	88	88
Σ	70	106	176	100	76	176	90	86	176	89	87	176	86	90	176

Results and Discussions

The evaluation results of unbalanced class labels are shown in Tables 14.4 and 14.5 shows the results of balanced class labels after applying the SMOTE. From the results, we observed that in both approaches, the machine learning algorithm Neural Network classified the dataset as Normal (N) or Altered (O) in the best way when compared to the other learning algorithms. Neural Network algorithm shows better results in terms of the considered performance metrics AUC, Classification Accuracy, F1-Score, Precision, and Recall (shown in bold in Tables 14.4 and 14.5).

Table 14.4 Evaluation Metrics (Unbalanced Class Labels)

Classifiers	Evaluation Metrics				
	AUC	CA (%)	F1-Score (%)	Precision (%)	Recall (%)
kNN	0.665	83.0	79.8	76.9	83.0
Tree	0.676	85.0	83.2	82.0	85.0
Neural Network	**0.764**	**88.0**	**84.0**	**84.1**	**88.0**
Naive Bayes	0.650	81.0	81.9	82.9	81.0
Random Forest	0.581	86.0	82.8	80.9	86.0

Table 14.5 Evaluation Metrics (Balanced Class Labels Using SMOTE)

Classifiers	Evaluation Metrics				
	AUC	CA (%)	F1-Score (%)	Precision (%)	Recall (%)
kNN	0.992	89.8	89.7	91.5	89.8
Tree	0.985	95.5	95.5	95.5	95.5
Neural Network	**1.0**	**98.9**	**98.9**	**98.9**	**98.9**
Naive Bayes	0.961	92.0	92.0	92.8	92.0
Random Forest	0.998	97.2	97.2	97.2	97.2

The ROC analysis of the proposed work is shown in Figure 14.4. From the graph, it is observed that the Neural Network algorithm performs well since its AUC value is 1.

The performance comparison of the evaluation metrics for the unbalanced class labels and the proposed balanced class labels using SMOTE are shown in Figures 14.5–14.9. It indicates that the proposed work performs well for all the considered metrics.

Table 14.6 shows the percentage of improvement for the proposed work Balanced-SMOTE than using an unbalanced dataset. From the table, it is clear that balanced-SMOTE shows the best values than the unbalanced dataset.

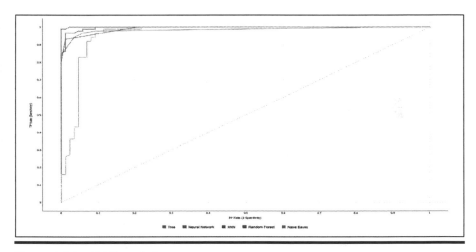

Figure 14.4   ROC analysis curve.

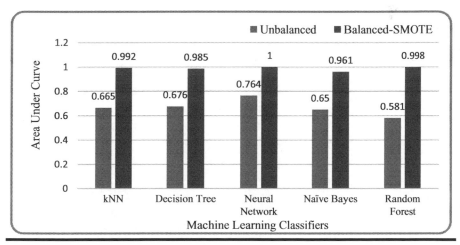

Figure 14.5   Area Under Curve – machine learning algorithms.

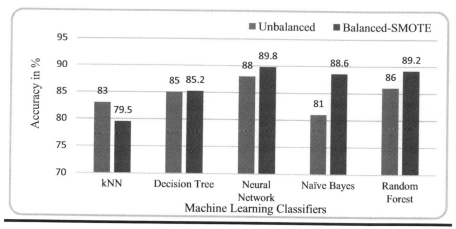

Figure 14.6   Accuracy.

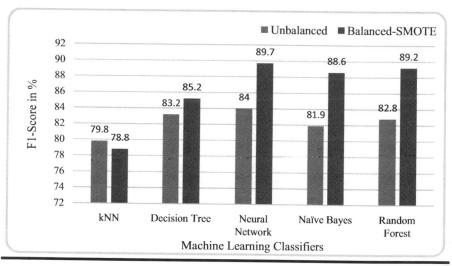

Figure 14.7   F1-Score.

Build the Proposed Model

Though the proposed work performed well in all the learning algorithms, the classifier model of this dataset is built using the Neural Network algorithm since it provides the best results when compared to the other algorithms. Hence, the proposed model of this fertility dataset is built using the Neural Network algorithm and it provides an accuracy of 98.9% with an AUC of 1.0. It indicates that the proposed model makes predictions in the fertility dataset in the best way.

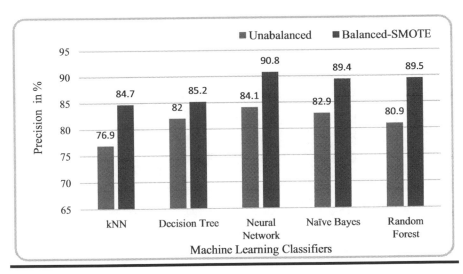

Figure 14.8 Precision.

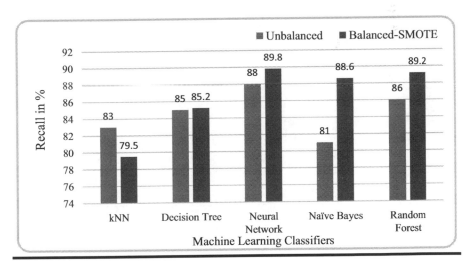

Figure 14.9 Recall.

Prediction Using the Proposed Model

Figure 14.10 shows the most influential attributes of the fertility dataset for making future predictions and this process is carried out using the decision tree. From the figure, we can observe the most influential attributes for predicting the success rate of IVF.

Table 14.6 Percentage Improvement of Balanced-SMOTE

Metrics	Unbalanced	Balanced-SMOTE	Percentage of Improvement (%)
AUC	0.764	1.0	30.89
Accuracy	88.0	98.9	12.39
F1-Score	84.0	98.9	17.74
Precision	84.1	98.9	17.60
Recall	88.0	98.9	12.39

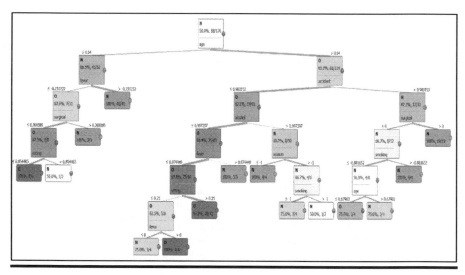

Figure 14.10   Identifying influential attributes of the dataset.

Conclusion

ML algorithms involve cautious investigation of the input data and the methods applied to the data. Applying the utmost suitable pre-processing techniques will yield a better performance of the ML algorithms. These ML algorithms will be most supportive in the medical domain to decide during bottlenecks. Infertility is the foremost issue faced by the couple and the problem can be overwhelmed by IVF treatment. But this IVF treatment is not affordable for all couples. This work aims to assist the couple to decide on undergoing the treatment based on their IVF success rate. Initially, the fertility dataset is well-adjusted using the resampling technique SMOTE and classified as training and test data using the Cross-Validation method. The dataset is analyzed using various machine learning classifiers such as kNN, Naive Bayes, Decision Tree, Random Forest, and Neural Networks. From the analysis, it was found that the machine learning algorithm Neural Networks performs well for the considered dataset. Hence, in this study, the Neural Networks algorithm is used to build the model and the results show 30.89% AUC, 12.39% Accuracy, and Recall 17.74% of F1-Score and 17.60% of Precision as the performance improvement than the unbalanced dataset. Finally, the most influential attributes that can be used for future predictions are identified using the decision tree.

References

1 https://www.parents.com/getting-pregnant/infertility/causes/health-101-infertility-in-men/
2 https://www.mayoclinic.org/diseases-conditions/infertility/diagnosis-treatment/drc-20354322
3 https://www.webmd.com/men/features/male-infertility-treatments#4
4 https://medlineplus.gov
5 https://images.app.goo.gl/VUL9zu3ni6qcPsbz5
6 https://monashivf.com/
7 https://www.dssimage.com/blog/understanding-in-vitro-fertilization-ivf-better/
8 Yildiz, M.S., Khan, M.M. "Opportunities for reproductive tourism: cost and quality advantages of Turkey in the provision of in-vitro Fertilization (IVF) services", *BMC Health Services Research* 16, (2016): 378. doi: 10.1186/s12913-016-1628-7.
9 https://americanpregnancy.org/infertility/in-vitro-fertilization/
10 https://archive.ics.uci.edu/ml/datasets/Fertility
11 Rani, A. Mercy, and S. Maheshwari, "Melanoma skin cancer analysis using thresholding method.", *International Journal of Computer Technology & Applications* 8 4 (2017): 507–511.
12 A. Mercy Rani, M. Kaleeswari, and M. Karpagam, "Diagnosing human diseases using toe tail", *International Journal of Engineering Research in Computer Science and Engineering (IJERCSE)*, 5 3 (2018): 217–220, ISSN (Online) 2394-2320.
13 Saranya, V., and A. Ranichitra, "Image segmentation techniques to detect nail abnormalities", *International Journal of Computer Technology & Applications*, 8 4 (2017):522–527.
14 D P Augustine, and Pethuru Raj, "Performance evaluation of parallel genetic algorithm for brain MRI segmentation in hadoop and spark", *Indian Journal of Science and Technology*, 9 48, (2016): 1–7.
15 https://www.sart.org/patients/fyi-videos/understanding-the-sart-clinic-report/
16 https://www.cdc.gov/art/index.html
17 Hassan, Md Rafiul, et al. "A machine learning approach for prediction of pregnancy outcome following IVF treatment," *Neural Computing and Applications,* 32 7 (2020): 2283–2297.
18 Nidhin R, Anita H B, and D P Augustine, "Identification of interstitial lung diseases using deep learning", *International Journal of Electrical and Computer Engineering (IJECE)*, 10 6 (2020): 6283–6291.
19 Khosravi, Pegah, et al. "Deep learning enables robust assessment and selection of human blastocysts after in vitro fertilization", *NPJ Digital Medicine* 2.1 (2019): 1–9.

20 Güvenir, H. Altay, et al. "Estimating the chance of success in IVF treatment using a ranking algorithm", *Medical & Biological Engineering & Computing* 53.9 (2015): 911–920.

21 Bidgoli, Azam Asilian, Hossein, Ebrahimpour Komleh, and Seyed Jalaleddin Mousavirad. "Seminal quality prediction using optimized artificial neural network with genetic algorithm." *2015 9th International Conference on Electrical and Electronics Engineering (ELECO).* IEEE, (2015).

22 J.L. Girela, D. Gil, M. Johnsson, M.J. Gomez-Torres, and J. De Juan, "Semen parameters can be predicted from environmental factors and lifestyle using artificial intelligence methods," *Biology of Reproduction,* 88, (2013): 99.

23 M. Durairaj, and R. Nandha Kumar, "Data mining application on IVF data for the selection of influential parameters on fertility", *International Journal of Engineering and Advanced Technology (IJEAT)* 2 6 (2013): pp. 262–266. ISSN: 2249–8958

24 David Gil, Jose Luis Girela, Joaquin De Juan, M. Jose Gomez-Torres, and Magnus Johnson. "Predicting seminal quality with artificial intelligence methods", *Expert Systems with Applications,* 39 16 (2012): 12564.

25 Uyar, Asli, et al. "3P:Personalized pregnancy prediction in IVF treatment process", *International Conference on Electronic Healthcare.* Springer, Berlin, Heidelberg, (2008).

26 Fernández, Alberto, Salvador García, and Francisco Herrera. "*Addressing the classification with imbalanced data: open problems and new challenges on class distribution*", *International conference on hybrid artificial intelligence systems.* Springer, Berlin, Heidelberg, (2011).

27 https://www.analyticsvidhya.com/blog/2017/03/imbalanced-data-classification/

28 Batista, G.E.A.P.A., Prati, R.C., Monard, M.C., "A study of the behaviour of several methods for balancing machine learning training data", *SIGKDD Explorations* 6 1 (2004): 20–29.

29 Fernández, Alberto, María José del Jesus, and Francisco Herrera. "On the 2-tuples based genetic tuning performance for fuzzy rule-based classification systems in imbalanced data-sets", *Information Sciences* 180 8 (2010): 1268–1291.

30 Fernández, Alberto, Salvador García, and Francisco Herrera. "*Addressing the classification with imbalanced data: open problems and new challenges on class distribution*", *International conference on hybrid artificial intelligence systems,* Springer, Berlin, Heidelberg, 2011.

31 https://towardsdatascience.com/machine-learning-basics-with-the-k-nearest-neighbors-algorithm-6a6e71d01761

32 https://techgrabyte.com/10-machine-learning-algorithms-application/

33 Namdev, Neeraj, Shikha Agrawal, and Sanjay Silkari. "Recent advancement in machine learning based internet traffic classification", *Procedia Computer Science* 60 (2015): 784–791.

34 https://www.analyticsvidhya.com/blog/2017/09/common-machine-learning-algorithms/

35 https://www.hackerearth.com/practice/machine-learning/machine-learning-algorithms/ml-decision-tree/tutorial/

36 https://builtin.com/data-science/random-forest-algorithm

37 https://www.verypossible.com/blog/machine-learning-algorithms-what-is-a-neural-network

38 Uddin, S., Khan, A., Hossain, M. et al. "Comparing different supervised machine learning algorithms for disease prediction", *BMC Medical Informatics and Decision Making,* 19, (2019): 281.

Chapter 15

Commuter Traffic Congestion Control Evasion in IoT-Based VANET Environment

A. Ranichitra and A. Mercy Rani

Sri S. Ramasamy Naidu Memorial College, Sattur, India

Contents

DOI: 10.1201/9781003119784-15

Introduction

Globally, every year, almost 1.3 million individuals die due to road traffic accidents that cause more than 3000 deaths consistently. Between 20 and 50 million additional individuals experience the ill effects of a mishap and such injuries are a significant reason for physical disabilities around the world. Most of those influenced are youngsters in developing countries. Road traffic crashes are catastrophes that throw their families into hopelessness and destitution. Except if a progressively far-reaching universal action is made, the quantity of deaths and injuries is probably going to rise altogether [1]. There are solutions to the road-safety problem. A wide scope of viable interventions is available, and associations in nations with long narratives of mechanized travel have shown that a coherent, "framework approach" to road safety is imperative to manage the issue. This methodology refers to the transport framework overall and looks at the interactions between vehicles, road users, and the road infrastructure to perceive the solutions.

The world is moving from a period of items to a time of administrations and encounters, from equipment to programming, from usefulness to data as the primary entity of significant worth construction, from diligence stockpiling to complicatedly associated eco-systems [2] and air pollution monitoring [3] with the assistance of Internet of Things(IoT). The IoT alludes to an association of billions of complex gadgets like hardware, sensors, doors, actuators, and hubs. These substantial gadgets associate and collaborate over a remote wireless system. Connected objects (or things) share information and work with no intercession from people.

The IoT empowers revolution, and there is a denial of doubt that the automotive division is shifting incredibly quickly. IoT-correlated advancements will portray the guide for the business to pursue, and the associated vehicle assumes a significant job on streets and in the financial system of things to come [4]. VANET has been introduced for improving the security and adequacy of transportation systems, which led to the creation of portable applications. VANET is a network that brings together the sensors and the ad-hoc networks. In VANET, vehicles work as nodes that can communicate information among each other with no physical establishment of the network. To be a part of such a network, a vehicle must be outfitted with an extraordinary electronic gadget that will give ad-hoc network access to the vehicles. Incorporating the IoT in VANET makes the transportation system VANET-IoT smarter. A sample VANET-IoT is shown in Figure 15.1.

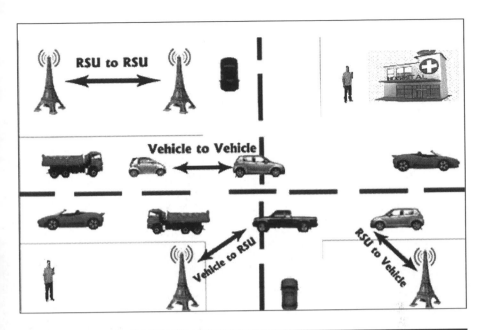

Figure 15.1 Sample VANET-IoT architecture.

VANET-IoT is a heterogeneous network that includes Vehicles, Road Side Units (RSUs), people, and other devices as the entity, with Vehicle-to-Vehicle (V2V), Vehicle-to-RSU (V2R), Vehicle-to-People (V2P), RSU-to-RSU (R2R), and Vehicle-to-Sensors (V2S) Communications. To play a part in such communication, every entity ought to be furnished with the essential radio correspondence device. Since every entity operates as a remote station and versatile switch simultaneously, unreachable vehicles can communicate with one another by utilizing middle vehicles for sending the packets. If there is no nearby vehicle within the coverage area, RSU stores the traffic details about the locality, and the same will be communicated once a vehicle enters the coverage area.

Vehicular networks are a type of ad-hoc network; however, highly dynamic behavior and the mobility pattern of the vehicles are the significant qualities [5]. VANETs also possess frequent disconnection of the network particularly when the swarm of vehicles is low, the movement of the vehicles can be predicted and the vehicles themselves have adequate energy and power to communicate in the communicating environment [6].

The communications that exist in a VANET are capable of several extraordinary inert applications with incredibly different necessities. Driver-assisted and business applications are the primary categories of applications in VANET. Driver-assisted applications will keep an eye on the nearby area, movements toward vehicles, traffic-lane-changing in the road, road maintenance, and caution of a probable collision.

Business applications will give the driver/voyager entertainment and facilities, for instance, Internet access, Electronic Toll Collection, vehicle garage, and travel information.

Transportation systems face several challenges, including traffic jams and poor road safety. The incorporation of the IoT and VANET is changing the transportation industry in providing prior and real-time traffic information to the commuter to reduce travel time and escape from congestion. The principal target of the work is to manage the traffic and reduce traffic congestion, and in the event of misfortunes, the sensors in the vehicles/RSUs are responsible for communicating the information with the approaching vehicles to evade traffic congestion in the interest of reducing the travel duration for the commuter. The proposed work utilizes the reactive protocol Ad-hoc On-demand Distance Vector (AODV) to observe the performance of the model. Initially, the performance of the model is analyzed by varying the transmission rate for IEEE 802.11 and IEEE 802.11p standards. To scale down the delay and to boost the efficiency of the proposed model, the Multi-Channel Multi-Interface (MCMI) is incorporated.

The chapter is formulated as follows: the next section of the chapter summarizes the works associated with congestion avoidance and framework related to VANET-IoT, followed by the initial study for the proposed model. The proposed model, the algorithms used to detect and avoid traffic congestion, and its analysis are summarized in the following section, and finally, the chapter is concluded.

State-of-the-Art Reviews

The advancements in the industry and the innovation are making each person move toward amazingly intellectual devices in our computerized world to make them smarter. Current vehicles are gradually turning out to be increasingly more self-governing with the assistance of sensors and communication techniques. VANET-IoT is an emerging innovation that targets to accomplish traffic efficiency by limiting traffic issues. A large number of researchers have contributed their research findings to create more smart applications in automated vehicles. Some of their contributions are summarized further.

Jayapal and Roy [7] proposed conveyed, collective traffic block identification and spread framework with the guide of Traffic APP that utilizes VANET. On distinguishing the blockage, the data are scattered to the end client telephone through RSUs. The Mobile App transmits the scope, longitude, the current time, and the area of the vehicle. Utilizing the data gathered, the distance moved by the vehicle is recognized and if the distance is less than the limit, congestion is suspected in the zone and the data will be imparted to the vehicles moving toward it through the display board and the Mobile App. The vehicles moving toward the congestion zone may take redirection and diminish congestion without human intervention. The proposed model uses the IEEE 802.11p convention for correspondence between vehicles. The framework utilizes the range between 0 and 10 as the congestion coefficient value with 0 showing the lowest congestion and 10 demonstrating the highest congestion. The framework is assessed to lessen the delay in routing the path.

Lu et al. [8] proposed a model to give the data to the vehicle's control unit preceding the congestion to avoid the accident. The principle point of the work is to dissect the driving behavior and give pre-cautioning data to decelerate the vehicle speed to maintain a strategic distance from the accident.

Kausar et al. [9] proposed a model that points toward a more secure and progressively effective transportation framework by giving ideal and solid data to drivers and concerned specialists. This model focuses just on the V2V correspondence and eliminates the utilization of RSUs. In this model, each vehicle is doled out with a special Car Identification Number. On accepting the messages from different vehicles, a priority is assigned to each message. The messages are organized in the line dependent on the priority and handled further. The microcontroller confers a sign to the bell or notices the driver that it is unnecessarily nearby or scatters an alert to various vehicles at genuine danger, or disagrees to forward an alert message. Along these lines, all the "N" vehicles in the region are inspected for the chance of a probable effect or mishap, where "N" is the number of endorsed nodes/hubs in the locale of the host vehicle.

Zhu et al. [10] proposed a Ready-to-Broadcast-Emergency-Message and Clear-to-Broadcast-Emergency-Message (RBEM/CBEM) handshake component to improve the communication convention in urban street conditions. The reliability of tragedy communication spread perhaps is enhanced by diminishing dropped packets brought about by the collisions. The proposed framework is intended to communicate emergency messages dependent on road characteristics and scalability requirements. [9] utilized distinctive handshake methodology for street intersections and street sections to keep up low signaling overhead. The model is assessed through simulations and shows the high unwavering quality and the framework keeps up over 70% of inclusion for short beacon intervals.

Tolba [11] proposed a strategy that depends on a universal trust server and vehicle conduct for keeping away from crash assaults. The projected strategy considers both vehicle-to-vehicle and within-vehicle correspondence. The creators have also proposed a CSRP to enhance the correspondence dependability amid the vehicles, which limits energy misuse and delay. TDA enhances the security of the system by recuperating the pace of collision acknowledgment and the communication pace. The CSRP chooses an ideal neighbor dependent on the channel state and the energy level of On-Board Units to continue the correspondence. The proposed model upgrades the security, guaranteeing secure information transmission among vehicles, and shows diminished delay and overhead with enhancements of 16% and 17% in the correspondence pace and protection, respectively, compared to ICWS [12] and CMAP [13] independently.

The primary point of the model [12] was to look at the impact of Collision Warning Systems at the intersection and traffic quieting metric concerning the drivers' conduct. The drivers' conduct was analyzed by the multivariate variance analysis methodology. ICWS helps the driver to begin before slowing down to escape the contention at the crossing points. From the examination, sound messages make the driver respond sooner than the visual messages, to escape the contention at the crossing points.

Lyu et al. [14] proposed a versatility-aware TDMA MAC convention for VANETs (MoMAC) to diminish impacts. The creators recognized two basic versatility situations that would acquire huge transmission collisions in vehicular conditions. The proposed framework utilizes a completely transmitted opening access and crash-recognition plan to dispense with the concealed terminal issue. Hypothetical examination and simulation results exhibit the productivity of MoMAC and contrasted and cutting-edge TDMA MACs, the collisions can be diminished by 59.2%, and the pace of wellbeing information communicated/gathered is extraordinarily improved.

Lyu et al. [15] proposed a completely conveyed beacon congestion control scheme, in which every vehicle adjusts an adequate beacon rate to stay away from a backside collision. ABC embraces a TDMA-based MAC convention and settles an NP-hard ideal distributed beacon-rate-adjusting issue with a voracious heuristic calculation. The proposed framework recognizes the congestion, adjust dispersed beacon rate, and the adjusting rates are coordinated and the model output demonstrates the proficiency of the projected model.

A Distributed Vehicular Re-Routing System for Congestion Avoidance (DIVERT) [16] off-loads an enormous piece of the re-routing calculation to the vehicles. In DIVERT, the vehicles trade messages over a VANET. DIVERT offsets client protection using re-direct viability. The model shows that a contrasted and unified framework expands user protection by 92%. As far as with normal travel time, DIVERT's exhibition is somewhat not as much as that of the incorporated framework, however, despite everything, it accomplishes a slight increase compared to no redirecting case. The model reduces the load on the server by 99.99% and 95%, individually.

Yaqoob et al. [17] expect to diminish congestion and message overhead and proposed a congestion evasion scheme Energy Efficient Message Dissemination (E²MD). Every vehicle needs to redesign the status to the server either straightforwardly or through middle vehicles. During a crisis, the server educates the approaching vehicles to back off, dispatch salvage groups to offer important types of assistance, and coordinate patrolling to clear the street. E²MD is analyzed utilizing NS 2.35 and contrasted and AFCS [18] and RMFF [19]. The proposed model is assessed utilizing different measurements like packet delivery, loss ratio, setback time, bandwidth, and overhead. E²MD improved the delivery cost by 108% than AFCS and RMFF, and at the same time, it declined the overhead expenses by 73% and 98% than AFCS and RMFF, respectively.

From the above-mentioned study, we can conclude that the vehicles on the road should be connected and communicating with other vehicles to transmit the information regarding the traffic to all the vehicles approaching the location. The main aim of the work is to identify the over-speed vehicles and decrease their speed, evade the congestion, and take diversion if there exists vehicle congestion to minimize the travel time for the commuter.

Preliminary Study for the Proposed Model

The IoT empowers vehicles, persons, and objects in VANET by helping them inform the traffic flows and make automated decisions to avoid congestion. Commuters can decide in advance in choosing the route and the time to travel. To participate and communicate in the VANET_IoT network, each vehicle should be equipped with Internet connectivity, sensors, onboard storage devices, and actuators. These associated vehicles can interact with different vehicles and RSUs and has to be updated with the information in the surrounding areas of the region.

Performance Metrics

In this study, the performance measures Packet Delivery Ratio (PDR), Delay, Packets Dropped, Overhead, and Throughput have been used to evaluate the proposed model.

■ *Packet Delivery Ratio* is the proportion of the absolute quantities of the information transmitted to the goal and all information sent by the vehicle.

$$PDR = \frac{\sum_{i=1}^{n} Received\ Packets}{\sum_{i=1}^{n} Sent\ Packets} \times 100 \tag{15.1}$$

■ *Dropped Packets* indicate the number of packets that have not successfully been delivered to the destination.

$$Dropped\ Packets = \sum_{i=1}^{n} Sent\ Packets - \sum_{i=1}^{n} Received\ Packetss \tag{15.2}$$

■ *Delay* determines the duration taken by the packet to arrive at the destination.

$$Delay\ (ms) = \frac{\sum_{i=1}^{n} Receivingtime\ of\ the\ packet - Senttime\ of\ the\ packet}{Total\ Packets\ Generated} \tag{15.3}$$

■ ***Routing Overhead*** is characterized as the proportion between the number of packets created and the number of packets received during the simulation.

$$RoutingOverhead = \frac{\sum_{i=1}^{n} RoutingPacketsGenerated}{\sum_{i=1}^{n} PacketsReceived} \qquad (15.4)$$

■ ***Throughput*** is the quantity of data received at the destination. It is measured in bits per second or data packets per time limit.

$$Throughput\,(Kbps) = \frac{Numberofreceivedbits}{Timetakenbythepackettoreachthedestination} \qquad (15.5)$$

Initial Evaluation of the Model

The assessment is completed utilizing the NS2 simulator [20] and the Test System parameters are summarized in Table 15.1. In [21, 22] the most widely used protocols, AODV and Destination Sequenced Distance Vector (DSDV) were studied and analyzed for various performance metrics. It is observed however that both the protocols are appropriate for VANET; the outcomes demonstrate that the reactive protocol AODV consistently outperforms the proactive protocol DSDV. Hence,

Table 15.1 Test System Parameters

Parameter	Value
Test System	NS-2
Duration	150 s
Vehicles	15,20,25,30,35,40,45
Connections	5,10,15,20,25,30,35,40
Vehicle Speed (m/sec)	50
Packet-Size	512KB
Rate of Transmission	0.064Mbps
Protocol	AODV(Reactive)
Study Area(m)	1000 × 1000
Transmitter	Omnidirectional Antenna

the reactive protocol AODV – which empowers dynamic, self-beginning, multi-hop routing – is considered for this study.

Initially, the model is evaluated using the reactive routing protocol AODV by varying the number of vehicles and maximum connections in an area of 1000 × 1000 m². It was assumed that the vehicles move at a uniform speed of 50 meters/second. The model is analyzed and evaluated using PDR, Percentage of packets dropped, Delay, Overhead, and Throughput. The performance analysis of the study is shown in Figure 15.2(a–e).

From the chart, it is evident that an increment in the connections raises PDR gradually, declines the packet loss, and shows maximum throughput, minimum delay, and minimum routing overhead for the number of connections less than 30 after which the simulation values are not stable.

In VANET, the messages that are to be communicated should be reliable and forwarded to the other vehicles on time to save the life of the individual. Hence,

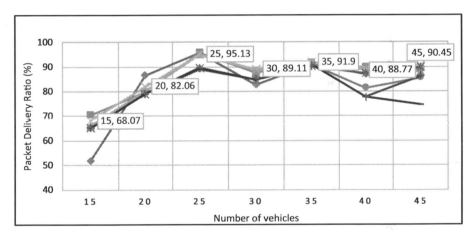

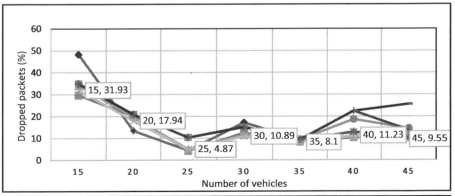

Figure 15.2 (a) Packet Delivery Ratio, (b) Dropped Packets (%), (c) Delay (ms), (d) Routing Overhead, and (e) Average Throughput.

(*Continued*)

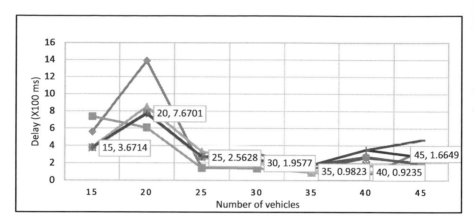

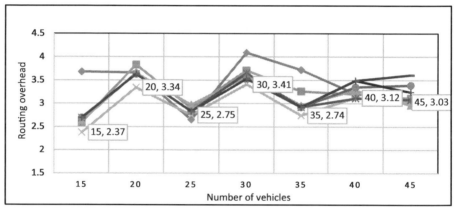

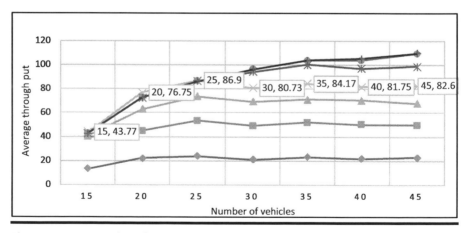

Figure 15.2 (Continued)

the PDR values should be maximum, the delay and routing overhead should be as minimum as possible. In the initial study, it is clear that the model shows acceptable performance for the number of connections as 20 irrespective of the number of vehicles. It also shows maximum PDR values for the number of vehicles 25 and 35 and the delay is less when the number of vehicles is 35. Hence, a further study of the proposed model is carried out with the maximum number of connections' Constant Bit Rate (CBR) as 20.

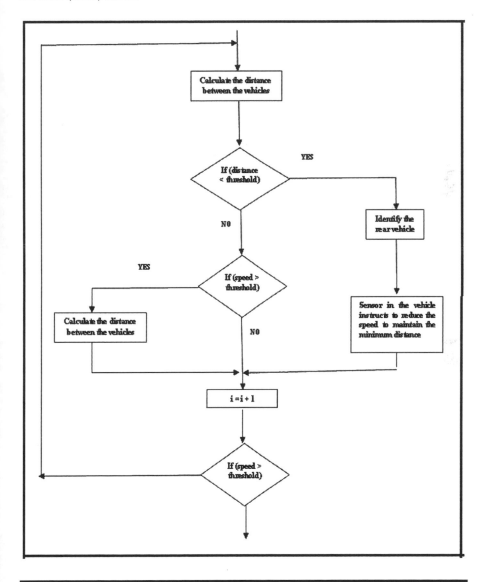

Figure 15.3   Working principle of CAV-AODV.

Implementation of the Proposed Model for Congestion Avoidance

In this section, a model, Congestion Avoidance in VANET (CAV-AODV) is proposed to assist the driver and to improve safety on the road by avoiding congestions between the vehicles. The model CAV-AODV considers speed, the distance between the vehicles, and the direction of the moving vehicles. The reactive routing protocol AODV is suitably modified to achieve the goal of eliminating the congestions between the vehicles. The working principle of CAV-AODV is shown in Figure 15.3. CAV-AODV uses the following procedures to avoid congestion between the vehicles.

- vehicles_speed() – identifies the speed of the vehicle.
- vehicles_distance() – calculates the distance between the vehicles.

Algorithms

Identifying the Vehicle Speed

The Procedure vehicles_speed() recognizes the moving vehicles' speed. At first, the index of every vehicle is recognized and the actual speed of the vehicle is recovered using the vehicles→speed( ) function. If the vehicle speed surpasses the limit value, at that point, the sensors fitted in the vehicle send a caution message to the driver to lessen the speed and sets it to the threshold speed. The procedure vehicles_speed( ) is called in the forward( ) strategy of AODV to discover the speed of the moving vehicles which is the next-hop neighbor in the way. The algorithm for vehicles_speed() is given as follows:

1: ALGORITHM: TO CALCULATE THE SPEED OF THE VEHICLES

```
1: // in forward( ) procedure
2: // cspeed represent the current speed of the vehicle
3: vehicles_speed( ){
4: do {
5: MobileNode * Vehicles =(MobileNode*) (Node::get_node_by_address(i));
6: cspeed = ((MobileNode *) Vehicles)→speed();
7: while (cspeed>speed_threshold) then {
8: Vehicles→min_speed = speed_threshold;
9: }
10: i=i+1;
11: } while (i<=n);
```

Calculating the Distance between the Vehicles

The procedure vehicles_distance() perceives the distance between the vehicles. This technique at first finds the location of each vehicle, the vehicle direction, and registers the distance between the adjoining vehicles

The procedure vehicles_distance() recognizes the distance between the vehicles. This procedure initially finds the location of every vehicle, the direction of the vehicle, and computes the distance between the neighboring vehicles. The algorithm for calculating the distance is given as follows:

1: ALGORITHM: TO CALCULATE THE DISTANCE BETWEEN THE VEHICLES

```
1: vehicle_distance()
2: do {
3: for every neighboring vehicle i and j{
4: (MobileNode *) Vehicles(i)→getLoc(xpos,ypos,zpos);
5: (MobileNode *) Vehicles(j)→getLoc(xpos,ypos,zpos);
6: int x1=Vehicles(i)→xpos;
7: int y1= Vehicles(i)→ypos;
8: int x2= Vehicles(j)→xpos;
9: int y2= Vehicles(j)→ypos;
10: distance =sqrt(power((x2-x1),2) + power((y2-y1),2));
11: if (distance <dist_threshold)
12: //Identify the direction of the vehicles
13: //Instruct the rear vehicle to lessen the speed with the intention of
       maintain the distance
14: vehicles→speed - - ; }
15: }while (i<=n);
```

In the vehicles_distance() algorithm, vehicles→getloc(xpos,ypos,zpos) is utilized to recognize the location of the vehicle, and xpos, ypos is used to identify the direction of the vehicles. If the two vehicles are having the same xpos values, at that point, they are moving along the Y-axis and on the off chance that they have the same ypos, they are moving along the X-axis. The distance between the vehicles is determined by utilizing the Euclidian equation. If the distance between them is less than the threshold distance (10 m), the sensor fitted in the vehicle instructs the rear vehicle to decrease the speed to keep up the minimum distance and to stay away from the collision.

Wireless Access in Vehicular Environment (WAVE)

VANET is a spontaneous network dependent on direct V2V communication with habitually adjusting topology due to the high versatility of vehicles on the road. To implement various applications of VANET such as safety, driver assistance, entertainment, and many other Intelligent Transport System applications, some protocols should be encouraged to take full benefit of the communication among the V2V, V2R, V2P, and V2S communications. Hence, the IEEE has proposed a family of standards called Wireless Access in the Vehicular Environment (WAVE) that can be used for establishing the communication between the entities of VANET. Hence, in this study, the IEEE 802.11p standards are incorporated to analyze the performance of the anticipated model CAV-AODV and compared with 802.11.

Physical and MAC Layer Parameters

IEEE 802.11p is an advancement made to IEEE 802.11 benchmark for vehicular communications, WAVE. It provides the parameters to aid Intelligent Transportation Systems (ITS) applications, which incorporates the communication among the vehicles and between the vehicles and RSUs. The physical and Mac layer simulation parameters used for analyzing CAV-AODV are summarized in Table 15.2.

The CAV-AODV model is evaluated with the maximum number of connections as 20 for the different number of vehicles by implementing WAVE architecture for vehicular communications. The performance results compared with AODV for the considered metrics are shown in Figures 15.4a–15.4e. The experimental values are summarized in Table 15.3.

Observed Results and Discussion

Packet Delivery Ratio

Figure 15.4a shows the PDR for AODV and CAV-AODV by altering vehicle density with maximum CBR traffic as 20. From the graph, it is clear that the CAV-AODV shows good results with a maximum value of 99.49% for the number of vehicles as 25(shown in bold font in Table 15.3).

Dropped Packets

Figure 15.4b shows the dropped packet values by varying the number of vehicles for AODV and CAV-AODV. From the graph, it is clear that the dropped packets value is comparatively less for the proposed model CAV-AODV than AODV irrespective of the number of vehicles and it is very less with the number of vehicles as 25(shown in bold font in Table 15.3).

Table 15.2 Physical and Mac Layer Simulation Parameters for 802.11p

Physical Layer Parameter	Value
Carrier Sensing Threshold	3.981e-13
Transmission Power	0.01
Frequency	5.9e+9
Noise_floor	1.26e-13
L	1.0
Power Monitor Thresh	3.981e-18
Header Duration	0.0000400
Preamble Capture Switch	1
SINR_Preamble Capture	3.1623
SINR_Data Capture	10.0
Trace_dist	1e6
Mac Layer Parameter	**Values**
CWMin	15
CWMax	1023
SlotTime	0.000013
SIFS	0.000032
ShortRetryLimit	7
LongRetryLimit	4
HeaderDuration	0.000040
SymbolDuration	0.000008
RTSThreshold	2346

Delay

The delays for AODV and CAV-AODV are shown in Figure 15.4c. From the graph, it is clear that initially, the delay is less for the projected model with the number of vehicles less than 20 and it gradually improves with a raise in vehicle density. CAV-AODV shows more delay compared to AODV.

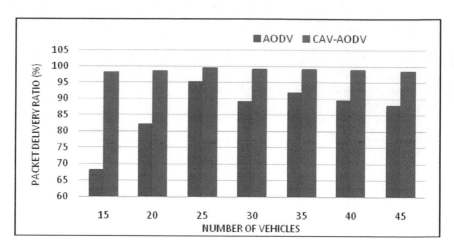

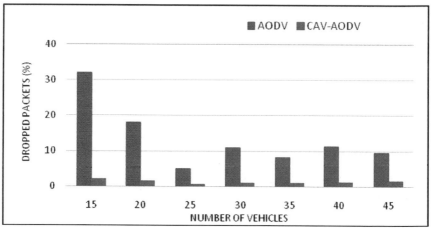

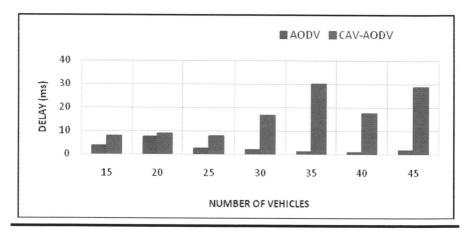

Figure 15.4 **(a) Packet delivery ratio (%), (b) dropped packets (%), (c) delay (ms), (d) routing overhead, and (e) throughput.**

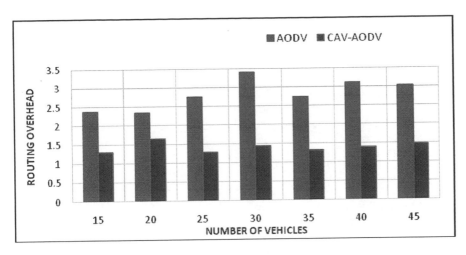

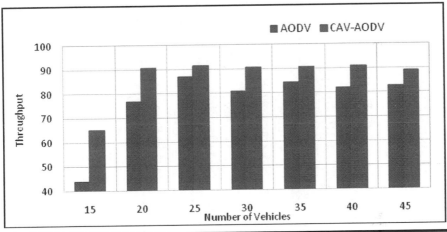

Figure 15.4 (Continued)

Routing Overhead

Figure 15.4d shows the Routing Overhead for AODV and CAV-AODV by varying the number of vehicles. The graph clearly explains that the proposed model CAV-AODV shows less routing overhead compared to AODV and it shows less routing overhead when the number of the vehicles is 25(shown in bold font in Table 15.3).

Throughput

Figure 15.4e shows the Throughput of AODV and CAV-AODV by altering the vehicle density with maximum CBR traffic as 20. From the graph, it is clear that

Table 15.3 Simulation Results of AODV and CAV-AODV

Vehicles	PDR (%)		Dropped Packets (%)		Delay (ms)		Overhead		Throughput	
	AODV	CAV-AODV	AODV	CAV-AODV	AODV	CAV-AODV	AODV	CAV-AODV	AODV	CAV-AODV
15	68.07	98.03	31.93	1.97	3.67	7.81	2.37	1.3	43.77	64.99
20	82.06	98.58	17.94	1.42	7.67	8.92	2.34	1.64	76.75	90.48
25	95.13	**99.49**	4.87	**0.51**	2.56	**7.71**	2.75	**1.28**	86.9	**91.37**
30	89.11	99.03	10.89	0.97	1.95	16.73	3.41	1.43	80.73	90.57
35	91.9	98.99	8.1	1.01	0.98	30.33	2.74	1.32	84.17	90.48
40	89.38	98.85	11.23	1.15	0.92	17.73	3.12	1.38	81.75	90.82
45	87.85	98.49	9.55	1.51	1.66	28.73	3.03	1.46	82.6	89.02

Table 15.4 Performance Improvement of CAV-AODV for the Considered Metrics

Metrics	AODV	CAV-AODV	Percentage of Improvement (%)
Packet Delivery Ratio (%)	95.13	99.49	4.58
Dropped Packets (%)	4.87	0.51	89.5
Delay (ms)	2.56	7.71	↓66.79
Routing Overhead	2.75	1.28	53.45
Throughput	86.9	91.37	5.14

the CAV-AODV shows good results and shows the maximum value of 91.37 for the number of vehicles as 25(shown in bold font in Table 15.3).

The following were the conclusions drawn from the study. The proposed model CAV-AODV performs well compared to AODV in avoiding collision between the vehicles by maintaining the vehicle's speed and distance between them and it shows

- Increased PDR values
- Decreased Dropped Packets
- Increased Delay
- Decreased Routing Overhead and
- Increased Throughput

The performance improvement of CAV-AODV than AODV with the number of vehicles as 25 is summarized in Table 15.4.

From the analysis, it is observed that CAV-AODV shows a 4.58% increase in PDR, 89.5% decrease in dropped packets, 66.79% more delay, 53.45%less routing overhead, and 5.14% increase in throughput compared to AODV.

Improved CAV-AODV

In the VANET environment, in case any traffic congestion is detected, the information related to the collision should be delivered promptly to save the life of the individual and hence the delay should be less. From the analysis, it is clear that CAV-AODV shows better performance than AODV for the considered metrics except for delay consequently CAV-AODV should be enhanced as Improved CAV-AODV (ICAV-AODV) to reduce the delay. Hence, in this section, the delay in the network is reduced by incorporating MCMI [23] approach and modifying the Direct-Sequence Spread Spectrum (DSSS) parameter values [24, 25] in the VANET

Table 15.5 MCMI Values and DSSS Parameters Values

Parameters	Values
Number of Interfaces and Channel	2
Carrier Sensing Threshold	3.162e-12
transmission Power	0.001
PowerMonitorThresh	6.310e-14
PreambleLength	96
SINR_PreambleCapture	2.5118
SlotTime	0.000009
PLCHeaderLength	128
basicRate	1.0e6
dataRate	11.0e6

Table 15.6 Percentage Improvement of ICAV-AODV for Delay

Number of Vehicles	CAV-AODV	ICAV-AODV	Percentage of improvement (%)
15	2.81	2.27	19.22
20	8.92	8.34	6.50
25	7.71	4.25	44.88
30	16.73	5.85	65.03
35	30.33	7.85	74.12
40	17.73	6.19	65.09
45	28.73	13.60	52.66

architecture. As traditional ad-hoc, routing protocol uses a single channel to confirm the connectivity among all the vehicles in the network, it does not utilize the bandwidth completely provided by the available interface spectrums. Moreover, the utilization of only one channel may lead to increased routing overhead with a raise in vehicle density. At the point when various channels are free, a vehicle with more than one interface performs correspondence all the while on various channels [26] to decrease the delay. The DSSS is a system essentially used to diminish

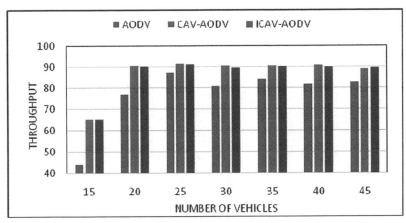

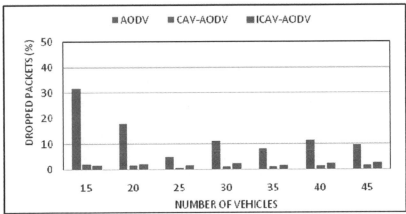

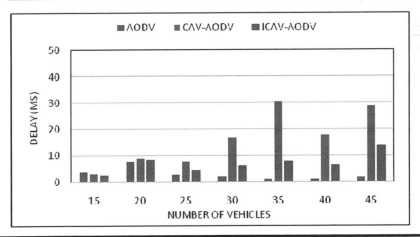

Figure 15.5 (a) Packet delivery ratio, (b) dropped packets, (c) delay (ms), (d) routing overhead, and (e) throughput.

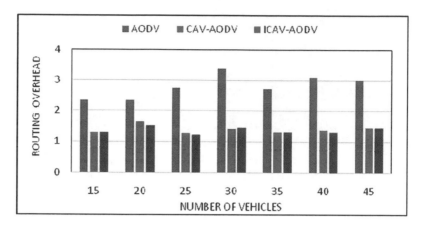

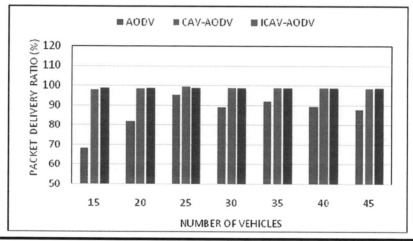

Figure 15.5 (Continued)

signal impediments. The immediate arrangement regulation makes the imparted signal more extensive in transmission capacity [27]. Thus, the performance of CAV-AODV can be improved by incorporating the MCMI Approach and altering the DSSS parameter to reduce the delay. The simulation values of MCMI values and DSSS parameters are summarized in Table 15.5.

The performance of AODV, CAV-AODV, and ICAV-AODV is shown in Figures 15.5a–15.5e with the maximum number of connections as 20 for the different number of vehicles. The models are evaluated and analyzed using PDR, Dropped Packets, Delay, Routing Overhead, and Throughput as the performance metrics.

From the above analysis, it is evident that ICAV-AODV performs well than CAV-AODV and ICAV-AODV shows minimum delay than CAV-AODV. The performance comparison of CAV-AODV and ICAV-AODV with regard to delay (ms)

Table 15.7 Performance Improvement of ICAV-AODV for the Considered Metrics

Performance Metrics	Performance of AODV	Performance of ↓ ICAV-AODV	Percentage of Increase/ Decrease (%)
Packet Delivery Ratio	95.13	98.73	3.78
Dropped Packets	4.87	1.27	73.92
Delay	2.56	4.25	39.76
Routing Overhead	2.75	1.2	56.36
Throughput	86.9	90.93	4.63

Table 15.8 Performance of CAV-AODV and ICAV-AODV

Performance Metrics	CAV-AODV	ICAV-AODV	Percentage of Increase/ Decrease (%)
Packet Delivery Ratio	99.49	98.73	0.76
Dropped Packets	0.51	1.27	59.84
Delay	7.71	4.25	44.88
Routing Overhead	1.28	1.2	6.25
Throughput	91.37	90.93	0.48

by varying the vehicle density with the number of connections as 20 are summarized in Table 15.5.

From the table, it is clear that ICAV-AODV shows an average of 46.79% less delay compared to CAV-AODV. As the proposed models show acceptable performance for the considered metrics with the number of vehicles as 25 (concerning Table 15.3), the performance improvement of ICAV-AODV than AODV for all the considered metrics with the number of vehicles as 25 is summarized in Table 15.7.

From the analysis, it is evident that the proposed models CAV-AODV and ICAV-AODV outperform AODV. ICAV-AODV shows a 3.78% increase in PDR, 73.92% decrease in Dropped Packets, 39.76% more Delay, 56.36% less Routing Overhead, and 4.43% increase in Throughput compared to AODV. The performance comparison of CAV-AODV, ICAV-AODV with the number of connections as 20, and the number of vehicles as 25 for the considered metrics are shown in Table 15.8.

From the analysis, it is clear that ICAV-AODV shows better performance with 44.88% less delay than CAV-AODV. However, there is a negligible increase in PDR (0.76%) and Throughput (0.48%) for CAV-AODV than ICAV-AODV, ICAV-AODV shows 44.88% less delay and 6.25% less routing overhead, which are the essential metrics for VANET-IoT in avoiding collision and saving the life of the individual.

Conclusion

VANET with the IoT is an imaginative standard with the progress in the field of wireless and mobile advancement. Vehicles in VANET share consistent information about the road status and zone of the vehicle. Traffic congestion is a major challenge in VANET and the messages that are to be communicated should reach the vehicles in the communication range without any delay. Hence, in this work, we have proposed a model CAV-AODV to assist the driver and to improve the safety on the road by avoiding congestions between the vehicles to reduce the travel time for the commuter.

The proposed model uses two procedures to identify the speed of the vehicles and to find the distance between the vehicles. These procedures are used to maintain a minimum threshold speed and distance to avoid traffic congestion between the vehicles in the VANET-IoT environment. From the analysis, it is observed that CAV-AODV shows a 4.58% increase in PDR, 89.5% decrease in dropped packets, 66.79% more delay, 53.45% less routing overhead, and 5.14% increase in throughput compared to AODV. But in VANET, the messages have to be communicated without any delay to save the life of the individuals. Hence, CAV-AODV is enhanced as ICAV-AODV to minimize the delay by implementing MCMI and modifying the DSSS parameters. ICAV-AODV shows an average of 46.79% less delay compared to CAV-AODV. The essential metrics for VANET-IoT in avoiding collision and saving the life of the individual are delay and routing overhead, which is 44.88% and 6.25%, respectively, less than CAV-AODV.

References

1 https://www.who.int/mediacentre/news/releases/2004/pr24/en/
2 https://camrojud.com/the-internet-of-things-in-automotive/
3 Wilson, S., Manuel, T., Augustine, D. P. (2019). "Smart pollution monitoring system", *International Journal of Recent Technology and Engineering (IJRTE)*, 7(6), 1131–1136.
4 https://www2.deloitte.com/tr/en/pages/technology-media-and-telecommunications/articles/internet-of-things-iot-in-automotive-industry.html
5 Praba, V. L., & Ranichitra, A. (2013). "*Isolating malicious vehicles and avoiding collision between vehicles in VANET*", In *2013 International Conference on Communication and Signal Processing* (811–815).IEEE.

6 Praba, V. L., & Ranichitra, A. (2012). "Detecting Malicious Vehicle in a VANET scenario by incorporating security in AODV Protocol", *ICTACT Journal on Communication Technology*, *3*(3).

7 Jayapal, C., & Roy, S. S. (2016). *"Road traffic congestion management using VANET"*, *In2016 International Conference on Advances in Human-Machine Interaction (HMI)* (1–7).IEEE.

8 Lu, S. N., Tseng, H. W., Lee, Y. H., Jan, Y. G., & Lee, W. C. (2010). "Intelligent safety warning and alert system for car driving", *Tamkang Journal of Science and Technology*, *13*(4), 395–404.

9 Kausar, T., Gupta, P., Arora, D., & Kumar, R. (2012). "A VANET based cooperative collision avoidance system for a 4-lane highway", *Notes on Engineering Research and Development, IIT Kanpur Technical Journal*, 4.

10 Zhu, W., Gao, D., Foh, C. H., Zhao, W., & Zhang, H. (2016). *"A collision avoidance mechanism for emergency message broadcast in urban VANET"*, *In 2016 IEEE 83rd Vehicular Technology Conference (VTC Spring)*(1–5).IEEE.

11 Tolba, A. M. R. (2018). "Trust-based distributed authentication method for collision attack avoidance in VANETs", *IEEE Access*, *6*, 62747–62755.

12 Silvestri, M., & Bella, F. (2017). "Effects of intersection collision warning systems and traffic calming measures on Driver's behavior at intersections", *In Advances in Human Aspects of Transportation*, *484*, 773–786.

13 Shen, W., Liu, L., Cao, X., Hao, Y., & Cheng, Y., (2013)."Cooperative message authentication in vehicular cyber-physical systems", *IEEE Transactions on Emerging Topics in Computing,*1(1), 84–97.

14 Lyu, F., Zhu, H., Zhou, H., Qian, L., Xu, W., Li, M., &Shen, X. (2018). "MoMAC: Mobility-aware and collision avoidance MAC for safety applications in VANETs", *IEEE Transactions on Vehicular Technology*, *67*(11), 10590–10602.

15 Lyu, F., Zhu, H., Cheng, N., Zhu, Y., Zhou, H., Xu, W., ... Li, M. (2018). *"ABC: adaptive beacon control for rear-end collision avoidance in VANETs"*, *In 2018 15th Annual IEEE International Conference on Sensing, Communication, and Networking (SECON)* (1–9). IEEE.

16 Pan, J., Popa, I. S., &Borcea, C. (2016). DIVERT: "A distributed vehicular traffic re-routing system for congestion avoidance", *IEEE Transactions on Mobile Computing*, *16*(1), 58–72.

17 Yaqoob, S., Ullah, A., Akbar, M., Imran, M., & Shoaib, M. (2019). "Congestion avoidance through fog computing in internet of vehicles", *Journal of Ambient Intelligence and Humanized Computing*, *10*(10), 3863–3877.

18 Chang, B. J., Liang, Y. H., &Huang, Y. D. (2015). "Adaptive message forwarding for avoiding broadcast storm and guaranteeing delay in active safe driving VANET", *Wireless Networks*, *21*(3), 739–756.

19 Sattar, S., Qureshi, H. K., Saleem, M., Mumtaz, S., &Rodriguez, J. (2018). "Reliability and energy-efficiency analysis of safety message broadcast in VANETs", *Computer Communications*, *119*, 118–126.

20 Network Simulatorhttp://www.isi,edu/nsnam/ns

21 Praba, V. L., & Ranichitra, A. (2011). "Reactive vs proactive in VANET scenarios", *International Journal of Advanced Research in Computer Science*, *2*(6).

22 Rani, M., & Praba, V. L. (2015), "Comparative analysis of AODV and DSDV protocols in hybrid wireless mesh network", *International Journal of Advanced Research in Computer Science*, *6*(5).

23 Li, H., Cheng, Y., Zhou, C., & Zhuang, W. (2012). "Routing metrics for minimizing end-to-end delay in multiradio multichannel wireless networks", *IEEE Transactions on Parallel and Distributed Systems*, *24*(11), 2293–2303.

24 Hakak, S., Latif, S. A., Anwar, F., Gilkar, G., & Alam, M. K. (2014, September). *"Performance Analysis of DSR protocol on the basis of DSSS rate"*, In *2014 International Conference on Computer and Communication Engineering* (48–51).IEEE.

25 Hakak, S., Abd Latif, S., Anwar, F., Alam, M. K., & Gilkar, G. (2014). "Effect of 3 key factors on average end to end delay and jitter in MANET", *Journal of ICT Research and Applications*, *8*(2), 113–125.

26 Raniwala, A., Gopalan, K., &Chiueh, T. C. (2004), "Centralized channel assignment and routing algorithms for multi-channel wireless mesh networks", *ACM SIGMOBILE Mobile Computing and Communications Review*, *8*(2), 50–65.

27 Torrieri, Don (2005). *Principles of Spread-Spectrum Communication Systems*, Vol. 1. Boston, MA: Springer.

Chapter 16

Dyad Deep Learning-Based Geometry and Color Attribute Codecs for 3D Airborne LiDAR Point Clouds

A. Christoper Tamilmathi and P. L. Chithra

University of Madras, Chennai, India

Contents

DOI: 10.1201/9781003119784-16

Introduction

The rapid growth of 3D technology improves the availability of the 3D acquiring system and the 3D model processing. The 3D model gives the perception of the real-world effect to understand and analyze the data. Nowadays, 3D technology has entered into-many fields like Medical, Geospace Systems, Games, Movies, Printers, etc. The raw data of the 3D model are point cloud data (PCD). In the 3D scanner, every object is captured in the form of PCD LiDAR technology.

LiDAR is an active optical sensor technology to capture the ground object image in a 3D point cloud format by calculating the vertical distance from the sensor to the target object. LiDAR throws the laser pulses to the ground target surface and calculates the time. It takes time to return to the sensors, which is mentioned as the distance to the ground surface object. The formula for calculating the distance of the ground object is the product of the time taken by the pulse to reach the sensor and the flight time from the start pulse to the return of the pulse, which is divided by the value of two ($d = (ft \times pt) / 2$) is shown in below figure. This LiDAR technique produces accurate 3D information about the ground surface objects with different distances. Most government and private data collection services use helicopters, airplanes, and drones for capturing the LiDAR data [1]. The LiDAR technique is grouped into two categories based on the functionality: Airborne LiDAR and Terrestrial LiDAR. Airborne LiDAR is the laser pulse-emitting gun that is mounted on to the airspace vehicle to collect the data. All the remote sensing PCD data are collected using this airborne LiDAR technique. The working of the Airborne LiDAR is displayed in the below figure.

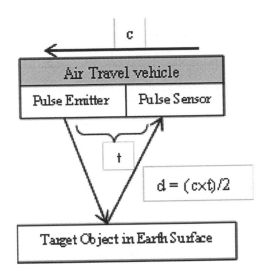

Unlike Airborne LiDAR, the Terrestrial LiDAR is attached to the ground-moving vehicle to capture the point cloud information of the surface objects like, inside and outside information of the building, information of the highways, etc. The 3D airborne LiDAR images play a vital role in the area of 3D remote-sensing objcct analysis. This is currently a very accurate and detailed capturing model to record the digital elevation of the earth's surface, which has replaced the photogrammetry technique. This airborne LiDAR PCD image helps to design a 3D digital elevation model (DEM) for forests, lakes, rivers, bridges, cities, etc., which are covered by trees in the image. This technique is applied to different areas such as Oceanography, Space Research, Health Industries, Medical Science, Agriculture, etc. [2]. Hence, the proposed compression work is developed for the 3D Airborne LiDAR datasets to reduce the cost of the memory space, bandwidth size, time of transmission. The proposed work has been implemented and tested on the two 3D Airborne LiDAR datasets and one Terrestrial dataset.

Point Cloud Image

A typical LiDAR can generate a point cloud image of up to approximately 2.2 million 3D points per second within a range of 120 meters [3]. This point cloud image has huge, unstructured, and unordered 3D points. The LiDAR technology generates the spatial information of x, y, and z coordinates of the target object on the ground surface. The collected points from the LiDAR are post-processed into the highly accurate geometry (spatial) references points x, y, and z by using laser time range, scanning angle, information of INS, and the GPS position [2]. The sensor records the information in different formats such as Laser format (LAS), point cloud format (PCD), ASCII format, coordinate format (XYZ), etc., which depends on the technology implemented on the sensor. In the proposed method, the collected 3D model datasets are converted into PCD format datasets. Each point in the point cloud image carries additional information along with spatial information (x, y, and z). The point cloud image (p) is expressed by the following equation (16.1).

$$p = \{[x_n, y_n, z_n], [R_n, G_n, B_n], Intensity, Scan\ Angle, \cdots\} \tag{16.1}$$

where p is a point cloud image with n number of 3D geometry (spatial) x, y, z information, color R (red), G (green), B (blue) attribute, and other additional attributes. The additional information (attributes) of a point cloud image are intensity, return number, point classification (from ground or water), Edge of the flight line, GPS time, number of returns, scan angle, scan direction, etc. [2]. The proposed DDLCPCD algorithm concentrates on spatial (x, y, z) and color (RGB) attributes.

Preprocessing Methods

The PCD information collected by the sensor from multiple reflections leads to the possible occurrences of the outliers data in the PCD information. The large volume of real-world geometry information (a distance of the object) is measured using these reflected pulses that have huge values. This massive real-world spatial information increases the complexity of computations, space, and time. To avoid these outliers and complexity problems, the PCD data are preprocessed before being fed into other analysis processes. There are plenty of preprocessing methods available for PCD images.

In this work, there are two preprocessing methods: downsampling and transformation are introduced to reduce the complexity of large volumes and large values of the real-world signal data. The bulk of signal data are segmented into a number of smaller-sized non-overlapped samples of data using the downsampling technique. The computation can easily be performed on the sampled data instead of the whole large data in an iterative manner. The signal downsampling techniques are the best suitable methods, for the PCD data downsampling process. The other preprocessing method is data transformation, in which the original PCD image data are transformed into the small compact window-based PCD data within a range of the minimum value. This transformation method reduces the complexity of the point cloud processing.

Deep Learning (DL) Model

Deep-structured learning is a subset of Machine Learning that learns from the algorithm to mimic the structure and functions of the human brain called Artificial

Intelligence. This Deep Learning (DL) consisting of large neural networks that auto-matically extract the features of the raw data is called feature learning. The DL can learn the features without human supervision on unstructured and unlabeled data. Hence, this DL technique has been chosen for our proposed work with unstructured PCD data. This proposed work is based on the DL model with multiple fully connected (dense) hidden layers to improve the learning of a model. The working of DL is shown in the below figure.

The deep learning process consists of four states. The first one is to design the model with parameters like the number of hidden layers with neurons, activation function, optimization function with learning rate and momentum value, etc. Then, the designed model is trained using the collected raw data. Next, the model is created depending on the training process; then, the model is tested using the test data with trained experience. Finally, the output is obtained from the testing model.

Dyad Deep Learning Model

There are three ways to design the DL by using the Keras library. The first one is a sequential model, in which the layers are arranged one-by-one, to create a DL model. The next one is the functional model, in which the layers are linked in a cascade manner. In the sequential DL model, more layers are linked in sequential order, increasing the depth of the DL model. There is a possibility of issues to occur, such as vanishing gradient and diminishing the features reuse; this may reduce the efficiency of the training process of the DL model. To overcome this problem, the proposed work moves on to the functional DL model to reduce the depth of a DL model. In this work, two DL models are connected in parallel from the shared input layer to the merged output layer. A single input is separated into two input layers and two outputs are merged to form a PCD image. The structure of the dyad DL model is shown in the below figure.

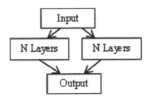

In this Dyad DL model, both the DL structures are sharing the same hyper-parameters for producing better training results. In the proposed work, the dyad model does the same process on the two different attributes of an input PCD image.

Point Cloud Compression and Decompression

Compression is a method to reduce the size of the data without changing the information. The point cloud compression is a compression technique applied to a point cloud to reduce the cost of storage and transmission. On the sender side, a PCD image is compressed by using a compression technique to reduce the size of the PCD and send it to the remote end. In the receiver end, the compressed form of a PCD is decompressed by using the reverse process of an applied compression technique, to produce a decompressed PCD, which is similar to the original PCD image. The proposed work compresses the 3D Airborne LiDAR PCD images using the dyad deep learning technique to improve the decompressed PCD image with a good compression ratio and better quality.

The proposed DDLCPCD work compresses the geometry and color attributes of the 3D Airborne LiDAR PCD image by using the Dyad Deep Learning model. The combination of Alternate Signal Sampling (ASiS) and Min-Max Signal Transformation (MiST) techniques was applied to the original PCD image to downsample and transform the signal data, respectively. The standardized signal data move into the Dyad Deep Learning model to compress the PCD data. This Dyad network has two group units: spatial and color information, and two sub-networks: compression and decompression. The main contributions of this work are as follows.

- The proposed cascaded structure of the Deep Learning model replaced the traditional point cloud compression technology to improve the speed and quality of the decompressed point cloud image.
- The proposed DDLCPCD compression method compresses both geometry and color attributes of the 3D Airborne LiDAR color point clouds with a constant high compression ratio and less distortion. The performance of the proposed work has been proved by subjective and objective analyses.

The rest of this chapter is organized as follows. The related work of the proposed method is discussed in the "Related Work" section. The Dyad Deep Learning-based compression method is explained in the "Proposed Methodology" section. The performance of the proposed methodology is described in the "Experimental Results" and the "Performance Analysis" sections. Finally, the summary is given in the "Conclusion" section.

Related Work

In this section, some of the research works related to the proposed model have been discussed. The captured raw PCD data have always had some abnormalities and noise values. This unwanted information has to be removed before they enter the processing methods.

Preprocessing Methods

A massive amount of PCD images have been downsampled using different techniques. The discrete-time point cloud signal is downsampled by the N factor, which means that it retains only every Nth signal and discards the reaming signal [4]. The unimportant point in the PCD data has been removed by the inbuilt point cloud library filtering functions [5]. In the building diagnostics techniques in PCD, retain only the information of concentrates on the cracks, and cavities. The other even surface points are eliminated during the downsampling method [6]. Most of the downsampling algorithm follows the voxel grid method [7]. Only the important points in the PCD are retained by the critical points dense layer [8]. The transformation function is applied on PCD data to squeeze the data range to produce better performance. Statistical methods play an important role in the transformation function [9]. The selection of the normalization function depends on the pulse divergence from the target object, atmospheric attenuation during the PCD capturing process [10]. The adaptive normalization method improves the training process in the convolutional neural network (CNN) [11]. Mainly, the compress ratio (CR) of a PCD is improved by applying the Z-score transformation method [12].

Point Cloud Compression

Earlier, the PCD images have been compressed using a conventional method [13]. The 3D PCD image is divided into the 2D local patches; then, the compression techniques are applied [14]. The probability-based Golon-Rice encoding method increases the value of the CR [15]. Predictive coding, variable length coding, and arithmetic coding increase the efficiency of a PCD compression algorithm [16]. The PCD compression method is based on the plane extraction method, in which it considers only the vertical plane points [17]. The MPEG PCD coding consists of the octree method, Euclidean-based level of detail function [18]. The overall geometric shape is retained using a uniform sampling method [19]. The spatial information of a PCD is compressed by using a set of graphs and the temporal redundancy is reduced by the prediction method [20]. 3D tensor-based unfolding method is used to reduce the dimension and the value of the PCD image [21] and the Tensor Tucker decomposition technique has been applied to reduce the dimension of the LiDAR PCD data [22]. The 3D blocks of PCD data have been reduced by applying sparse representation, and the predictive method is applied to remove the redundancy between the blocks [23]. The mapping algorithm is used to map the 2D folded PCD with the original PCD data to reduce the unimportant points in a PCD image [24]. To avoid the direct reduction of points, the polynomial function fits each pixel to find the difference of the points, which is considered as compressed data points [25]. The traditional Discrete Wavelet transform (DWT) method helps to retain the information of a PCD [26].

Deep Learning on Point Clouds

Nowadays, most of the PCD processing research has been implemented using the Deep Learning model. The DL model performs well on the different PCD processing like segmentation, Classification, Detection, etc., but only a few works explored the DL on the large-scale 3D scene [27]. Machine learning is an ocean; it contains plenty of concepts and real-world applications [28]. Very little research work is going on in a PCD coding based on DL [3]. Many real-world applications mainly focus on classification problems based on DL. PointNet++ with the octree grouping method improves the classification efficiency [29]. CNN-based Semantic3D.Net model helps to label the large PCD dataset [30]. The spatial information of a PCD is compressed by a well-trained DL model [31]. In disaster-detection applications, the 3D PCD features are extracted by the DL-based CNN [32]. The local neighborhood of 3D points is enhanced by the point web net based on the adaptive feature adjustment method [33]. Each 3D point in the point cloud is labeled using fully convolutional networks [34]. The geometry information of a PCD is compressed by a 3D stacked autoencoder model [35]. The Recurrent neural network improves the PCD compression methods by using the residual blocks [36]. The U-Net architecture eliminates the temporal redundancy of the dynamic PCD data [37]. The sequential hyper-prior model improves DL-based geometry compression [38]. A very few of the DL-based PCD processing are directly working on PCD data [27]. Autoencoder-based DL model performs well on a PCD image compression [39]. The CNN model replaces the transformation and quantization methods in the compression process [40]. The sparse encoder and the compressed sensing method increase the speed of the compression method [41]. The dimension of the PCD data is reduced using the symmetric-based autoencoder [42]. The coarse and sparse latent vectors are generated by applying the graph CNN model [43].

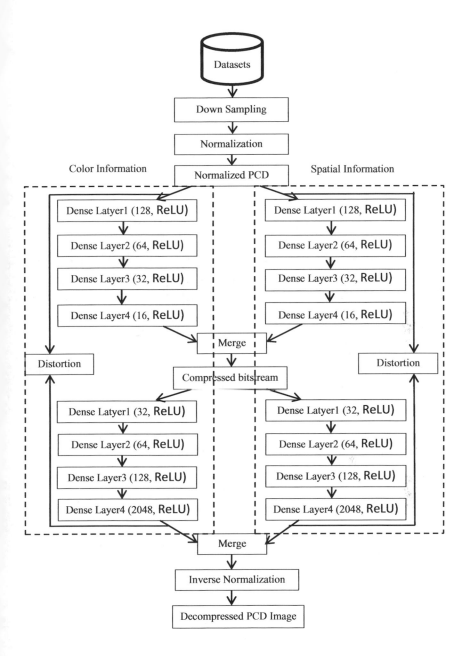

Proposed Methodology

The architecture of the DDLCPCD algorithm is shown in the above figure. The proposed algorithm consists of three modules. The first two modules focus on the preprocessing steps: ASiS and MiST techniques. The third module is Dyad Deep

Learning-Based Codec (DDLC) that reduces the dimension and the number of bytes required to store the 3D PCD images. This DDLC has two sub-networks: compression stage and decompression stage on both spatial and color information of the testing PCD images. A detailed explanation of the proposed DDLCPCD algorithm is given below. The input layer in the DDLC model has been shared by the two groups of units such as geometry and color.

Alternate Signal Sampling (ASiS)

Generally, the PCD data are very huge and inconsistent due to the speed, height, and angle of the vehicle, which carries the LiDAR sensor that records the sample of the earth's surface. Hence, the recorded PCD in the datasets is unbalanced in the number of points and the density of an image. The dense PCD image depends on the number of 3D points that have been acquired per meter by the sensor in the LiDAR [44]. The PCD image p_i in the dataset P is denoted by the following equation (16.2).

$$\forall_{i=1}^{2} P_i = \forall_{i=1}^{N} \left\{ p_{i1}, p_{i2}, p_{i3}, \cdots, p_{iN} \right\} \qquad (16.2)$$

where N is the number of PCD images in the ith dataset. The proposed work has been implemented and tested on two 3D airborne LiDAR PCD datasets: Building and Landscape. Hence, the maximum of i value is 2. Each point cloud image p_i contains many attributes. From that, this work focuses on only the two important attributes spatial information (3D coordinates) and color information (R, G, B). A PCD image can be represented by the following equation.

$$\forall_{j=1}^{N} p_j = \left\{ \begin{array}{l} \left[[x_1,y_1,z_1], [x_2,y_2,z_2], [x_3,y_3,z_3], \cdots, [x_k,y_k,z_k] \right], \\ \left[[R_1,G_1,B_1], [R_2,G_2,B_2], [R_3,G_3,B_3], \cdots, [R_k,G_k,B_k] \right], \cdots \end{array} \right\} \qquad (16.3)$$

where p_j is a jth PCD image that consists of k number of spatial and color information. k is an unbalanced value, which varies in every image and depends on the capturing speed and density of a PCD image. Hence, the first module ASiS in the proposed work overcomes the inconsistent problem of the PCD images in the datasets, to make a balanced dataset with all the PCD images having the same number of points. This process improves the efficiency of the training process in the dyad deep learning model. This method is based on the Nyquist signal sampling technique. The sampling points have been selected based on the factor of the Nyquist frequency and interval period in the Nyquist sampling technique. In the proposed ASiS method, the alternate signal values have been selected with the help of the time period (Λ_s) and the maximum frequency (δ_s) of the signal in the spatial and color information of a PCD and is mentioned in the equation (16.4).

$$\left(\delta_s\right) = \frac{1}{\Delta_t} * \left(k\right) \tag{16.4}$$

where δ_s is the number of frequency signals (samples) selected for the time period (Δ_t) and number of maximum signal (k) in the particular pcd for the proposed algorithm. In this ASiS method, the value of Δ_t is two (alternate). Hence, the δ_s value in all the pcd images is constant. Thus, the sampled pcd p_j' is as described by equation (16.5).

$$\forall_{j=1}^{N} p_j' = \left\{ \begin{array}{l} \left[\left[x_1,y_1,z_1\right],\left[x_3,y_3,z_3\right],\left[x_5,y_5,z_5\right],\cdots,\left[x_{\delta_s},y_{\delta_s},z_{\delta_s}\right]\right], \\ \left[\left[R_1,G_1,B_1\right],\left[R_3,G_3,B_3\right],\left[R_5,G_5,B_5\right],\cdots,\left[R_{\delta_s},G_{\delta_s},B_{\delta_s}\right]\right],\cdots \end{array} \right\} \tag{16.5}$$

where p_j' is an outcome of an ASiS method, fed into the next preprocessing module to improve the signal data for efficient learning of a DDLC network model.

Min-Max Signal Transformation (MiST)

The MiST process transforms the recorded world coordinate PCD values into the window coordinate values to reduce the computation, memory space, and time complexity of the proposed system. When the captured raw PCD attributes values in the datasets are very large, it is a very challenging task to manipulate, analyze, and maintain the data. Hence, the large world 3D coordinate data have to transform into the compact window 3D coordinate values. The MiST is a technique, to standardize each signal value of the spatial and color information into a suitable format for the DDLC training process. The proposed preprocessing method is based on the minimum and maximum frequency signal values of a PCD. The calculation of MiST is given in equations (16.6) and (16.7).

$$\omega_s = \max\left[\left[x_1,y_1,z_1\right],\left[x_3,y_3,z_3\right],\left[x_5,y_5,z_5\right],\cdots,\left[x_{\delta_s},y_{\delta_s},z_{\delta_s}\right]\right] \tag{16.6}$$

$$\gamma_s = \min\left[\left[x_1,y_1,z_1\right],\left[x_3,y_3,z_3\right],\left[x_5,y_5,z_5\right],\cdots,\left[x_{\delta_s},y_{\delta_s},z_{\delta_s}\right]\right] \tag{16.7}$$

where ω_s and γ_s are the maximum and minimum frequency signal from the spatial information domain, calculated by *max* and *min* mathematical functions.

$$\omega_c = \max\left[\left[R_1,G_1,B_1\right],\left[R_3,G_3,B_3\right],\left[R_5,G_5,B_5\right],\cdots,\left[R_{\delta_s},G_{\delta_s},B_{\delta_s}\right]\right] \tag{16.8}$$

$$\gamma_c = \min\left[\left[R_1,G_1,B_1\right],\left[R_3,G_3,B_3\right],\left[R_5,G_5,B_5\right],\cdots,\left[R_{\delta_s},G_{\delta_s},B_{\delta_s}\right]\right] \tag{16.9}$$

where ω_c and γ_c are the maximum and minimum frequency signals from the color information domain, calculated by *max* and *min* mathematical functions in equations (16.8) and (16.9). Then, the range of signal values on both domains has been calculated using equations (16.10) and (16.11).

$$\rho_s = \omega_s - \gamma_s \qquad (16.10)$$

$$\rho_c = \omega_c - \gamma_c \qquad (16.11)$$

The transformed spatial information S_i and color information R_i are computed using equations (16.12) and (16.13).

$$\forall_{i=1}^{\delta_s} S_i = [x_i, y_i, z_i] / \rho_s \qquad (16.12)$$

$$\forall_{i=1}^{\delta_s} R_i = [R_i, G_i, B_i] / \rho_c \qquad (16.13)$$

$$\forall_{i=1}^{N} p_i'' = \{ [[S_i], [R_i]] \} \qquad (16.14)$$

where p_i'' is a transformed ith PCD in a datasets with spatial information S_i and color information R_i. In the transformed pcd, all the signal values are in the range of 0-1. This algorithm is a distortion-free, perfect reverse process. This MiST process has also retained the original structure of the point cloud. This transformed PCD p_i'' moves to the input of the DDLC model.

Dyad Deep Learning Codec (DDLC)

The proposed DDLC model overcomes the two main issues of the sequence deep learning networks, namely diminishing feature reuse in forwarding propagation and the vanishing gradient problem in back propagation [45]. The proposed algorithm aims to compress both geometry (spatial) and color attributes of a PCD in the given datasets. Hence, the sequential deep learning architecture for both attributes would be complex by nature to produce a better-compressed and reconstructed image. This sequential DL architecture is forced to increase the training of the model multiple times. This multiple number of layers and the training process reduce the back-propagated gradient value for balancing the weight in a model [45, 46]. Hence, the model was not able to learn properly on the given dataset. The result of the vanishing gradient value is to produce a premature convergence state to a bad solution. The diminishing feature reuse problem occurs due to the long training process with a large number of layers in the sequential DL model. This is because of the increase in the computation and transformation with multiple numbers of weight matrices. This continuous process washed out the [45] original information from the earlier layer: the resultant of this missing information, would not calculate the proper gradient value in the back-propagation process. This situation misleads the direction of the convergence state. Then, the model could not learn properly from the given dataset with its structure. To avoid these two problems, the proposed DDLCPCD algorithm introduces the DDLC network model with a cascade connection of fewer layers. The basic structure of the DDLC is shown in the below figure. In this model, the output layer is very near to the processing layers. Hence, the original information need not go for the long process; this helps to alleviate both the problems.

The structure of DDLC is effective in reducing the number of layers in sequential order, and it is shown in above figure. The proposed network model splits into two groups: one group for spatial information and the other one for color information. The topology of the DDLC contains two symmetric sub-networks: compression subnet and decompression subnet. The key idea behind the structure of the DDLC model is to reduce the number of layers and the computations to reach out to the output layer, very near to avoid the occurrence of the problems. In both the sub-networks, the layers are linked in a sequential manner. The transformed PCD data are split into spatial information and color information for the independent compression process. This network has two shared input layers for both spatial and color information processing in compression and decompression sub-nets, and two concatenate layers for both compression and decompression networks. The spatial group unit takes the input from a PCD and starts to train the perceptions in each layer one by one until all the layers in the architecture have been trained. The color group unit starts the training process once the spatial group has completed the training work. The color group unit takes the input from the transformed PCD data, and not from the output of the spatial process due to the topology of the DDLC. Both the group of units complete their process in the compression network and then their output values of the latent vectors have been merged into a single vector and considered as the compressed bitstream data for the internal storage and transmission process. At the receiver end, the compressed bitstream is split into spatial information and color information for the decompression sub-network process. This sub-network has the inverse process of the compression network. Finally, the outputs of both groups of units in the decompression network are merged into decompressed PCD signal data.

The spatial (S) and color (R) groups have four fully connected layers with 128, 64, 32, 16 neurons for each process in the compression sub-network. The transformed PCD data have been split and the data structure is flattened before entering the DDLC network for improving the efficiency of the training process in the dense layer. The transformed PCD from the MiST process has been described by equation (16.15).

$$\forall_{i=1}^{N} p_i'' = \left\{ \left[[S_i], [R_i] \right] \right\} \qquad (16.15)$$

where S_i and R_i are the ith spatial and color information, respectively. Then, the transformed ith PCD p_i'' segmented and flattened for the input of DDLC process is given equation (16.16).

$$\forall_{i=1}^{N} p_i'' = [S],[R]$$
$$= \left[x_1, y_1, z_1, x_2, y_2, z_2, \cdots, x_{\delta_s}, y_{\delta_s}, z_{\delta_s} \right], \left[R_1, G_1, B_1, R_2, G_2, B_2, \cdots, R_{\delta_s}, G_{\delta_s}, B_{\delta_s} \right] \quad (16.16)$$

where S and R are the segmented and flattened data, respectively, from equation (16.15). The compression process in the spatial domain is denoted by equation (16.17).

$$\Psi_S = \left(D_{s4}, \left(D_{s3}, \left(D_{s2}, \left(D_{s1}, S, \theta_1 \right), \theta_2 \right) \theta_3 \right), \theta_4 \right) \quad (16.17)$$

where Ψ_S is a 16-bit latent vector (compressed bitstream) from the spatial compression sub-network model. This vector is calculated from four spatial dense layers D_{s1}, D_{s2}, D_{s3}, and D_{s4}, working on the spatial input S with ith dense layer compression hyperparameter θ_i. In the same way, the color information has been compressed by the function, and it is given in equation (16.18).

$$\Psi_R = \left(D_{r4}, \left(D_{r3}, \left(D_{r2}, \left(D_{r1}, R, \theta_1 \right), \theta_2 \right) \theta_3 \right), \theta_4 \right) \quad (16.18)$$

where Ψ_R is a 16-bit latent vector (compressed bitstream) from the color compression sub-network model. Then, merge the Ψ_S vector and the Ψ_R vector to form the compressed bitstream of a corresponding pcd image for internal storage and transmission process. The decompressed sub-network has a reverse process of compression. The reverse process of spatial and color information has been done using the following equations (16.19) and (16.20).

$$\Omega_S = \left(D_{s1}, \left(D_{s2}, \left(D_{s3}, \left(D_{s4}, \Psi_S, \varphi_4 \right), \varphi_3 \right) \varphi_2 \right), \varphi_1 \right) \quad (16.19)$$

$$\Omega_R = \left(D_{r1}, \left(D_{r2}, \left(D_{r3}, \left(D_{r4}, \Psi_R, \varphi_4 \right), \varphi_3 \right) \varphi_2 \right), \varphi_1 \right) \quad (16.20)$$

$$\forall_{i=1}^{N} p_i''' = \left\{ \left[[\Omega_{Si}], [\Omega_{Ri}] \right] \right\} \quad (16.21)$$

where Ω_S, Ω_R are the decompressed vector of spatial and color domain from the compressed vectors in equations (16.17) and (16.18) by using ith dense layer hyperparameter φ_i. Then, the decompressed vectors are merged to form a 3D pcd structure p_i''' denoted in equation (16.21). Finally, these 3D PCD data are transformed into the inverse MiST function to get back the original sampled PCD image.

The Mean Squared Error (MSE) loss function is the most suitable function to find the error value in between the target and the actual output of the proposed model during the forward-propagation process. This MSE value leads to the Peak

Signal-to-Noise Ratio (PSNR) characteristics of the output PCD image. The MSE loss function calculation is given in equation (16.22).

$$\text{MSE} = \sum_{i=1}^{\delta_s} \frac{\left(S_i - \Omega_{Si}\right)^2}{\delta_s} \qquad (16.22)$$

In equation (16.22), S_i is an ith target output, Ω_{Si} is an ith actual output from the proposed DDLC model, and δ_s is the total number of sampled points in a point cloud. Depending on the MSE value, the gradient factor is generated by using Stochastic Gradient Descent (SGD) algorithm to balance the weight matrix values to reduce the error during the back-propagation process. This SGD works with the learning rate and the momentum factor to adjust the quantity of weight updation and increases the speed to the meet converge state with minimum error and good quality of decompressed PCD image. The SGD calculation is given in equation (16.24).

$$\Theta = \Theta - \left(\alpha \times G\right) \qquad (16.23)$$

$$\Theta i = \Theta i - \alpha \left(P_i - P_i'\right) x_j^i \qquad (16.24)$$

where α is a learning rate and Θ_i is an ith random point selected for the gradient calculation, and G is a gradient value. The hyperparameters (θ, φ) such as activation function (ReLU), epochs (1500), loss function (MSE), optimizer (SGD), learning rate ($\alpha = 0.3$) with momentum ($\eta = 0.9$), and batch size (5) are similar in both the networks except the last dense layer in decompression network having a Sigmoid activation function for making the real-valued output PCD image.

Performance Metrics

The performance of the proposed DDLCPCD algorithm has been implemented and tested on two different dense datasets by using objective quality metrics. In the point cloud compression algorithm, the performance of the algorithm is generally measured by the correlation relationship between the original and the decompressed point clouds. In the proposed work, V_{org} is considered as an original (reference) point cloud image and V_{deg} is considered as a decompressed (degraded) point cloud image. The performance of the DDLC module has been measured by the distortion between the input and output PCD of the DDLC model. This calculation has been done using a popular method, Chamfer pseudo-distance. The performance of the whole DDLCPCD algorithm has been measured using the point-to-point (p2p) evaluation. Generally, the distance of the point clouds is measured by the Euclidean distance metrics. A detailed explanation of the performance metrics of the compression algorithm is given further.

Chamfer Pseudo-Distance (CPD)

This method measures the squared distance between each point in one point cloud V_{org} and its nearest neighbor in the other point cloud V_{deg}. This can be expressed by the following equation (16.25) [47].

$$CPD\left(V_{org}, V_{deg}\right) = \sum_{x \in V_{org,}} \min_{y \in V_{deg}} \|x - y\|_2^2 + \sum_{y \in V_{deg,}} \min_{x \in V_{org}} \|x - y\|_2^2 \qquad (16.25)$$

where x and y are the 3D points in V_{org} and the V_{deg} point cloud image.

Hausdorff Distance (HD)

The Hausdorff distance measures the distance between the set of two point clouds. First, calculate is the maximum value of the minimum distance from V_{org} to V_{deg} and V_{deg} to V_{org}. Then, selected is the maximum value of these two maximum distances. This maximum distance is called the Hausdorff distance between these two point clouds. This can be expressed by the following equation (16.26) [48].

$$HD\left(V_{org}, V_{deg}\right) = \max\left\{\max_{x \in V_{org}} \min_{y \in V_{deg}} d\left(x,y\right), \right.$$
$$\left. \max_{y \in V_{deg}} \min_{x \in V_{org}} d\left(x,y\right)\right\} \qquad (16.26)$$

where x, y are the 3D points present in V_{org} and V_{deg} point clouds, respectively. The $d(x,y)$ is a Euclidean distance between the points x and y.

Point-to-Point Metrics (p2p)

These metrics measure the distance error between the point in the V_{org} and the same point in the V_{deg} by using the equations (16.27) to (16.29) [49].

$$RMSE = \sqrt{\frac{1}{N} \sum_{i=1}^{N} \left(V_{org} - V_{deg}\right)^2} \qquad (16.27)$$

$$d_{rms}\left(V_{org}, V_{deg}\right) = \max\left(RMSE\left(V_{org}, V_{deg}\right), RMSE\left(V_{deg}, V_{org}\right)\right) \qquad (16.28)$$

$$PSNR = 10 \log_{10} \left\|\max_{x,y,z}\left(V_{deg}\right)\right\|_2^2 / d_{rms}\left(V_{org}, V_{deg}\right)^2 \qquad (16.29)$$

Experimental Results

The proposed DDLCPCD model has been implemented and tested on two inconsistent 3D Airborne LiDAR point cloud datasets by using the Jupyter environment in Python 3.7.3 on Windows 10 with a 64-bit operating system, x64-based processor, and 12 GB RAM. For the performance comparison process, the proposed work was implemented on the Terrestrial point cloud set, which is used to test the existing DWT-based compression model [26].

Datasets

The proposed model tested two inconsistent, different dense, unlabeled, 3D model datasets such as the Building dataset and the Landscape dataset. The Landscape dataset contains a huge seven landscape 3D models in ASCII format. The Building dataset contains huge eight 3D models of buildings in ASCII format. These two datasets are in different formats that are converted into PCD format using the CloudCompare tool to work on 3D points and color attributes. The PCD images in the datasets have been divided into training (80%) and testing (20%) process. Each PCD in the datasets is a very huge and unbalanced number of 3D points. Some of the sample PCD images are shown in the below figure.

The above figure shows a) Szymbarkmodel (B), b) Weglowka_v1 (B), c) London test (B), d) Linabobardi (L), e) Skelling (L), f) Ibirapuera (L). Each PCD image name is specified with dataset name, B describes the Building dataset, and L denotes the Landscape dataset.

Implementation of the Proposed DDLCPCD Algorithm

Initially, the PCD images in the datasets have a different number of 3D points. It is very difficult to train the proposed model with these PCD images. Hence, the PCD images have been downsampled by the ASiS method, to make all the PCD images with the same number of 3D points to improve the training process of the DDLC model. The below figure shows the 3D scatter plot of the resultant signal data of the two proposed preprocess modules, ASiS, and MiST. figures (a) and (d) denote the original spatial and color information of an input point cloud image Szymbarkmodel (B). The original PCD image has been downsampled using the proposed ASiS method. The downsampled spatial and color information of a Szymbarkmodel (B) PCD data are shown in the below figures (b) and (e). Then, the original value of the downsampled PCD data has been transformed by using the proposed MiST method to standardize the data for the training process. The transformed spatial and color information of PCD data are described in the below figures (c) and (f). From the below figure, it is observed that the MiST method transforms the value of the spatial and color data in the range of 0–1 without affecting the structure of the sampled PCD image.

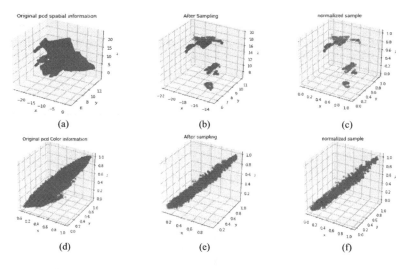

(a)   (b)   (c)

(d)   (e)   (f)

The transformed data of a PCD image feed into the DDLC model for the training process. The DDLC model has a separate dyad deep learning model for spatial and color information. Hence, both information of a PCD have been split and flattened before entering into the DDLC model to reduce the complexity of the training process of the proposed model. The first proposed DDLC model has been designed with four dense layers with 128, 64, 32, 16 neurons. Then, it started the spatial training by using the ReLU activation function, MSE loss function, SGD optimizer with a batch size five for 1500 epochs. Next, the color training process is started after their training process is completed. Both the training processes take the input from the earlier transformed flattened PCD data from the given datasets. These two training processes share the same hyperparameters to produce a better reconstruction image. The model has been trained well; then, the DDLC model has been created and tested on the testing PCD images. In each epoch, the loss has been measured and it has been reduced by using the optimization function SGD with learning rate (0.3) and the momentum (0.9). The below figure shows the loss value for both the training and validation process of the given two datasets.

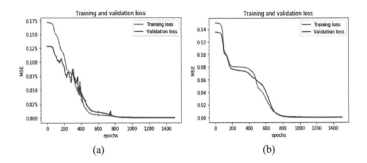

(a)   (b)

From the above figure, it is observed that the proposed DDLC model has been trained and performed well on the given two datasets and reached out to convergence state in the earlier stage of the epochs. The below figure illustrates the target and actual outcome of the proposed DDLC model on the two sampled point cloud images in the Building dataset.

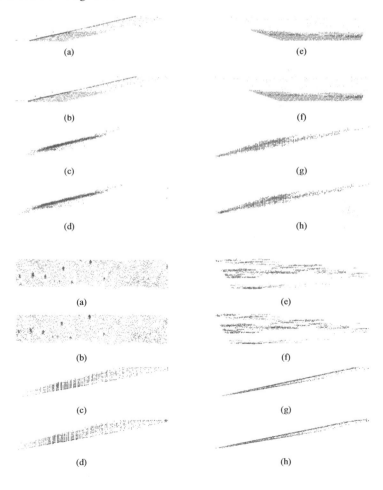

In the above two sets of figures, (a) and (c) are the target spatial and color information of the point cloud images Washington Square (B) and Mine near Riga, Lavatia (L), (b) and (d) are the actual outputs of proposed DDLC model for the corresponding spatial and color information of the point cloud images Washington Square (B) and Mine near Riga, Lavatia (L), (e) and (g) are the target spatial and color information of the point cloud images Weglowka_v1(B) and Skelling (L), (f) and (h) are the actual outputs of the proposed DDLC model for the corresponding spatial and color information of the point cloud images Weglowka_v1(B), Skelling (L).

From the above two sets of figures, we observe that there is no subjective distortion between the target and output images of the two datasets. Hence, the proposed model is well trained and outperforms the given two datasets.

Performance Analysis

In this section, the performance of the proposed DDLCPCD algorithm has been analyzed with the different functions and metrics using the given two airborne datasets. This dyad deep learning-based compression model output has been compared with the existing traditional DWT-based compression algorithm by using the Terrestrial LiDAR PCD dataset.

Subjective Analysis

In the proposed DDLCPCD model, the MiST function outperforms the other existing functions as a well-known normalizer function norm. The below figures show the 3D scatter plot, for comparing the MiST with the existing norm function.

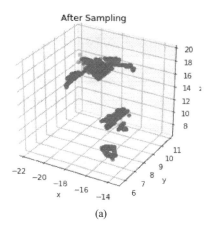

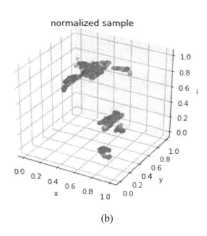

(a)   (b)

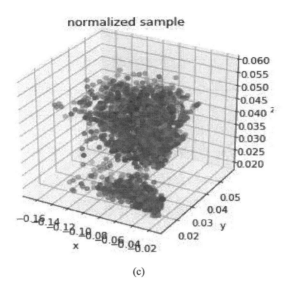

(c)

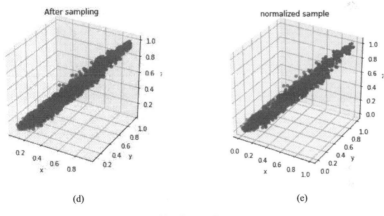

(d)

(e)

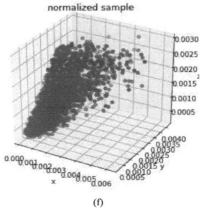

(f)

This analysis work has been compared the transformed spatial and color information in the above figures (b) and (e) with the information in figures (c) and (f). It is observed that the MiST function transforms the information data without affecting the structure of the PCD image but the norm function transforms the data and structure of the PCD image. From this, it can be concluded that the MiST outperforms the norm function.

Next, the analysis process concentrates on the design of the DDLC model. The performance of the proposed model with suggested loss and optimization function compared with the DDLC models designed by using different combinations of loss and optimization functions. The following figures display the different loss values acquired from the model with different loss and optimization functions, MSE Logarithmic (MSEL) loss function, Mean Absolute Error (MAE) loss function, and Root Mean-Squared Property Optimization (RMS PROP) function.

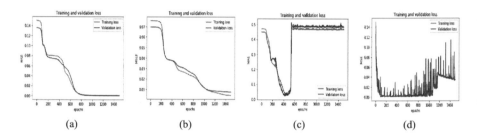

(a)   (b)   (c)   (d)

The observed loss values from different DDLC models from the different combinations of functions are expressed in graph notation in the following figure. We compared figure (a) with the remaining figures; it shows that the proposed model trained better than the other models. From the following figure, we conclude that the suggested combination (SGD, MSE) of the functions in the proposed model trained and performed better than the model with the other combinations of functions.

The above table compares the actual output from different models with a target output pcd image, Mine near Riga, Lavatia (L). The actual output from the proposed model is subjectively similar to the target output. From the above table, we conclude that the actual output from the proposed model most is likely similar to the target output than the other model's output.

Objective Analysis

The various objective quality metrics mentioned in the performance metric section, have been applied on the target and the actual output, produced from the different combinations of the models, and the resultant values are tabulated in the following two tables.

Functions	Spatial Information	Color Information
Target Sampled Point cloud Image Mine near Riga, Lavatia		
From Proposed Method (MSE + SGD)		
From (MSLE +SGD)		
From (MAE + SGD)		
From (MSE + RMS PROP)		

Dataset Name	Point Cloud Image Name	Functions	MSE	PSNR	HMSE	HPSNR
Banana Point Cloud Image		Existing DWT	0.12	43	0.2	54.2
		Proposed DDLCPCD	5.15E-07	111.01	0.10	57.75
Building	Washington Square	Proposed DDLCPCD	7.47E-08	119.39	0.09	58.53
		MSLE+SGD	1.15E-07	117.52	0.15	56.30
		MAE+SGD	0.0005	80.83	0.53	50.82
		RMS PROP+MSE	0.001	78.11	0.15	56.18
	Weglowka_v1	Proposed DDLCPCD	1.38E-07	116.73	0.04	61.46
		MSLE+SGD	3.47E-07	112.73	0.15	56.21
		MAE+SGD	0.000183	85.49	0.10	57.72
		RMS PROP+MSE	0.004	71.80	0.55	50.65
Landscape	Mine near Riga, Lavatia	Proposed DDLCPCD	1.62E-08	126.03	0.07	59.65
		MSLE+SGD	9.39E-07	108.40	0.12	57.30
		MAE+SGD	1.18E-06	107.42	0.03	62.39
		RMS PROP+MSE	5.47E-05	90.74	0.08	58.65
	Skelling	Proposed DDLCPCD	2.31E-07	114.49	0.05	60.77
		MSLE+SGD	2.08E-06	104.94	0.17	55.72
		MAE+SGD	1.44E-06	106.56	0.03	62.41
		RMS PROP+MSE	6.19E-07	110.21	0.037	62.35

Dataset Name	Point Cloud Image Name	Functions	MSE	PSNR	HMSE	HPSNR
Banana Point Cloud Image		Existing DWT	0.02	48.36	0.1	52.8
		Proposed DDLCPCD	**3.82E-08**	**122.3**	**0.032**	**63.02**
Building	Washington Square	Proposed DDLCPCD	**1.72E-09**	**135.7**	**0.07**	**59.64**
		MSLE+SGD	5.76E-08	120.5	0.14	56.44
		MAE+SGD	0.03	62.4	0.67	49.83
		RMS PROP+MSE	0.005	70.9	0.58	50.49
	Weglowka_v1	Proposed DDLCPCD	**4.54E-08**	**121.5**	**0.03**	**62.67**
		MSLE+SGD	1.05E-07	117.9	0.13	56.80
		MAE+SGD	0.05	60.99	0.71	49.57
		RMS PROP+MSE	0.0115	67.50	0.56	50.62
Landscape	Mine near Riga, Lavatia	Proposed DDLCPCD	**6.33E-07**	**110.1**	**0.06**	**60.16**
		MSLE+SGD	4.56E-05	91.54	0.20	55.03
		MAE+SGD	0.0007	79.53	0.79	49.12
		RMS PROP+MSE	0.002	73.46	0.61	50.25
	Skelling	Proposed DDLCPCD	**9.93E-09**	**128.1**	**0.06**	**60.31**
		MSLE+SGD	2.17E-05	94.77	0.19	55.15
		MAE+SGD	0.0004	81.89	0.79	49.14
		RMS PROP+MSE	0.002	74.55	0.58	50.44

The Spatial Objective Quality Metrics (SOQM) of MSE, PSNR, Hausdorff Distance (HMSE), and a Hausdorff PSNR (HPSNR) are given in the above table. The QOM of the proposed DDLCDPCD algorithm has been measured and compared with the existing traditional DWT-based algorithm by using a Terrestrial LiDAR PCD dataset and the different combination dyad deep learning model by using the two given datasets. In the above table, the first line illustrates that the SOQM values of the existing DWT-based compression algorithm. Next, the proposed DDLCPCD technique has been implemented on the same Terrestrial dataset, which is used by the existing DWT algorithm and placed in the second row of the above table. Here, the proposed method on the existing algorithm's dataset compared with a DWT algorithm shows that the proposed DDLCPCD algorithm produced less error (MSE, HMSE) and good quality (PSNR, HPSNR) of the decompressed (actual) PCD image than the existing method. From the above table, we conclude that the SOQM from the proposed DDLCPCD method with the suggested hyperparameter on the given two datasets produced the more similar actual output (PSNR, HPSNR) with less distortion (MSE, HMSE) values than the other models and an existing algorithm. In the same way, the color objective quality metrics (COQM) of the proposed and existing algorithms have been measured and tabulated in the table given below.

The proposed algorithm on the color information produced less MSE and high PSNR values than the other existing and different combination models. From the above two tables, we conclude that the proposed DDLCPCD method performed well on both geometry and color information than the other mentioned methods. Hence, the proposed compression model is well suited for the given 3D airborne LiDAR PCD datasets.

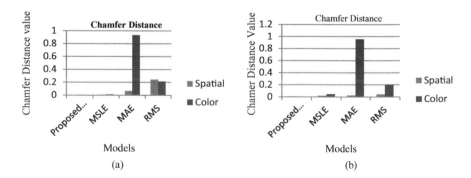

(a) (b)

The above figures show the graphical representation of the measured Chamfer distance of proposed and existing methods on the given datasets. It is observed that the proposed model produced less Chamfer distance (distortion) than the other models, and the MAE model produces the high Chamfer distance on both color information of the two given datasets. The RMS model produced a high spatial Chamfer distance on both datasets. From the above output figures, we conclude that the proposed method produces the actual images with less distortion than the other mentioned models.

From the subjective analysis, figures, and tables, it is proved that the proposed DDLCPCD model outperforms other compression models. From the objective analysis, the calculated values in the tables and figures prove that the proposed method works better than the other combination models. From both analyses, we proved that our proposed DDLCPCD model is the best-suited compression model for the 3D Airborne LiDAR point cloud datasets.

Conclusion

A novel 3D airborne LiDAR point cloud image codec based on the Dyad Deep Learning algorithm has been introduced in this work. The raw point cloud image has been downsampled and transformed by applying ASiS and MiST techniques, respectively. Then, the transformed data have been fed to the dyad deep learning model for compressing both the geometry and the color attributes of the point cloud images. This DDLC network consists of compression and decompression sub-networks. This model has been trained well with suggested optimal hyperparameters to produce constant compressed 128 bytes of data for each information and better quality decompressed image. The performance of the proposed DDLCPCD model is compared with the different models and existing DWT-based compression algorithms. The experimental result shows that the proposed algorithm improves the constant compressed image with 128 bytes of data for each information and increases the PSNR value averagely by 1.6 times than the existing methods. The analysis part states that the proposed DDLCPCD algorithm outperforms the existing algorithms and proves that the proposed algorithm is the best-suited model for 3D airborne LiDAR color point clouds.

References

[1] "What is a Point Cloud? What is LiDAR?" https://community.safe.com/s/article/what-is-a-point-cloud-what-is-lidar (accessed September 5, 2020).

[2] "What is lidar data?—Help | ArcGIS Desktop." https://desktop.arcgis.com/en/arc-map/10.3/manage-data/las-dataset/what-is-lidar-data-.htm (accessed September 5, 2020).

[3] W. Liu, J. Sun, W. Li, T. Hu, and P. Wang, "Deep learning on point clouds and its application: A survey," *Sensors – MDPI.* Vol. 19, no. 19, 2019, doi: 10.3390/s19194188.

[4] O. Gazi, "Multirate signal processing," *Digit. Signal Process*, vol. 13, pp. 71–144, 2018, doi: 10.1007/978-981-10-4962-0_2.

[5] C. Moreno and M. Li, "A comparative study of filtering methods for point clouds in real-time video streaming," *Lect. Notes Eng. Comput. Sci.*, vol. 2225, pp. 389–393, 2016.

[6] C. Suchocki and W. Błaszczak-Bąk, "Down-sampling of point clouds for the technical diagnostics of buildings and structures," *Geosci.*, vol. 9, no. 2, 2019, doi: 10.3390/geosciences9020070.

[7] M. Miknis, R. Davies, P. Plassmann, and A. Ware, *"Near real-time point cloud processing using the PCL,"* 2015 22nd International Conference on Systems, Signals and Image Processing - Proceedings of IWSSIP 2015, London (UK), no. section C, pp. 153–156, 2015, doi: 10.1109/IWSSIP.2015.7314200.

[8] E. Nezhadarya, E. Taghavi, R. Razani, B. Liu, and J. Luo, "Adaptive Hierarchical Down-Sampling for Point Cloud Classification," *Comput. Vis. Pattern Recognit.*, arXiv:1904.08506, pp. 12953–12961, 2020, doi: 10.1109/cvpr42600.2020.01297.

[9] R. Gautam, S. Vanga, F. Ariese, and S. Umapathy, "Review of multidimensional data processing approaches for raman and infrared spectroscopy," *EPJ Tech. Instrum.*, vol. 2, no. 1, 2015, doi: 10.1140/epjti/s40485-015-0018-6.

[10] B. Jutzi and H. Gross, "Normalization of lidar intensity data based on range and surface incidence angle," *Int. Arch. Photogramm. Remote Sens.*, vol. 38, no. 3/W8, pp. 213–218, 2009.

[11] D. Bommes, H. Huang, I. Lim, M. Ibing, and L. Kobbelt, "A convolutional decoder for point clouds using adaptive instance normalization," *Eurographics Symp. Geom. Process.*, vol. 38, no. 5, pp. 99–108, 2019.

[12] M. Courbariaux, I. Hubara, D. Soudry, R. El-Yaniv, and Y. Bengio, "Binarized Neural Networks: Training Deep Neural Networks with Weights and Activations Constrained to +1 or -1," pp. 2019–2020, 2016, [Online]. Available: http://arxiv.org/abs/1602.02830.

[13] H. Houshiar and A. Nuchter, *"3D point cloud compression using conventional image compression for efficient data transmission,"* 2015 25th International Conference on Information, Communication and Automation Technologies, ICAT 2015 – Proceedings, Sarajevo, Bosnia and Herzegovina, 2015, doi: 10.1109/ICAT.2015.7340499.

[14] T. Golla and R. Klein, *"Real-time point cloud compression,"* International Conference on Intelligent Robots and System, Kyoto, Japan, vol. 2015-Decem, pp. 5087–5092, 2015, doi: 10.1109/IROS.2015.7354093.

[15] I. Maksymova, C. Steger, and N. Druml, "Review of LiDAR sensor data acquisition and compression for automotive applications," *Proceedings*, vol. 2, no. 13, p. 852, 2018, doi: 10.3390/proceedings2130852.

[16] D. Mongus and B. Žalik, "Efficient method for lossless LIDAR data compression," *Int. J. Remote Sens.*, vol. 32, no. 9, pp. 2507–2518, 2011, doi: 10.1080/01431161003698385.

[17] V. Morell, S. Orts, M. Cazorla, and J. Garcia-Rodriguez, "Geometric 3D point cloud compression," *Pattern Recognit. Lett.*, vol. 50, pp. 55–62, 2014, doi: 10.1016/j.patrec.2014.05.016.

[18] S. Schwarz et al., "Emerging MPEG standards for point cloud compression," *IEEE J. Emerg. Sel. Top. Circuits Syst.*, vol. 9, no. 1, pp. 133–148, 2019, doi: 10.1109/JETCAS.2018.2885981.

[19] D. Tian, H. Ochimizu, C. Feng, R. Cohen, and A. Vetro, *"Geometric distortion metrics for point cloud compression,"* Proceedings - International Conference on Image Processing ICIP, China, vol. 2017-Septe, pp. 3460–3464, 2018, doi: 10.1109/ICIP.2017.8296925.

[20] D. Thanou, P. A. Chou, and P. Frossard, "Graph-based compression of dynamic 3D point cloud sequences," *IEEE Trans. Image Process.*, vol. 25, no. 4, pp. 1765–1778, 2016, doi: 10.1109/TIP.2016.2529506.

[21] P. L. Chithra and A. C. Tamilmathi, "3D LiDAR point cloud image codec based on Tensor," *Imaging Sci. J.*, vol. 68, no. 1, pp. 1–10, 2020, doi: 10.1080/13682199.2020.1719747.

[22] P. L. Chithra and A. C. Tamilmathi, "Tensor tucker decomposition based geometry compression on three dimensional LiDAR point cloud image," *Int. J. Innov. Technol. Explor. Eng.*, vol. 9, no. 3, pp. 1897–1903, 2020, doi: 10.35940/ijitee.c8551.019320.

[23] S. Gu, J. Hou, H. Zeng, H. Yuan, and K. K. Ma, "3D point cloud attribute compression using geometry-guided sparse representation," *IEEE Trans. Image Process.*, vol. 29, no. c, pp. 796–808, 2020, doi: 10.1109/TIP.2019.2936738.

[24] M. Quach, G. Valenzise, and F. Dufaux, "Folding-based compression of point cloud attributes," 2020, [Online]. Available: http://arxiv.org/abs/2002.04439.

[25] Y. Xu, W. Zhu, Y. Xu, and Z. Li, "*Dynamic point cloud geometry compression via patch-wise polynomial fitting*," *IEEE International Conference on Acoustics, Speech and Signal Processing – Proceedings*, Brighton, UK, vol. 2019-May, pp. 2287–2291, 2019, doi: 10.1109/ICASSP.2019.8682413.

[26] P. L. Chithra and T. A. Christoper, "*3D color point cloud compression with plane fitting and discrete wavelet transform*," *2018 10th International Conference on Advanced Computing ICoAC, Chennai, India*, 2018, pp. 20–26, 2018, doi: 10.1109/ICoAC44903.2018.8939106.

[27] S. A. Bello, S. Yu, C. Wang, J. M. Adam, and J. Li, "Review: Deep learning on 3D point clouds," *Remote Sens.*, vol. 12, no. 11, pp. 1–34, 2020, doi: 10.3390/rs12111729.

[28] P. Mehta et al., "A high-bias, low-variance introduction to machine learning for physicists," *Phys. Rep.*, vol. 810, pp. 1–124, 2019, doi: 10.1016/j.physrep.2019.03.001.

[29] X. Yao, J. Guo, J. Hu, and Q. Cao, "Using deep learning in semantic classification for point cloud data," *IEEE Access*, vol. 7, pp. 37121–37130, 2019, doi: 10.1109/ACCESS.2019.2905546.

[30] T. Hackel, N. Savinov, L. Ladicky, J. D. Wegner, K. Schindler, and M. Pollefeys, "Semantic 3D.net: A new large-scale point cloud classification benchmark," *ISPRS Ann. Photogramm. Remote Sens. Spat. Inf. Sci.*, vol. 4, no. 1W1, pp. 91–98, 2017, doi: 10.5194/isprs-annals-IV-1-W1-91-2017.

[31] T. Huang and Y. Liu, "*3D point cloud geometry compression on deep learning*," *MM 2019 – Proceedings of the 7th ACM International Conference Multimedia*, Nice, France, pp. 890–898, 2019, doi: 10.1145/3343031.3351061.

[32] A. Vetrivel, M. Gerke, N. Kerle, F. Nex, and G. Vosselman, "Disaster damage detection through synergistic use of deep learning and 3D point cloud features derived from very high resolution oblique aerial images, and multiple-kernel-learning," *ISPRS J. Photogramm. Remote Sens.*, vol. 140, no. May, pp. 45–59, 2018, doi: 10.1016/j.isprsjprs.2017.03.001.

[33] H. Zhao, L. Jiang, C. W. Fu, and J. Jia, "*Pointweb: Enhancing local neighborhood features for point cloud processing*," *Proceedings of the IEEE Computer Society Conference on Computer Vision and Pattern Recognition, California, USA*, vol. 2019-June, pp. 5560–5568, 2019, doi: 10.1109/CVPR.2019.00571.

[34] A. Boulch, B. Le Saux, and N. Audebert, "Unstructured point cloud semantic labeling using deep segmentation networks," *Eurographics Work. 3D Object Retrieval, EG 3DOR*, vol. 2017-April, pp. 17–24, 2017, doi: 10.2312/3dor.20171047.

[35] J. Wang, H. Zhu, Z. Ma, T. Chen, H. Liu, and Q. Shen, "Learned point cloud geometry compression," pp. 1–13, 2019, [Online]. Available: http://arxiv.org/abs/1909.12037.

[36] C. Tu, E. Takeuchi, A. Carballo, and K. Takeda, "*Point cloud compression for 3d lidar sensor using recurrent neural network with residual blocks*," *Proceedings of International Conference on Robotics and Automation, QC, Canada*, vol. 2019-May, pp. 3274–3280, 2019, doi: 10.1109/ICRA.2019.8794264.

[37] C. Tu, E. Takeuchi, A. Carballo, and K. Takeda, "Real-time streaming point cloud compression for 3D LiDAR sensor using U-Net," *IEEE Access*, vol. 7, pp. 113616–113625, 2019, doi: 10.1109/access.2019.2935253.

[38] M. Quach, G. Valenzise, and F. Dufaux, "Improved deep point cloud geometry compression," 2020, [Online]. Available: http://arxiv.org/abs/2006.09043.

[39] W. Yan, Y. Shao, S. Liu, T. H. Li, Z. Li, and G. Li, "Deep auto encoder-based lossy geome-try compression for point clouds," *Comput. Vis. Pattern Recognit.*, arXiv:1905.03691, 2019, [Online]. Available: http://arxiv.org/abs/1905.03691.

[40] M. Quach, G. Valenzise, and F. Dufaux, "*Learning Convolutional Transforms for Lossy Point Cloud Geometry Compression,*" in *Proceedings - International Conference on Image Processing, ICIP,* Alaska, USA, vol. 2019-Septe, pp. 4320–4324, 2019, doi: 10.1109/ICIP.2019.8803413.

[41] X. Chen et al., "A fast reconstruction method of the dense point-cloud model for cultural heritage artifacts based on compressed sensing and sparse auto-encoder," *Opt. Quantum Electron.*, vol. 51, no. 10, pp. 1–16, 2019, doi: 10.1007/s11082-019-2038-y.

[42] J. Wang, H. He, and D. V. Prokhorov, "A folded neural network autoencoder for dimen-sionality reduction," *Procedia Comput. Sci.*, vol. 13, pp. 120–127, 2012, doi: 10.1016/j.procs.2012.09.120.

[43] Z. Yuhui, G. Gutmann, and K. Akihiko, "Irregular convolutional auto-encoder on point clouds," pp. 1–20, 2019, [Online]. Available: http://arxiv.org/abs/1910.02686.

[44] L. Graham, "How dense are you, anyway?", *The LAS 1.4 Specification*, vol. 4, no. 5, pp. 4–6, 2014. https://www.asprs.org/wp-content/uploads/2010/12/LAS_Specification.pdf

[45] G. Huang, Y. Sun, Z. Liu, D. Sedra, and K. Q. Weinberger, "Deep networks with stochas-tic depth," *Lect. Notes Comput. Sci. (including Subser. Lect. Notes Artif. Intell. Lect. Notes Bioinformatics),* vol. 9908, pp. 646–661, 2016, doi: 10.1007/978-3-319-46493-0_39.

[46] E. S. Marquez, J. S. Hare, and M. Niranjan, "Deep cascade learning," *IEEE Trans. Neural Networks Learn. Syst.*, vol. 29, no. 11, pp. 5475–5485, 2018, doi: 10.1109/TNNLS.2018.2805098.

[47] M. Zamorski et al., "Adversarial autoencoders for compact representations of 3D point clouds," *Comput. Vis. Image Underst.*, vol. 193, 2020, doi: 10.1016/j.cviu.2020.102921.

[48] T. Marošević, "The hausdorff distance between some sets of points," *Math. Commun.*, vol. 23, no. 2, pp. 247–257, 2018.

[49] R. Mekuria, S. Laserre, and C. Tulvan, "*Performance assessment of point cloud compression,*" *2017 IEEE Vision and Communication. Image Processing VCIP,* St. Petersburg, FL, vol. 2018-January, no. 1, pp. 1–4, 2018, doi: 10.1109/VCIP.2017.8305132.

Chapter 17

Digital Enterprise Software Productivity Metrics and Enhancing Their Business Impacts Using Machine Learning

Vipul Gaurav and Savita Choudhary

Sir M Visvesvaraya Institute of Technology, Bengaluru, India

Contents

Introduction

The rise of software engineering dates back to the times when giants such as IBM, Microsoft, and Oracle were in their premature phase. The computation power available was limited, and these companies started as nothing more than startups which evolved eventually into the technology giants we witness today. This evolution in the computing industry has happened only in a matter of four to five decades, and as we slowly reach the saturation stage of the increasing computational power, the focus quickly shifted to making this computation power more readily available to the society and compacting the large machines to a neat portable device for use. The software industry is the most rapid-evolving industry to date and is still expanding. The digitization of these startups helped them become enterprises, and their products not only made our lives easier, but also created a massive number of jobs, to become one of the most influential industries in the modern era for developed and developing countries across the world. The rapid development of the software industry led to the need for more innovation, different roles within each of these organizations, ranging from creative engineers to trained business professionals and fluent legal advisors.

The modern era witnessed the introduction of object-oriented programming, with the need to provide better security to the user's data, and the industry transitioned from the procedural programming paradigm to the more efficient coding practices, with developer collaborations, and by creating unique products. Each company that came into existence tried its hands on innovation, as well as aggregation of existing technologies, thus becoming a powerhouse of computation. However, in all these times with evolving coding practices, the dilemma of evaluating good quality code has been thriving with all the managers.

Code Productivity has been an extensive subject of study for software engineers, computer experts, business managers, analysts, and even doctorate researchers. Each company developing a different product has different requirements and these needs evolve with times, with changing customer needs, adapting to new technologies, and transforming developer jobs. In the earlier times, collaboration monitoring was a huge responsibility of the managers and they employed traditional software metrics to evaluate the software performance and development process. With the launch of GitHub in April 2008, versioning systems became open-sourced, and thus all organizations adopted it as part of their development teams and slowly it became an essential skill in the industry.

Software productivity can be primarily explained as the ratio of software produced to the expense and labor of producing it. In the early days, software productivity was measured as lines of code (LOC) per man-hour but a modern-day approach could be obtained by considering factors like Function Point Analysis, Cost Component Modeling, Cyclomatic Complexity, Fan-Out Complexity, and Program Performance Metrics into the account with applied machine learning models to predict their nature. The idea of software productivity is not a theoretical abstract; it should be considered as a software engineering process. Comprehension of software productivity is important for the industry as it would ease the process of system analysis and hence result in the growth of the software industry. The contemporary software industry struggles with productivity measurement and with the onset of version control systems, it becomes difficult to monitor the value of commits and determine software productivity. With different parameters and attributes, a comparison of their production rates would not be conclusive and would eventually become meaningless.

The Need for Business-Oriented Software Metrics

The value of a productivity measurement system is not confined to only its technical aspects and must have a business focus too. Traditional software metrics are evergreen; however, they do not matter at all if we have not combined them with business goals. The era of digital transformation started with the onset of cloud computing that made computational power more accessible to the masses and paved the way for projects that built upon the business insights and needs of the people thriving into products. A software product is completely useless if we do not make use of business metrics and do not meet the customer requirements. A good product does not complicate tasks; it is supposed to simplify them.

The selection of productivity metrics requires a very careful thought process, filtering business needs, balancing technical requirements, and studying the trends, fluctuations in the objective metrics present in the data. In versioning systems, every company commits huge amounts of data at each sprint cycle or on a daily basis in the local branches of the developers, which can be analyzed to not only predict the code nature, but also predict the timeline of the entire sprint cycle and eventually provide enhanced monitoring of the software development process from idea brainstorming to product delivery. This is why modern software development focuses on subjective metrics, attached to certain features and supporting specific business goals, thus allowing us to use metrics as an effective tool for continuous learning and improvement.

Companies that practiced the traditional waterfall approach model to software development are starting to become irrelevant in the industry as we are transitioning toward version-based software with better delivery with continuous integration and continuous delivery of the product that provides room for evolving customer requirements at the same time. A business model will treat the entire project as a **Snowflake**. Each component in the product is treated as a snowflake since we do not come across components having the same needs or the same functionality often. Each person with a different skill brings something new to the table, ranging from their interests, programming capabilities, and communication skills. A good team with collaboration and effective communication abilities is also a snowflake. It can consist of weak developers at an individual level but they become an effective team after collaborating with each other. Thus, we can conclude that any project which becomes a product is also a snowflake whose requirements evolve with time. Hence, we cannot determine the exact metrics we want to measure productivity except individual history that relates to eventual business goals.

This has helped in a number of ways, including accommodation of customer needs and continuous feedback on the development of the system. This will ensure a reduction in customer support services later and also working in close collaboration with the customer will help establish better relationships professionally with them that would prove beneficial to the organization in the long run. So, till now, the software metrics dealt with technical parameters to determine the productivity of the programmers. Now, we have to include business-based metrics to determine whether the product made by the developers is actually proving to be beneficial for the company or not.

The business metric is aimed at increasing the quality of the product and services offered by the organization. A very simple approach to any software business metric involves studying the structural and logical structure of the pipeline program. The academic approach of ease of maintenance, elegance in terms of design patterns, reliability, throughput, and time efficiency of the software developed will lead to stability in the production environment. From a business feedback perspective, we need ratings and user happiness as satisfaction feedback to gauge whether the developed product delivered the requirements stated at the beginning of the project and accommodated the changing requirements or not. Hence, the metrics which actually matter in the end are not just subjective but objective success metrics that give us an idea of the deliverables and system engagement by the users.

In traditional waterfall software projects, it was assumed that software could be specified in advance and quantified by estimates. It was also assumed that the software specification would meet end-user requirements which often was not the case. Hence, we need better monitoring metrics which are more data-driven and business-oriented. Team velocity is one such metric to determine the collaboration quality of the team, set by the deliverables promised by them in every sprint cycle. Team velocity measures the number of story points, quantifying the number and size of product features, completed by the team in the previous sprints. It helps to understand how much value the team is providing to the customers in a given time period. To measure the amount of time to complete the pending tasks in the product development cycle, we make use of burndown charts that quantify the works to be done as a release burndown. It gives a brief idea to the managers about the amount of time needed to complete the project and release the minimal version of the product. We make use of escape defects to track the number of bugs present in the project before the first release, and the managers are supposed to track and resolve all these issues in coherence with the customer requirements. This is a major feedback mechanism for the user and an increasing trend in the escape defect can indicate a faulty process being followed by the developer team.

Testing is an integral part of the cycle of development too. However, traditional testing methods involved unit testing followed by system testing; now there is a need for release testing which identifies bugs in the system at every release stage in order to provide more insight into the product development to the team as well as incorporate better customer feedback and best practices. We call this metric true test coverage as opposed to the regular test coverage metric which only measures unit tests. This is a metric that tells you how much of your codebase or feature set is covered by all types of tests ranging from unit, integration, UI automation, manual tests, and end-to-end acceptance tests. This can give insight into the irrelevant components of the software. This is where a data-driven system is the need of the hour and machine learning comes into the picture to implement such intelligence systems that can effectively monitor the product development cycles along with measuring the productivity of the code.

Traditional Software Productivity Metrics

The traditional software productivity metrics are evergreen in determining the quality of code, structure of programming done by developers. It also focuses on the various parameters a developer should follow ideally in order to deliver modular code into the product pipeline, and it is unavoidable in the prediction of the productivity of the code. Every organization wishes to follow best practices and an agile methodology in order to accelerate the product development process. An intelligence system that involves tools providing visibility for development managers through monitoring tests across all test frameworks, collecting test execution data, and correlating it with data about code changes and frequently used features. This can help compute a True Test Coverage metric which can expose quality gaps in a software product.

The traditional metrics can be classified into process-based and product-based metrics. Process metrics assess the state and resource usage of the development process, while product metrics assess the state and complexity of the artifacts (e.g., requirements, architectures, designs, and implementations) resulting from executing a software process [1]. The field of software architecture addresses the development of large-scale, complex software systems. Software architectures provide high-level abstractions for representing the structure, behavior, and key properties of a software system. These abstractions involve (1) descriptions of the elements from which systems are built, (2) interactions among those elements, (3) patterns that guide their composition, and (4) constraints on these patterns [2]. The product metrics can be classified into static and dynamic types. The static metrics have a structural and designing component to them while the dynamic metrics are used for only testability. The static metrics can be further classified into size-based, design, control, information, weighted, data-structure–based, and software-science-based metrics.

There are various size metrics present in the software codes completed by developers. In a very general sense, the number of LOC and the count of the number of tokens is a good quantitative measure of the size of the program. In recent times, with better practices coming into the picture, the focus on well-documented and commented code is considered as not just healthy but also an essential practice today. Hence, the number of comments with respect to the LOC becomes a new size metric. The number of methods or functions in the program is also a parameter of utmost importance, indicating not just modularity but also that its number of calls also affects the memory complexity that ultimately comes under the size metric as well. Next, comes the control metric which refers to the change in flow control of the program. It is also measured by the number of functions declared and studying the number of calls to them.

These metrics are wonderfully defined by the following terminologies:

1. **Cyclomatic Complexity:** There has been no obvious relationship between the LOC and the module complexity in programming; hence, to depend on the LOC and comments with respect to them is a naive idea, hence, we determine the control flow present in the program. The control flow of any procedural piece of software can be depicted as a directed graph, by representing each executable statement (or group of statements where the flow of control is sequential) as a node, and the flow of control as the edges between them [3, 4]. Mathematically,
   Cyclomatic Complexity:

$$M = E - N + 2P \tag{17.1}$$

   where:
   E = the number of edges in the control flow graph
   N = the number of nodes in the control flow graph
   P = the number of connected components.

2. **Halstead Complexity:** Halstead measurements rely on program execution and its measures, which are analyzed specifically from the operators and operands from the source code. Halstead measurements permit assessing testing time, vocabulary, estimate, trouble, mistakes, and endeavors for the source code of any programming dialect.

   Halstead measurements were intended to think of each program as a grouping of operators with its related operands. The targets of Halstead measurements are to gauge certain qualities, for example, vocabulary, volume, level, trouble, programming exertion, and required programming time. As per Halstead, 'A PC program is an execution of a calculation thought to be an accumulation of tokens which can be named either operators or operands'[5].

Mathematically, we can define it as:
Halstead's Program Length:

$$N^\wedge = n_1 \log_2 n_1 + n_2 \log_2 n_2 \qquad (17.2)$$

$$N = N1 + N2 \qquad (17.3)$$

where:

n_1 = the number of distinct operators
n_2 = the number of distinct operands
$N1$ = total number of occurrences of operators
$N2$ = total number of occurrences of operands

3. **Fan-In and Fan-Out Complexity:** The Fan-In and Fan-Out Complexity is a measure of the flow of information within a program with Fan-In being simply defined as the total sum of the input variables in the program ranging from local variable declarations to global variables and parameters reading. While, the Fan-Out will be the sum of the output flow of information present in the data, ranging from the reference parameter written, reading parameter written, and global variable written.

Fan-In-Out Metric is the sum of both the Fan-In and Fan-Out complexity, and thus mathematically, we can represent them as follows:

$$\text{Fan} - \text{In Complexity} = LR + GR + PR \qquad (17.4)$$

where:

LR = Local Variable Reading
GR = Global Variable Reading
PR = Parameter Reading

$$\text{Fan} - \text{out Complexity} = RPW + GW + LW \qquad (17.5)$$

where:

RPW = Reference Parameter Written (RPW)
GW = Global Variable Written
LW = Local Variable Written

4. **Number of Methods or Procedural Calls (P):** The total number of functions declared in the program and the number of times each of those are called by the program modules, is called the number of methods or more formally procedural call count (P-C).

5. **Data Abstraction Coupling (DAC):** Data Abstraction Coupling is the measure of the correlation between two code modules mathematically. A high value indicates a strong relationship and similarity between the code modules and a low value means both of the modules have a low dependency on each other. This makes the code modules having low DAC values more flexible as the erroneous sections within the code can be easily detected and any additional dependency issues can be resolved by the developer teams efficiently. In case the code modules have a high DAC value, the erroneous code is hard to detect and making the entire project bug-free and functional is more challenging due to the additional dependencies that may create issues. Code isolation is integral in maintaining the health of a functional system. The idea of containers and Docker originated from the need to isolate code along with its additional dependencies. A healthy industrial practice is to ensure code isolation even on small modules to ensure that maintenance and configuration changes do not become a challenge. Further, this ensures better scalability of the product and can also be used to generate build images effectively using any execution tool like Jenkins. A step-by-step module creation through a traditional waterfall approach [6] is also a possible solution. In simple words, Data-coupling methods refer to passing all the information as parameters in the procedural calls and expecting suitable return values for the same. This can be utilized in the scalability testing of any code module.

Thus, these traditional metrics have to be considered in the measurement of software productivity and are an essential part of the product that is supposed to be monitoring the progress of software development.

Productivity Metrics in Software Engineering

Business managers try to keep track of their teams by measuring the number of LOC written by each member of the team that has many shortcomings. Starting from the fact that the complexity of a program cannot be determined with help of the number of lines coded, we are also neglecting the end-to-end product deliverables, and this is actually micromanaging the employees who prove to be highly harmful. The idea of any product is to have met the customer requirements and also provide additional services as desired, and at the same time, it should have technical prowess ranging from security measures to preserving the client privacy and maintaining the dignity and reputation of the organization.

Hence, in order to gauge the productivity of employees, the first thing we need to do is to identify our goals properly which is in a balance with the technical capabilities and the customer expectations. We, thus, defined a few goal-based metrics.

Goal-Question Metrics are defined as follows [7]:

1. Conceptualize goals aimed at understanding or improving software engineering tools and processes
2. Specify research questions to operationalize those goals
3. Define metrics for understanding or measuring tools and processes

Thus, the productivity of the employees can be measured with the following concepts for tracking progress in the product development cycle:

1. **Project or Burnt Sprint Rate:** A good manager will divide the tasks assigned to each member of the team based on their technical knowledge and capabilities to handle work. Another good idea used actively is to divide the tasks as story points where each story point is related to a bug, a production task, or a testing work. The important component of having such best practices is the risk mitigation that is associated with it. The managers can gauge how much time period is needed to deliver the product and at the same time, track the risks involved in the project releases.
2. **Ticket Close Relevance Rate:** It refers to the number of story points completed by a developer and how relevant that particular task is to the project. This should not be taken as gospel by the manager in evaluating an employee's potential, as it is a subjective metric. A task can vary from creating a new pipeline to solving the bug in the program and thus it should be assigned a weighted score based on the relevance of the task to the nearby milestone. This can be used as a metric to identify issues present in the project and discuss upcoming issues with collaboration regarding the work.
3. **Lines of Code (LOC):** A very naive metric as aforementioned, it cannot be directly used to relate to productivity; hence, it is combined with other factors such as the number of comments (to gauge whether the developer follows the guidelines and best practices), to determine the number of code changes made by the developer in a single project, and the impact it has on the memory complexity. All these factors can be combined into a single impactful metric that can be related to software productivity.
4. **Code Churn Rate:** It is basically a measure of the developer's confidence, and it is the number of edits, configuration changes, or codebase reviews after pushing the code into the pipeline, and it indicates a programmer's efficiency and rate of correctness. Code churn rate should be used only when the requirements of the product are very clear and especially during the finishing stage of software development. It is not a very good metric in the beginning stages of product development because the user requirements will change; many times the client is not clear in what they want and there is a lack of balance between the understanding of the work by the manager and expectation of the client.

5. **Refactoring Rate:** The rate of changes made in the code with complete replacement of the old code and changing the codebase itself is called the refactoring rate. It can potentially indicate either inefficiency on part of the team who did not understand the user requirements in the first go, or if the user is lacking an understanding of the product they need, and hence, if entire code replacement was needed.

These metrics are used for product management in the organizations by managers along with their instincts to check the team's progress and employee performance. However, a manager's instincts and tracking over traditional software metrics are not completely evasive from a self-induced bias. These can be used effectively by them to promote good culture and customer satisfaction, and can also be a backlash if used to promote nepotism, or favoritism among the employees. Hence, the need of the hour is to automate the process of identifying productivity through data mining on traditional metrics and providing an assistive tool to the management who can use a mix of such a tool and their chosen instinctive business metrics in order to efficiently and effectively deliver products. With the development of versioning systems and cloud computing, many developers make use of bots and many other means to avoid writing code at all, which becomes a huge task in measuring the effective effort of a programmer. Hence, keeping all these factors into consideration, it is imperative that a manager rewards genuine human-coded efforts and accelerates the morale of their teams toward swift delivery.

Data Mining in Software Productivity Measurement

Data Collection

With the objective of measuring the productivity of tasks completed by a programmer, we can utilize the versioning systems used by them for this purpose. The versioning systems have ID for each unique commit with details on the time of commit along with their description. We collected data indicating comments in a program, the total number of lines of code and wrote a separate program for calculating the traditional software metrics within the same module. Hence, we created these programs as a single module component. This data collection facilitated the need to identify better production-ready code and transformed the problem into a simple binary classification.

Data Understanding

We scraped over a million entries of commits and processed them to obtain multiple software metrics used to measure the productivity of the code. The modern versioning systems suffer from the inability to distinguish between human-written and bot-generated code. Hence, we scraped different commits to obtain a collection of data with the following parameters:

1. Transaction ID: A unique primary key assigned to each commit
2. API_Code: A unique key generated for each commit
3. Commit_ID: A non-unique parameter composed of multiple commits
4. commit_date: Date of the commit made
5. submit_time: Time of submission
6. Commit_Status: Indicates the status of the commit
7. count_loc_added: Number of LOC added in the commit
8. count_loc_removed: Number of LOC removed in the commit
9. count_loc_total: Total number of LOC in the commit
10. count_com_change: Change in the number of comments before and after the commit
11. change_filesize: Total change in the file size
12. count_filesize_total: Total file size
13. count_cyclo_change: Change in cyclomatic complexity
14. count_cyclo_total: Total cyclomatic complexity
15. count_dac_change: Change in DAC
16. count_dac_total: Total DAC
17. count_halstead_change: Change in Halstead complexity
18. count_halstead_total: Total Halstead complexity
19. count_fanout_change: Change in Fan-Out Complexity
20. count_fanout_total: Total Fan-Out Complexity
21. count_nom_change: Change in the number of methods
22. count_nom_total: Total number of methods in commit
23. filetype: Extension and nature of files
24. Employee_ID: ID assigned to a user
25. target: Label assigned to indicate that the work is of a human indicating greater productivity (False) or a bot indicating less productivity (True)

A better insight into each of the relevant features is as follows:

1. **Cyclomatic Complexity:** We develop a control graph of the code and calculate the number of linearly independent paths to judge the code complexity. The code written by a human can be distinguished from the code written by a bot by analyzing the complexity of a program. Since code written by a human would be more complex, i.e., having more nested statements and a large number of defined classes/methods. This provides an apparent distinction between a code written by a human and that by a bot.
2. **Halstead's Complexity Measures:** Halstead's metrics can be computed directly from the number of operators and operands used in the source code.

Some of the metrics include Halstead program length, Halstead vocabulary, program volume, program difficulty, and programming effort.

3. **Fan-Out Complexity:** Fan-out complexity can be explained as an association of one class with the other class. Also, the fan-out complexity is directly dependent on the amount of maintenance required in functional programs. Hence, this feature can be more influential for determining the target variable.

4. **Number of Methods:** This contains the number of methods used in the source code. If the number of methods is relatively low with respect to the number of lines, then it could be assumed to be a human whereas if the number of methods is large, then it could be a bot. On the contrary, we can assume that a human writes code in a structured way using a large number of methods; this comes under the topic of class imbalance. This has been addressed in the model using MICE.

5. **Lines of Code:** Counting LOC is the oldest and most widely used software metric to judge the size of the software system. It has been debated and also shown that this method is not appropriate to measure productivity. We considered this parameter in our model but it only reflects a good result when combined with other dependent factors like the number of comments which otherwise showed a poor result.

6. **Number of Comments:** This is a metric that is used to indicate the number of comments in the source code. The more the number of comments with respect to the number of lines, the more likely they are to be written by a bot. On the other hand, a human is expected to write fewer comments with respect to the number of lines, making the code readable and optimal.

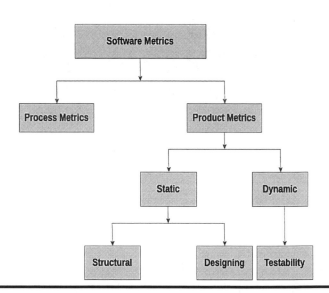

Figure 17.1   Flow diagram for the proposed system.

Exploratory Data Analysis (EDA)

The data are largely imbalanced by nature; if we observe the frequency of human-written code and bot-generated code, we can see that there is quite a difference between them. Hence, in order to make a generalized model, we need to first resolve the problem of imbalance in the target variable (Figure 17.2).

The data have a large number of missing values as well. The dataset was raw initially, owing to manual scraping from versioned commits of different repositories and had a large number of missing values. There are plenty of ways by which we can tackle missing values. We experimented with multiple techniques to impute the missing values. Dropping the missing values was found to be inefficient and prone to array shape-based errors later in processing, and we also tried replacing the NaN values with the mean and median of the respective feature. However, the sheer scale of the missing values leads to the creation of bias in the dataset toward the mean or median used for imputation. We also tried using k-nearest neighbors (kNN) as an imputation technique. However, it suffered from the problem of majoritarian instance prediction and led to creating another bias in the dataset. We, therefore, tried out Multiple Imputation by Chained Equations (MICE) which proved to be better at handling the missing data without introducing much bias in the data. In this technique, we fill the missing value by doing multiple imputations rather than single imputation which increases the probability of getting better results as compared to all other models. It considers missing values to be at random in the dataset, thereby increasing the variance of replacing them and ensuring equitable handling of all the missing values, ensuring uniformity in handling them throughout the raw data to deliver preprocessed data.

Initially, the heatmap is plotted for visualizing the correlation between different features. The correlation plots were analyzed and the most relevant features whose contribution to the target variable is higher were identified. The data seemed to suffer from the class imbalance problem. The number of bot-produced code was much

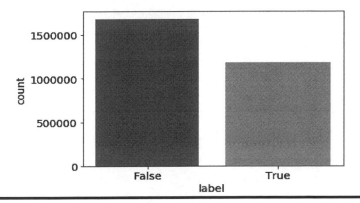

Figure 17.2 Count plot of the target variable.

lower than the number of human-coded efforts; thereby, the data needed to be balanced before being dealt with further.

The following count plot displays the count of the human-coded and bot-coded target variables in the dataset. The label 'True' indicates that it is coded by a bot and the label 'False' means it is coded by humans. Thus, we observe that there are many misclassifications in the form of identifying human efforts in data.

To overcome the class imbalance problem, we explore the use of Synthetic Minority Oversampling (SMOTE). SMOTE performs oversampling of the minority classes to balance the data. This can be achieved by simply duplicating examples from the minority class in the training dataset prior to fitting a model. This can balance the class distribution but does not provide any additional information to the model which is desirable. Thus, after applying SMOTE to the data, we obtain a balanced sample with an equal number of instances taken from both values of the target variables.

The correlations are represented using the Pearson correlation coefficient as a numerical value. As shown in Figure 17.3, 'cyclo' (Cyclomatic Complexity) has shown a good correlation with the 'nom' which is the Number of Methods feature with a value of 0.94. At the same time 'halstead_total' shows a good correlation with 'nom' Number of Methods with a value of 0.92. 'halstead_total' Halstead Complexity shows a good correlation with 'cyclo' Cyclomatic Complexity with a value of 0.96. The DAC shows a good correlation (0.82) with fan-out complexity which infers the coupling between classes. The correlation between the number of comments and the number of LOC is quite high and therefore, we can simply neutralize the effect by taking the mean of both the features and making a new strong feature in the data. Similarly, the number of methods is highly correlated with the cyclomatic complexity which is an expected pattern since the cyclomatic complexity indicates the change in the flow of the program execution and whenever a method is called then the flow of the program gets changed immediately. We also note that the Halstead complexity is also highly correlated to the number of methods, which is an unusual pattern but indicates distinct operators and the occurrence of operands that are used in the methods. The fan-out complexity is also highly correlated with the number of methods which is expected since it is the measure of the association between different classes and the number of distinct methods that must be belonging to different classes as well. A general pattern of the programming languages preferred by bots is as follows: (Figure 17.3).

Feature Scaling

The data consisted of features which could not be compared directly and required standardization to transform them into comparable features. The features undergo Z-Score Normalization which rescales them to a standard normal distribution having a mean of zero and a unit standard deviation. An alternative approach can be in the form of Min-Max Normalization to rescale the data between 0 and 1 and make

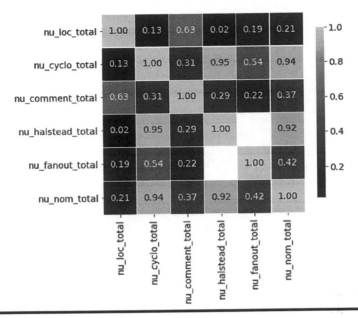

Figure 17.3   **Programming languages used by humans (left) and bots (right).**

two distinct features comparable. The size of the dataset is huge and therefore it is necessary to draw a meaningful sample of features from it thus we make use of the Principal Component Analysis (PCA) further on the standardized data to obtain more strong contributing features to the output classification.

Model Selection

The aim of the classification task is to identify the human-coded efforts out of the dataset. We experiment with various models available for classification including Logistic Regression, Gradient Boosting Classifier, Ridge Classifier, Support Vector Classifier, Gaussian Naive Bayes, and Multi-Perceptron Classifier. We found out the Gradient Boosting Classifier to have the highest mean test accuracy of 97.98%. This is accountable for the fact that the Gradient Boosting combined various weak learners to form strong learners based on the concept of Probability Approximately Correct (PAC) Learning and Hypothesis Boosting which keeps all the correctly classified observations and prunes out others from the decision tree, thereby handling any additional correlations present in the set of reduced feature vectors. Logistic Regression fails to construct a proper decision boundary to separate the classes and hence converges to the lowest mean test accuracy of 80.73%. The Ridge Classifier yields an optimal performance based on the use of regularization to prevent any overfitting of the model. The Multi-Layer Perceptron also delivered an optimal performance owing to the efficient use of neural networks but could not handle the correlations automatically and thus ended up having comparatively lower performance than the Gradient Boosting. The custom data collected through random version control commits were preprocessed by handling missing values with MICE which randomly impute continuous two-level data and maintain consistency between imputations by means of passive imputation. This method worked well with the data collected and proved to be a better method than replacing the missing values with mean or median or dropping them as a whole. To handle class imbalance, SMOTE was used to oversample the minority classes that produced class-balanced data. The data got structured after applying SMOTE and was followed by the standardization of a few features to make them comparable. After preprocessing the data, the high-dimensional data were subjected to PCA, which emphasizes variation and brought out strong patterns in the dataset. With the dimensionality reduction achieved through PCA, we experimented with various classification models as a comparative analysis. Out of all the models, Gradient Boosting Classifier yields the best output in classifying actual human-coded efforts with a mean test accuracy of 97.98%. The classification reports for the evaluation of the different classifier models are given as follows (Tables 17.1–17.6).

A comparison of the mean test accuracy given by the different models is as follows.

Table 17.1 Classification Report of Gradient Boosting Classifier on Data

	Precision	Recall	F1-score	Support
False	1.00	1.00	1.00	503753
True	1.00	1.00	1.00	355634
Accuracy			1.00	859357
Macro-Average	1.00	1.00	1.00	859357
Weighted Average	1.00	1.00	1.00	859357

Table 17.2 Classification Report of Ridge Classifier on Data

	Precision	Recall	F1-score	Support
False	0.92	0.94	0.93	494398
True	0.91	0.89	0.90	364959
Accuracy			0.92	859357
Macro-Average	0.91	0.91	0.91	859357
Weighted Average	0.91	0.92	0.91	859357

Table 17.3 Classification Report of Logistic Regression on Data

	Precision	Recall	F1-score	Support
False	0.79	0.90	0.84	438154
True	0.88	0.74	0.81	421403
Accuracy			0.83	859357
Macro-Average	0.83	0.82	0.82	859357
Weighted Average	0.83	0.82	0.82	859357

Table 17.4 Classification Report of Gaussian Naive Bayes on Data

	Precision	Recall	F1-score	Support
False	0.95	0.84	0.89	572411
True	0.74	0.92	0.82	286946
Accuracy			0.87	859357
Macro-Average	0.85	0.88	0.86	859357
Weighted Average	0.88	0.87	0.87	859357

Table 17.5 Classification Report of Multi-Layer Perceptron Classifier on Data

	Precision	Recall	F1-score	Support
False	0.89	0.88	0.86	638154
True	0.88	0.87	0.86	521403
Accuracy			0.85	859357
Macro-Average	0.86	0.87	0.87	859357
Weighted Average	0.87	0.86	0.86	859357

Table 17.6 Classification Report of Logistic Regression on Data

Classifier	Mean Test Accuracy (%)
Logistic Regression	80.73
Gradient Boosting Classifier	97.98
Ridge Classifier	84.77
Support Vector Classifier	84.71
Gaussian Naive Bayes	82.03
Multi-Layer Perceptron	85.77

Conclusions

Software development is one of the most dynamic industries in the new era and its evolving nature makes it the most productive as well as challenging industry at the same time. As a result, software productivity also becomes transitional by nature, and with the onset of versioning systems, it becomes easier to collaborate with other developers and also monitor progress easily. The changing needs of the customers and better optimizations in the software industry will eventually introduce new parameters and metrics to measure the productivity of the programmer; however, the essence of the object-oriented metrics will always remain at the heart of computer science.

References

1 André van der Hoek, Ebru Dincel, Nenad Medvidovic, Using service utilization metrics to assess and improve product line architectures, Article, University of California, Irvine (2012)

2 N. Medvidovic, R.N. Taylor, A classification and comparison framework for software architecture description languages. *IEEE Transactions on Software Engineering* 26(1), 70–93, 2000.

3 M. Shaw, D. Garlan eds. *Software Architecture: Perspectives on an Emerging Discipline.* Upper Saddle River: Prentice-Hall (1996).

4 Martin Shepperd, A critique of cyclomatic complexity as a software metric, *IEEE Software Engineering Journal* 3(2), 30–36 (1988).

5 T Hariprasad, K Seenu, Vidhyagaran G, Chandrasegar Thirumalai: *Software complexity analysis using halstead metrics, International Conference on Trends in Electronics and Informatics* IEEE (2017).

6 Ravi Arora, Mukul Kumar: Dynamic coupling metrics for object oriented software, *IJRAR* 5, 1–8 (2018).

7 Caitlin Sadowski, Margaret-Anne Storey, Robert Feldt: A software development productivity framework, *Rethinking Productivity in Software Engineering* 2, 39–47, (2019).

Index

Page numbers in **bold** indicate tables.